THE CORPORATE PARADOX

THE CORPORATE PARADOX

Economic Realities of the Corporate Form of Organization

by

WOUTER H. F. M. CORTENRAAD

Loeff Claeys Verbeke, Amsterdam,
The Netherlands

SPRINGER SCIENCE+BUSINESS, MEDIA, B.V.

A C.I.P. Catalogue record for this book is available from the Library of Congress.

ISBN 978-0-7923-8695-7 ISBN 978-1-4615-4619-1 (eBook)
DOI 10.1007/978-1-4615-4619-1

Printed on acid-free paper

"Legal control is future physical control."

John R. Commons, *Institutional Economics – Its Place in Political Economy*, Volume 1, page 87, 1990 (New Brunswick: Transaction Publishers), originally published in 1934.

Contents

Acknowledgments

THE SUBJECT MATTER of this book intersects the realms of law, economics and organization. Its purpose is to review and discuss the economics underlying the corporate form of business organization, thus attempting to contribute to a better understanding of both the rationales and the effects of the corporation as a legally endorsed concept of organization.

Using modern microeconomic theory, this work examines, in particular, how the corporate form affects organizational behavior and the behavior of the human agents that control the organization (managers and investors). As we shall see, the corporation's well acknowledged status as *the* dominant vehicle for organizing economic activity in contemporary market economies should not conceal the social costs arising from several conflicts of interests attending the corporate form, which market mechanisms have failed to eliminate, and on account of which the concept of the corporation deserves qualified praise only.

Although this book draws heavily on economic theory, including organization theory, and uses economic analysis as its leading analytical tool, readers are not required to have extensive prior economic training. Economic concepts are explained as and when they are introduced into the text, so as to ensure the book's accessibility to non-economists. No mathematical or econometric methods of analysis are applied. Similarly, as the most important legal terms figuring in the text are also explained, little legal understanding is required of the reader.

I was first acquainted with the use of economics to analyze matters traditionally associated with the domain of law and with its application to corporate law and organization when I was a graduate student at the law school of the University of Toronto in the academic year 1988-1989. I am much indebted to Professor Bruce Chapman of that university who, apart from promoting the value of alternative approaches to legal scholarship in his teachings, supervised my thesis for the degree of Master of Laws, which contained my first steps in economic analysis of corporate law and organization. His comments and suggestions were most valuable to the shaping of my initial ideas on the use of economic theory in relation to the study of corporate legal matters.

I elaborated on my graduate study in Toronto as a John M. Olin Visiting Research Fellow in Law and Economics at Harvard Law School in the second half of 1989. I am grateful to the Law School, the John M. Olin Program in Law and Economics and to Professor Steven Shavell for having provided me with this opportunity. During my stay at Harvard, I particularly benefited from discussions with Professor Reinier H. Kraakman relating to economic aspects of United States corporate law and theories of firms and organizations and I would like to express my gratitude to him for this.

Subsequently I was able to relate theory to practice, in particular, to relate academic concepts concerning organizational and individual behavior and the presumed impact of legal rules thereupon to the actual operation of large corporations, first as in-house legal counsel with the Royal Dutch/Shell Group (1991-1995) at its principal offices in The Hague, the Netherlands and later in private practice (since 1995) as an associate of Loeff Claeys Verbeke (Nederland), a leading Dutch international law firm, in their Amsterdam offices. This dual experience as a practitioner has greatly influenced my perception of, and hopefully deepened my insight into, the economic forces bearing on firms operated in corporate form and directing managerial and investor behavior. My firm Loeff Claeys Verbeke generously allowed me to spend a substantial number of office hours in the completion of the manuscript for this book, for which I am most grateful.

I am also much indebted to Professors Jürgen G. Backhaus and Nico H.M. Roos of the University of Maastricht, the Netherlands (Faculty of Economics and Faculty of Law, respectively), who critically read the entire manuscript and made various suggestions for improvement, not merely for their valuable advice but also for their encouragement during the years which have lapsed between my first ideas about writing this book until its completion. Furthermore, I am grateful to Michael G. Faure and Gerrit Meijer of the same university and to L.R.T. van der Goot of the University of Amsterdam (Faculty of Economics and Econometrics) for their constructive and most helpful comments relating to parts of the manuscript. Finally, I thank Frank M.P. van Dun and Jacques L.M. Elders (emeritus) of the University of Maastricht who kindly commented on an early draft of Chapters 1 and 2 of this book, and several anonymous referees engaged by the publisher whose advices on contents and exposition have also been highly appreciated.

Without prejudice to the debts of gratitude expressed above, I assume full responsibility for the contents of this book and for any remaining inadequacies it may contain.

Amsterdam, July 1999
Wouter H.F.M. Cortenraad

Note on Citations

THIS BOOK does not contain footnotes. Instead, abbreviated references are inserted in the text (between square brackets) when a proposition contained in, or a citation taken from, the work of other authors is used. The full source is stated in the list of references at the end of this book.

All references are to the number(s) of the page(s) containing the relevant proposition or citation, except for the references to Dutch case law in Chapters 6 and 9; such references refer to the number in the relevant case law reporter (the "*Nederlandse Jurisprudentie*") under which the cited case has been published.

To illustrate the system of citations: [Manne (1975), 516] refers to: Manne, H.G., 1975, *Our Two Corporation Systems: Law and Economics*, in: Idem (ed.), The Economics of Legal Relationships – Readings in the Theory of Property Rights, page 516.

INTRODUCTION

THE PAST DECADE witnessed a number of collapses and scandals in the world of big business that hit the global headlines. These included several spectacular bankruptcies, cases of appalling mismanagement, sometimes accompanied by fraud, as well as several environmental disasters. Such cases were not limited to one particular country but occurred at several unconnected places on the world map. Moreover, they almost invariably involved companies with a more or less respectable record of previous performance.

As regards widely publicized business collapses and instances of mismanagement, one may think of, for instance, the failure of the Bank of Credit and Commerce International (nicknamed by some the "Bank of Crooks and Cocaine International") in 1991, whose principal holding company was registered in Luxembourg, after more than 5 billion U.S. dollars had disappeared from the bank's accounts, the fall of Canadian mining company Bre-X Minerals in 1997, which purported to have discovered an exceptionally rich gold deposit in the jungle of Kalimantan, Indonesia, at a site which proved to be primarily composed of mud, the failure of British business bank Barings in 1995, after top management had allowed a single employee to put the fate of the entire bank at stake by engaging in high risk futures transactions in the Singapore stock market, and the collapse of major German retail group Co-op in 1989, which was accompanied by fraud accusations against the group's top management amounting to some DEM 100 million.

Widely reported also were instances of fraud in the Japanese Sumitomo company in 1996, which lost over 2.5 billion U.S. dollars in a copper trading gamble by a member of its senior staff, and in the Spanish bank Banco Banesto, which was put under the guardianship of the country's central bank in 1993 after it had failed to account for an amount approximating several billions of U.S. dollars and the president of which was subsequently tried in criminal proceedings following allegations of fraud. Less outrageous, but also upsetting local public opinion were the failures of the Ogem (real estate development), RSV (ship building) and Fokker (aircraft construction) concerns in the Netherlands, the first two of which (in the 1980s) were reportedly caused in significant part by mismanagement of top managers, whilst the bankruptcy of aircraft manufacturer Fokker in 1996 has been attributed to the over-ambition of the company's top management and failure to adjust to market developments.

Other cases involving big business which caused general public indignation included the massive mineral oil pollution which resulted when the Exxon Valdez, a tanker of the Exxon group, ran aground off the coast of Alaska in March 1989 and the poisoning disaster which had occurred a few years earlier when toxic gas escaped from a Union Carbide factory nearby Bhopal, India, which reportedly caused thousands of casualties. To a related category belong the allegations that tobacco companies such as Philip Morris and R.J. Reynolds damaged the health of numerous people by putting cigarettes on the market knowing that they could cause lung disease, without properly warning the public, and claims directed against Dow Chemical and Dow Corning for having manufactured and marketed silicone implants, which allegedly caused injury to hundreds of thousands of women who had such implants inserted into their bodies. The tobacco and silicone cases have meanwhile given rise to settlement proposals involving multi-*billion* U.S. dollar payments by the industries concerned.

Although the events described above vary in nature and in dimension, they are united, not only through the public indignation each of them prompted but also through the fact that in one way or another they produced a substantial number of victims. Such victims have included in their number investors and creditors, who sustained losses as a consequence of the collapse or failing management of the company in question, and third parties (including the public at large in the Exxon Valdez case), who were harmed as a result of the company's activities.

Yet the above-mentioned cases are united in one more respect: all cases involved businesses legally organized as corporations, or as a group of affiliated corporations. Although in common parlance the word "corporation" is frequently used as a synonym for company, business enterprise or firm, strictly it denotes only one of the legal forms in which a business may be organized. Throughout this book, we will use the term "corporation" in its legal sense, that is, as a legally endorsed concept for the organization of a business firm.

In brief, when a business enterprise is legally organized as a corporation it means (i) that the enterprise is able to have rights and obligations in basically the same way as an individual (thus, the enterprise has "legal personality"), (ii) that it can raise funds to finance its operations by the sale of transferable shares in its capital, (iii) that the holders of such shares, who are entitled to the enterprise's profits and to the excess of its assets over liabilities when the business is dissolved, are not liable for its debts, and (iv) that the management function is legally separate from the providers of the share capital. (We will further discuss these features in Chapter 2.) Thus, the corporation embodies the basic "rules of the game" for the organization of a business enterprise operating in corporate form.

Is the fact that the companies referred to above were organized according to the aforesaid corporate principles merely a consequence, or an illustration, of the corporate form's frequency? Or could there be a relation between the unfavorable performances of these companies and the fact that they were dressed up as corporations? These questions, which touch the very heart of the corporation as a method of organizing a business, refer to the relationship between the firm, as an economic entity, and the corporate form of organization. This relationship is examined in this study.

More precisely, we intend to examine whether, and how, the corporate form of organization relates to the functioning of the firm it organizes. For this purpose, we will discuss both the economic rationales underlying the basic legal principles of the corporate concept (as summarized above) and the behavioral incentives these principles create for the individuals controlling the organization (*i.e.* managers and shareholders). Through this exercise, we endeavor to contribute to a fuller understanding of how the corporate form of organization may affect the behavior of the firm and its controlling individuals and in effect, the use that firms operated in this form make of society's valuable resources.

The Victims

As indicated, apart from the fact that they all concerned firms operated in corporate form, the cases quoted above have in common that each of them created victims who sustained injury as a result of the activities of the firm or the management in question. These victims can be divided into two categories.

The first category consists of shareholders who sustained accounting or opportunity losses as a consequence of improper or inadequate performance by the company's management, which resulted in or contributed to the company's eventual collapse, or which caused large losses to the company. Shareholders incur "accounting losses" when they lose all or part of their invested wealth in a particular firm, whilst "opportunity losses" refer to the forgone returns the shareholders would have earned if management had taken appropriate action.

Shareholders are a party internal to the company's organization. They have agreed to participate in the firm by supplying equity capital to it in exchange for shares. Moreover, they have agreed to bear the risk of the company's success or failure: they have accepted that they may lose their entire invested wealth in the event of bankruptcy and that the value of their shares as well as the reward they receive for their investment is contingent upon the success of the business. The shareholders have also agreed that their invested wealth and their risk be primarily controlled by a specialized management. However, they have *not* agreed that management waste their capital investment, or that management use their invested money so ineffectively that the shareholders would have been better off if they had managed their capital themselves.

The second category of victims consists of parties external to the firm and includes creditors, tort victims and other members of society not belonging to one of these classes, who suffered injury as a result of the firm's activities, including its failure to satisfy contractual obligations or to repair damage outside the firm resulting from its operations. Such external victims had either agreed to furnish the firm with certain inputs (money, raw materials, intermediate goods) on credit, usually in exchange for a fixed return (interest), or had not agreed to provide inputs to the firm (tort victims, victims of pollution, casualty or illness attributable to the activities of the firm). Tort victims, for example, involuntarily supplied "inputs" to the firm by exposing their health, safety or welfare to its operations. Unlike the shareholders, the cited external parties have not agreed to bear the risk of the company's fortune or misfortune. Still, they face losses from the company's failure to properly pay its debts or to pay compensation for external injury ensuing from its operations.

When it comes to the *causes* of the injury sustained by the victims in either one of the above-mentioned categories, frequently the blame is put on one or more factors belonging to the same limited range of potential triggers: mismanagement by the firm's top management, failure by management to install effective systems for monitoring employee behavior, fraud, failure to properly respond to developments in product or factor markets, an ineffective, non-competitive, unsafe or unhealthy organization of productive activity, business adversities, or disappointing macroeconomic developments. However, most of the time the corporate form as such appears to be above suspicion, and would only occasionally seem subject to critical analysis. The corporation's status of apparent immunity is amazing, not merely because it furnishes firms with their essential principles of organization but also because the corporate form is broadly acknowledged to be the dominant form of organization among large business firms. The present study may be regarded as an attempt to focus more closely on the corporate form, its merits and demerits.

In analyzing the corporate form and its effects, we will distinguish between its potential relevance to losses sustained by shareholders as a result of management's behavior on the one hand (which will be discussed in Part II of this book), and injury sustained by parties external to the corporation (creditors, tort victims) as a consequence of the activities of the corporate firm on the other (to be addressed in Part III). Our exercise is limited to the class of for-profit corporations, as the vast majority of incorporated firms are operated to earn profits for the shareholders.

Furthermore, with few exceptions, we concentrate on publicly held corporations given that they organize or control, directly or through subsidiary corporations, the larger businesses and that they, therefore, tend to affect large numbers of people (shareholders, employees, creditors and other parties outside the firm). A publicly held corporation is defined by the fact that its equity shares ordinarily are owned by numerous dispersed shareholders and that there is a possibility for active trading in its shares, either in an organized securities exchange or in an over-the-counter or other private market. This type of corporation has traditionally been at the focus of attention in United States state corporation statutes; in the Netherlands, the other country to whose corporate law we will refer, this type of corporation is incorporated as a "*Naamloze Vennootschap*" under the special chapter on publicly held corporations in the country's Civil Code. Its counterpart is the closely held or close corporation, the stock ownership of which is concentrated among a relatively small number of shareholders and for whose shares no active trading market exists. When hereinafter referring to "corporation", we mean publicly held corporation as defined above, unless the context indicates otherwise.

The Methodology

In this book, we examine the relationship between the corporate form and the behavior of the firm and the individuals controlling it from the perspective of microeconomic theory. The use of economic theory and tools of analysis to understand a legal concept places our study in the line of scholarship known as "law and economics". Since both the concept of the corporation and the firm organized by it are parts of the institutional framework of the modern market economy, the object of our study also belongs to the area known as neoinstitutionalist economics.

Economic analysis distinguishes between empirical and conceptual analysis. Empirical analysis centers on the use of factual data to explain and understand a given subject. Conceptual analysis endeavors to examine a given theme or problem by theoretical analysis based on assumptions, paradigms and methodological tools generally accepted in economic theory. We apply the second form of analysis and refer to empirical findings by others only when such findings clarify economic theory concerning the rationales and effects of the corporate concept.

Nobel laureate Ronald H. Coase [1993, 360] maintained that "it is impossible to undertake good empirical work without a theory and difficult to formulate theories without good empirical work". The same author also emphasized the importance of theory when he criticized the institutionalist school in American economic scholarship during the first decades of the twentieth century, for being "anti-theoretical" and for having produced "nothing to pass on except a mass of descriptive material waiting for a theory, or a fire" [Coase (1984), 230]. Taking Coase's exhortation seriously, we will endeavor to bring together elements relevant to the formulation of an economic theory of the corporate form of business organization.

When lawyers study a particular case for the purpose of establishing its legal consequences and implications, they require a full and detailed understanding of all relevant facts pertaining to that case. Economists, by contrast, tend to narrowly define the subject or problem they examine and to confine themselves to analyzing those aspects of the subject or problem which fall within that definition. They apply the same method when analyzing matters traditionally belonging to the realm of law. This approach may be less complete than that of lawyers, but it is indispensable for the purpose of ascertaining the effects of a given legal rule or concept on behavior patterns and consequent allocations of resources. Following the economists' approach, we define a corporation by the four characteristics mentioned earlier (legal personality, transferable equity shares, limited liability of shareholders and separation between management and share ownership), which distinguish the corporation from other legal forms of organization. We acknowledge that this definition ignores much of the corporate law governing the corporation and the relationships between the individuals involved in it, but it is not the corporate *law* as a branch of law which we are expounding: our focus is on the corporate form as a method of *organization* of economic activity, and this form of organization is characterized by the cited features.

Lawyers usually analyze cases on the basis of the facts as they are perceived to have occurred. Thus, their starting point is the *fact*, and they apply rules to facts once occurred. Economists trespassing onto the field of law, on the other hand, examine the effects of a legal *rule* or concept on human and organizational behavior. The question then is what facts may result from or be attributable to a given rule. Thus, their starting point is the legal rule rather than facts. In other words, whilst lawyers' perspective is *ex post*, *i.e.* after-the-fact, economists tend to proceed from an *ex ante* perspective [Hol (1990), 632]. The *ex ante* perspective enables them to make predictions and explanations in the abstract concerning a rule's probable effects. We will examine the effects of the rules that make up the concept of the corporation (as defined above) in the same manner.

The use of express or implied assumptions is another element common to economic analysis that is alien to lawyers' traditional methods of analysis (except for attorneys in criminal trials and for attorneys in civil proceedings invoking the mythical notion of "the reasonable man"). Economic theories often involve express or implied assumptions concerning the institutional structure of the economy and the behavior of individuals and firms. For instance, much neoclassical economic analysis is based on the assumption that markets are perfectly competitive. The perfect competition model assumes that there are numerous buyers and sellers in the market, all of whom have perfect information on prices and products available, that the products offered for sale are homogeneous, so that the product of one firm cannot be distinguished from the competing product offered by another firm, that there is complete freedom to enter and to exit the market, and that the prevailing market price is given to all parties in the market. Economists realize that real markets to a greater or lesser degree differ from this model, but the model still enables them to analyze the operation of markets and the behavior of consumers and producers. We will use the economists' technique of making assumptions as an analytical tool throughout this book.

A common assumption in mainstream neoclassical economics is the assumption that people are rational utility maximizers. This assumption is frequently criticized by non-economists, partly, we presume, because its meaning is not always clearly understood. It does *not* mean that all human beings always act perfectly rationally in a psychological sense, or that they have no regard for other people. Nor does it mean that people are consciously and systematically exploring markets for goods and services all the time in search of maximum personal utility. Opponents of the assumption of rational utility maximization tend to depict the notion's meaning in this incorrect and rather caricatural way in order to make it appear controversial.

Rational utility maximization assumes solely that, in a world in which total resources available are insufficient to meet everybody's wants, people can and do rank their wants on the basis of evaluations independent of budget constraints (*i.e.* preferences) and make decisions (choices) on the basis of such preferences and relative prices in the markets facing them, so as to maximize their total satisfaction (*i.e.* utility) from a given budget and a given range of possible decisions. Maximum utility requires equation of marginal utilities per dollar spent on disparate goods and services. "Rational utility maximization" does *not*, however, require that in reality people consciously act in the manner described; it is only maintained that human behavior can be understood and explained in that way. The assumption is concerned with the explanation of the *outcomes* of human behavior, not a purportedly accurate description of mental processes [Ekelund and Tollison (1991), 159]. As a hypothesis, therefore, rational utility maximization, in our view, is neither far-fetched nor controversial.

In addition, the test of any economic theory is not in the realism of its assumptions but in its ability to explain or to predict real world phenomena, as Friedman [1953] has set forth, and in the theory's internal coherence including, in particular, logical consistency between the assumptions used and the conclusions reached. In Friedman's own words [1953, 15], "the relevant question to ask about the "assumptions" of a theory is not whether they are descriptively "realistic", for they never are, but whether they are sufficiently good approximations for the purpose in hand. And this question can be answered only by seeing whether the theory works, which means whether it yields sufficiently accurate predictions".

Throughout this book, we assume that the human actors involved in or affected by the corporate form of organization are rational utility maximizers in the sense described above. A person's utility function, representing his preferences based on the utility that he derives or expects to derive from different goods and services, may include both pecuniary and non-pecuniary components. Wealth is only one source of utility. For instance, a manager of a firm may prefer both a high salary and a fair amount of leisure. (We will further discuss managers' utility functions in Chapter 4.) It is difficult to see, however, how a shareholder, who is not at the same time a manager of the corporation in which he owns shares, could maximize his utility as a shareholder other than through maximization of his pecuniary benefit from owning the shares. Therefore, as for shareholders, but not for managers, we will equate maximum utility with maximum wealth.

Finally, economic analysis distinguishes between positive – "what is" – and normative – "what ought to be" – analysis. In *positive* analysis the emphasis is on the explanation and prediction of behavior patterns in a given institutional environment, and on how such behavior patterns and the given institutional environment affect the allocation of scarce resources among alternative ends. Positive analysis also extends to predicting the effects of potential changes in circumstances relevant to economic agents' choices between alternative uses of scarce resources, including potential modifications of the economy's institutional structure. Positive economics is independent of any particular normative judgment or preconception [Friedman (1953), 4]. *Normative* analysis concentrates on changes in the allocation of resources in order to increase the satisfaction of human wants, given that total resources are limited, and on developing changes in the institutional framework of the economy intended for this purpose.

The major part of the economic analysis in this book is positive analysis. Normative analysis is largely confined to Chapters 5 and 8 (discussing possible remedies to certain deficiencies that we will associate with the concept of the corporation).

The Plan

The first part of this book (Chapters 1 through 3) is dedicated to a general discussion of the economics underlying the corporate form of organization. An examination of the relationship between the corporate framework and the business firm it organizes involves two parameters, viz. the corporate form and the firm. Understanding the relationship between these parameters requires us to first examine each parameter individually. In Chapter 1, therefore, we survey economic theories on the nature and rationales of the business firm. Chapter 2 does the same for the corporation as a method of organization. We shall see that the corporate form is a product of market forces as much as the firm it organizes.

Subsequently we examine in some detail what is, as we shall see, the most peculiar characteristic of the corporate concept: the statutory principle of limited shareholder liability. Generally the law induces persons entitled to the fruits of an activity to take into account the effects of that activity on other people by making them liable for injury imposed on others. Limited liability for shareholders, however, has the opposite effect: it removes liability from those entitled to the corporation's profits. Why are shareholders treated differently, and how does their limited liability fit in with the economic functions of the corporation as described in Chapter 2? We will seek to answer these questions in Chapter 3.

Part II of this book (Chapters 4 through 6) deals with the possible impact of the corporate form on managerial behavior. Chapter 4 examines the effects of the separation of the functions of management of the firm and supply of investment capital, which is inherent in the corporate concept. In particular, we will review whether this separation provides top managers with the discretion to sacrifice shareholders' wealth-maximizing interests in favor of the maximization of managers' personal utility. Having concluded that managers are likely to have such discretion indeed given imperfections in the mechanisms that operate to discipline them, Chapter 5 addresses several potential cures from a theoretical point of view.

Chapter 6 then describes legal remedies, and their consistency with our economic analysis, which are currently applied under United States corporate law, having originated from a common law background, and under Dutch corporate law, as a rather rigid exponent of the civil law tradition on the European continent. This approach will enable comparison between United States common law and Dutch civil law solutions and, so, between the approaches developed from contrasting legal traditions.

Finally, Part III (Chapters 7 through 9) examines whether, and how, the corporate form of organization and in particular, the limited liability principle, affects the behavior of the firm itself in relation to parties external to it (including creditors and tort victims). In Chapter 7, we discuss the effects of the limited liability rule on other members of society. As we shall see, limited liability of shareholders may promote activities and behavior patterns on the part of the firm that are desirable from the shareholders' point of view but that adversely affect parties outside the firm. Chapter 8 discusses several potential remedies to this phenomenon from the perspective of economic theory, whilst Chapter 9 surveys where and when the limited liability principle is set aside under United States law and under Dutch law to remedy adverse effects on third parties.

Throughout this book, when referring to United States statute law on corporations, we refer to the provisions of the Model Business Corporation Act, which was first promulgated by the Section of Business Law, Committee on Corporate Laws, of the American Bar Association in 1950 and which had its most recent complete revision in 1984 (with some later modifications of a relatively minor nature). The Model Business Corporation Act has served as a model for many state corporation statutes or parts thereof and has been influential on corporation statutes enacted by other states. It has now been adopted more or less in its entirety as a general corporation statute in twenty-four state jurisdictions, including Connecticut, Florida, Georgia, Tennessee and Virginia, whilst other states have adopted selected parts or provisions from it. Therefore, the Model Act can be safely assumed to reflect the general tenor of state corporation statutes in the United States. In addition, according to the introduction by the Committee on Corporate Laws to the 1984 revised edition, the Model Act has deliberately been designed so as to reflect "current views as to the appropriate accommodation of the various commercial and social interests involved in modern business corporations".

PART I

THE CORPORATE FORM OF ORGANIZATION

1. ON BUTTERMILK AND ISLANDS OF CONSCIOUS POWER

THE LEGAL CONCEPT of the corporation embodies the basic institutional framework of many business enterprises. It is widely employed to structure an enterprise according to certain legally endorsed principles of organization, enshrined in the corporate concept. In essence, the corporation is nothing but a cocoon enveloping a business enterprise.

A biologist desirous to understand how a cocoon relates to the species it encloses must know first the characteristics of the species contained in the cocoon. Likewise, if we desire to find out if and how the corporate framework relates to the enterprise it enwraps, we need to understand, as a preliminary matter, what exactly the corporation organizes. Therefore, our inquiry into the relationship between the concept of the corporation and the business enterprise organized by it starts with a description of the object of the corporation, the business enterprise or, as it is commonly called by economic scholars, the "firm". What defines an "enterprise" or "firm", and what are its particular advantages causing economic activity to be organized in firms?

Economic theory has developed various answers to these questions. In this chapter we survey the most influential contributions.

The Firm – A Production Function

The way in which a "firm" is defined largely depends on the academic field from which the definition has emerged.

From a sociological angle, a firm frequently is described as a social organization. In this approach, emphasis is put on the inter-human relationships inside the firm and on various aspects of the cooperation between the human actors whose productive efforts the firm combines. Attention is paid also to the firm's interaction with other social institutions and to its place and functions in society as a whole [Vanberg (1982); Nutzinger (1978)].

In mainstream neoclassical economics, on the other hand, a firm is defined by its constituent economic activity. Neoclassical economics generally views the firm as a production function, that means, as a series of inputs from which output (goods or services) is produced.

A production function summarizes the relationship between a number of inputs (the factors of production: raw materials, labor and capital) on the one hand and the maximum amount of output on the other, which can be obtained from given quantities of these inputs. It indicates how much output can be produced from different combinations of inputs, given the state of technology and knowledge. The firm captures this input-output relationship and is, thus, properly defined as "a set of feasible production plans" [Hart (1989), 1758].

The activities of the neoclassical firm consist of three components, which together make up the firm: it obtains resources (inputs) from the owners of production factors, it transforms such inputs into one or more products (output) by combining different inputs, and it disposes of the resulting output to parties external to the firm (the product market) [Grossack and Martin (1973), 13]. Accordingly, a firm has been described as "a vehicle of organizing an input-output process" [Kwang and Wu (1971), 6] and as "an input-output system" [Albach (1981), 718]. Based on the same conception, Stigler [1951, 187] has referred to the firm as "purchasing a series of inputs, from which it obtains one or more salable products, the quantities of which are related to the quantities of the inputs by a production function".

The Firm – A Coalition

Neoclassical economists are increasingly inclined to broaden the approach outlined above and to view a firm not merely as a set of inputs put together for the purpose of producing goods or services.

It has been suggested, in particular, that the essence of a firm is cooperative activity, or teamwork, by different resource owners. From this perspective the firm has been defined as a *coalition*, or a team, consisting of owners of inputs whose joint efforts produce output, such output being the product of the inputs collectively rather than the sum of individually created products by different resource owners [Alchian and Demsetz (1972); Alchian (1991), 233; Alchian (1993), 367].

The key premise underlying this approach is that there is a gain from cooperation, which motivates individual input owners to unite their efforts in a coalition or team; the latter is termed a "firm". It is maintained that by cooperating in a firm, inputs are able to enhance their individual productivities: through teamwork the joint inputs will yield a larger output than separately used inputs could otherwise achieve [Alchian and Demsetz (1972); Alchian (1991), 233; Alchian (1993), 367]. Similarly, Arrow [1974, 53] has phrased the principal function of the firm in terms of its ability "to take advantage of the superior productivity of joint actions". We return to this point later in this chapter.

If the firm is described as a coalition of jointly producing inputs, generally it is also assumed that the owner of a resource (a production factor) suited to serve as an input into a team productive process has certain rights entitling him to determine how his resource is used, to reap the fruits it yields and to encash the value others may attach thereto, and to exchange these rights. In other words, a resource owner has the right to take decisions affecting the value of his resource, the right to bear the value consequences of the resource concerned, and the right to alienate these rights. In microeconomic theory, this bundle of rights is collectively referred to as a "property right" [Alchian (1977), 129-132; Alchian (1984), 34; Demsetz (1966), 62].

In the theory which approaches a firm as a coalition of cooperative input owners, it is usually implied that the latter contract among each other about how their respective inputs are to be combined with other inputs, *i.e.* about the use of their resources in the coalition (the firm). More accurately, the owners of *property rights* (as defined above) in resources to be used in the coalition are deemed to contract among themselves about the exercise of these rights so as to effect joint production [Alchian and Demsetz (1972); Jensen and Meckling (1976); Alchian (1984)]. Jensen and Meckling [1979, 470] have argued, therefore, that the very notion that inputs are supplied into a firm implies "the existence of a system of "rights" in resources".

The view of the firm as a coalition between contracting input owners has culminated into the thesis that what is called a "firm", is what comes into being as a result of the contracting process between owners of property rights in resources.

The Firm – A Nexus of Contracts

Thus, a firm has come to be regarded as a set of contracts among individual input owners devised to organize joint production [Alchian (1984), 34]. Accordingly, Jensen and Meckling [1976, 310] have concluded: "Contractual relations are the essence of the firm". Such contractual relations emerge because each contracting input owner expects to be better off by cooperating with others in a firm than by working on an individual basis. A firm, then, connects various contracts between input owners and by doing so, it serves as "*a nexus for contracting relationships*" [Jensen and Meckling (1976), 311; emphasis by the authors].

Within the firm, all contracting individuals are deemed to be motivated by their personal self-interests and the behavior of the firm, including the output it produces, will therefore reflect the equilibrium emerging from such individual self-interests [Jensen (1983), 327].

In brief, by the above-mentioned theory, a "firm" is the place where contracts between input owners come together. The contracts which make up the firm cover "the way inputs are joined to create outputs and the way receipts from outputs are shared among inputs", as Fama [1980, 290] has explained. It is not always understood, especially by lawyers, however, that the "nexus of contracts" concept of the firm does not exclusively refer to contracts in a strictly legal context.

The term "contract" has different connotations in law and economics, respectively [Gordon (1989), 1549; Hart (1989), 1764 fn. 30]. A lawyer tends to define a contract according to the rules of contract formation specified in the relevant contract law. As a rule, therefore, he is inclined to think more formally of what constitutes a contract than an economist would tend to do.

Traditionally, to a lawyer a contract is essentially made up of one or more promises, enforceable by law and ordinarily based on an offer made by one party followed by its acceptance by another party. Williston's definition stated long ago is still the core of many lawyers' thinking about what constitutes a contract: "A contract is a promise, or set of promises, to which the law attaches legal obligation" [Williston (1927), 1]. Similarly, Section 1 of the American Law Institute's Restatement (Second) of Contracts defines a contract as "a promise or the set of promises for the breach of which the law gives a remedy, or the performance of which the law in some way recognizes as a duty".

From a legal angle, the distinguishing mark of a contract is the creation of one or more legally enforceable rights, founded on such promises, to another party's conduct in the future [Pollock (1946), 1]. One party's *right* to a particular performance is mirrored in another party's *obligation* to act accordingly. The legal notion of contract requires that the rights and obligations between the contracting parties be "specified and fixed by their own voluntary and actual agreement", as Clark [1985, 60] has stated.

To an economist, on the other hand, a contract is rather a manner to denote an arrangement characterized by reciprocal expectations and behavior, directed toward and induced by a common interest in the realization of a mutual benefit [Gordon (1989), 1549; Hart (1989), 1764 fn. 30]. Unlike the lawyer, the economist does not focus on the legal requirements with regard to contract formation. In his view a contract is simply where supply and demand meet.

From an economist's point of view, spirit rather than letter (legal rules) determines whether there is a contract [Williamson (1993), 45]. His emphasis is not so much on legally enforceable *promises* but on a mutually understood joint *interest* and on reciprocal *expectations* that each contracting party will behave according to a particular course of action beneficial to the other party. Economists tend to assume that in a "contract" such a common interest and such expectations are reflected in one or more commitments about future action, in this rather informal way [Alchian (1993), 368].

In the definition of the firm as a "nexus of contracts", a contract should be conceived of in accordance with the above-mentioned economic concept rather than in strictly legal terms. Therefore, when a firm is said to be "a nexus for a complex set of contracts among individuals" [Jensen and Meckling (1979), 470], this description primarily points to the premise that the individuals involved have a mutually understood common interest in and reciprocal expectations about bringing together inputs for the purpose of jointly producing output, which are deemed to be reflected in a set of (more or less informal) commitments about collective action made for this purpose. Such commitments may be formalized through binding contracts in a legal sense, but they do not need to. Thus, the firm as a "nexus of contracts" may include both "implicit" (*i.e.* legally unenforceable) and "explicit" (*i.e.* legally enforceable) contracts.

Furthermore, it should be noted that economists, as well as lawyers, often distinguish between two types of contracts. A *spot contract* (or *discrete contract*) refers to a single exchange, that is, a transaction by which a resource is traded outright or by which a service is provided on one occasion, usually in exchange for money, or in exchange for some other resource or service (in barter transactions). A spot contract, by definition, is a short-term contract.

A *relational contract*, on the other hand, refers to a relationship by which parties engage in cooperative action for an agreed purpose. It does not refer to cooperation to bring about a single exchange, or a series of such exchanges, but to some longer lasting cooperative action [Macneil (1981); Macneil (1985); Williamson (1986), 104-105]. The emphasis here is on continuity of the parties' cooperation. A relational contract, therefore, refers to an intended long-term relationship. In the "nexus of contracts" definition of the firm, the term "contracts" is to be understood as primarily including relational contracts. The "nexus of contracts" concept assumes a set of *relationships* between resource owners cooperating for the purpose of jointly producing output, rather than a series of separate spot contracts.

The "nexus of contracts" approach is complementary to the definition of a firm as a series of inputs from which output is obtained, *i.e.* the firm as a production function. It extends the production function concept by indicating *what* brings such inputs together so as to produce output: a set of implicit and explicit contracts between owners of property rights in resources.

The extent and nature of the output a firm can produce depend on the nature and substance of these rights and contracts. Hence, the composition of the firm's production function and, so, the production opportunities available to it depend on the rights input owners have and on the terms of the contracts among them [Jensen and Meckling (1979), 470]. Otherwise said, the production function the firm embodies is itself a function of the rights of input owners and the contracts between them, and this insight is what the "nexus of contracts" theory adds to the description of the firm as a production function.

The "nexus of contracts" concept emphasizes the essentially contractual nature of the firm, the term "contractual" being used in the sense discussed above. The firm's contractual nature is relevant to our question of how the corporate structure may relate to the operation of the firm, given that the set of contracts from which a firm emanates may also determine its organizational structure and provide incentives to the individuals in the firm to engage in particular courses of conduct. In Chapter 2 we will examine the particular contractual arrangements represented in the organizational concept of the corporation.

The Firm – An Alternative to the Market

The "nexus of contracts" concept of the firm has emerged largely in reaction to another theory in which the firm is approached as an alternative to a series of market exchange transactions (spot contracts) [Jensen and Meckling (1976), 310]. The starting point in the latter theory is the observation that there is a paradox between the existence of firms and standard (neo)classical theory of how the economic system of a market economy works.

(Neo)classical economics teaches that the market mechanism, meaning exchange transactions directed by relative prices, coordinates economic activity by directing scarce resources to their highest valued uses. It does so by permitting owners of property rights in resources to trade freely at whatever prices they agree. The operation of the market mechanism is illustrated by the following example.

If B, desiring to use a resource x for a particular purpose, attaches a higher value to x than the value of x to its current owner A and to other market participants, resource owner A would increase his wealth by selling x to B. Such a transaction would make each of A and B better off, since A would only sell at a price exceeding the value of x to A and since it would only make sense for B to purchase x if B's expected benefit from x outweighs its price.

In sum, for both A and B there is a potential gain from trade, being the difference between the transaction price and the utility each of them attaches to x. To obtain this gain A and B, conceived of as utility maximizing individuals, will enter into a transaction as described. As a result, resource x will flow from a place where it is valued comparatively low to a higher valued use.

Relative prices emerging in the market indicate a resource's market value in relation to the value of other resources. A resource's relative price is determined by the availability of and demand for that resource relative to the availability of and demand for other resources. Relative prices prevailing in the market together with personal preferences – a person's evaluations independent of price and budget considerations – reveal to individual participants in the market potential gains from trade. Utility, or wealth, maximizing participants buy and sell to obtain such gains, like A and B in our example. In this manner the "invisible hand" of the market mechanism [Smith (1981; orig. 1776), 456] directs resources to their highest value in use.

The market mechanism can, and to a large extent does, in the same way serve to allocate factors of production to their highest valued uses. If in the above example x is substituted by, for example, labor, the example demonstrates that it would be beneficial to both A and B if A would sell his labor to B.

Acquiring A's labor could be beneficial to B, for instance, if B would be able to use A's labor to operate a machine in order to manufacture a product y. Suppose that C would be willing to purchase y from B at a price which exceeds the costs to B of obtaining A's labor as well as the operating costs of B's machine. In these circumstances, B will increase his wealth if he hires A's labor to manufacture y and if he subsequently sells y to C. If more people like C show up, B may further increase his wealth if he hires more labor (and perhaps more machines) to raise the production of y (until B's marginal cost and marginal revenue from manufacturing an additional unit of y become equal). In this way the market mechanism serves to direct inputs into products.

Within a firm, however, the use of inputs is typically *not* governed by market exchange transactions directed by relative prices. In our example, B acquires A's labor with a view to having A operate a machine, but how exactly A is to perform once hired will depend on B's directives. Within the firm it is not exchange transactions between A and B of the kind described above which determine how A's labor is used, but B's instructions. In Arrow's words [1970, 140], within the firm "the price system, which the economist tends to regard as essential to the rational allocation of resources, is not used (...) at all".

The different manner in which *within* a firm the use of resources is determined, is what distinguishes a firm from the allocative system of the market. In a firm normally the "visible hand of management" [Chandler (1977), 1] coordinates the allocation of production factors among alternative ends. It is the firm's management which decides to which production opportunity set available to the firm resources (for example, workers) shall be dedicated, that means, where on its production function the firm shall produce.

As described, (neo)classical economic theory tells us that the market mechanism directs the use of resources by means of bilateral transactions between resource owners, the buying and selling decisions of market participants being made on the basis of relative prices. However, within firms there are "intra-firm coordinators" (commonly referred to as entrepreneurs or managers) who allocate production factors between different uses, in place of exchange transactions among resource owners acting across the market. In effect, the firm constitutes an alternative mode of coordinating economic activity.

This fundamental insight has been set forth by Coase in his seminal paper on "The Nature of the Firm" [1937], pointing out that organizing economic activity in a firm is an alternative to using the market mechanism. In his own words, firm and market are "alternative methods of coordinating production" [Coase (1937), 388].

The Firm – An Allocative System

What makes up the alternative coordinating mechanism within a firm has not, however, been defined without ambiguity.

Coase [1937, 388] has stated that within a firm market transactions are substituted by an "entrepreneur-co-ordinator, who directs production". In his view, within a firm the orders of such an "entrepreneur-co-ordinator" determine the use of resources, including the tasks that workers are to perform. In a firm the market mechanism is superseded and it is entrepreneurial authority that takes its place, so Coase maintains. Judging from the popularity which the association of the firm with such entrepreneurial "supervision" over productive activity meanwhile has achieved, Cohen [1979, 589] has concluded that "the presence of supervision [is] perhaps the most commonly ascribed characteristic of firms".

On the basis of Coase's insight, others have proceeded to describe the intra-firm allocation of resources as a "hierarchy", suggesting that the mark of a firm is a system of superiors and subordinates, the former instructing the latter on how to employ productive resources. In this approach, the use of resources within a firm is determined by the hierarchy in the firm, which selects its appropriate production plan. The opposite of the hierarchy in the firm, then, is everybody's freedom to engage or not to engage in a transaction, which is characteristic of the market [Williamson (1973); (1975)]. Coase has meanwhile explained that his term "entrepreneur-co-ordinator" is to be understood as a catch-all term referring to all hierarchy in a firm replacing the market mechanism, viz. "the hierarchy in a business which directs resources and includes not only management but also foremen and many workmen" [1988b, 31].

The "hierarchy" or "entrepreneur" concept suggests that within a firm there is an authority (or a hierarchical system of authority) which has some rather autocratic power to instruct and to discipline others, so as to direct the use of resources. This perception has been challenged by Alchian and Demsetz [1972]. They have explained the firm's internal allocative system from the perspective of the contractual nature of the firm previously discussed.

In their view, an intra-firm coordinator has no superior authoritarian power at all to instruct and to discipline inputs. Approaching a firm as a set of contracts among diverse cooperating input owners, they argue that his position is that of a "*central contractual agent in a team productive process*" [Alchian and Demsetz (1972), 778; emphasis by the authors]: he is conceived of as a party common to the various contracts between input owners from which the firm has emerged.

To direct resources within the firm and to discipline cooperating inputs, Alchian and Demsetz assume that this "central contractual agent" continually renegotiates with individual input owners about the use of the resources they supply, that means, about the contractual terms governing their cooperation in the firm. Thus, when a manager allocates a production factor (for example, a worker) to a different use (task), according to Alchian and Demsetz this means that the terms of the contractual relationship between the resource owner (the worker) concerned and other participating input owners are adjusted through the manager as their common agent. No managerial *command* is involved.

The process of renegotiating the various contracts among input owners that constitute the firm does not require every individual input owner's consent to every contractual change. In order to enable him to enhance joint productivity, Alchian and Demsetz assume that input owners bestow on the firm's central agent the right to revise contract terms of individual input owners independently of contracts with other inputs, that is, without having to terminate or alter every other input's contract.

In principle, so Alchian and Demsetz maintain, this process of renegotiating contractual relationships among input owners does not differ from contracting across the market, except that within a firm renegotiations and contract adjustments take place through a specialized central agent and not through bilateral negotiations like in the ordinary market. They have, therefore, called a firm a "specialized surrogate" of the market, and "a privately owned market" of input owners for team use of inputs [1972, 793, 795].

The Firm – A Market?

The Alchian-Demsetz analysis summarized above does not, however, refute Coase's basic proposition that the allocative system of the firm is different from the allocation of resources by means of bilateral exchange transactions across the market.

They may have termed it a "surrogate market", but the continuous renegotiation through a common agent of contracting relationships among input owners, which in the Alchian-Demsetz hypothesis marks a firm, is not equal to carrying out transactions via the market. Within a firm, the ordinary market mechanism consisting in exchange transactions directed by relative prices, does not operate. Coase [1937, 389] therefore concluded, "the distinguishing mark of the firm is the supersession of the price mechanism".

Alchian and Demsetz assume that the contractual relationships between cooperating input owners in a firm do not materially differ from contracting in the market place. While agreeing to the firm's contractual nature, Cheung [1983], by contrast, has argued that within a firm market exchange transactions have been replaced by another type of contract. A firm, he states, should be conceived of as "a way to organize activities under contractual arrangements that differ from those of ordinary product markets" [1983, 3].

In a market exchange contract a resource is usually traded outright, in its entirety, or, more accurately, the entire property right in a resource is transferred. In a firm, Cheung [1983, 10] argues, this type of contract is substituted by a contract by which an input owner transfers only a delimited bundle of rights to use his input (referred to as a "limited set of use rights" [1983, 3]). By such a contract, the input owner entitles the acquirer of these rights to allocate his input, largely at the latter's discretion, in exchange for future income. Therefore, within the firm no further transactions are needed to direct resources between alternative uses. Although in Cheung's opinion [1983, 10] the point is not that a firm supersedes the market mechanism but that in a firm bilateral exchange contracts are superseded by another type of contract, his conclusion is similar to the observation made by Coase [1937, 391].

Jensen and Meckling [1976, 310-311; 1979, 470] suggest that the set of contracting relationships which constitutes a firm, does not merely include contracts among cooperative input owners but also contracts with consumers. The insight that the firm differs from the market in that within a firm the allocation of resources is not governed by the ordinary market mechanism, implies that this thesis is conceptually incorrect.

As far as contracts with consumers are concerned, these are transactions between parties that trade in the market. The firm, or the joint input owners, enters into such contracts as a participant in the output market and so do consumers. On the premise that the activities inside the firm are not directed by the market mechanism, in our view contracts between the firm, or the joint input owners, and consumers, which *are* directed by the market mechanism, fall outside the allocative system established by the firm.

Such contracts belong to the domain of the market as they are no different from other bilateral exchange transactions between parties transacting across markets. They deal with the distribution of the firm's output and not with the allocation of resources into products. The allocative system of the firm, by contrast, deals with the allocation of production factors into output, the latter being disposed of through the market, and thus comprises contracts among resource owners only.

The Specialization Argument

Since the market mechanism serves to allocate resources between different uses and since in that way it is technically able to direct factors of production into output, one may be tempted to ask: why have firms emerged at all? Why do we, apart from exchange transactions coordinated by relative prices directing scarce resources into their highest value in use, observe firms within which the ordinary market mechanism does not function? Why have firms come into existence, as "islands of conscious power in this ocean of unconscious co-operation like lumps of butter coagulating in a pail of buttermilk", as Robertson [1923, 85], quoted by Coase [1937, 388], has posed the question?

It has been asserted that neoclassical theory has "failed to provide a full rationale for the firm's role in the economic system" [McNulty (1984), 245]. Similarly, Boulding [1960, 1] has stated that in neoclassical economics the firm remains "a shadowy entity (...) and most of the problems which are connected with it simply do not arise". The relative lack of interest in neoclassical economic theory in the role of firms ensues from the fact that in the theory's dominant perfect competition model, which was briefly described in the Introduction to this book, the existence and operation of firms is simply taken for granted. In that model, all production is *assumed* to occur in firms as opposed to consumption, which occurs in households. Firms produce goods and services for exchange in the market, with market prices dictating the use firms make of productive resources, assuming a given level of technology and knowledge.

Demsetz [1997, 426-428] has made it clear that in conventional neoclassical theory the relevant distinction is not between the firm and the market, but between production for the market, *i.e.* for sale to others, which is done by firms, on the one hand and production for oneself, *i.e.* self-sufficiency, which is *not* regarded as production by a firm and which is excluded from the perfect competition model, on the other hand. Market and firm then are complementary concepts, not potential substitutes, given that firms need markets to sell output and to acquire inputs. The Coasian distinction between managerial (entrepreneurial, hierarchical) coordination within firms and coordination of productive activity by the price mechanism, is not made. Yet it is this *second* distinction which brings into question the matter of the firm's origins and determinants.

However, as we elaborate below, various explanations of the emergence of firms have been advanced. Each of them endeavors to demonstrate that organizing productive activity in a firm has certain advantages peculiar to this form of economic organization which are responsible for the firm's emergence. What, therefore, are the merits of organizing production in a firm which may account for its existence?

Although the classical economists, too, have been accused of having failed to develop a plausible explanation of the emergence of firms [Blaug (1958), 226], Adam Smith [1981] did take a first step towards the formulation of an explanatory theory of the firm. He associated the existence of firms with cooperation between owners of production factors to accomplish production on a large scale, which in turn enabled specialization of production factors in different activities.

Illustrated by his famous pin manufacturing example [1981, 14-15], Smith noted that if production takes place on a sufficiently large scale, factors of production can become specialized in different tasks, thereby improving their dexterity and productivity through increased experience in a particular activity. Specialization also enables workers to save time in passing between different tasks and it fosters invention by concentrating workers' minds on a single activity, so Smith observed. Consequently, specialization increases the amount of output which can be obtained from a given level of input of production factors, and concurrently enables production to take place at a lower cost per unit of output than if production were in small volumes and unspecialized.

Briefly, through specialization of labor and equipment, large-scale production results in productivity advances and consequent reductions in unit production costs. In Smith's description of how the economy works, firms emerge to take advantage of such *economies of scale*. In his theory, they are vehicles facilitating the production of large quantities of output by specialized equipment and specialized workers. It is Smith's reasoning that has caused specialization to become regarded as "a fundamental principle of economic organization" [Stigler (1951), 193].

The Division of Risks Argument

A second explanation of the origin of firms has been developed by Frank Knight [1921]. His theory of the firm also hinges on specialization, but in a different way to the way in which Smith construed it. Smith thought of specialization in technical terms, *i.e.* specialization in different parts of the production process and in different technical skills. Knight, however, centers on specialization in the assessment of the *risks* to which economic activity is inherently subject.

He argues that such risks inevitably result from the existence of uncertainty, particularly with regard to the future development of technology and knowledge, future demand for outputs, availability of production factors, price fluctuations in output and factor markets and so on. According to Knight, business ventures are affected by a large degree of uncertainty, as various contingencies influence their success or failure. Consequently, there is ordinarily substantial risk involved in putting resources together in order to produce and market goods or services.

Knight submits that some people are better able to assess such business risks than others. They have "greater ability to forecast the future and greater power to control the course of events" [1921, 265]. Because of their superior ability to appraise risks, these individuals have an advantage over others in organizing productive activity. Therefore, they will both specialize in "risk-taking or uncertainty bearing" [1942, 129] and organize production. To organize production, they acquire labor and other inputs from third parties and as risk-takers they earn the profits (the excess of earnings over costs) and suffer the losses arising from productive activities. Knight refers to these people as "entrepreneurs".

Others who are less able and, hence, less willing to take risks, will furnish productive services to the former in exchange for a fixed remuneration. They agree to carry out the entrepreneur's instructions, while in return he provides them with security of income. Those who dislike risk will become employees. By submitting to the directives of an entrepreneur in exchange for a fixed remuneration, they shift business risks to the latter and are relieved of uncertainty. In Knight's view, firms come into being as a result of this shifting of risks to entrepreneurs who direct economic activity.

If there were no uncertainty, according to Knight, firms simply would not arise. If uncertainty were absent, every individual would have "perfect knowledge of the situation", so that there would be no need for specialists in risk assessment to assume control of productive activity. In effect, Knight asserts, in the absence of uncertainty the "flow of raw materials and productive services to the consumer would be entirely automatic" [1921, 267].

Knight's entrepreneurial concept comprises two functions [1921, 271]. First, the entrepreneur bears the *responsibility* for the success or failure of business operations. If a venture becomes a success, he will reap its profits; if it becomes a failure, he will suffer the losses. Second, he has *control* of the use of resources in the firm. He decides in which way resources shall be allocated and which activities workers are to perform. In summary, the entrepreneur is a specialist in both risk-taking and "leadership or economic pioneering" [1942, 128]. In the latter capacity his primary task is "to initiate useful changes or innovations" [1942, 128]. The firm emerges as a consequence of this dual specialization.

Thus, along with the separation between risk-taking and risk-avoidance Knight noticed the separation between *direction* and *execution*. Risk-taking individuals direct economic activity and bear the wealth effects of the various contingencies that affect business operations. Risk-avoiding people execute the directives of the former. Knight regards such separation between direction (leadership) and execution as the "most important differentiation in function, or division of labor, between individuals" [1951, 17].

From his observation that firms place specialists in leadership in the position to direct economic activity, he concludes that "undoubtedly the largest single source of the increased efficiency through organization results from having work planned and directed by the exceptionally capable individuals, while the mass of people follow instructions" [1951, 17].

The Transaction Costs Argument

Ronald Coase [1937] has given a third reason for the emergence of firms. Coase does not deny the productivity advances that Smith associated with specialization. Nor does he object to Knight's assertion that some people have superior abilities to assess business risks. He does claim, however, that neither argument provides a sufficient and convincing explanation for the existence of firms.

Coase's explanatory theory of the firm starts with a reference to the ability of the market mechanism to coordinate the use of productive resources. To comprehend his reasoning, we must revert briefly to the working of the market mechanism. As we saw earlier, in a market economy people enter into transactions on the basis of relative prices in order to obtain gains from trade. Gains from trade arise mainly where people specialize in different activities; trade is to a large degree the counterpart of specialization. If a person specializes in producing a particular good or service that he sells on the market, he can use the revenues to purchase other goods and services. In this way he will be able to satisfy his wants to a greater extent than if he were to attempt to produce everything he desires by himself.

Market prices induce individuals to specialize in a particular activity, according to comparative advantage. Suppose that A could earn USD 6 per hour as an unskilled laborer. Suppose also that the market price for interpreting services is USD 12 per hour and that A has a gift for languages. In these circumstances, A would maximize his revenues if he would specialize as an interpreter. People, and production factors in general, have different qualities. A utility maximizing individual may seek to maximize revenue by specializing in an activity in which he has an advantage over other people. By specializing in an activity in which he has such a comparative advantage (more accurately, an activity in which his comparative advantage over other people is greatest), he will maximize his revenues, which he can subsequently exchange for other goods and services to satisfy his desires. All of this is elementary economic theory.

As people can and do trade and as market prices induce individuals to specialize in activities in which they have a comparative advantage, technically an institution such as the firm is not required to bring about the advantages connected with specialization. People specializing in different activities could simply trade the results of their specialized productive efforts through the market, which would make resources flow to their highest value in use. This is the starting point in Coase's argument.

For instance, a specialist in a particular part of a production process could sell his output, as an intermediate good, to a specialist in the next stage and so on. Hence, Smith's pin manufacturing could, in principle, be organized by means of market transactions between specialists in different parts of the pin making process.

Coase [1937, 398] argues that there is no need for a special "integrating force" to organize and control specialized production (as had been suggested by Dobb [1928, 10]), given that such a force already exists in the form of the market mechanism which directs the use of resources, including people's productive efforts. Because of the coordinating function of the market mechanism, Coase contends that "there is no reason to suppose that specialization must lead to chaos" [1937, 398].

Also, Knight's specialists in the assessment of business risks could sell their superior judgment on the market as advice, for instance, to those interested to know how demand for a particular good or service is likely to develop. There is no need for them to engage actively in organizing productive processes [Coase (1937), 400]. From these observations Coase concludes that specialization *per se* is not a satisfactory explanation for the existence of firms.

As described, in Coase's view a firm is an alternative to organizing economic activity by means of exchange transactions across the market; firm and market are regarded as alternative means of economic organization [1937, 388]. A firm, he maintains, consists of "the system of relationships which comes into existence when the direction of resources is dependent on an entrepreneur" instead of market transactions [1937, 393]. Coase proceeds to explain why one coordinating mechanism (the entrepreneur) is substituted for another one (the market mechanism). His answer is that firms arise because there is a cost of using the market mechanism, viz. the costs of carrying out transactions in the market. Organizing production in a firm serves to avoid these costs [1937, 392; 1988c, 40; 1992, 715]. If the costs of carrying out market transactions were zero, in Coase's view firms would have no purpose [1988c, 34] and would therefore simply not exist.

In his 1937 paper, Coase was not very explicit about what he meant by the costs of using the market, although he did give some indications. First, transacting in the market involves the cost of "discovering what the relevant prices are" [1937, 390]. Second, there are costs of negotiating and specifying exchange contracts [1937, 391]. Coase later clarified that "to carry out a market transaction it is necessary to discover who it is that one wishes to deal with, to inform people that one wishes to deal and on what terms, to conduct negotiations leading up to a bargain, to draw up the contract, to undertake the inspection needed to make sure that the terms of the contract are being observed, and so on" [1960, 15; 1988d, 6].

The costs of carrying out market transactions have come to be known as *transaction costs*. "Transaction costs" is a catch-all term referring to *any* costs that people considering to engage in and to implement a transaction across a market have to incur, apart from the contract price of the good or service which is the subject of the transaction concerned and apart from the production costs of the particular good or service. Accordingly, transaction costs have been interpreted as the costs of "*any* activity undertaken to use the price system" [Demsetz (1997), 426; emphasis by the author]. They are the costs of bringing buyers and sellers together and of organizing and enforcing exchange transactions.

Stephen [1988, 31] has defined transaction costs as "the cost of finding transactors, negotiating the transaction and policing and enforcing its terms". Similar definitions have been given, *inter alia*, by Dahlman [1979, 152] and Polinsky [1983, 12]. Other commentators have referred to such costs as the "costs of running the economic system" [Arrow (1969), 48] and as the "economic equivalent of friction in physical systems" [Williamson (1985), 19].

By organizing economic activity in a firm, transactions are taken out of the market place and shifted into a firm. Coase argues that within a firm, transaction costs are saved by allowing some authority to direct the use of resources through instructions [1937, 392]. The direction of resources by such an authority, the "entrepreneur-co-ordinator" previously referred to, is held to avoid transaction costs as it avoids transactions between individual resource owners.

Within the firm cooperating factors of production do not have to incur the cost of identifying parties with whom they could transact, or the cost of negotiating and enforcing contracts for separate contributions to the production process. This is because within the firm, such a series of separate transactions is substituted by one contract, viz. an employment contract under which a production factor agrees to obey the directions of an entrepreneur within the limits of the employment contract in exchange for a certain remuneration [1937, 391]. As Coase [1960, 16] stated in a later paper, "within the firm individual bargains between the various cooperating factors of production are eliminated and for a market transaction is substituted an administrative decision".

In Coase's theory, the firm emerges to economize on transaction costs. It arises when it is possible to organize an activity within a firm at less cost than would be incurred if the same activity were organized through market transactions [1988b, 19; 1988d, 7]. In other words, a firm exists if it is able to allocate resources at a lower cost than the cost of allocation by means of the market mechanism. How an activity is organized, through the market or in a firm, depends on a comparison of the costs of organizing the activity within a firm with the costs of carrying out market transactions [1988a, 17; 1988b, 32].

If, for instance, Smith's pin manufacturing process were to be organized by the market mechanism, a large number of separate transactions would have to be negotiated between specialists in various parts of the pin production process. Or imagine the number of transactions that would need to be concluded in order to manufacture an automobile if market transactions were used to organize production. In such instances, the amount of transaction costs incurred by using the market mechanism would unquestionably be enormous. Substituting a series of market transactions by entrepreneurial direction, in other words, organizing production in a firm, serves to save such transaction costs.

In conclusion, Coase argues that production will be organized in a firm "until the costs of organising an extra transaction within the firm become equal to the costs of carrying out the same transaction by means of an exchange on the open market or the costs of organising in another firm" [1937, 395]. Thus, the boundaries of firms are not regarded as technologically determined [Williamson (1985), 4], but a firm will tend to extend its activities as long as its organizational costs are less than "the costs of achieving the same result by market transactions or by means of operations within some other firm" [1988c, 47; 1988c, 38].

The Team Production Argument

A fourth explanation of the firm has been advanced by Alchian and Demsetz [1972]. They do not reject Coase's proposition that economic activity is organized in a firm when this method of organization serves to economize on the costs of carrying out exchange transactions across markets. However, they do criticize Coase for failure to identify the factors which determine *when* the cost of organizing economic activity in a firm is low relative to the cost of carrying out market transactions [1972, 783-784].

The market mechanism operates at a cost but there is also a cost accompanying the allocation of resources within a firm. Alchian and Demsetz submit that Coase did not explain when the cost of directing resources within a firm would be less than the cost of using market transactions. In a similar criticism, Williamson [1975, 3; 1985, 4; 1986, 175] has maintained that Coase failed to "operationalize" the notion of transaction costs: he has not developed a comprehensive theory concerning the factors which account for differences in the respective costs of organizing economic activity through the market or within a firm and which, thus, determine the outcome of the choice between organization of an activity in a firm or by means of market transactions. Meanwhile, Coase has conceded this criticism [1992, 718].

The theory of the firm developed by Alchian and Demsetz [1972] can be regarded as an attempt to make up this deficiency. They have identified one source of cost differences between the firm and the market as methods of organization, viz. team use of inputs and shirking problems connected with team production.

The starting point in the Alchian-Demsetz analysis is that much productive activity involves teamwork of production factors. "Teamwork" refers to a production process involving multiple inputs which are owned by more than one supplier, and yielding an output which is not simply the sum of identifiable products of the individual inputs [1972, 779]. Team productive activity is moreover defined by the fact that "a union, or joint use, of inputs yields a larger output than the sum of the products of the separately used inputs" [1972, 794]. Thus, with team production, the productivity of the joint inputs is larger than if each of them were to perform independently of the others. This surplus is the gain resulting from cooperation as a team.

The output of a team productive process is the result of the *joint* efforts of the cooperating factors of production; it is *team* output, not an aggregate of separately produced components [Alchian (1993), 367]. In order to induce each *individual* input to a team productive process (a "team member") to make maximum use of its comparative advantage over others, each team member is to be rewarded in accordance with his contribution to the team's total output [Alchian and Demsetz (1972), 778]. If an input's reward were not reflecting its actual contribution to the team, *i.e.* its marginal product, individual team members would not have proper incentives to productive action. If a team member were to earn less than his marginal product, he would have insufficient incentive to improve his effort. And if a team member were to earn more than his marginal product, he would receive a reward for bad performance and would therefore have an incentive to shirk.

To reward each cooperating production factor in accordance with his contribution to the team's total output, it is necessary to determine the actual contributions of the individual team members to the team's output. However, it is difficult and costly to measure individual contributions, as they are not separately reflected in the team's output. By definition, a team's output is not the sum of the separable outputs of each of its members or, in the words of Alchian and Demsetz, the "individual cooperating inputs do not yield identifiable, separate products which can be *summed* to measure the total output" [1972, 779; emphasis by the authors].

As individual contributions of team members to the team's output are not directly and cheaply observable, it is both difficult and costly to determine each individual team member's reward in accordance with his marginal product. This difficulty gives rise to *shirking* problems: a team member may be able to shirk without the resulting decrease in his productivity being detected and without his reward being reduced proportionately to his neglect of duty. Individual team members have incentives to shirk in so far as shirking is likely to result in a net increase in their utility (for example, by affording extra leisure).

Shirking by individual team members leads to a decrease in team productivity, which will be reflected in a decrease of the team's total output and in a decline in net team earnings (profits). Note that the survival of any team (and any firm) requires that team earnings be at least sufficiently high to offset the opportunity costs of the inputs, *i.e.* the amount they could earn elsewhere which is given up by joining or staying on the team.

To detect shirking and to prevent shirking losses, team members would have to incur costs to monitor fellow team members; such costs discourage monitoring by individual members. Because of the difficulty of measuring a team member's marginal product and the cost of detecting shirking, the reward to a shirking team member may well be reduced by less than the reduction in team output and income for which he is responsible. In this manner a team member may be able to shift at least a part of the costs of his shirking to the team as a whole, the costs of his neglect of duty being shared by the team members collectively in the form of a reduction of total team output and profit [1972, 780].

In the theory of Alchian and Demsetz, a firm arises to cope with the above-mentioned shirking problem. As noted earlier in this chapter, in their approach within a firm there is some central common party to the contractual arrangements between the various cooperating inputs. This central agent monitors the performance of cooperating team members and apportions rewards to team members in accordance with each member's marginal product. He measures individual productivities, detects shirking, disciplines team members, assigns tasks, and may change the team's composition to improve team productivity. For these purposes he has been given the authority to revise the contract terms of individual team members independently of contracts with other members [1972, 782].

By monitoring the members of the team so as to detect undesirable actions and by adjusting the contract terms on which the team members cooperate so as to enforce desired actions, the team's central agent (the "monitor") manages the use of resources. He does not merely keep track of individual team members' performance but he also directs their efforts, explores productive opportunities and takes business decisions, thereby coordinating the activities of the team. In order to motivate the monitor to act in a manner which reduces shirking and which maximizes the team's productivity and, consequently, team profit, he is given the "residual claim" on team assets and cash flows: he is entitled to the residue amount remaining after all other cooperating inputs have been remunerated. The monitor will earn his residual reward by diminishing the amount of shirking by the team members.

"Shirking" is a special cost connected with team effort and arising from the difficulty to measure individual productivities in a team production process [Demsetz (1987), 5]. Alchian and Demsetz submit that this cost is reduced more effectively and more cheaply within a firm than if production were organized by means of market transactions, because in a system of bilateral exchange transactions there is no central agent to measure marginal productivities, to detect shirking, to discipline shirking team members and to revise the team. Although input owners could in principle perform the same tasks by bargaining across markets, for team productive processes, in which the marginal products of the individual team members are not readily and separably observable, matching rewards to marginal productivities and reducing shirking can be achieved "more economically" in a firm, *i.e.* by an intra-firm monitor [1972, 794, 782].

True, market competition by outsiders would (and to a certain extent does) deter incumbent team members from shirking, but not entirely. Outside input owners might offer to replace shirking team members by promising better performance, or in exchange for a lower share of the team's total income than the reward given to the shirking member. By refraining from shirking, new team members could raise team productivity, which would be reflected in their rewards (on the assumption that rewards are paid in conformity with individual team members' contributions to the team).

For competition to be effective, however, competitors must be willing to incur the cost of detecting the amount of shirking by incumbent team members in order to ascertain whether, and to what extent, opportunities exist for productivity increases. In addition, once a shirking team member is replaced by a new one, the latter will also have an incentive to shirk since he, too, will probably face less than the total reduction in team output and profit for which he is responsible, because of the same difficulty and cost of measuring shirking [1972, 781].

Alchian and Demsetz suggest that team productive activity will be organized in a firm if a net increase in productivity can be achieved, net of the costs associated with the shirking problem (including monitoring expenses), in comparison with a multitude of bilateral bargains between individual inputs [1972, 780; Demsetz (1987), 5]. They argue that team production can be organized in a firm at less cost than by means of bilateral transactions across markets, because of the firm's superior ability to tackle the shirking problem. The firm's device to cope with shirking costs, an intra-firm monitor motivated by the possession of the residual claim, is presumed to be superior to bilateral bargaining between input owners across the market and competition by non-team members. Thus, the firm is essentially viewed as "a means of achieving the benefits of collective action in situations in which the price system fails", as Arrow has put it [1974, 33].

The Asset Specificity Argument

A second reason for differences in the magnitude of the costs associated with organizing productive activity in a firm or by means of market transactions has been identified by Klein, Crawford and Alchian [1978]. In short, they argue that specificity of assets used in production processes gives rise to postcontractual opportunistic behavior, the costs of which can be reduced to a larger extent by the creation of a firm than by contracts between resource owners across markets. Their argument runs as follows.

A resource owner may possess an asset (for example, a piece of equipment) which is specialized to the productive activities of another individual, or to the operations of a team of cooperating production factors. The value of such an asset is likely to be higher to the individual, or the team, to whose activities the asset is specialized than to other parties. In other words, the value of a specialized asset elsewhere (the "salvage value") will be less than its value to the individual, or the team, to whose activities it is specialized.

Non-specialized assets typically have values that are not dependent on a particular user. If their current user would disappear, such assets would be able to earn an equal remuneration elsewhere. The return on the investment made to create a *specialized* asset, however, is dependent on its use by a particular individual or team. Therefore, the value of such a "specific" asset depends on the behavior of the individual or team to whose activities it is specialized [Alchian (1984), 36].

Suppose that the specialized asset is rented to the individual (or the team) on whose activities its value is dependent. If the individual (or team) to whom the asset is specialized were to stop renting it, the asset would lose a part of its value. It would lose the value in excess of its salvage value, *i.e.* the excess of its value over the value in its next best use to another renter, which has been labeled the "quasi-rent value of the asset" [Klein, Crawford and Alchian (1978), 298].

If an asset is specific to the activities of its renter in the manner described above, the renter may attempt to have his rent reduced after the rental contract is agreed. He may try to negotiate a lower remuneration to be paid to the asset's owner, opportunistically manipulating the situation on the basis of his knowledge that the owner is unlikely to have a comparable demand for the asset concerned from third parties willing to pay the same rent. Therefore, if the present renter would stop renting the asset, the owner would be left with the asset's salvage value and would forfeit the excess of the investment cost incurred to create the asset over the asset's salvage value.

By threatening to renege on the rental contract unless the specific asset's owner agrees to lower the rent, the renter of a specific asset may be able to reduce his cost of using the asset. In this manner he might effectively appropriate a part of the return on the asset owner's investment which is non-salvageable if the renter would disappear (*i.e.* the rent from the asset's specific value to the activities of that renter). In other words, he might appropriate a part of the quasi-rent to the asset owner.

Similarly, if an asset is specifically tailored to the activities of a particular user, the asset *owner* could attempt to renegotiate a higher rent by threatening to withdraw the asset. If comparable assets specialized to the user's activities are not readily available, by withdrawing his asset the asset owner could impose a cost on the asset's user, for example, by causing a production delay. Thus, by exercising credible threats of withdrawal and by carrying out such threats, the asset owner could renege on the rental contract in order to have his remuneration increased.

For instance, once a firm has become dependent upon supplies from one particular factory, the factory's owner may attempt to raise prices by threatening to cut off supplies to that firm. On the other hand, once a supplier has made an investment in a machine producing a product for which there is only one possible customer, the buyer could seek to obtain a price cut by threatening to reduce his purchases.

In summary, when an investment is made in an asset specialized to a particular user, a "hold-up" potential is created [Klein (1988), 199]: Asset specificity so creates prospects for opportunistic behavior, that is, self-interest seeking with little regard for principles or consequences [Macneil (1981), 87 fn. 17] and not restrained by consideration for rights and duties previously agreed. This type of behavior may result in the unanticipated non-fulfillment of contracts.

Williamson has related opportunism to "self-interest seeking with guile" [Williamson (1975), 26; (1981), 45-46; (1985), 47]. Somewhat more precisely, Macneil has defined opportunism as "self-interest seeking contrary to the principles of the relation in which it occurs" [1981, 87 fn. 17]. The relationship between owner and renter of a specific asset is susceptible to self-interest seeking contrary to the principles embodied in their rental contract. In particular, as set forth above, it is susceptible to postcontractual reneging in order to obtain individual advantage in the form of a rent reduction or increase. Incentives for opportunistic reneging exist where the owner of a specific asset and its user have conflicting wealth or utility maximizing objectives.

The prospect of postcontractual opportunistic behavior by the other party exposes both the owner and the renter of a specific asset to the risk of unanticipated losses resulting from unanticipated breaches of contract. Therefore, if there were no cost-effective means of avoiding postcontractual reneging, the possibility of postcontractual opportunistic behavior would discourage investments to create specific assets of the kind described above (relationship-specific investments), as a part of the value of the investment would be subject to the risk of appropriation.

Opportunistic behavior is likely to result in high transaction costs, if the relationship between the owner of the specific asset and its user (the renter) is organized by transactions made in the market place. High transaction costs would result not only from postcontractual reneging *per se*, but they would also be incurred by designing and enforcing contractual devices to reduce the prospects for such opportunistic behavior. Detailed contractual arrangements, together with a payment arrangement directed to align incentives, would be necessary to assure non-opportunistic behavior. However, in the event that such contracts do not completely eliminate prospects for opportunistic behavior, the potential for unanticipated costs from postcontractual hold-ups will continue to exist. In this event, *ex post* contracting hazards will discourage investments to create specific assets.

Even though a contract may be evidently legally enforceable, it may still be subject to postcontractual opportunistic behavior. For instance, by reneging a party may be able to impose substantial enforcement costs (entailing a postcontractual loss) on the other party, the threat of which may induce the latter to accept the demands of the reneging party. Also, "the threat of production delay during litigation may be an effective bargaining device" [Klein, Crawford and Alchian (1978), 301]. Hence, threats to breach a contract may be credible and effective even when they lack legal basis.

Klein, Crawford and Alchian argue that organizing the relationship between the specific asset and its user within a firm will serve to economize on transaction costs associated with postcontractual opportunistic behavior. Intra-firm coordination of asset use eliminates the prospect for gains from reneging on market contracts involving asset specificity, and so removes either party's incentive to behave opportunistically. Thus, the firm serves to align interests and behavior. To avoid market transaction costs, both the owner of a specific asset and its user have incentives to organize their relationship in a firm instead of across the market.

Thus, the problem of postcontractual opportunistic actions can be resolved by substituting a firm (in other words, imposing vertical integration) for market transactions. The more specific one party's investment would be to another party, the higher will be the market transaction costs associated with opportunistic behavior relative to the costs of organizing resources in a firm, and the more likely their relationship will be organized within a firm.

In the reasoning of Klein, Crawford and Alchian summarized above, asset specificity is a constraint on transacting in the market place which leads to an intra-firm relationship in place of market transactions. Coase [1988c, 42-46], however, has objected to asset specificity as a force causing market transaction costs to exceed the costs of organizing resources in a firm. First, he submits that the market discourages opportunistic actions by inducing individuals to take account of the adverse effects of such behavior on their chances of doing business in the future. Even if immediate gains are available, opportunities for future business may be lost.

Second, Coase points to the availability of contractual arrangements "which reduce the profitability of opportunistic behavior and therefore make it even more unlikely" [1988c, 44]. He suggests that the costs connected with opportunistic behavior in situations where there is asset specificity could effectively be reduced by means of properly tailored long-term contracts. Therefore, in his view there is no reason to assume that the hold-up potential created by asset specificity is more likely to lead to a firm than to a detailed long-term contract.

Likewise, Demsetz [1988, 150] has suggested that organizing resources within a firm does not have a significant advantage over bilateral contracts between resource owners to resolve the problems of opportunism to which asset specificity gives rise. He is skeptical about asset specificity as a factor affecting the relative amount of transaction costs. Demsetz questions whether it would cost more "to detail the terms of a contract when asset specificity is involved than when it is not" [1988, 150].

Instead, he argues, the relevant presumption of the asset specificity theory is that the presence of asset specificity increases each party's loss if the other party were to fail to comply with the terms of the rental agreement, relative to failure of an agreement involving non-specialized assets [1988, 150]. This observation suggests that it is not high transaction costs but the incentive to avoid the risk of such greater losses in situations involving asset specificity which induce a specific asset and the resource to which it is specialized to be organized within the same firm. This would then be the "true" rationale of the firm from an asset specificity perspective.

2. THE CORPORATE VEHICLE – A VIEW FROM ORGANIZATION THEORY

MANY BUSINESS FIRMS are legally organized as corporations. The corporation, including both its publicly held and its close manifestation, has over the past century come to be "the dominant organizational form for conducting business", as Scherer has noted [1988a, 61]. Its dominance does not so much appear from the absolute number of corporations that can be counted but, rather, from the percentage of total sales and business revenue for which corporations account and from the numbers of people they employ. In the United States, for instance, corporations are responsible for over 80 percent of annual business revenue. Accordingly, in market economies firms organized as corporations are usually responsible for the greater part of gross national product. In their famous 1932 treatise on "The Modern Corporation and Private Property", Berle and Means [1991, 313] already concluded that the business corporation may be regarded "not simply as one form of social organization but potentially (if not yet actually) as the dominant institution of the modern world". In a similar observation, Chayes [1959, 27] described the corporation as "the dominant nongovernmental institution of modern American life".

For quite a long time economists have studied the firm without particular reference to the corporation as its predominant form of organization in many parts of the economy. Similarly, legal scholars tend to study corporate legal problems without paying much attention to the economic entity that the corporation organizes. Thus, the corporation, as a form of organization, and the firm as its object of organization, are treated largely as separate subjects. Notable exceptions are Wolfson [1984], Easterbrook and Fischel [1991] and Romano [1993].

Economists studying the firm tend to regard the availability of instruments to set up a firm as given. They assume that organizational devices such as the corporation exist and usually do not discuss the particular features of the corporate concept. Likewise, lawyers refrain from entering the area of the economics of the business firm structured as a corporation. In general, they simply take for granted that the corporate form helps to finance the firm's operations by enabling the sale of equity shares and by insulating investors from liability. This observation is unquestionably true but it provides by no means a full and comprehensive insight into the relation between the firm and the corporation as an organizational concept embedded in the law.

As long ago as 1911, Nicholas Murray Butler, at that time president of Columbia University, said: "I weigh my words when I say that in my judgment the limited liability corporation is the greatest single discovery of modern times. (...) Even steam and electricity are far less important than the limited liability corporation, and they would be reduced to comparative impotence without it" [Meiners, Mofsky and Tollison (1979), 351]. However, it seems less clear *why* the corporate form should deserve so much praise.

In this chapter we examine in what ways the concept of the corporation is related to the firm as an economic institution. For this purpose, we examine the various functions of the corporation in organizing a business enterprise. What does the corporate concept contribute to the firm or, in other words, why does the corporation organize a firm as it does? As indicated in the introductory chapter, our focus is on publicly held corporations as generally they organize the larger businesses and as, therefore, they frequently affect large numbers of people.

Transaction Costs Revisited

In the preceding chapter we investigated first, what economists mean by a firm. We saw that the starting point in neoclassical microeconomics is that a firm comprises a series of inputs from which outputs are obtained, *i.e.* a production function. In the "nexus of contracts" theory the inputs represented in this production function are assumed to be linked together by a series of implicit and explicit contractual relations among owners of property rights in resources. These resource owners cooperate for the purpose of jointly producing output.

The relationships between input owners within a firm differ from bilateral exchange transactions across markets. Within the firm, the ordinary market mechanism does not function and the use of resources is directed by some alternative coordinating mechanism called either entrepreneur [Coase (1937)], hierarchy [Williamson (1975)] or monitor [Alchian and Demsetz (1972)]. The institutional setting of the firm has come to be viewed as an alternative to a multitude of exchange transactions directed by the market [Coase (1937)].

We explored various reasons that have been given in order to explain why economic activity is organized in a firm. Smith [1981] associated the firm with productivity advances from specialization enabled by large-scale production. Knight [1921] argued that firms emerge as a result of the organization of production by specialists in the assessment of business risks. Coase [1937] explained that the firm serves to economize on the costs of carrying out exchange transactions through the market. Alchian and Demsetz [1972] approached the firm as a means to ensure effective monitoring of input behavior in a team productive process. Klein, Crawford and Alchian [1978] argued that the firm eliminates prospects for postcontractual opportunistic behavior in situations in which the value of an asset (resource) depends on the behavior of some other agent.

As discussed in the previous chapter, both team effort and shirking problems arising from it and the hold-up potential to which asset specificity gives rise, have been identified as forces which occasion differences in the respective costs of organizing economic activity by means of market transactions or within a firm. Whether or not transactions will be shifted out of the market into a firm depends on market transaction costs in relation to the costs which would have to be incurred to operate a firm. In Coase's words, the firm has "a role to play in the economic system" when it is possible for transactions "to be organized within the firm at less cost than would be incurred if the same transactions were carried out through the market" [1988b, 19].

If market transaction costs were zero, potential gains from trade could be attained at no cost. Resources would flow to their highest value in use automatically, provided that rights in resources are well defined and freely transferable (and regardless of the choice of legal entitlements). This is what, again, Coase has pointed out in his now classic article on "The Problem of Social Cost" [1960]. There would be no reason for the existence of firms [1988d, 14] in view of the fact that exchange transactions across markets would serve to direct resources into products and services without cost. The market mechanism invariably would organize production by means of exchange transactions between resource owners.

However, transaction costs do exist and their existence entails that resources are absorbed in the making of transactions needed to bring about gains from trade. If the expected gain from a transaction is less than the transaction costs which would have to be incurred to carry out the transaction, the transaction will not take place [Coase (1960), 15-16; Coase

(1992), 716]. Thus, the existence of transaction costs implies that certain transactions are not carried out although they would make parties better off in the absence of those costs. In this event the wealth, or utility, maximizing allocation of resources will not be reached.

In other words, transaction costs are a barrier to the realization of gains from trade; they prevent potential gains from trade from being fully exploited. In this way the magnitude of transaction costs influences the economic outcomes obtained [Furubotn and Pejovich (1974), 46].

Demand for Organization

Suppose the market were the only method of economic organization available. If every productive activity involving different input owners were to be organized by means of market exchange transactions, a large amount of resources would inevitably be absorbed by the transaction costs which would have to be incurred in order to bring about the exchanges needed to organize production. Every contribution to the production process would require a separate transaction and would necessitate the cost of identifying a co-transactor, the cost of the bargaining process itself and the cost of specifying and enforcing contract terms. Owing to such costs certain productive arrangements would not be organized at all: a utility maximizing input owner will not exchange the resource he owns if the magnitude of the transaction costs involved in an exchange exceeds the size of the utility improvement which he would expect from an exchange transaction ignoring transaction costs. In such a case, on balance a transaction would not make him better off, and as a result his resource would *not* come to serve as an input to productive activity, whereas he would have supplied it in order to exploit gains from trade if transaction costs were zero or less.

Assuming that all resource owners participating in the market face transaction costs in one way or another, certain transactions needed to generate productive activity would not be carried out, although they would bring about wealth improvements if transaction costs were left out of the account. Transaction costs, then, would inhibit the organization of productive arrangements that would be organized in the absence of such costs. It follows that the existence and the magnitude of transaction costs has a negative effect on the amount of output which would become available for the satisfaction of consumer needs. In addition, in respect of those productive arrangements that would still be organized, transaction costs would be reflected in the costs of generating output and, consequently, in the prices consumers would have to pay.

In brief, if market exchange transactions were the only possible way to organize production, the existence of transaction costs would imply that certain production processes (output) would not come about at all, or at high costs (and correspondingly high prices) only. Thus, transaction costs would not merely affect the transactions that would take place but also the goods and services that would be produced and their prices [Coase (1992), 716].

When transaction costs absorb potential gains from trade, it does not pay resource owners to specialize. The amount of transaction costs they would have to incur in order to sell their specialized output to other parties might be larger than the extra income they could earn by specialized performance. In this way market transaction costs would inhibit the attainment of productivity advances from specialization. Hence, if all production were to be organized by transacting in the marketplace, the larger output quantities and the reductions in unit production costs that could technically be effected by specialization would simply not be realized. For instance, given the multitude of transactions that would need to be carried out to set up Smith's specialized pin manufacturing process, the magnitude of transaction costs would almost certainly inhibit the attainment of the same degree of specialization if it had to be achieved by means of bilateral bargains across the market.

If market transactions were the only way to organize production, transaction costs would similarly impair the organization of production by Knight's specialists in the assessment of business risks. Also, the transaction costs of ascertaining input performance might offset productivity increases from team production and in effect, they would preclude the exploitation of the superior productivity connected with team productive processes. Furthermore, the costs of potential postcontractual opportunistic behavior in situations of asset specificity would seriously discourage the making of investments to create specialized assets. If the anticipated cost of postcontractual reneging, including the cost of designing and enforcing contractual arrangements to prevent postcontractual hold-ups, were to exceed the expected return on the investment required to create a specific asset, the investment would not be made [Klein, Crawford and Alchian (1978), 301].

Organizing productive activity in a firm serves as a means to avoid the above-mentioned effects of market transaction costs, but it only does so if the cost of organizing a firm is lower than the cost of a series of bilateral exchanges through the market. The firm surmounts the impediments raised by market transaction costs – provided that it is possible to establish a firm at less cost. In as far as a firm avoids the costs of market transactions, organizing productive activity by establishing a firm serves to secure productivity gains from specialization of equipment and labor, from having production organized by specialist risk-takers, from team production and from investments in specific assets. Thus the reduction in transaction costs effected by the firm is the source of all other gains associated with the emergence of firms.

A firm does not, however, come into being as a creature of its own. It needs to be organized. Robertson's "islands of conscious power" [1923, 85] are not true islands raised by the forces of nature but polders which are intentionally created by men amidst the "ocean of unconscious co-operation" constituted by the market. In addition, the cost of shifting a market transaction into a firm is not *inherently* less than the market transaction costs that would so be avoided. The existence of firms, therefore, requires organizational devices that enable them to replace market exchange transactions and to economize on the costs of such transactions. This point is often overlooked in mainstream neoclassical economics, which tends to deal with "firms without organization" [Coase (1988d), 3]. The prevalence of market transaction costs can be conceptualized as having triggered a demand for organizational instruments suited to organize a firm at less cost than would be incurred if production were organized by means of market transactions.

The higher the costs of organizing production in a firm relative to market transaction costs, the less attractive it will become to shift market transactions into firms. When the cost of operating a firm would exceed the cost of carrying out exchange transactions through the market, the firm would lose its comparative advantage over the market as a means of economic organization. The alternative of organizing productive arrangements by means of market transactions, however, would inevitably face the transaction costs and the consequences of such costs on productive activity discussed above. Thus, the higher the cost of organizing production in a firm, the lower the number of productive arrangements which will be organized and, hence, the lower the amount of output which will become available to satisfy consumer needs, and the higher will be the prices consumers will have to pay for what is offered in the market.

Supply of Corporate Features

The legal concept of the corporation is essentially that of an organizational instrument which enables economic activity to be organized in a firm at costs lower than those incurred by carrying out transactions in the market place.

Yet it is not the *only* legal concept available to employ in the setting up of a firm. Other organizational devices embodied in the law include, for instance, the sole proprietorship, the partnership, the limited partnership and, in a steadily increasing number of United States state jurisdictions, the limited liability company. As noted earlier, however, the *corporation* has become the dominant form of business organization in many parts of the economy.

The explanations advanced for the existence of firms cannot simultaneously be used to explain the emergence of the corporation as a means to organize a firm. In the preceding section we argued that the existence of market transaction costs has occasioned a demand for organization in order to avoid the costs associated with using the market mechanism. The mere observation that the corporate form is such an organizational instrument does not explain why the corporation in particular has emerged to meet this demand. Nor does it explain the success of the corporation as a form of organization.

Before examining in some detail the economic functions of the corporate form, let us briefly describe the principal organizational features that characterize it.

Legal Personality

First, the corporation enjoys "legal personality". This means that the corporation is entitled to have rights and obligations on its own behalf and in its own name, independent of the rights and obligations of its constituent human beings. For example, it may acquire and alienate property as an entity and it may contract debts in its own name. "Legal personality" means that in the eyes of the law the corporation is treated as if it were an individual, with similar ability to have rights and obligations of its own.

For instance, Section 3.02 of the Model Business Corporation Act confers on corporations "the same powers as an individual to do all things necessary or convenient to carry out its business and affairs". Similarly, Section 2:5 of the Dutch Civil Code provides that for the purposes of the law of obligations and property law, a corporation is equated with a human being, except where statute law provides otherwise.

The corporation's "legal personality" is predominantly displayed in two ways: the corporation is able to act in the market as an entity distinct from its shareholders and it has access to the judiciary in its own right. It can buy and sell in product and factor markets, own property and incur debts as if it were an individual, and it can sue and be sued in the courts in its own name. The corporate form of organization, hence, does not merely serve to establish an economic entity (a firm) but it also constitutes an entity for the purposes of the law (*i.e.* a legal entity).

Pursuant to the concept of "legal personality" (or "legal entity") as embedded in corporate law, the corporation has a life of its own, separate from that of its constituent human beings (including shareholders), and so the life span of the corporation may exceed that of the constituent human beings at a given time. Therefore, corporations are sometimes said to enjoy "perpetual existence and succession": a corporation may continue to exist long after the initial shareholders and managers have passed away or have left the organization. Yet this statement is misleading as it does not take into account the possibility that corporations can be terminated. Shareholders *can* dissolve a corporation if the requisite majority vote accordingly. Moreover, the law may provide that a corporation can be involuntarily dissolved by a court order under certain conditions.

Transferable Shares

A second characteristic of the corporation is the division of its equity capital into transferable shares. The owners of these shares, the shareholders, are entitled to the profits, net of taxes, earned by the business firm organized in corporate form. Shareholders receive profits in the form of dividends paid by the corporation. In addition, in the event of dissolution of the corporation they are entitled to any excess yielded by the corporation's assets once its liabilities to creditors have been satisfied. Furthermore, the shareholders are entitled to the money value of increases in the market value of the firm as measured by the market price of their shares.

A share represents a part of the equity capital put up by investors to finance the ventures of the corporate firm. The return on the shares, that is, dividends as well as potential value increases (capital gains), are not fixed but contingent on the success and profitability of the firm's operations. The same applies to the eventual repayment of the shareholders' capital contribution at the corporation's dissolution: whether their investment will be repaid is contingent on the amount remaining, if any, once all liabilities have been settled. Thus, unlike lenders, shareholders do not have a *fixed* claim on the corporation's earnings and assets.

Shareholders' claim, by definition, is subordinate to the claims of the corporation's creditors, including tax claims. Since shareholders' return on investment depends on the fortune of the firm and since they may lose their entire investment if the business fails, share capital is referred to as *risk capital*. The shares reflect the risks to which a firm operated in corporate form is subject. The profitability of a business and, thus, shareholders' reward is inevitably subject to a certain degree of risk. A share is a stake in the business risk of the corporate firm and the shareholders, by definition, have agreed to bear that risk.

Shareholders can primarily influence the risk to which they are exposed in two ways: they can vote in shareholders' meetings and they can relieve themselves of continued risk exposure by transferring their shares to a third party. A share, thus, carries a right to vote and a right to transfer the share. Both rights enable shareholders to protect their investment. In the analysis to follow we will assume that both of these rights are inherent in the shares. (We acknowledge that United States jurisdictions following Section 6.01 (c) (1) of the Model Business Corporation Act permit the articles of incorporation to provide for the issue of non-voting shares. For the purpose of our analysis, however, we assume that shares do carry voting rights, as is the general rule in both the United States and the Netherlands.) Also, we will not distinguish between different classes of shares but assume that all shares in a particular corporation have equal attributes, including equal voting rights.

The scope of shareholders' voting rights (the issues on which shareholders may vote) is defined by the applicable corporate statute, whilst the corporation's articles of incorporation may confer additional voting rights on the shareholders to the extent permitted by the law. According to United States state corporation statutes, shareholders' voting rights ordinarily include the right to vote on the appointment and removal of directors. Similarly, in the Netherlands, statute law bestows on the shareholders the right to vote on the appointment and removal of the members of the corporation's management board and supervisory board. However, in the Netherlands a special type of corporation exists in which shareholders' voting rights do *not* extend to such appointments and removals; we will describe this type of corporation in Chapter 5 and until then we assume that the shareholders do possess the above-mentioned voting rights. In both countries, shareholders' voting rights moreover include, *inter alia*, the right to vote on amendments of the corporation's articles of incorporation (Section 10.03 of the Model Business Corporation Act; Section 2:121 of the Dutch Civil Code) and on dissolution of the corporation (Section 14.02 Model Business Corporation Act; Section 2:19 Dutch Civil Code), for instance, in the event of merger with another company.

Although we acknowledge that shareholders' right to transfer their shares may be subject to restrictions ensuing from statute law or from the articles of incorporation (especially in the event of statutory close corporations), our analysis will assume that shares are freely transferable throughout. This assumption is justified as for publicly held corporations, free transferability of shares is the rule, not the exception, in both United States jurisdictions and the Netherlands. In addition, if transfer restrictions do apply, generally the laws do not, and the articles may not, render transfer of shares completely impossible. We will briefly discuss restrictions on share transferability and their rationales in Chapter 5.

Limited Liability

The statutory principle of limited liability of shareholders is the third feature of the corporate form. Apart from their voting rights and the right to alienate their shares, limited liability, too, protects the interests of the suppliers of equity capital. The principle of limited liability means that the shareholders are neither liable for the fulfillment of the corporation's contractual obligations, nor for torts attributable to the corporation or any of its employees.

Section 6.22 (b) of the Model Business Corporation Act phrases this principle as follows: "Unless otherwise provided in the articles of incorporation, a shareholder of a corporation is not personally liable for the acts or debts of the corporation except that he may become personally liable by reason of his own acts or conduct". Section 2:64 (1) of the Dutch Civil Code expresses the same principle, stating that a shareholder is not liable for acts performed in the name of the corporation and is not subject to any liability for corporate losses beyond the subscription price for his shares.

Shareholders have an obligation towards the corporation to pay the amount for which they subscribed when committing themselves to purchase shares but they have no further financial obligations towards the corporation or towards its creditors. If the corporation were to fail to repay a loan extended to it, they are not liable for the deficit. Also, if the corporation were unable to pay damages to tort victims, shareholders do not have to pay the unsettled amounts. The principle of limited liability means, therefore, that if the corporation fails, a shareholder will never lose more than his invested wealth. Thus, "limited liability" limits the risk to which shareholders are exposed to the purchase price of their shares.

Although the statutory principle of limited liability may be set aside, either by the law (as we will see in Chapter 9) or by private contracts between the shareholders and the creditors of a corporation, limited liability for shareholders is the prevalent legal rule and in our analysis of the corporate form we will treat it as such.

Centralized Management

Finally, the legal concept of the corporation separates the management of the corporate firm from the provision of equity capital; management of the firm and supply of equity capital are treated as distinct functions, with specialized roles for the actors in each category. The suppliers of equity capital, the shareholders, have a claim on the profits earned by the corporation and on the excess of its assets over liabilities in the event of dissolution, but they are not entitled to run the corporate firm. Instead, the direction of the firm is assigned to a specialized management body which is legally separate from the shareholders. Managerial power is centralized in this body, which is clothed with specific managerial rights and duties for this purpose. The centralization of managerial power is the fourth distinguishing mark of the corporate form [Manne (1975), 512].

State corporation statutes in the United States traditionally provide for a single governance body, the "board of directors", in which the management function is formally vested. Section 8.01 (b) of the Model Business Corporation Act provides that all corporate powers be exercised "by or under the authority of" the board of directors and that the business and affairs of the corporation be managed "under the direction of" the board. However, this provision does not require active involvement by the individual directors in the day-to-day management of the corporate firm [Clark (1986), 108]: the directors may, and frequently do, appoint officers to whom managerial authority is delegated, if the corporation's bylaws allow them to make such appointments (Section 8.40 (a) of the Model Business Corporation Act).

The officers then actually run the corporate firm as its full-time top managers, under the supervision ("direction") of the board of directors. A corporation's officers usually include, in any event, its president, vice presidents, secretary and treasurer, whilst other senior executives may be designated officers as well [Clark (1986), 113]. The board of directors may include both executive directors (who are at the same time officers) and non-executive directors (*i.e.* "outside directors"), who have a supervisory role only and who usually dedicate only a small part of their time to the firm. Outside directors, unlike officers and executive directors, typically are not employed by the corporation. Technically, the board may also be entirely composed of non-executive directors or of directors who do actively manage the corporate firm.

Dutch corporate law, by contrast, has institutionalized a two-tier structure of corporate governance, consisting of a "management board" (known as the "*bestuur*") and a "supervisory board" (the "*raad van commissarissen*"). In this governance structure, the firm's day-to-day management is entrusted to the management board in which executive power is concentrated and which is responsible for the monitoring of the other inputs in the firm (Section 2:129 of the Dutch Civil Code). The supervisory board in turn monitors the performance of the management board and the firm in general and gives advice to the management board when appropriate (Section 2:140 (2) of the Civil Code).

Each Dutch corporation *must* have a management board and it *may* have a supervisory board if the articles of incorporation so provide. However, a supervisory board is mandatory for large corporations (as identified by Dutch legal standards) that satisfy certain statutorily defined quantitative criteria (Sections 2:153 (2) and 2:158 (1) of the Civil Code). The role of the supervisory board is comparable to that of the non-executive directors in the United States governance model, whilst the management board performs the functions of the executive directors and the (traditional) officer positions in the governance structure of United States corporations.

Thus, although the *form* of both corporate governance models is different, practically they each distinguish between functionaries in charge of the firm's day-to-day management (executive directors and officers in the United Stated model versus members of the management board in the Dutch model) and functionaries supervising the former (non-executive directors in the United States versus members of the supervisory board in the Netherlands). Given the similarity of the functions performed, throughout this book we refer to "managers" to denote directors exercising executive power and officers in the United States governance model as well as members of the management board in the Dutch model, and to "supervisory directors" to denote both non-executive directors in the first model and members of the supervisory board in the second.

In both United States and Dutch corporate statutes, the distinction between share ownership (*i.e.* the supply of risk capital) and management of the corporate firm is the key principle of corporate governance. Shareholders may be appointed as managers or as supervisory directors and managers and supervisory directors may also own shares in the corporation they manage or supervise, but such combinations of roles do not alter the legal premise that share ownership is legally distinct from managerial powers. Managers, and not shareholders *per se*, are to make business decisions.

The Monitorial Model

In summary, the corporation is characterized by legal personality, transferable shares in its equity capital to which voting rights are attached, limited liability of shareholders, and separation of share ownership and managerial responsibilities. What are the economic functions of the corporation as a vehicle to organize a business enterprise?

Below we elaborate on the premise that the merits of the corporate form of organization should be considered in two ways. On the one hand, it facilitates effective monitoring of input activity and on the other, it is beneficial to the raising of funds to finance business ventures.

We will first examine the corporation from a monitoring perspective. The monitorial approach to the corporate form of organization originates with Alchian and Demsetz [1972]. Their thoughts on the corporate firm will therefore be the starting points for our analysis. The concept of monitoring, which was introduced in Chapter 1, refers to the collection of information about individual productivities and about productive opportunities in team production processes, the detection of undesirable input behavior (shirking), and the enforcement of desired actions so as to enhance team productivity and team profits. It encompasses the right to direct the actions of the individual team members and the right to apportion rewards [Alchian and Demsetz (1972), 782].

The Corporate Team

Alchian and Demsetz [1972] have emphasized the necessity of monitoring input behavior in team production processes in order to oppose shirking and, thereby, to improve team productivity. They have argued that within a firm, the monitoring function is assigned to a specialized monitor. This monitor manages the use of cooperative inputs and has the right to revise the team's composition. To motivate the monitor to enhance team performance, he is given the residual claim on the team's assets and cash flows: the monitor is entitled to team earnings, net of payments to other inputs, and to the team's remaining assets, net of outstanding debts, when the team is wound up. The monitor earns his residual award by optimizing input performance. The Alchian-Demsetz theory of the firm was discussed in detail in Chapter 1.

As described in that chapter, in a team productive process, individual team members do not yield identifiable, separable products that can be disposed of through the market. The output sold is that of the team members collectively and by definition no individual products are observable in the team's output. The team operates in the market as an entity: it sells *team* output and it acquires resources for *team* use by the joint cooperative inputs. "Legal personality" permits the team (the firm) to act as such an entity.

It recognizes the fact that a firm does not consist of a series of individuals carrying out individual businesses, and that the individuals in a firm work as a union to effect joint productive activity. "Legal personality" recognizes the team nature of the firm by enabling the firm to buy and sell and to sue and be sued as a union. In addition, as teamwork yields a larger output than the team's separately used inputs could otherwise achieve, "legal personality" can be understood as the law's recognition of the superior productivity of team production.

"Legal personality" furthermore enables the team to select as an entity a central agent to monitor the performance of the cooperative inputs in the team. In the absence of "legal personality", it would be for individual input owners to select a monitor. By implication, the monitor may look at the performance and the interests of the particular team members who designated him rather than at those of the team as a whole. With legal personality, however, the monitor is assigned to the team as such for the enhancement of the productivity of the joint team members so that ideally the whole of the team will benefit.

Monitoring Services

Who will be the most effective monitor of a team, *i.e.* the monitor best able to direct team members so as to take full advantage of the superior productivity of joint productive efforts? Alchian and Demsetz [1972] assume that the most effective monitor will be that team member who has the greatest pecuniary incentive to optimize team performance, that is, the team member who has the residual claim. But this leaves us with the question: which member shall be given the residual claim?

In the framework of the corporation the residual claim resides in the shareholders. They are entitled to what is left over after the corporation's obligations to other parties have been fulfilled. Firms organized as corporations grant the residual claim by issuing shares in their equity capital. A share is a portion of the residual claim combined with a right to vote and a right to transfer that particular portion and the voting right attached to it.

As noted, shareholders provide risk capital to the corporate firm. In their capacity as providers of risk capital they would have a clear incentive to monitor input behavior even if there were no residual claim. This incentive stems from the fact that, by definition, suppliers of risk capital are not protected by security for the repayment of their capital contribution (whereas lenders frequently are) and may lose their entire invested wealth if the firm in which they have invested fails. They, therefore, have well-defined, loss-minimizing incentives to monitor other team members in order to protect their investment. Designating the suppliers of risk capital (the shareholders) as the team's monitor, serves to take advantage of such initial monitoring incentives.

Alchian and Demsetz identify the monitor of a team with the residual claimant. Accordingly, by allocating the residual claim to the shareholders, the corporate form designates them as the team's monitors. The allocation of the residual claim means that the shareholders have a dual incentive to monitor the actions of the other team members: to protect their invested wealth and to enhance their earnings from the possession of the residual claim. The residual claim on the team's assets and cash flows, net of pay-outs to other inputs, is shareholders' reward for the supply of risk capital *plus* monitoring services to the team.

Shareholders can monitor team performance directly or by appointing one or more intermediaries. Direct monitoring by shareholders occurs when they also run the corporate firm, that is, when the shareholders concurrently have managerial positions that entitle them to conduct the firm's day-to-day management. Alternatively, shareholders may appoint specialized managers to manage the team. In that event they may confine themselves to monitoring the performance of such specialized managers (monitors). The factors determining *when* shareholders will delegate the monitoring function to a separate management are discussed on pages 59-61 *infra*.

The possession of the residual claim entails that shareholders' reward is dependent on the profitability of the team. More accurately, shareholders do not merely receive a reward positively correlated to team profitability, but collectively they are entitled to *all* team profits (net of taxes). As their remuneration depends on the profits earned by the team, shareholders have wealth-maximizing incentives to optimize team performance, either through direct monitoring or by appointing capable managers to the team.

In principle, however, shareholders would not need to be given title to *all* of the team's profits to make their reward depend on team profitability. They could also be motivated by a promise of a certain *percentage* of future team profits. Such a promise would not entitle them to all team profits, as does the residual claim, but only to a part thereof. The remainder could, for instance, be distributed among other inputs. In that event, shareholders' reward would still depend on team profits, which would induce them to monitor other team members so as to enhance team performance.

If the residual claim is not in its entirety given to the shareholders but if instead they have to share team profits with other members under some profit-sharing scheme, a shirking problem would arise among the various team members who would be entitled to the team's profits [Alchian and Demsetz (1972), 786]. A member entitled to only a percentage of team profits would have utility-maximizing incentives to rely on the efforts of other claimants to monitor input behavior. By shirking as a monitor, he may be able to benefit from monitoring by other team members without having to incur monitoring expenses himself, and without a proportionate reduction in the size of his earnings as a residual claimant.

The prospects to individual claimants for gains from shirking as a monitor would endanger the adequate provision of monitoring services to the team. By allocating the residual claim to one input category (the suppliers of risk capital), the corporate form serves to mitigate this problem.

To find the most effective monitor, a corporate firm may (and corporate firms frequently do) exploit competition among potential monitors. (Neo)classical economics tells us that competition among suppliers of a particular product compels suppliers to sell high quality products: competition will drive suppliers of bad products out of business, and induces suppliers to offer products which meet demand in a manner maximizing consumer satisfaction. The same principle applies to the supply of monitoring services.

A firm can take advantage of competition among potential monitors by selling all or part of the residual claim to the highest bidder(s). Firms operated in corporate form do so by selling equity shares. The residual claim (the shares) is likely to be purchased by the most effective monitor or by an investor able to assign the most effective monitor (management) to the firm. The monitor best suited to enhance team performance, or the investor able to assign the best monitor to the firm, will expect the highest return from the residual claim and he will therefore be prepared to pay the highest amount to obtain the residual claim.

Selling the residual claim (the shares) as a method for acquiring monitoring services will be beneficial to the team, given that the highest bidder is likely to be the monitor, or the investor, who will make the best use of each team member's comparative advantage in order to maximize his earnings as residual claimant. This bidder will maximize team productivity and profits, to the benefit of the joint team members.

Divisible Residual Claims

The corporate form assigns the residual claim jointly with the function of monitor to the suppliers of risk capital. A team in which one particular member has the residual claim and monitors all other cooperative inputs, is representative of a corporation with a single shareholder who also manages the corporate firm.

However, the amount of risk capital put up to finance a firm's operations may be furnished by more than one supplier. If the size of his investment in a particular firm increases, the risk to which an investor is exposed (that is, his potential loss) also goes up. The larger the amount of capital a firm demands, the larger the risk to which a single supplier is exposed and the less likely it will be that one particular investor will be prepared to provide the entire amount.

The possibility that *several* suppliers will provide risk capital to the firm is what establishes the need for the division of the residual claim on the firm's earnings and assets into portions (shares). The division of the residual claim into shares enables each supplier of risk capital to obtain a portion of the residual claim in proportion to the relative size of his investment. As indicated, in the Alchian-Demsetz model, the function of residual claimant and monitor is joined. Consequently, the division of the residual claim results in the dispersal of the monitorial function among the various owners of portions of the residual claim.

To protect their investment and to enhance their reward, each owner of a portion of the residual claim (*i.e.* each shareholder) may demand rights enabling him to monitor the team's activities. Thus the possibility of multiple suppliers of risk capital does not merely result in divisible residual claims, but also in proportionate monitoring (*i.e.* voting) rights attached to each portion of the residual claim.

The existence of multiple residual claimants with monitoring powers necessitates flexible transferability of shares. Different residual claimants may have different views on the exercise of monitoring powers, for example, with regard to the activities the firm should undertake. Suppose decisions are taken by vote, with each residual claimant's voting rights being proportional to his portion of the residual claim. In this event, any investor's invested wealth becomes subject to the firm's course of action as determined by the majority vote.

To protect his interests, a residual claimant who disagrees with the majority decision may wish to remove his investment from control by the other residual claimants [Alchian and Demsetz (1972), 788]. The ability to transfer his shares, without the permission of fellow residual claimants, makes such a removal possible. If they were exposed to the risk of becoming locked in, *i.e.* if shares were not transferable, potential suppliers of risk capital may not be willing to invest in the firm's operations at all, given that they might then lose all or part of their invested wealth as a result of decisions adopted by their fellow residual claimants in spite of their opposition.

In addition, if a team has several residual claimants with equal voting rights and irreconcilable views on how to use them, votes may be evenly divided. The ability to transfer shares and the voting rights they carry is a method for resolving such deadlocks in intra-firm decision-making processes. Alchian and Woodward [1987, 121] capture the same point, stating that "without transferable shares the potential for shareholder conflicts over investment and dividend policy could kill the corporation".

There is a second reason for flexible transferability of shares. The activities of a firm are not static and neither is the economic and technical environment in which it operates. A firm's activities may expand and the nature of the firm's business may change. Technology may develop in a way affecting the firm's operations or opportunities. Relevant product markets as well as factor markets may change over time; prices may go up or down, competition by other firms may increase, and demand for the goods or services manufactured by the firm may change. In such a dynamic environment the most effective monitor(s) to a firm at one point in time may no longer be the best monitor(s) when circumstances change.

Transferability of residual claims and monitoring powers attached thereto allows them to flow to superior monitors [Manne (1964); (1965)]. If a third party were able to monitor the corporate firm more effectively than its current residual claimant(s), he will anticipate a higher future income stream from the residual claim than its current owner(s) do and be prepared to pay a higher price for it than its value to the latter. In this event existing residual claimants can improve their wealth by selling their residual claim. As the most effective monitor will expect the highest reward from the residual claim, he will normally offer the highest price and so obtain the claim (and thereby the monitorial function). In this way flexible transferability of residual claims (shares) is a mechanism ensuring that firms will always be able to attract effective monitors, that is, monitors having a comparative advantage in monitoring the firm concerned.

A third reason calling for flexible transferability of shares originates in the fact that residual claimants do not live in perpetuity. To a residual claimant, his residual claim is an asset which may be inherited by his descendants (provided the law of succession applies). Heirs may not always have the same gifts as the deceased and, hence, they may not have similar abilities to monitor input activity.

Heirs unable to optimize team productivity and profits have wealth-maximizing incentives to transfer their inherited residual claim to more effective monitors [Ekelund and Tollison (1980), 717]. Because of their superior abilities as monitors, the latter are likely to offer a higher price for the residual claim than the net present value to the heir of his anticipated future earnings from the residual claim. By enabling the transfer of the residual claim to superior monitors, flexible transferability of shares serves as a means to ensure effective monitoring over the long run.

Specialized Monitors

The principle of easy transferability of shares makes use of across-market competition from potential monitors outside the firm to attain effective monitoring within the firm. Centralization of management, meaning management of the firm by (a limited number of) specialized managers, is an instrument internal to the firm designed to secure effective monitoring of input behavior. Several forces are responsible for the emergence of centralized management as a monitoring device.

First, as noted above, if the amount of capital required to finance a team's operations increases, the number of suppliers is also likely to rise. Hence, teams demanding large amounts of risk capital tend to have several team members who furnish such capital in exchange for a portion of the residual claim. If all, or most, of the suppliers of risk capital to a firm would actively participate in the firm's management in order to protect their investment and to enhance their earnings as residual claimants, decision-making to direct the firm's activities would become more complicated as the number of suppliers rises. Also, the costs of decision-making would rise concurrently with the rise in the number of residual claimants [Buchanan and Tullock (1965), 68]. In other words, if a firm with many shareholders were to be managed by the shareholders, high costs of decision-making would be incurred. Centralized management serves to economize on these costs [Demsetz (1975), 33].

Easy transferability of shares is a requirement for centralized management [Woodward (1985), 602]. Without it, shareholders would need to participate actively in the management of the firm in order to protect their investment from managerial decisions that they consider undesirable. The transferability of shares enables shareholders to evade the effects of such decisions by selling their shares and so avoids the costs of shareholder interference in the firm's management. Accordingly, transferability of shares does not only promote effective monitoring by facilitating competition from would-be monitors outside the firm, but it also promotes centralized management.

Second, if the number of residual claimants increases, individual claimants will have an incentive to shirk as monitors, that is, to rely on the efforts of others to monitor input behavior. By shirking as monitors they would avoid monitoring expenses, while still being able to benefit from monitoring by fellow shareholders. The appointment of specialized managers to conduct the firm's day-to-day management is a way to cope with this shirking problem among larger numbers of shareholders [Alchian and Demsetz (1972), 788]. Instead of monitoring the behavior of every cooperative input, shareholders may now limit themselves to the monitoring of these specialized managers only.

But then a potential new shirking problem would arise, viz. shirking by the members of the management, as individual shareholders may rely upon others to monitor the performance of the firm's centralized management. The actual possibilities for specialist *managers* in multi-shareholder firms to shirk are discussed in detail in Chapter 4. The introduction of supervisory directors is an attempt to secure effective monitoring of the firm's day-to-day management where shareholders may fail to properly monitor managerial performance. Moreover, if the residual claim is diffused among many different shareholders, high costs will be incurred if all or most of them were to concern themselves with the monitoring of the firm's management. Therefore, to the extent that individual shareholders were to expend resources to monitor the firm's day-to-day management, the monitoring of the firm's management by a limited number of supervisory directors may well bring about a net reduction in the costs of monitoring managerial performance which would be incurred if many dispersed shareholders actively monitored the management.

Third, in the Alchian-Demsetz theory of the firm it is largely assumed that those having the greatest pecuniary *incentive* to monitor input activity (the residual claimants) will also be the most *effective* monitors. But this need not necessarily be so. Residual claimants might be better off by hiring outside managers to run the corporate firm. Specialized managers may have a comparative advantage in monitoring (for example, as a result of education and training appropriate to the job) and, so, may be able to enhance team income and rewards to the residual claimants in greater measure than the latter themselves may be able to accomplish. If the extra earnings professional managers effect exceed their costs to the shareholders, it pays the shareholders to appoint such managers to run the corporate firm. In these circumstances, possession of the residual claim can be thought of as a means for inducing shareholders to select capable managers, to be watchful of the performance of those managers, and to revise the composition of the management team if incumbent managers fail to maximize team income.

Centralized management by specialized managers may yield a higher return to shareholders than management by the shareholders themselves, because centralized management yields the advantages commonly connected with specialization of labor, viz. greater dexterity and productivity and, hence, more output at less cost per unit of production. Therefore, specialized managers are likely to produce more effective management at a lower cost per unit of management than unspecialized shareholders may be able to accomplish. Specialized management will particularly pay when a large amount of managerial input is required, *i.e.* in large firms or conglomerates, in firms operating in various product or geographical markets and in firms with complex businesses. This explains why management tends to be entrusted to specialized managers more and more as the size and complexity of a firm's operations increase.

There may not only be gains from specialization with regard to the firm's day-to-day management, but also with respect to the monitoring of the performance of hired managers. Supervisory directors are specialized monitor-monitors, who may be able to monitor managerial performance more efficaciously than shareholders could do. Thus, as well as being both a device to resolve the shirking problem among large numbers of shareholders and a cost-saving device, the introduction of supervisory directors may also be a method to take advantage of specialization in monitor-monitoring.

Above we have attempted to identify factors accounting for the centralization of management into the hands of a limited number of specialized individuals. Frank Knight [1921], by contrast, has regarded the management (control) of a business and the bearing of the business risks as inseparable. As described in Chapter 1, according to Knight, those having control of the use of resources in a firm will also bear the financial risk of its success or failure. In Knight's words: "Any degree of effective exercise of judgment, or making decisions, is in a free society coupled with a corresponding degree of uncertainty-bearing, of taking the responsibility for those decisions" [1921, 271]. The functions of control and risk-bearing are joined in his concept of "*responsible direction*" [1921, 271; emphasis by Knight], which he has called the "essence of enterprise". Knight's approach seems to ignore the benefits attainable by specialized management we have discussed above.

Principals and Agents

Some particularities of the relationship between residual claimants (shareholders) and managers are addressed by the economic theory of agency. This theory views managers and supervisory directors as "agents" of the shareholders who in turn are considered to be their "principals". Lawyers, on the other hand, may object to that perception on the basis that although shareholders have the right to elect and to remove managers (in the Netherlands) or supervisory directors who appoint the day-to-day management (in the United States), the managers and the supervisory directors are *not* shareholders' agents in a legal sense [Clark (1985), 56].

For the legal concept of agency to be met, it is essential first that the principal has the authority to direct (control) the activities of the agent. For example, under Section 1 (1) of the American Law Institute's Restatement (Second) of Agency the existence of an agency relationship requires "the manifestation of consent by one person to another that the other shall act on his behalf and subject to his *control*, and consent by the other so to act" (emphasis added). Likewise, Section 7:402 (1) of the Dutch Civil Code obliges the agent to obey the directions given by the principal.

A second component of the legal concept of agency is that, as a rule, the principal assumes liability for the acts of the agent which are performed on behalf of the principal and are within the agent's scope of authority as conferred upon him by the principal (see, for example, Sections 140 and 219 (1) of the Restatement (Second) of Agency and Sections 6:171 and 6:172 of the Dutch Civil Code).

According to the legal concept of agency, managers are the agents of the *corporate entity*, and not of the shareholders. They act on behalf of the corporate entity and it is, at least in theory, the corporate entity that controls their activities. Shareholders do not have a right to determine or to command specific managerial actions. As Clark [1985, 56] has observed, the "power of the principal to direct the activities of the agent does not apply to the stockholders as against the directors or officers of their corporation". Moreover, the *corporation* is liable for the acts performed by the management on behalf of the corporation and not the shareholders. Shareholders experience wealth effects of managerial actions through their residual claim on the corporation's assets and cash flows but shareholders are not liable for the acts of the corporation's management. Thus, the relationship between shareholders and managers is not an agency relationship as understood by agency law.

The economist's conception of agency, however, is different from its legal definition. In economic theory, an agency relationship is assumed to exist whenever one person (the agent) performs an action which affects the wealth or utility of some other person (the principal), and which *implies* (or, better, *presupposes*) the delegation of some decision-making authority by the principal to the agent whose actions affect the former's wealth or utility. The principal does not need to define the powers of the agent expressly, nor is the principal required to direct the activities of the agent. What is decisive, is whether the agent has the power to take decisions and to perform actions that influence the interests of the principal. Pratt and Zeckhauser [1985, 2; emphasis by the authors] have given a simple but characteristic definition of agency as an economic concept: "Whenever one individual depends on the action of another, an *agency relationship* arises. The individual taking the action is called the *agent*. The affected party is the *principal*".

According to the economic concept of agency, managers (and supervisory directors) *are* agents of the shareholders [Arrow (1985), 39; Jensen and Warner (1988), 15] as the market value of shareholders' residual claim, the returns from the possession of that claim and the ultimate repayment of their invested wealth depend on whether management (as monitored by the supervisory directors) is taking appropriate decisions to enhance shareholders' wealth. Such an agency relationship is created by the separation of the functions of management and residual risk-bearing present in the corporate form.

However, the interests of principals (shareholders) and agents (managers) may diverge. As Jensen [1986, 323] has put it, the agency relationship between managers and shareholders is "fraught with conflicting interests". Shareholders may desire, for instance, that managers maximize dividends in the short term and maximize the value of the residual claim in the long run. But managers may shirk the pursuit of shareholders' objectives and seek to maximize their personal utility instead [Alchian (1975a)]. To this end managers may attempt to manage the corporation in their own self-interest, with the sacrifice of shareholders' interests, for example, by appropriating corporate resources in the form of perquisites, by exploiting corporate opportunities for their personal benefit, or by pursuing leisure instead of maximizing returns to shareholders. In Chapter 4 we will discuss managerial deviations from shareholders' interests in greater detail.

The divergence of interests between managers and shareholders is responsible for the existence of *agency costs* [Jensen and Meckling (1976), 308]. Agency costs are the costs arising from the possibility that agents (managers) may not always act in the best interests of their principals (shareholders). They are the costs of separating management from residual risk-bearing. Agency costs tend to exist in any agency relationship since principal-agent contracts are not written and enforced without cost [Fama and Jensen (1983a), 304; (1983b), 327]. Jensen and Meckling [1976, 308] have identified three components which together make up agency costs.

First, shareholders are likely to incur costs to monitor managers in order to ensure that the latter will faithfully and efficaciously act to advance the interests of the shareholders and will refrain from pursuing competing interests. Second, managers may expend resources to commit themselves to shareholders' interests (bonding costs), since if they fail to convince shareholders that they will serve them faithfully, shareholders may not hire them or may only be prepared to hire them at a lower remuneration. Third, given the existence of positive monitoring and bonding costs, some divergence is likely to remain between *actual* managerial decisions and those decisions which would be optimal from shareholders' viewpoint (as the costs of ensuring full compliance with shareholders' interests would exceed the benefits). Consequently, shareholders may experience wealth reductions relative to a situation in which managers would always act in the pursuit of shareholders' objectives (*i.e.* shareholders' "residual loss"). It will only pay shareholders to appoint specialized managers if the anticipated benefits to shareholders from specialized management outweigh the costs of managerial rewards (salaries) plus agency costs.

The legal concept of the corporation comprises several devices protecting shareholders from self-interested managers who seek to pursue managerial objectives at the expense of shareholders' interests: shareholders' voting rights, transferability of shares, monitoring of management by supervisory directors and limited liability of shareholders. These devices serve to mitigate agency costs, although they do not eliminate such costs altogether. In other words, they serve to diminish the costs of the separation between management and residual risk-bearing [Fama and Jensen (1983a), 312-315; Jensen (1983), 328]. By mitigating the agency costs arising from the divergence of interests between shareholders and managers, the corporate form encourages shareholders to make use of the benefits of centralized management by specialist managers – as we discussed in the preceding section – and encourages investors to invest in the equity of corporations with centralized management.

Shareholders' voting rights enable them to displace ineffective managers or supervisory directors, for example, if they fail to manage the firm (or to supervise the management) in a manner maximizing shareholders' earnings from the residual claim. Moreover, shareholders' voting rights ordinarily entitle them to approve or to reject managerial proposals relating to issues of paramount importance to the firm (in other words, which potentially have large impact on the value of their residual claim).

The monitoring of the management by supervisory directors imposes a further constraint on managers' discretion. Fama and Jensen [1983a] have argued that the monitoring of managerial decisions by supervisory directors serves to separate decision management (the initiation and implementation of decisions) from decision control (the ratification and monitoring of decisions) at the firm's top level. They have interpreted this separation as a mechanism for controlling agency problems and regard it as a major device for limiting the costs arising from divergences between shareholders' interests and those of managers.

Furthermore, the principle of limited liability creates a ceiling for shareholders' potential loss from managerial failure to serve their interests (and other causes). Limited liability ensures that shareholders are not exposed to potentially unlimited costs should managers neglect shareholders' interests. As Franke [1987, 143] has stated, limited liability gives shareholders "protection against large losses of private wealth arising from imprudent behavior by managers".

Finally, the easy transferability of shares does not merely enable shareholders to withdraw their invested wealth from control by managers with whom they have become dissatisfied but it also imposes a market constraint on managerial discretion to ignore shareholders' interests: if managers fail to act in shareholders' best interests, third parties may observe potential gains from acquiring the corporation's shares and subsequently replacing incumbent managers by more effective ones. This threat of displacement deters managerial shirking.

The Financial Model

In the preceding pages we explained the corporate form as a means to ensure effective monitoring of input activity. As our discussion reveals, the emergence of corporate features can be explained solely on the basis of the monitoring needs inherent in team production processes. The non-separability of marginal productivities in team production processes creates information (measurement), shirking (supervision) and decision-making (coordination) problems, which in turn have created a demand for sophisticated monitoring to secure the superior productivity of team production and to ensure that team earnings be sufficiently high to offset the opportunity costs of the inputs. The corporate form facilitates the supply of such monitoring within the firm.

An alternative, more traditional, approach explains the corporation as an instrument to raise large sums of capital through the sale of equity shares in order to finance large-scale, capital-intensive production processes. For instance, Scott [1951, 442] has described the corporation as "no more than the ready means for improving production by arranging for the ready inflow of capital". Similarly, Posner [1992, 409] has defined the corporate form of organization as "a method (...) for attracting capital into the firm". And Cutler [1979, 346] has judged the corporation to be "a remarkable method of assembling and deploying capital and of turning it into an engine of economic efficiency and growth". The financial approach and the monitorial model described above comprise complementary, not competing, theories of the corporation.

Firms demand both monitoring of input behavior and capital to finance the operations of the business. The concept of the corporation serves to provide both. Yet as the monitorial model in itself is capable of explaining all four distinguishing characteristics of the corporate form, even without a theory based on corporate finance considerations we would still have a comprehensive genetic theory of the corporate form. This is illustrated, for instance, by the adoption of the corporate form by large professional service providers such as auditing firms and management consultancy firms, which initially began and developed to considerable size as partnerships. The incorporation of such firms is not motivated by the desire to attract outside equity capital. It can be explained, however, by the monitorial theory described in this chapter.

The work in such service firms has gradually changed from the provision of services on an individual basis to teamwork, requiring more intensive monitoring of input behavior (supervision). Legal personality facilitates the firm's operation in the market as a team provider. As the number of partners (*i.e.* the residual claimants) rises, decision-making costs may be reduced by centralizing managerial decision-making, and as the organization grows larger and becomes more complex, a centralized management specializing in the job may more effectively run the organization than the joint partners. Limited liability, then, is instrumental in encouraging individual partners to delegate decision-making power to such a management and a flexible exit mechanism, as supplied by the transferability of residual claims, protects individual partners from becoming subject to the effects of decisions which they are unwilling to accept. The same mechanism allows for the smooth entry of new residual claimants who may enhance total team earnings. Attempts to refine the partnership contracts underlying large professional partnerships in order to provide substantially similar rules of organization would be on a scale of undertaking tantamount to the reinvention of the corporate form.

The monitorial model, as indicated, views the corporation as a vehicle facilitating the supply of appropriate monitoring services to team productive processes. The financial model adds that the corporate form also serves as a mechanism for the supply of capital inputs into a firm. The corporation as a capital raising mechanism, too, may be understood (in the economic sense) as a principal-agent relationship, capital suppliers (including both shareholders and creditors) being the principals and capital managers (hired managers as well as shareholder-managers in control of debt) being their agents, as the returns capital suppliers will receive depend on the performance of the capital managers.

The significance of the corporate form to the raising of capital for investment is discussed below.

Equity Capital

The amount of capital a firm desires to invest may exceed the resources of its founder(s). In particular, substantial funds may be required to organize large-scale production enabling specialization of labor and equipment. And some firms will be unable to produce at all unless huge investments are made to create the assets required to manufacture output. To organize production so as to take full advantage of economies of scale, the organizers of a firm may seek to acquire capital from third parties.

Suppose the organizers of a firm would attempt to raise funds by borrowing in credit markets. Suppose further that the security they could offer for the repayment of loans would be limited, as will normally be the case. The larger the amount of credit sought relative to the security the firm's organizers can give, the higher the risk to which lenders are exposed and the higher the compensation (interest) the latter are likely to demand. In addition, the less security a firm's organizers can offer, the lower will be the total amount of credit lenders will generally be prepared to provide [Hicks (1982), 11].

Moreover, since debt charges are fixed costs to a firm which it cannot unilaterally reduce, the amount of the firm's debt will affect the risk of failure, as firms with heavy fixed costs are more likely to go bankrupt in the event of business adversities than firms with low fixed costs. High costs of debt, that is, interest charges and amortization, imposing high fixed costs on a firm, tend to increase the firm's default risk [Posner (1992), 393]. Consequently, the higher a firm's indebtedness, the less eager lenders will be to increase credit and the higher will be the interest rates they will charge.

The corporate form enables firms to surmount the above-mentioned impediments to borrowing in capital markets. It does so by permitting a firm to raise funds by the sale of equity shares to those willing to provide risk capital to finance its activities. By definition, no interest is payable on funds obtained in this way and no security for repayment is given. Purchasers of shares put up capital in exchange for promises of future rewards, the size of which depends on the firm's profitability, whereas lenders provide capital in exchange for a fixed interest or a fluctuating interest depending on market interest percentages.

The sale of equity shares enables firms operated in corporate form to acquire large amounts of capital through the accumulation of small investments from a relatively large number of investors. The funds so raised permit the acquisition of the many resources that are needed to organize large-scale production processes. From this observation, John Stuart Mill [1965 (orig. 1848), 137] has concluded: "Production on a large scale is greatly promoted by the practice of forming a large capital by the combination of many small contributions; or, in other words, by the formation of joint stock companies" (*i.e.* corporations).

We do not discuss why businesses raise funds by borrowing in some instances and by raising equity capital in other cases, for we do not intend to enter the domain of (the determinants of) the capital structure of a firm. For the present purpose, it is sufficient to note that these different forms of obtaining capital exist and that the corporate form makes it possible for firms to finance all or part of their ventures by means of the sale of equity shares.

The investors providing the equity capital accept that their remuneration as well as the eventual repayment of their contribution will depend on the success or failure of the operations of the corporate firm. However, if they were entirely unprotected from business failure and from wrong expectations with regard to the firm's profitability, investors might not be prepared to invest in the firm. Thus, the absence of protective devices might endanger the firm's capital raising opportunities. As previously discussed, voting rights, monitoring of the firm's management by supervisory directors, limited liability and transferability of shares all serve to protect investors.

The operation of a firm requires investment in the equipment of the business for the full lifetime of the business or the assets in which the investment is made. Rather than making long-term financial commitments for the purpose of such permanent or semi-permanent investments, investors, however, want to be able to liquefy their investment at short notice in order to be able to shift their invested wealth to more profitable investment opportunities or to avoid losses [Scherer (1988a), 55]. Flexible transferability of shares allows investors to do so: it allows them, at their own discretion, to exchange their investment for cash by selling their shares in the stock market. Thus, it gives them the opportunity to recover their investment, not from the firm's assets, but from potential purchasers of their shares. The possibility to liquefy their investment by selling their shares enables investors to reallocate their invested wealth to different uses from which they expect greater pecuniary returns or utility [Manne (1975), 514].

Asset Ownership

Firms, to a greater or lesser extent, invest in assets to carry on a business. Legal personality enables a firm to own such assets and to conduct the business in its own name.

If a firm were unable to own property as an entity, its assets would have to be owned by individual investors and transactions and other legal acts in respect of the assets would, in principle, require the involvement of the individual asset owners. For instance, the cooperation of the individual owners would be required for the transfer of ownership or the lease, mortgage, or pledge of assets. In addition, if a firm could not own property in its own name, every single purchase of an asset would require an investor to own the asset concerned.

When the number of investors and assets increases, the costs of organizing and administering the ownership of assets and the costs of carrying out legal acts in respect of the assets would rise accordingly. These transaction costs would absorb a part of the earnings of the firm and in this way they would effectively set a limit to the number of investors in the firm as well as to the number of assets. Legal personality economizes on such transaction costs. In place of a number of individual owners is substituted one owner, namely the corporate entity, which is entitled to purchase, own, transfer and encumber the assets in the firm in its own right and in its own name, and without the involvement of individual investors being required.

Moreover, if individual investors owned the assets in a firm, its business may be disrupted if an investor chooses to withdraw his assets from the firm. He may do so, for instance, if he desires to sell his assets in order to obtain liquid funds for investment elsewhere. Alternatively, an investor desirous of withdrawing could demand payment of the net value of his assets, after deduction of his proportionate share in the firm's aggregate liabilities. To ensure liquidity of their investment, prior to making an investment, investors may even demand a *right* to be bought out of the firm whenever it suits them.

If an investor invokes such a right, a proportion of the assets in the firm may have to be sold in order to obtain cash to buy out the investor concerned. By withdrawing their investment, either through the withdrawal of assets or by forcing a buyout, individual investors might unilaterally provoke the termination or curtailment of the operations of the firm.

Disruption of a firm as the result of one or more investors' exit would deprive other investors of the expected return on their investment. To avoid such an effect, the remaining investors would have to make up the withdrawing investor's contribution, either by putting up additional resources themselves, by finding one or more other investors to replace the former or by additional borrowing, which in turn would raise the interest and debt repayment obligations incumbent on the firm. Both the risk that their expected return may not materialize due to the firm's potential disruption through another investor's withdrawal and the expenses they may have to incur to preclude such an effect, may discourage potential investors and, thus, harm the firm's prospects for raising funds for investment.

Legal personality is a mechanism to avoid disruption and the above-mentioned effects thereof, and it also eliminates the costs which would otherwise need to be incurred to ensure continuity of the firm, should an investor withdraw his investment. Since legal personality provides a firm with an existence of its own, distinct from the investors, individual investors can no longer cause the disruption of the firm (except if they own the requisite majority of shares). In this way, legal personality serves to preserve the continuity of the firm and minimizes the costs to investors of other investors' withdrawal.

Legal personality serves investors' interests in yet another way. The assets in the firm frequently have greater value collectively, *i.e.* as an integrated business, than the sum of their separate values if each asset were appraised independently of the others. In other words, the "going concern" value of a firm may well exceed the marketable values of the various assets separately. If an individual investor (or several investors acting jointly) were able to cause the disruption of a firm, such added going concern value might easily be sacrificed. In that event *all* investors would be deprived of their share in the firm's going concern value in excess of the independent market values of the assets.

The risk of losing value because of another investor's decision to withdraw would, again, discourage potential investors and harm the firm's ability to raise capital. By eliminating the possibility that individual investors could force the firm's disruption, legal personality serves to preserve the going concern value of a firm [Clark (1986), 19], which enhances its appeal to investors.

Instead of the withdrawal of their contribution, the corporate form provides investors with an alternative mechanism to recover their investment: the division of a firm's equity capital into transferable shares. As indicated in the preceding section, share transferability is a means to attain investment liquidity other than through the withdrawal of the investment from the firm. The alienation of shares maintains the firm's going concern value, given that share transfers, unlike the withdrawal of investments (separately owned assets or their money value), will not affect the firm's existence in itself. The transferability of shares permits investors, through the stock market, to encash a stake in the firm's going concern value proportionate to their investment, whilst maintaining that value for the remaining investors (and for successive shareholders).

In addition, the transferability of shares simply provides investors with a method for attaining investment liquidity that is less cumbersome and less expensive than the withdrawal and sale of the assets of a business or the withdrawal of the money value of their investment from the business. Thus, apart from being a protective device for investors, the existence of transferable shares in a corporation's equity capital economizes on the transaction costs of investment withdrawals.

Shareholders' Liability

Suppose the owners of the shares in the firm's equity capital were personally liable to the full extent of their personal wealth for the debts of the corporate entity.

Under a rule of joint and several liability, personal liability means that the risk to which any one shareholder would be exposed is negatively correlated to the wealth of other shareholders relative to his own personal wealth. The poorer are the other shareholders, the larger will be the amount a wealthy investor may eventually have to put up to settle corporate debts and vice versa. In other words, unlimited shareholder liability would imply that relatively wealthy investors may bear a larger part of the burden than relatively poor shareholders, should the corporation fail to fulfill its financial obligations.

Consequently, under a rule of unlimited joint and several shareholder liability, shareholders would be induced to expend resources in order to monitor the wealth of other shareholders. Since their costs in the event of corporate default would not merely depend on the liabilities of the corporate firm but also on the wealth of other shareholders relative to their own, shareholders would have loss-minimizing incentives to monitor (developments in) other shareholders' wealth [Jensen and Meckling (1976), 331]. The costs of monitoring other shareholders' wealth will reduce a shareholder's net return on his investment and will thereby render investment in corporate equity less attractive than if there were no such costs.

Moreover, shareholders would have loss-minimizing incentives to demand organizational devices preventing the entrance of poorer and the exit of richer investors. However, devices restricting the entrance of investors of relatively modest means would reduce the amount of risk capital a firm may be able to attract. Devices restricting relatively wealthy shareholders from alienating their shares would have similar effect, as such devices would discourage investment in corporate stock by wealthy investors.

The principle of limited liability, which insulates shareholders from liability for debts of the corporate entity, renders the relative wealth of other shareholders irrelevant with regard to the amount of a shareholder's potential loss. Therefore, it removes the need for shareholders to incur costs to monitor other shareholders' wealth [Demsetz (1975), 34] and it takes away their incentive to demand devices restricting the entry of poorer and the exit of relatively wealthy shareholders. Apart from encouraging investment merely by reducing investors' risk, in both ways limited liability promotes the supply of risk capital to the corporate firm.

Limited shareholder liability does not merely economize on the resources shareholders would otherwise expend in monitoring each other's wealth, but also on the transaction costs facing potential providers of credit (for example, loans).

If shareholders were personally liable for the debts of the corporation, creditors would be entitled to collect corporate debts not only from the assets of the corporation but also from the individual property of its shareholders. Therefore, to assess their risk, potential creditors would have to evaluate the personal wealth of a corporation's shareholders. The larger the number of shareholders, the larger the costs potential creditors would have to incur to assess shareholders' capacity to repay credit (loans) granted to and to pay interest due by, the corporation. Similarly, the larger the number of shareholders, the larger the costs to creditors of enforcing liability for corporate debts against individual shareholders [Clark (1986), 8-9].

Limited shareholder liability avoids the aforesaid costs to creditors: potential creditors have to evaluate only the corporation's payment capacity and enforcement costs are, as a rule, limited to the costs of collecting from the corporation. By reducing the costs of credit evaluation and the costs of contract enforcement, limited shareholder liability may enhance the supply of credit and lower the cost of credit to firms operated in corporate form (to the extent that those costs would be reflected in interest rates).

(Please note that above, we have only partially reviewed the functions of limited liability. We have reserved Chapter 3 for an in-depth examination of the limited liability principle.)

Diversified Investments

Centralized management is another device that promotes the supply of capital to the corporate firm. In the discussion of the monitorial model of the corporation we argued, *inter alia*, that centralized management by specialist managers economizes on the cost to investors of making decisions with regard to the running of the corporate firm. Also, we argued that specialist managers may be able to effect higher returns on investment than unspecialized shareholders. However, the operation of a firm by specialized managers enhances the firm's ability to obtain funds for investment in yet another way.

An investor who purchases shares in only one firm will lose his entire invested wealth if that firm goes bankrupt. Modern portfolio theory teaches that investors in corporate equity are able to reduce their risk by spreading investments over a number of firms, provided that the prospects of success for each of these firms do not depend on the same set of contingencies. Based on this premise, the larger the number of holdings, the less an investor is likely to lose as the result of any one company's failure and the less will be the variability in returns on his aggregate investment. Accordingly, investors may seek to reduce their risk of suffering losses through diversification of investments [Brealey and Myers (1988), 132; Ross and Westerfield (1988), 148]. As, for example, Kripke [1976, 39] has observed, "much of the risk of individual securities can be eliminated by appropriate diversification".

When holding shares in various unrelated firms in order to avoid dependence on one firm's fortune, individual shareholders will have no particular interest in becoming personally involved in the day-to-day management of the activities of any one firm in their portfolio [Fama (1980), 291]. Suppose an investor would participate in the management of each company in the stock of which he has invested. In this event his ability to reduce risk through diversification would be limited in two ways. First, there is a practical limit to the number of companies someone can manage simultaneously; this limit would constrain an investor's ability to eliminate risk by increasing the number of his holdings. Second, an investor's costs of participating in the management of the firms in his portfolio would increase concurrently with the number of investments. Ultimately these costs will offset an investor's anticipated gain from bearing less risk, *i.e.* the reduction in his potential loss from investment misfortune effected by means of diversification.

Management by hired specialist managers enables investors to hold diversified portfolios without having to become involved in the management of the companies in which they invest [Morgan (1978), 93]. In this way centralized management permits investors to reduce risk by diversification without having to incur the costs of participating in the management of the firms in their portfolio, and without a limit determined by the number of companies an investor is technically able to manage. The costs of hiring specialized managers (and agency costs) are shared by the investors in a company's stock collectively, and wealth maximizing investors will incur such costs until they outweigh the anticipated reduction of potential losses further diversification (*i.e.* increasing the number of holdings) would accomplish.

In summary, centralized management is an instrument that resolves the management problems attending diversified investment portfolios. By enabling investors to reduce their risk through diversification without having to participate in the management of each company in their portfolio, centralized management renders the provision of equity capital less risky, therefore more attractive to investors. In this way it supports the supply of risk capital to firms operated in corporate form.

(As we shall discuss in Chapter 3, limited liability of shareholders is also a requisite for risk reduction through diversification.)

The Corporate Firm

Monitoring and capital are inputs to production processes, in the same way that raw materials and workers' labor are. The corporate form is a vehicle for the ready input of large amounts of capital and specialized monitoring services to production processes.

Jensen [1983, 323] has argued that organizational forms tend to be related to the type of activities the organization undertakes. The corporate form and in particular the publicly held corporation, is specifically suited to organize activities requiring large amounts of capital and specialized monitoring of input behavior. Activities requiring such inputs include capital-intensive and complex production processes. They may also include other economic activities such as trade and the provision of services, especially when these activities are carried out on a large scale, that is, by large and complex enterprises.

The more resources (assets) a firm seeks to own, the larger will be the funds it needs to attract for investment in the assets of the business. In particular, (the organizers of) a firm will seek to own those assets that are specific to the firm's activities, *i.e.* that will lose value if employed elsewhere. If such specific assets are rented, this may give rise to problems of postcontractual opportunistic reneging (hold-up situations), as discussed in Chapter 1. The firm's ownership of assets that are specialized with respect to its activities serves to avoid the transaction costs connected with the possibility of such opportunistic behavior [Klein, Crawford and Alchian (1978)]. Therefore, the larger the number of firm-specific assets required to carry on the business (and the more expensive is their creation), the larger the amount of capital a firm will need in order to obtain the ownership of those assets and the more likely it is that the firm's organizers will choose to take advantage of the corporate form as a capital raising mechanism.

Moreover, the more inputs (workers) a firm employs, the larger the potential losses from shirking by individual inputs if they are not monitored properly to counter shirking. In any team production process, individual team members have an incentive to shirk since the benefits of less effort or lower quality effort by an individual member are enjoyed exclusively by that particular member, whereas the costs of his shirking will be shared by the team as a whole in the form of productivity losses and forgone profits [Manne (1981), 689].

Not only does the *number* of potential shirkers rise with the number of workers employed, but *individual* team members will also have more incentive to shirk as a firm grows larger. This increased incentive to shirk ensues from the fact that as the number of team members rises, a shirking member would have to shoulder a smaller part of the costs of his shirking himself, since a greater part of its effects would be borne by others in the team. In addition, when the total number of a team's members rises, the return to each individual member from spending resources in order to detect shirking by fellow team members will be diluted proportionately, which in turn diminishes individual members' incentives to incur such expenditure as well as a shirking member's chance of being caught. Accordingly, as firms grow in size, overall shirking problems tend to grow larger [Jensen (1983), 327] and the total costs of shirking to the firm tend to rise. Because of these increased shirking problems, the larger a firm grows, the larger is the need for effective monitoring of input behavior to reduce losses from shirking, and the more likely it is that the firm's organizers will seek the benefits of the corporate form as a means facilitating the ready input of specialized monitoring services.

The corporation's capital raising ability and its ability to arrange for the inflow of effective monitoring services are key elements of an organizational theory explaining why it has become the dominant form of organization in those sectors of the economy requiring such inputs. In particular, these factors yield an organizational explanation of why, for example, manufacturing companies, transportation companies demanding substantial funds to invest in aircraft, trucks or ships, companies engaged in trading activities on a large scale, and commercial banks and other financial institutions which require large amounts of capital, are predominantly organized as corporations.

The Concession Theory

The corporate form has come to flourish as a result of both the technological developments of the Industrial Revolution and its aftermath which made possible the production (*i.e.* the *supply*) of goods on a large scale, and the demographical developments (the population explosion) of the nineteenth and twentieth centuries which created a *demand* for large quantities of products for consumption. Both developments called for the organization of production on a large scale, requiring the input of substantial amounts of capital and resulting in sizeable and complex firms demanding elaborate monitoring of input behavior. In this chapter we have endeavored to demonstrate that the corporate form of business organization facilitates the raising of large amounts of capital as well as the intensive monitoring of input activity in team productive processes. Similarly, Chayes [1959, 28] observed that "[t]he corporate form fostered not only the aggregation of capital but the altered social organization for work implicit in large-scale enterprise".

Among lawyers, the corporate form of organization is often viewed as a creation of the state that has grown popular in response to the above-mentioned developments. In its most rudimentary form, this view originates in the fact that a state permit is required to incorporate a firm. A business can be legally operated as a corporation only after a certificate of incorporation has been obtained, confirming the state's permission to incorporate. Thus a corporation is deemed to come into existence upon the successful completion of the formal procedure resulting in the issuance of a certificate of incorporation [Clark (1986), 5]. It is frequently maintained, therefore, that the corporate form is essentially a *concession* granted by the state.

The much cited statement of the Chief Justice of the United States Supreme Court, John Marshall, in 1819 in *Trustees of Dartmouth College* v. *Woodward* [17 U.S. (4 Wheat). 518, 636 (1819)], is illustrative of the view of the corporation as a creation of the state. In the opinion of the court, Marshall stated: "A corporation is an artificial being, invisible, intangible, and existing only in contemplation of law. Being the mere creature of law, it possesses only those properties which the charter of its creation confers upon it, either expressly, or as incidental to its very existence". And as recently as in 1987, in *CTS Corp.* v. *Dynamics Corp. of America* [107 S.Ct. 1637, 1649 (1987)], the United States Supreme Court described corporations as "entities whose very existence and attributes are a product of state law".

The theory of the corporation as a concession of the state has its roots in medieval England [Chayes (1959), 32-35; Hessen (1979), 3-11]. In particular, from around the eleventh century, the English Crown developed the practice of granting special privileges to institutions such as boroughs, guilds, churches, hospitals and charities. Such privileges were generally granted notwithstanding potential future changes in the membership of the organization concerned. That is to say, they were vested in the institution rather than in its constituent human beings at a given time. In this way the institution receiving the privilege obtained quasi-perpetual existence comparable with that of the modern corporation.

The privileges granted by the Crown varied between different beneficiaries. For instance, a borough might obtain the right to collect taxes, while guilds were usually granted certain rights to fix and enforce prices and quality standards of products, and related rights to regulate trade (*i.e.* monopoly or quasi-monopoly privileges). Churches, hospitals and charitable institutions might be permitted to acquire and to alienate property as an entity. The organizations which obtained such privileges independent of their membership at a given time were known as corporations, although they cannot be compared with the private business corporations of today [Hessen (1979), 4-5].

In order to obtain privileges of the kinds referred to above, a special legislative act was required. In exchange for the grant of privileges the Crown often demanded something in return, generally a sum of money. In this way the granting of privileges served to meet the financial needs of the Crown.

In the Mercantilist era, the Crown and later also Parliament started to grant special privileges to trading companies on a similar basis. Originally the organizers of such companies petitioned for a royal charter to obtain monopoly privileges in respect of trade to specific territories and governmental power over those territories [Butler (1986), 170; Anderson and Tollison (1983), 112-113]. As of the seventeenth century, promoters of trading companies would also request that the charter included provisions entitling their company to act as a legal entity distinct from the merchant-venturers involved and to raise capital by the sale of transferable equity shares, and granting limited liability to the investors putting up the equity capital intended to finance business ventures. Such charters were primarily sold as a means to raise money for the state [Butler (1986), 171], just as the earlier medieval grants of privileges did. Like the medieval grants, every separate incorporation of this type required a special legislative act.

The method of establishing corporations by a special act of Crown or Parliament was abandoned by the adoption of general incorporation statutes in the nineteenth century, which provided "a revolutionary new method of creating corporations" [Hessen (1979), 3]. General incorporation statutes were enacted prior to 1860 in England, the United States and the Netherlands. As a result of this legislation the incorporation of a business no longer required a legislative act by the state. To create a corporation, it became sufficient to comply with the formalities prescribed by the general statute, and this situation has prevailed until today.

As contemporary incorporation statutes set forth rather formal procedures which may technically be complied with by anyone desirous to do business as a corporation, the theory of the corporation as a privilege from the state has lost much of its ground: the historical foundations on which this theory is based no longer accord with the realities of today's general incorporation legislation which makes the privilege of doing business as a corporation available to anyone who fulfills the formalities prescribed by the law [Berle (1950), 198]. Under the current legislation, the choice for the corporate form is a decision by private parties and not contingent on some discretionary act of the state. As Berle [1950, 217] has put it, under today's general incorporation statutes "[t]he Government, for all practical purposes, no longer creates a corporate entity".

In the Netherlands, the theory of the corporation as a creature of the state is often associated with the birth in 1602 of the Vereenigde Oost-Indische Compagnie (the "VOC"), a joint-stock trading company [Van der Grinten (1992), 2; Van Schilfgaarde (1995), 29]. The VOC was established pursuant to a concession granted by the state, which, *inter alia*, bestowed corporate features upon it. However, in our view, the essence of that concession was not the bestowal of corporate features but the granting of a trade monopoly relating to trading with what is now known as Indonesia and other parts of Eastern Asia and the conferral of governmental powers over corresponding

East Asian territories, backed by the right to use military force for these purposes [Gaastra (1991), 20-23]. Likewise, Gaastra [1991, 21] has regarded the assignment of sovereign powers to the VOC as the company's distinguishing characteristic. Both before and after the establishment of the VOC, trading companies were established in the Netherlands which had corporate characteristics based upon private contracts between the parties involved, and which did not ensue from any concession or privilege granted by the state [Gaastra (1991), 16-19; Van der Grinten (1992), 2-6; Maeijer (1994), 2-3].

Sections 2:64 (2) and 2:175 (2) of the current Dutch Civil Code require that a "statement of no objections" be given by the Minister of Justice before a business can be incorporated. However, this requirement should *not* be conceived of as evidence for, or as a reminiscence of, the corporation as a creature (concession) of the state. Ignoring for the moment differences in the legal history of the corporation in the Netherlands, on the one hand, and England and the United States on the other, the requisite ministerial "statement of no objections" is a merely formal requirement: the grounds on which it may be obtained are generally available to the public (Sections 2:68 (2) and 2:179 (2) of the Civil Code and the Guidelines on incorporation published by the Ministry of Justice, most recently in 1985) and the Minister of Justice is legally obliged to issue the statement upon request if these grounds are duly complied with. Thus, the ministerial statement of no objections is part of the formal procedure of incorporation, and does not provide the Minister with substantive discretion to permit or to refuse incorporation as would have been typical of the granting of a "privilege"-like concession.

The Contractual Theory

The view of the corporation as a creation of the state has encountered fundamental criticism because it largely ignores the role of voluntary agreements among private individuals in the emergence and the prevalence of the corporate form [Anderson and Tollison (1983); Butler (1986); Butler and Ribstein (1988)]. Based on that criticism, an alternative theory has arisen which explains the corporation as a result of private contracting and not as a product of governmental activity. According to this theory, the corporation is a creature of market forces, particularly of the demand for capital and monitoring services by some and the supply thereof by others. Where such demand and supply meet, contracts arise which are considered to be reflected in the characteristics of the corporation. Accordingly, the corporate form, just as the firm it organizes, has been construed as a set of contractual relationships among various cooperating individuals [Jensen and Meckling (1976), 310-311; Jensen (1983), 326]. The contractual theory of the corporation has come to be the dominant view among neoinstitutionalist economists.

In the previous chapter we discussed the "nexus of contracts" concept of the firm, which views the *firm* as a result of the contracting process between cooperative input owners aimed at enabling joint production. Likewise, the corporate *form* of organization has been conceptualized as a set of contracts among cooperative individuals, including providers of risk capital, specialized managers and creditors. The leading definition comes from Jensen and Meckling, who described the corporation as a "*legal fiction which serves as a nexus for contracting relationships and which is also characterized by the existence of divisible residual claims on the assets and cash flows of the organization which can generally be sold without permission of the other contracting individuals*" [1976, 311; emphasis by the authors]. The contractual relationships which make up the corporate concept specify "the rules of the game within the organization" [Jensen (1983), 326], *i.e.* the basic organizational framework within which a firm structured as a corporation is to operate.

In Chapter 1 we described the different meanings of the term "contract" in law and economics, respectively. This difference is crucial to understanding the contractual concept of the corporation as embraced by economists. As described, while lawyers tend to define a contract as one or more legally binding promises, to an economist a contract is properly, and more broadly, defined as "an arrangement between two or more actors supported by reciprocal expectations and behavior", as Gordon [1989, 1549] has stated. The "nexus of contracts" theory of the corporation is predominantly based on the economists' conception of a contract. The corporation is viewed as a gathering point for a series of commitments, express and implied, among individuals desirous to cooperate according to certain principles structuring their relationship, which are comprised in the corporate form. According to this approach, the corporation is a compilation of voluntary arrangements among private parties accompanied by the parties' reciprocal expectations that each of them will behave accordingly. No explicit, legally enforceable contracts are required.

The "nexus of contracts" view has its legal counterpart in the inherence theory, which views the concept of the corporation as the inherent result of purely private contracts requiring legal recognition [Henn and Alexander

(1983), 146; Butler and Ribstein (1988), 622]. The inherence theory assumes that the voluntary associative activities of individuals demanded recognition by the law, which is provided by the legal concept of the corporation. This approach does suggest that a corporation could technically be organized by means of *actual*, legally binding agreements among private individuals.

For instance, to enable a firm to enter into contracts in the market as an entity, the firm's constituent human beings could appoint a central agent (for example, a trustee) to represent them and authorize him to conclude contracts on their behalf. Legal title to the assets of the business could also be placed in the name of this agent. Similarly, the organizers of the firm could contract among themselves to channel legal actions by the firm through this central agent. In order that third parties wishing to take legal action against the firm would sue the firm and not individual input owners, they could include provisions to this effect in contracts with third parties. And if the judiciary would not uphold such provisions, contractual arrangements providing for arbitration by private arbitrators could perhaps provide an alternative means of dispute resolution. The corporation's "legal personality" formalizes such arrangements, and replaces a multitude of separate contracts among individuals that would be necessary to produce a similar result.

Also, investors could agree with other input owners to put up capital in exchange for (a portion of) the residual claim on the firm's assets and cash flows. They could further agree that separate portions of the residual claim should be transferable by their respective owners without the permission of the other contracting individuals. The concept of transferable shares in the corporation's equity capital reflects such arrangements.

Limited liability for investors in corporate equity is another device which, to a large extent, could be accomplished by means of contractual instruments. Limited liability is a risk-sharing arrangement between the suppliers of risk capital and the corporation's creditors. The former agree that both their remuneration and the ultimate repayment of their capital contribution be contingent on the firm's success and that their claims for repayment be subordinated to creditors' claims, provided that their total risk is limited to the value of their investment, that is to say, provided that they will not have to make up for the corporation's debts to its creditors. Creditors, on the other hand, consent to seeking repayment from the corporation's assets and cash flows only on condition that they themselves are given a fixed claim on the corporation's resources with priority over equity claims.

Shareholders and creditors could contract for limited shareholder liability as a part of the credit agreement. To provide shareholders with limited liability, standard clauses to this effect may be included on a regular basis in contracts entered into on behalf of the firm. However, there may also be creditors who involuntarily provide credit, that is, who have not entered into a prior contract. This category includes, in particular, the victims of torts generated by the operations of the firm. Such tort victims are creditors of the firm to the extent that the latter is liable to pay damages to them after the tort is committed, but unlike voluntary creditors they have not *agreed* to provide credit.

One could hypothesize, however, that involuntary creditors and shareholders may enter into contracts by which the creditors agree not to seek payment of damages from the personal (*i.e.* non-invested) assets of the shareholders, on condition that their claim for damages is given priority over shareholders' residual claim on the corporation's resources. Such contracts might be concluded before a liability in tort arises in as far as shareholders could identify potential tort victims in anticipation. The corporate principle of limited shareholder liability reflects such an arrangement to protect shareholders' non-invested wealth from tortious liabilities generated by the firm. (Whether contracts limiting shareholders' liability to tort creditors would be *likely* to arise is a different question, but technically such contractual limitations are possible.)

Centralized management, too, could be achieved by means of contracts. To achieve the advantages of centralized management the residual claimants could contract among themselves so as to hire one or more specialized agents to manage the business. Through the appointment of one or more of such agents they could seek to maximize their earnings from the possession of the residual claim. The contractual arrangements needed to separate the function of residual claimant from the management of the firm are represented in the concept of the corporation where it provides for centralized management by a governing body.

Note that the use of contractual instruments to achieve corporate characteristics is not merely a theoretical construct. Anderson and Tollison [1983] and Butler [1986] have produced historical evidence demonstrating that in England and in the United States, prior to the coming of general incorporation legislation in the nineteenth century, it was not uncommon for firms to be given corporate characteristics by means of contractual arrangements of the kinds described above. In this way companies were created which, although not legally incorporated, enjoyed the essential organizational features of a corporation. Contractual arrangements were used to establish corporate characteristics in order to avoid the costs of formal incorporation through a special legislative act by Crown or Parliament (or, in the early United States, state legislature). Anderson and Tollison [1983, 116] therefore conclude that the "emergence and spread of the corporation did not depend on legislation. (...) The corporation emerged because it was an efficiency instrument".

The Corporation as a Standard Contract

If the main organizational features characterizing a corporation can be achieved, at least in theory, by means of private contracts among the individuals concerned, then what is the function of the *legal* concept of the corporation? In other words, if individuals can contract to establish an organization with corporate attributes, why does the law expressly provide for the corporate form in a public corporation statute? And why do corporation statutes provide for a formal procedure to establish a corporation through a certificate of incorporation issued by the state?

The answer, again, rests on transaction costs. If transaction costs were zero, an organizational structure with corporate attributes could be created at no cost by means of contractual arrangements among the individuals involved in the manner described above. However, given the existence of positive transaction costs, considerable resources would inevitably be absorbed by the costs of making the various arrangements that would be needed to bring about corporate characteristics. The amount of such transaction costs may be prohibitive.

If transaction costs would prevent the necessary contractual arrangements, the advantages of the corporate form in the raising of capital and the attainment of effective monitoring of input behavior would not be realized. In as far as this would inhibit firms from obtaining the capital inputs and monitoring services required to maximize output and to minimize unit production costs, consumer interests would be harmed. And where notwithstanding the existence of positive transaction costs, parties would contract to create corporate features, high transaction costs would be reflected in the prices consumers will have to pay for the firm's output. In the second case, to the extent that high transaction costs would reduce net returns to investors, they would also adversely affect levels of investment, with similar effect on output levels and prices. In short, if corporate characteristics were to be created by a multitude of separate contracts, the existence of positive transaction costs would imply that the requisite arrangements might not come about at all, or at high costs (prices) only.

In general, the higher the cost of operating a firm in corporate form, the more likely the firm will be organized in an alternative way (*i.e.* without the benefits of the corporate form). And, as noted earlier, the higher the cost of organizing production in a firm in whatever way relative to the cost of using market transactions, the less likely production will be organized in a firm. Either way, transaction costs have a negative effect on the amount of output that will become available for the satisfaction of consumer needs and on the prices consumers have to pay.

The legal concept of the corporation and the procedure of incorporation under a public statute serve to economize on the transaction costs associated with the creation of corporate features by means of a variety of private contracts. Instead of the transaction costs of numerous contractual arrangements, individuals desiring to organize a firm in corporate form merely have to incur the cost of the formal procedure with which they have to comply in order to receive a certificate of incorporation from the state (pursuant to the applicable corporate statute). As the cost of compliance with this legal procedure is most likely less than the costs of separate contracts among private individuals, a net reduction in the costs of organizing a corporation is achieved.

The corporation as recognized by corporate law is a standard-form contract that unites the various contractual arrangements that would be required to bring about corporate features if no corporate statute and no incorporation procedure existed. Accordingly, the primary utility of corporate law has been said to lie in the provision of "a set of standard, implied contract terms" [Posner (1976), 506]. These standard contract terms specify the rights and duties of the parties to the contract comprising the corporation, which are summarized in the four cornerstones of the corporate form, viz. legal personality, transferable shares, limited shareholder liability and centralized management. As Posner [1992, 396] has observed, the corporation as a standard contract serves "to economize on transaction costs by supplying standard contract terms that the parties would otherwise have to adopt by express agreement". By compliance with the procedure for incorporating a business prescribed by the law, the parties can opt into the standard contract terms embodied in the corporate law.

The above reasoning suggests that if the costs of incorporation under a public statute were to exceed the costs of obtaining corporate characteristics through the use of contractual instruments, parties seeking the benefits of corporate characteristics would apply the latter instead. Indeed, Anderson and Tollison [1983, 110-112] have found evidence indicating that in the eighteenth century in England, the high costs of the legal procedure required for incorporation motivated the use of contractual arrangements to organize unincorporated firms with corporate features as a substitute for the specially chartered corporation. High costs of formal incorporation have also been reported by Amsler, Bartlett and Bolton [1981, 776] who found that the costs of obtaining a corporate charter from the Crown or Parliament at the time were prohibitive for "all but the largest enterprises" because of "the elaborate and uncertain political procedures" which the chartering process required. Private contracting then afforded an alternative means for obtaining corporate characteristics.

As the concept of the corporation is essentially the reflection of a voluntary contracting process among private individuals, it is not a creation of the state. By embodying the corporate concept in a statute establishing a formal procedure for obtaining corporate features through a state certificate of incorporation, the state recognizes the result attainable by private contracting. Given that the state does not create the corporate form but merely recognizes it, Butler and Ribstein [1988, 620] conclude that "a state corporate filing no more creates a corporation than a birth certificate creates a baby". Incorporation under a corporate statute *affirms* the arrangements private parties consent to but it does not *create* them.

The contractual approach set out above and the more traditional view of the corporation as a concession granted by the state both have different normative connotations.

The concession theory suggests first that the terms on which individuals may do business as a corporation are determined by the *state* rather than by the will of the private parties concerned. When the corporation is defined as a concession by the state, the state granting the corporate privilege (*i.e.* the state in which the firm is incorporated) is deemed free to decide the content of the privilege as it pleases, and it may unilaterally modify the terms of the privilege as embodied in the corporate law. Second, the conception of the corporation as a grant from the state suggests that the beneficiaries of the corporate privilege should adhere to the terms which govern it, and are not free to agree on deviations from the otherwise governing rules without the permission of the state [Henn and Alexander (1983), 145-146]. In other words, the concession theory supports the view that the legal rules governing the corporate form are *mandatory* rather than *enabling*.

On the other hand, the contractual theory of the corporation suggests that since the corporation is the result of private contracting, corporate law should seek to standardize the contractual arrangements which private parties would normally arrive at if they could bargain without obstacles, in other words, if transaction costs were zero. Such standardized contract terms implied by the law reduce the cost of attaining corporate attributes and so economize on the cost of economic organization, to the extent that the standard terms properly accommodate the desires of the private parties concerned [Posner (1976), 506]. From this perspective the role of the state is limited to the creation of standard-form contract terms which minimize the effects of transaction costs [Butler and Ribstein (1988), 617, 619].

Moreover, since from the contractual viewpoint corporation law is deemed to be a reflection of purely private agreements, parties should be free to "opt out", that is to say, they should be free to agree on terms different from those provided by corporation law. As Gordon [1989, 1551] has put it, according to this theory corporation law should function as "an "off the rack" set of terms that parties may use for their convenience but may also freely alter". Thus corporation law is primarily thought of as being of an *enabling* nature.

The Dutch corporation statute, by contrast, provides that departures from statute law are allowed only if and to the extent permitted by the statute (Section 2:25 of the Civil Code). The mandatory nature of Dutch corporate law is based on the premise that the corporate form is a concession from the state, a premise that defies the essentially voluntary associative nature of the relationships between the various parties involved in the corporation.

In relation to corporations incorporated in United States state jurisdictions, finally, Butler and Ribstein [1988] have construed the contractual nature of the corporate form to imply that the private arrangements embodied in corporate charters deserve the protection of the "Contract Clause" of Article I, Section 10, of the United States Constitution, providing: "No State shall (...) pass any (...) Law impairing the obligation of Contracts (...)". Application of the Contract Clause to the associative arrangements which make up the corporation would considerably restrain the power of state legislatures to enact corporate legislation unilaterally dictating changes into the terms governing previously established corporate charters. According to this interpretation, state legislation impairing the rights that private parties have under corporate charters in existence when the particular legislation is introduced, might face challenges on the basis of unconstitutionality, and from the corporation's contractual nature would ensue a constitutionally protected right to structure corporate relations basically free from post-incorporation regulatory interference by the states.

3. A PARADOX NAMED LIMITED LIABILITY

THE CORPORATION IS a legal method for organizing a firm that comprises contractual and quasi-contractual relationships between the firm's various constituents. The corporate form does not merely serve to organize economic activity in a manner avoiding the costs of carrying out exchange transactions in the market, but it also makes available to the firm the advantages of legal entity status, transferable equity shares, limited shareholder liability and centralized management. Incorporation under a corporate statute serves to avoid the transaction costs that would be incurred if the same characteristics had to be accomplished by means of private bargaining.

Limited liability for equity investors is often regarded as the "hallmark of the corporation" [Sowards (1974), 2]. At the same time, it is presumably the least understood and most puzzling feature of the corporate concept. The owners of equity shares assume the risk of the firm's success or failure as both the return on their investment and the repayment of their capital contribution at the corporation's dissolution are contingent upon the prosperity of the business. However, whereas share owners, in principle, are entitled to all of the firm's profits, they assume the risk of the firm's failure to a limited extent only: the statutory principle of limited liability limits a shareholder's risk to the value of his investment. The risk that the corporation performs so poorly that it ultimately proves unable to fulfil its obligations to creditors is shifted to the latter.

Limited liability means that shareholders bear all of the positive wealth effects of the activities of a firm operated in corporate form, but only part of the negative wealth effects that the operations of the firm may generate. They have unlimited title to the profits which the firm may accumulate but their stake in the firm's losses is limited to the amount of their investment. Why do we observe this distinction, and what is its function in the context of the organizational concept the corporation embodies?

In the preceding chapter we examined the ways in which the distinctive organizational characteristics of the corporate form relate to the operation of a firm. In the present chapter we examine in greater detail the role of one of these characteristics, the principle of limited liability for shareholders. Our analysis centers, as before, on the particular functions of this principle in relation to publicly held corporations.

The Principle of Limited Liability

As a legal entity, the corporation itself is liable for any debts attributable to it which are incurred in the course of its business. The corporation is liable for obligations arising from contracts which employees or agents have entered into on behalf of the corporation, for torts generated by the corporate firm's operations, for taxes imposed on it by fiscal authorities and for social security premiums payable under social statutes. Thus a corporation is subject to civil liability in the same way as a private individual.

"Corporate liability" refers to the corporation's ability to be liable as one entity, and this ability is inherent in the corporate form. Corporate liability ensures that those dealing with the corporation and those injured by its activities need to make one stop only in order to claim damages or to demand the performance of a contract, and have access to one "deep pocket" from which damages may be obtained.

In general, the corporation's constituent human beings are not liable for obligations incumbent on the corporate entity. This principle applies to shareholders, directors, officers and workers alike. It does not, however, relieve these persons of the possibility that they become subject to liability as an individual. For instance, a worker who commits a tort while acting in the course of his employment may well be personally liable for the harm done to the victim, albeit that in many cases he has recourse to the corporate entity for reimbursement. Similarly, officers defrauding the corporation's creditors may become subject to personal liability.

The corporation's legal personality, enabling it to have obligations in its own name and on its own behalf, does not by nature absolve its constituent human beings from liability for the obligations of the corporation. One could conceive of an arrangement imposing liability on the corporation with vicarious liability of some or all of its constituent persons for corporate debts. The non-liability of shareholders, managers and workers for the obligations of the corporation, therefore, is complementary to the concept of corporate liability.

Non-liability of managers is consistent with, and ensues from, the principles of agency law. Managers acting on behalf of the corporation are legal agents of the corporation (*i.e.* the legal entity), the latter being their principal. Generally, a principal assumes liability for the actions of his agent that are within the scope of the authority conferred upon him, but not vice versa. Accordingly, managers may contract debts, the payment of which the corporation is liable for, but they are not personally liable for the latter's obligations. Similarly, an employer is usually obliged to compensate workers for liabilities they incur when acting in the course of their employment, but not the other way round. Therefore, the non-liability of managers and workers for corporate debts is not peculiar to corporations but it is the prevailing rule with any agency or employment relationship.

Suppose that the corporation would not enjoy legal personality, and that managers would act directly on behalf of the shareholders. Managers would then be the legal agents of the shareholders. In this event the latter, as their principals, would be liable for obligations entered into by managers (provided they acted within the scope of their authority) and managers would be relieved of personal liability. Non-liability of managers, thus, is in fact independent of the corporation's legal personality.

Shareholders are neither agents nor employees of the corporation. Therefore, shareholders' non-liability for corporate debts once they have paid full consideration for their shares cannot be explained by the existence of an agency or employment relationship. Non-liability of shareholders is a distinct legal rule that has emerged by its own merits.

The term "limited shareholder liability", as the above suggests, is, strictly speaking, inaccurate. Upon payment of the subscription price of their shares, shareholders are under no obligation whatsoever to pay any more to the corporation or its creditors. In other words, shareholders who have paid full consideration for their shares are relieved of any liability whatsoever. We will continue to speak of "limited liability" instead of "non-liability" (which would be more accurate) only because the former term is the more current one.

As noted in Chapter 2, limited shareholder liability is a risk-sharing arrangement between shareholders and creditors [Easterbrook and Fischel (1985), 101]. It effects that the risk (including the cost) of the corporation's failure is borne by the shareholders to the extent of their investment and that the remainder is borne by the corporation's creditors. Because of shareholders' limited liability, creditors cannot collect debts of the corporation from shareholders' personal assets (except if they contract around the rule of limited liability), and will be unpaid if corporate debts cannot be satisfied out of the corporation's assets. Limited liability of shareholders has been described, therefore, as "an arrangement under which the loss largely lies where it falls" [Easterbrook and Fischel (1985), 98].

If a prize were awarded to the most celebrated corporate feature, limited liability would win it with distinction. For instance, Eliot has depicted limited liability of shareholders as "the corporation's most precious characteristic" [Cook (1921), 583], Henn [1970, 96] has called it "the most attractive feature of the corporation", while Posner [1976, 502] has denoted limited liability as the "basic principle of corporation law". Warner Fuller [1938, 1376] has asserted that in "the historical development of the corporation probably no single attribute has been more significant than that of limited liability". Even more emphatically, the commentator of The Economist of December 18, 1926, wrote: "The economic historian of the future may assign to the nameless inventor of the principle of limited liability, as applied to trading corporations, a place of honour with Watt and Stephenson, and other pioneers of the Industrial Revolution" [Halpern, Trebilcock and Turnbull (1980), 118; Hunt (1936), 116]. Similarly, Hicks [1982, 12] has said that "it must be regarded as a major achievement of limited liability that it has made much of our economic progress possible".

The Limited Liability Paradox

The favorable appraisals cited above should not conceal the fact that, in a way, the statutory principle of limited liability for shareholders is a stepchild of the law.

Both tort and property law contain rules to the effect that the person who is entitled to the benefits from an activity or a piece of property is also subject to full personal liability for the costs the activity or property imposes on others, once the legal requirements for establishing liability have been fulfilled. The principle of limited shareholder liability, however, has the opposite effect. As indicated, it results in the fact that those who are entitled to the benefits ensuing from a firm's operations (the profits earned), are not liable for the costs these operations would impose on creditors if the corporation's assets fall short of its debts.

As a rule, the owner of an asset (a piece of equipment, a building, an animal) is entitled to the fruits the asset produces but, at the same time, he is liable to the full extent of his personal wealth for harm the asset concerned may cause to others. Likewise, a person who chooses to engage in a particular course of action also has to make up in full for harm done to third parties attributable to the action concerned (in particular, in the event a tort is committed). A car driver enjoys the benefit of driving but if he injures a pedestrian through his fault, he will be fully liable for damages payable.

Similarly, an employer who earns the benefits from his employees' labor is in most cases obliged to assume the liabilities incurred by the employees in the course of their work.

In each of these instances, the law establishes that the person who has the benefits from an activity or an asset also has to bear its costs to third parties (provided the conditions for imposing liability as determined by the law are fulfilled). The economic rationale underlying such rules is that a person will behave efficiently only if he bears the full social costs (*i.e.* the costs to himself *and* the costs to other members of society) of the asset or the activity of which he enjoys the fruits.

Suppose a person does not, or not entirely, have to pay for the adverse effects of his behavior on others. In this event he will be induced to leave potential costs to third parties out of account, in whole or in part, when choosing between alternative ways of behaving. Consequently, his decisions will most likely be inconsistent with the social costs they may generate. He will be inclined to undertake too much of a particular activity or to employ too much of a particular asset in proportion to its total costs to society as a whole. For instance, if a car driver were not liable for harm caused by careless driving, he would have little or no incentive to exercise care for others. Therefore, the level of careless driving he would be likely to undertake would be too high in relation to the potential costs thereof to others, especially the costs to the victims of traffic accidents.

In general terms, microeconomic theory teaches that a person maximizes his utility by engaging in those activities in which his marginal anticipated benefits equal the marginal anticipated costs to himself (*i.e.* marginal *private* costs). If a person does not bear the costs of his actions to other members of society, however, he will ignore such costs when deciding on how to act. In consequence, he will select actions that maximize his personal utility but of which the marginal costs to society as a whole may well outweigh the marginal benefits to society.

Where the law makes a person liable for costs (injury) imposed on others, he is given an incentive to take such costs into account when making decisions as they will now be relevant to the calculation of his net private gain from a contemplated activity. Accordingly, he will compare his anticipated benefits from a particular course of action to the *full* costs the action is likely to generate (including its costs to other members of society). Hence, his behavior will now reflect cost-benefit calculations at which his marginal anticipated benefits will be equal to marginal *social* costs. When private participants in the economy select activities at which marginal social benefits equal marginal social costs, their behavior is considered to be socially efficient.

Limited liability for shareholders defies the above reasoning. Shareholders enjoy the benefits from the activities of the firm in which they invest through their claim on its profits, but the principle of limited liability sets a maximum to shareholders' potential costs from the firm's operations. Therefore, their investment decisions, including the activities they desire the firm to undertake, have to take account of the potential costs of the firm's operations only up to the extent of shareholders' investment. Thus, although elsewhere the law provides that persons entitled to the benefits from an activity or an asset are liable in full for its costs to third parties, shareholders, in contrast, have full title to the profits earned by the firm in which they own shares but they are not liable for the costs of its operations beyond the subscription price of their shares. Why is it that shareholders are treated differently?

The popular belief is that limited liability promotes investments by risk averse investors [Manne (1975), 513; Posner (1976), 502; Barber (1981), 371; Thompson (1991), 1039]. Risk-aversion – a common assumption in microeconomics with respect to individuals – presupposes that a person attaches greater utility to a certain prospect of wealth than to an uncertain prospect of equal monetary value (for instance, he would prefer a 100 percent chance of receiving USD 10 to a 10 percent chance of receiving USD 100). Expressed negatively, risk averse individuals are assumed to dislike uncertainty about the potential magnitude of the losses that they might suffer (they would prefer, for instance, a 20 percent chance of incurring a loss of USD 100 on an investment to a 10 percent chance of losing USD 200 as the latter situation would involve a larger possible loss, although both situations represent the same monetary value, viz. USD 20) [Shavell (1987), 186]. According to the theory that risk-aversion on the part of investors explains limited liability, the possibility that creditors could reach a shareholder's non-invested assets would deter risk-averse individuals from making equity investments as it would create uncertainty about the possible size of their loss. By setting a limit on investors' maximum potential loss, limited liability reduces such uncertainty and, in effect, is deemed to alleviate this impediment to raising capital. Indeed, Blumberg [1993, 337], among others, has stated that one of the important advantages of limited liability lies in "its encouragement of entrepreneurial risk taking and new investment". True as this undoubtedly be, it does not provide us with a full explanation of the principle of limited shareholder liability.

The risk-aversion argument is incomplete as lenders also enjoy limited liability. Lenders' risk is limited in three ways: their potential loss is limited to the amount of their loan, they have a fixed claim on the corporation's assets and cash flows which is preferential to shareholders' residual claim, and they may further limit their risk by stipulating security for the repayment of their loan. Thus, if shareholders were personally liable for the debts of the corporation, risk averse investors unwilling to assume unlimited liability could provide capital by *lending* money. Rather than purchasing equity shares, they could, for example, invest in bonds issued by the corporation. Limited liability may be a necessary condition for explaining investment in equity by risk averse investors but, as lenders also have limited liability, it is not a *sufficient* condition [Jensen and Meckling (1976), 331].

The risk-aversion argument is incomplete moreover, because it ignores the possibility that with unlimited liability, risk averse investors might choose to take out liability insurance if and to the extent that such insurance were available [Halpern, Trebilcock and Turnbull (1980), 128; Shavell (1987), 176 fn. 17]. For instance, when subscribing to equity shares carrying unlimited liability, they could concurrently purchase third party liability insurance protecting them against tortious liabilities generated by the firm. If full insurance were available to cover investors' risk of personal liability, limited liability would not even be a necessary condition for investments by risk averse investors. (We will discuss the issue of unlimited liability and insurance in more detail in Chapter 8.) Thus, on the whole, risk-aversion would seem to be a largely *ad hoc* argument to explain limited liability in situations in which the firm has attracted capital from *supposedly* risk averse investors not merely in the form of debt and in which insurance would not provide such investors with suitable protection against unlimited liability.

Another popular belief is that limited shareholder liability somehow lowers the costs to a firm of obtaining capital. Granted, with limited liability investors presumably pay more for a share as their losses in the event of corporate failure are less and, therefore, the relationship between risk incurred and anticipated returns is more favorable to them. However, the limited liability of share owners reduces the number (and thus the value) of the assets from which lenders may seek repayment of a loan in comparison with the assets which would be available were a rule of unlimited shareholder liability to apply. If shareholders were subject to unlimited liability, lenders could collect the loan out of both the assets of the corporation and shareholders' personal wealth, whereas under a rule of limited liability they are unable to reach shareholders' non-invested assets.

As limited shareholder liability reduces the assets from which lenders may collect payment of the corporation's debts, they will probably demand higher interest rates, or collateral for the repayment of loans extended to the corporation, or both [Meiners, Mofsky and Tollison (1979), 359-362]. In this manner, when a shareholder is protected by a limited liability rule, "market conditions force him to pay a price for the limited liability", as Meiners, Mofsky and Tollison [1979, 361] have observed. Therefore, at this point the thesis that limited liability lowers a firm's cost of capital would seem to be, at best, an unproven proposition.

What, then, does limited liability do?

Limited Liability in the Monitorial Model

In Chapter 2 we described two economic models of the corporate form of organization. The monitorial model explains the corporation as a mechanism for achieving effective monitoring of input performance in a team production process. The complementary financial model approaches the corporate form as an instrument for attracting capital into a firm. Below we discuss the functions of limited shareholder liability in both models, starting with the monitorial model.

Costs of Monitoring

In the monitorial model, the function of monitor of the other inputs in the firm is assigned to the joint shareholders, motivated by the possession of the residual claim. They may delegate a substantial part of their monitoring task to specialized, hired managers and monitor the performance of these managers instead of monitoring *all* cooperative inputs. Specialized managers will then direct the use of resources within the firm, measure individual productivities, apportion rewards, and discipline individual inputs. In brief, they will be responsible for the day-to-day management of the firm's operations.

The larger the risk to which an individual is exposed, the greater, in all likelihood, will be his desire to control the factors that determine his exposure. Likewise, the larger the amount of an investor's potential loss relative to his total wealth, the greater will be his incentive to actively monitor the performance of the firm in which he has invested with a view to controlling the liabilities it incurs. Thus, shareholders' risk is positively related to their desire to monitor the other inputs in the firm: "The more risk they bear, the more they will monitor" [Easterbrook and Fischel (1985), 94].

Accordingly, shareholders' incentives to participate in the actual decision-making with regard to the operations of the firm are likely to correspond to the amount of risk to which they are exposed.

Shareholders' risk is determined by a variety of factors, including the nature of the activities of the firm in which they hold shares, its perceived chances of commercial success, and the legal rule which governs shareholders' liability for the tortious and contractual liabilities generated by the firm. Therefore, the form of the liability rule determining their liability for the obligations of the corporation affects shareholders' incentives to become involved in the making of business decisions, and affects the degree of participation in the management of the firm shareholders will demand [Halpern, Trebilcock and Turnbull (1980), 125].

Since under a rule of unlimited liability, shareholders are subject to the risk of losing their entire wealth, they would be motivated to participate actively in the management of the firm in order to protect their wealth. In other words, they would have risk-minimizing incentives to be closely involved in the direction of the firm's operations so as to see that they would not be "ruined by the mistakes that it made" [Hicks (1982), 11]. As Posner [1992, 393] has put it, with unlimited liability an investor may want "to participate in the actual management of the firm to make sure it does not run up huge debts for which he would be liable".

The larger the number of shareholders, the greater will be the number of bargains needed to take decisions and the larger will be the costs of operating the firm, if all or most of the shareholders were involved in managerial decision-making. Substantial resources would be absorbed in making decisions to direct the use of resources in the firm, and in the acquisition and digestion of information by the shareholders on the basis of which such decisions are made. Consequently, Demsetz [1975, 33] concludes that if the individual shareholders participate in each decision that needs to be made to run the company, "the scale economies of operating the company will be overcome quickly by high negotiating cost".

As limited liability sets a maximum on the losses managers may cause shareholders, it mitigates the risk shareholders take when entrusting their investment to specialized managers. Given that limited liability reduces their risk, it lessens shareholders' incentives to participate actively in the firm's management and increases their willingness to delegate the day-to-day management to a limited number of managers. Thus, limited liability is likely to lower the degree of participation in managerial decision-making by the individual shareholders. In this way, it serves to economize on the costs of operating the firm relative to operating costs under a rule of unlimited shareholder liability.

The larger the number of shareholders, the larger will be the reduction in the costs of business decision-making which is achieved when shareholders delegate the firm's day-to-day management to a relatively small group of managers. Therefore, the larger the number of shareholders, the more important is the cost-saving function of limited liability as a means of promoting centralized management by a limited management group.

Specialization in Monitoring

In the preceding section we noticed that under the rule of limited liability, wealth maximizing shareholders are more inclined to entrust their investment to a relatively small number of managers than they would be were a rule of unlimited liability to apply. In this way limited liability does not merely economize on the costs of business decision-making, it also encourages *specialization* in management, that is, it encourages the separation of the functions of residual risk-bearing and management of the firm. Limited liability encourages such a functional specialization by limiting the costs which managers may impose on shareholders through inadequate business decisions and, in particular, by limiting the potential costs to shareholders of any divergence of interests between shareholders and specialized managers which may result from the separation of management and risk-bearing [Ekelund and Tollison (1980), 718 fn. 5].

In Chapter 2 we argued that specialized management yields the same gains that are usually associated with specialization. Apart from bringing about a reduction in the aggregate costs of decision-making, then, management by specialized managers is likely to produce more extensive and better skilled monitoring of input behavior, at a lower cost per unit of monitoring, than management by unspecialized shareholders. This will not merely result in higher returns to shareholders but it is also beneficial to society as a whole: better management at less cost per unit will be reflected in increased productivity of the firm, resulting in the availability of more output for the satisfaction of consumer needs, at lower costs (prices) to consumers. By reducing the risk shareholders take when assigning the day-to-day management of the firm to specialized managers, limited liability supports the realization of these benefits.

The monitoring of input activity typically has characteristics associated with economies of scale [Manne (1981), 689]: a large volume of monitoring can be produced at a lower cost per unit than a small volume, because greater volumes allow a larger degree of specialization. The larger the amount of monitoring required, the larger the productivity gains attainable by specialization and the greater the value of limited liability as a device promoting functional specialization in monitoring. Therefore, the benefit of limited liability as a device for encouraging specialized management is greatest in large firms that organize complex businesses requiring a large input of monitoring.

Limited liability not only encourages delegation of a firm's day-to-day management to specialized managers, it also bears upon the supervision over the firm's managers. Suppose that shareholders hired specialized managers even under a rule of unlimited liability. As these managers might impose indefinite costs on shareholders, the latter would have risk-minimizing incentives to exercise detailed supervision over the management team. They would be reluctant to entrust the monitoring of the day-to-day management to specialized monitor-monitors (*i.e.* non-managing, supervisory directors).

The exercise of effective supervision over the management by the individual shareholders would probably absorb higher costs than would be incurred if the same task were carried out by a limited number of specialized monitor-monitors. Moreover, apart from a reduction in the overall costs of monitor-monitoring, supervision of the management team by specialist supervisors yields advantages of specialization similar to those discussed with regard to specialized day-to-day management: they presumably monitor managerial performance more effectively and at a lower cost per unit of monitor-monitoring than shareholders themselves would be able to do.

Limited liability reduces the risk shareholders take if they refrain from exercising detailed supervision over the firm's managers. In effect, limited liability promotes delegation of the monitoring of managerial performance to specialized monitor-monitors. Thus it serves to reduce the costs of monitoring the management team and encourages realization of the benefits of specialization in monitor-monitoring.

Monitorial Shirking

Under a rule of unlimited liability, shareholders would have risk-minimizing incentives to demand detailed involvement in the management of the firm. However, regardless even of the liability rule to which they are subject, if the number of shareholders increases, *individual* shareholders may gain by shirking as a monitor.

Consider a firm that is managed by its shareholders. If a corporation has multiple shareholders, individual shareholders have wealth-maximizing incentives to rely upon their fellow shareholders to monitor the cooperative inputs in the firm. In other words, individual shareholders may attempt to "free-ride" on the efforts other shareholders dedicate to monitoring input behavior. In this manner they could save effort and costs and still benefit from monitoring done by others, at no charge.

For instance, individual shareholders could save the costs of obtaining or digesting the information required to take soundly based business decisions. They could avoid the effort of acquiring and analyzing relevant data, examining business opportunities, studying the performance of different parts of the business, comparing the firm's performance to that of its competitors, and so on. They might simply sit back and wait for others to do the job. The costs of shirking by individual shareholders are shared by the joint shareholders in the form of less effective overall monitoring, while the benefits of less effort (or lower quality effort) and saved costs are enjoyed exclusively by the individual shareholder concerned.

If enough shareholders shirk the task of monitoring, the effective performance of the monitoring function *per se* will be threatened: the amount of shirking by individual shareholders may become so large that, as a consequence, input activity is not adequately monitored. This would bring about opportunity losses to *all* shareholders (lower firm productivity and lower profits) and may ultimately result in the firm's failure.

In particular, the larger the number of shareholders, the greater becomes the probability that individual shareholders assume that their fellow shareholders will act as monitors and that they will benefit from their efforts in any case. Hence, the larger the number of shareholders, the greater will be an *individual* shareholder's incentive to shirk the task of monitoring. On the assumption that monitoring expenditures are a function of the risk borne, the larger a shareholder's potential loss, the more he could save by relying upon others to monitor input activity. Moreover, the more extensive monitoring required (that is, the larger and the more complex the business to be monitored), the more significant will be the costs and effort an individual shareholder could save by shirking as a monitor, and the higher will be his incentive to shirk.

Centralized management is one device that serves to cope with the shirking problem among relatively large numbers of shareholders. Limited liability for shareholders is another, as Alchian and Demsetz [1972, 788] have noted. Limited liability mitigates the shirking problem among multiple shareholders in two ways. First, by limiting their potential losses from inadequate monitoring, it reduces the costs individual shareholders may impose on one another by shirking as a monitor. Second, since with limited liability, a shareholder's potential loss is smaller than with unlimited liability, he is likely to spend fewer resources in monitoring and, consequently, the expenses any shareholder would expect to save by relying upon others to do the work would be less.

Alchian and Demsetz [1972, 788] suggest that individual shareholders are inclined to shirk as a monitor "since the losses associated with unexpectedly bad decisions will be borne in large part by the many other corporate shareholders". This statement is, in our view, incorrect both under a rule of unlimited liability and under limited shareholder liability. Indeed, a shirking shareholder may bear less than the entire (opportunity) loss attributable to his shirking as a monitor. However, under *unlimited* joint and several liability, shareholders cannot be so sure that losses will be borne in large part by other shareholders as under this rule, each individual shareholder would be potentially liable for all of the debts of the corporation. Under *limited* liability, on the other hand, any particular shareholder is still subject to the risk of losing his investment in the firm concerned. The fact that other shareholders in aggregate might lose more than an individual shareholder would not preclude or make less serious the latter's loss of his invested wealth.

A shareholder's benefit from shirking the task of monitoring is not reflected in the size of his potential loss of wealth, as Alchian and Demsetz suggest, but in saved costs and effort. Limited liability is related to shirking in that it limits a shareholder's costs in the event of ineffective monitoring by the joint shareholders, and reduces the costs he may save by shirking as a monitor to the extent that monitoring expenditures would be higher under unlimited liability.

Limited liability mitigates the shirking problem among multiple shareholders regardless of whether shareholders have delegated the day-to-day management of the firm to a limited number of managers. If there is no such centralized management, it limits shareholders' losses that may arise when individual shareholders shirk the monitoring of the other inputs in the firm. If shareholders have entrusted the day-to-day management to a specialized management team, limited liability reduces the losses managers might impose on shareholders by inadequate performance, should shareholders fail to properly monitor the management (or the non-managing, supervisory directors they may have appointed for this purpose).

Transferability of Shares

Another function of limited liability is that it facilitates the transferability of shares. As described in Chapter 2, flexible transferability of shares is a mechanism for ensuring effective monitoring of input activity over time which operates through across-market competition from potential monitors external to the firm.

If would-be monitors outside a firm are able to employ the firm's inputs in more profitable ways than the incumbent monitors do, they will anticipate higher future earnings from possession of the residual claim than existing shareholders. Accordingly, in order to obtain the residual claim they will be prepared to pay a higher price for the company's shares than their value to the existing shareholders. Thus, flexible transferability of shares allows superior monitors, or investors able to replace incumbent managers by more effective ones, to take over control of poorly or sub-optimally managed firms [Manne (1964); (1965)]. As more effective monitors are better able to direct productive activity so as to satisfy the wants of consumers, unimpeded transferability of shares is not only beneficial to the parties obtaining wealth improvements in takeover transactions but also to society as a whole.

Limited liability is considered to be essential to the operation of a market in which shares can be readily traded, that is, a market that enables shares to smoothly flow to superior monitors [Halpern, Trebilcock and Turnbull (1980); Easterbrook and Fischel (1985); Woodward (1985)]. How does the liability rule to which shareholders are subject relate to the operation of a market for equity shares?

Suppose that shareholders are subject to a rule of unlimited joint and several liability, meaning that in the event of corporate insolvency, every single shareholder could be held liable for the full amount of the corporation's indebtedness. Under such a liability regime, the amount a particular shareholder actually has to pay in the event of the corporation's default is not only determined by the extent of the latter's debts, but also by the wealth of his fellow shareholders. The poorer the other shareholders, the larger the part of the corporation's unsettled debts a relatively wealthy shareholder may have to shoulder. Also, if other shareholders are richer, the probability becomes smaller that a shareholder of modest wealth will be pursued by the corporation's creditors. Thus, the relative wealth of other shareholders is relevant to the extent of each shareholder's potential loss in the event of corporate failure.

(Indeed, under a rule of joint and several liability, a shareholder who is made liable for the corporation's unpaid debts in excess of his proportion of the total shares issued, has recourse to reimbursement from other shareholders to the extent of the excess. However, the amount he will be able to recover from such other shareholders depends on the wealth of the latter and on the individual shareholder's ability to overcome the costs of collecting other shareholders' proportionate share of the corporation's debts; enforcement costs will be high and potentially prohibitive, especially if there are many other shareholders of relatively modest wealth.)

Under joint and several liability, the poorer the other shareholders, the larger the risk a wealthy investor will take by acquiring shares in a particular firm (*i.e.* the amount he might lose), and vice versa. Hence, the relative wealth levels of the other shareholders in a company influence the risk-return relationship a share in that company poses to a particular investor and, thus, the value investors will attach to the shares. Since, *ceteris paribus*, wealth maximizing investors are likely to attach less value to the shares in a firm as the risk they would take by becoming a shareholder rises, that is, as the underlying risk-return relationship becomes less favorable to them, the value a potential investor places on a share will be less, the greater his personal wealth relative to the wealth of existing shareholders, and vice versa. Under a rule of joint and several liability, then, an investor's valuation of a share would not merely depend on the prospects of the firm concerned but also on the magnitude of his wealth in proportion to the wealth of the other shareholders. This argument has been advanced by Halpern, Trebilcock and Turnbull [1980, 130-131] in a seminal essay on the economics underlying limited liability for shareholders.

As a relatively wealthy investor would anticipate a higher loss in the event of the corporation's default, he would therefore attach less value to a share than an investor of modest wealth in comparison with the wealth levels of the other shareholders. In other words, wealthy investors and investors of modest means relative to the levels of wealth of the other shareholders will arrive at a different valuation of the same shares. From this observation, Halpern and his co-authors [1980, 131] have concluded that if unlimited liability is the rule, "there will not be a single price for all shares of a particular company": prices will differ among investors of different wealth, and a separate price may have to be negotiated for each share transfer. Easterbrook and Fischel [1985, 96] recapitulate their argument in the phrase: "With unlimited liability, shares would not be homogeneous commodities, so they would no longer have one market price". The alleged absence of a single market price for the shares in one company will threaten the functioning of a liquid stock market as it forces would-be buyers and sellers to engage in costly private bargaining over the price of every separate transaction.

Unlimited liability may impair the smooth transferability of shares in yet another way. To determine the value he places on a share, taking into account his potential loss in the event of the corporation's default, a would-be investor has to examine the wealth levels of existing shareholders no less than the liabilities of the firm. In addition, in order to keep track of his risk exposure, an investor will also have to examine changes in other shareholders' wealth relative to his own after his purchase of shares since the magnitude of a shareholder's potential loss in the event of the corporation's default will change as the relative wealth of his fellow shareholders changes. Trading in equity shares will only take place if and to the extent that investors are willing to incur the transaction costs associated with monitoring other shareholders' wealth.

Halpern, Trebilcock and Turnbull argue that the costs of ascertaining other shareholders' wealth levels would induce wealthy investors to refrain from purchasing a small number of shares in a particular corporation. Under a rule of joint and several liability, a shareholder's maximum potential loss depends on the relative wealth of his fellow shareholders, and not on the number of shares he owns. Therefore, a wealthy shareholder owning only a few shares may have to incur high costs in order to obtain information on other shareholders' wealth, especially when there are many other shareholders. Halpern and his co-authors reason that a wealthy shareholder would rather buy "a large number of shares so as to have some control over the operations of the company" because this would permit him "to protect his investment and limit his potential loss through a close scrutiny over the company's operations" [1980, 136].

The consequent concentration of share ownership by rich investors would, in their view, probably preclude the operation of a market in which there is active trading in shares: "In the extreme, securities markets will not exist" [1980, 136]. More generally, they conclude that by skewing the distribution of risks among different shareholders, an unlimited liability regime would create "a significant measure of uncertainty in the valuation of securities and threaten the existence of organized securities markets" [1980, 147].

How does limited liability, according to the reasoning set out above, promote the transferability of shares?

First, given that the limited liability rule limits each shareholder's potential loss to a maximum equal to the amount of his investment, the size of other shareholders' wealth is irrelevant to the magnitude of an investor's potential loss in the event of the corporation's default. With limited liability, an investor's maximum potential loss is determined by the extent of his investment only, and the value investors attach to shares will now be based exclusively on the expected future income stream from the firm's assets. Therefore, it is maintained that the shares in a corporation will now have a single price at which share transfers will take place. In this way, limited liability is considered to make possible securities markets in which shares can be readily traded [Halpern, Trebilcock and Turnbull (1980), 137, 147;

Easterbrook and Fischel (1985), 92, 96].

The existence of one market price facilitates trade by economizing on the costs of exchanging shares. As the prevailing market price of its shares reflects the publicly available information about the prospects of a firm, it is unnecessary for many, especially small, investors to incur substantial expenditure in order to examine in detail the firm's prospects [Easterbrook and Fischel (1985), 96]. Generally, the market equilibrium price of the shares in a firm reflects the collective knowledge and expectations of investors with regard to that firm, thus greatly reducing the need for individual investors to expend resources in examining the firm's liabilities and its chances of commercial success. If the shares in a company did not have a single market price but a price had to be negotiated for each separate transaction involving a share transfer, investors would have to incur larger costs to collect and to examine information about the firm in order to determine a proper price. Moreover, if shares have one market price reflecting relevant information about the firm, buyers and sellers can avoid the costs of extensive negotiations to fix a price and simply trade at the prevailing market price.

Secondly, since limited liability renders other shareholders' wealth irrelevant to the risk a particular shareholder bears, it avoids the expenses investors would otherwise have to incur to evaluate the wealth levels of other shareholders. The larger the number of other shareholders, the greater would be an investor's cost of monitoring other shareholders' wealth under an unlimited liability regime. By avoiding the costs of monitoring other shareholders' wealth, limited liability lowers the transaction costs inherent in stock acquisitions. In effect, it encourages the realization of gains from trade in the stock market and thus facilitates the transfer of shares to superior monitors.

The Multiple Prices Thesis

We support the second explanation of limited liability described above but are rather skeptical about the first. We agree that a single market price economizes on the resources potential investors need to expend in order to ascertain the proper price for a share. However, we doubt that limited liability is necessary to arrive at one market price for all shares in a particular company.

Standard economic theory teaches that the price an individual is willing to pay for a good corresponds to his expected marginal utility from that good, that is, his expected increase in utility from increasing consumption of that good by one unit. Prices reflect *marginal* rather than *total* utility as utility maximizing individuals seek to achieve maximum satisfaction by equating marginal utilities per dollar spent on diverse goods and services. Accordingly, they spend their budget in such a manner that the prices they pay will reflect the marginal utilities of the goods and services purchased rather than the total utility they derive from acquiring a given quantity of such goods or services. The same principles apply to the purchase of shares in a given company.

The fact that with unlimited liability, a wealthy investor may suffer a greater loss than a relatively poor investor suggests that the anticipated *total* utility (benefit) from obtaining a given set of shares in a particular company may be different for investors of different wealth. However, total utility from a given quantity of shares is irrelevant to investors' valuations of the shares concerned since for the attainment of maximum satisfaction, only investors' expected extra utility (wealth improvement) from purchasing one or more shares is relevant as compared to the *extra* utility from using the same amount for a different purpose. Thus, investors' valuations and consequent bidding prices will be based upon the anticipated marginal utility (wealth increase) from purchasing one or more shares in a particular firm.

The existence of one market price does not require that all potential purchasers derive the same total utility from a given set of shares or attach exactly the same value to it. It merely requires that buyers' expected utility (benefit) from acquiring a share shall be equal *at the margin*, *i.e.* that different buyers derive equal utility from the last single share they obtain in a particular company. This requirement can be met under limited and unlimited liability alike. Potential investors expecting high benefits from acquiring one or more shares (or small losses in the event of a default) will attach a high marginal value to a share and therefore bid prices higher, whereas investors expecting a smaller benefit (or a higher default loss) will offer relatively low prices. From this competitive bidding process a single equilibrium price will emerge reflecting a share's *marginal* utility (benefit) to all investors, even though individual investors may have placed different values on the shares. Different valuations will be discounted in the various bidding prices that eventually culminate in one market price. A relatively high market price then indicates high marginal utility to investors in the aggregate, and a low market price indicates low marginal utility.

Contrary to Easterbrook and Fischel's [1985, 96] suggestion, the fact that under unlimited liability, a wealthy investor bears more risk than an investor of relatively modest means does not imply that the shares in a particular company would not be homogeneous goods. Under *any* liability rule, the shares in a particular company represent the residual claim on the same set of assets and cash flows. The fact that with unlimited liability, a wealthy investor takes more risk by purchasing equity shares in a firm than a poor one does not render the firm's assets and the income stream they generate any different. Thus the shares in one company remain homogeneous goods, capable of being traded at one price, regardless of shareholders' liability rule. The law of one price, defined by Kindleberger [1997, 67] as "the law (...) that in one market there is one price", will continue to apply. Different risk levels will be discounted in different bidding prices, as are other differences in a good's appreciation, and do not thwart the operation of the price mechanism yielding a single equilibrium price.

It is quite usual that different individuals will value a particular good or service differently as consumer preferences are not identical. The competitive bidding process among potential purchasers, then, enables the emergence of a single market price at which the good's or service's marginal utility measured in money terms is equal to all buyers. Also, differences in risk exposure among different purchasers are not peculiar to shares carrying unlimited liability. Such differences can be observed in respect of other goods as well, and they have not resulted in multiple prices for the same good.

Imagine a non-diversified investor who invests USD 100,000 of his wealth in a limited liability corporation. This investor runs a larger risk per dollar invested than an investor of equal wealth holding a properly diversified investment portfolio who makes an investment in the same firm. The first investor is subject to firm-specific risk that the second investor has diversified away. Still, following the approach criticized above, given limited liability, the shares would be homogeneous goods and would therefore have one market equilibrium price. Hence, both investors pay the same price for a share, at which the marginal benefit of the investment is equal to each of them, despite the difference in risk exposure. This confirms that differences in the risk borne are as such unlikely to produce multiple prices.

Another illustration of the unlikelihood of differences in risk exposure resulting in different prices can be observed under Dutch environmental law. The Dutch Soil Protection Act bestows extensive powers on the public authorities either to order the clean-up of polluted land, or to effect the clean-up of polluted land themselves. Under the conditions stated in the Act, the state may subsequently collect the costs of clean-up that the authorities have incurred from the relevant polluter (Sections 75 (1) and (2) of the Soil Protection Act). However, reimbursement of clean-up costs may also be sought from owners of contaminated land who did not cause the pollution concerned, if and to the extent that the clean-up has increased the market value of the land and so enriched the owners (Section 75 (3) of the Act). Both wealthy owners and owners of modest means are fully liable to reimburse the state for the added value by which they are enriched. One may safely assume that the prospect of the state seeking reimbursement from a poor individual whose land is cleaned up is less than the chance of the state pursuing a wealthy owner. Hence, the risk of having to pay clean-up costs is different for owners of different wealth. However, one does not observe different prices for polluted land among purchasers of different wealth levels. The same land is still being traded at one price for rich and poor buyers alike.

Furthermore, the risk taken by buyers of potentially hazardous products also tends to vary with their personal wealth. When a successful lawyer charging USD 500 per hour buys a bottle of cola of an inferior brand, he takes greater financial risk than an unemployed laborer buying the same product. If the bottle were to explode in the face of the purchaser or if its contents make him sick, he may be unable to work for some time. The amount of income so lost would be greater for the lawyer than for the unemployed worker. If the injured person is not duly compensated for his entire loss of income, the lawyer will suffer greater pecuniary loss than the unemployed person. Still, we do not see potentially hazardous products being traded at different prices depending on the magnitude of individual buyers' potential losses.

The risk that with unlimited liability, an investor's personal wealth may be reached in the event of the corporation's default, is in fact a risk of a hidden liability facing all potential purchasers which is no different from any other risk of a hidden liability. Therefore, like other hidden liability risks it will be discounted in investors' bids and in the resulting market price. As with unlimited liability, *every* investor's risk is higher than under a limited liability rule, under unlimited liability all investors will attach a lower value to a share, thereby lowering its equilibrium price. In this way the market price of shares will respond to the liability rule to which shareholders are subject.

The proposition that limited liability is not a necessary condition for the transferability of shares at a single market price is empirically supported, to some extent, by Grossman's study of market trading in the shares of the American Express Company during the 1950s [Grossman (1995)]. In the years reviewed (1951-1959), the shares in the American Express Company carried unlimited liability with respect to both contractual and tortious liabilities incurred by the company. It should be noted, however, that the shares did not expose shareholders to joint and several liability but (merely) to *pro rata* liability, that is, liability in proportion to the percentage of the company's total shares each shareholder owned. Thus, although his entire non-invested wealth would be exposed, a 2 percent shareholder, for instance, would never be liable for more than a 2 percent portion of the company's total liabilities. American Express shares carrying *pro rata* liability were traded on the New York Stock Exchange, whilst investors could have easily ascertained that share ownership would subject them to unlimited liability as this information was publicly available [Grossman (1995), 75].

Grossman [1995, 75-77] found that despite unlimited liability, throughout the 1950s the shares in the American Express Company were actively traded on the exchange and had a single market price, with no evidence appearing of prices varying across investors depending on their personal wealth. In addition, he did not find any indication that stock ownership was concentrated in a small group of shareholders, which could have disrupted the functioning of a market for American Express shares: one investor was found to control approximately 10 percent of the company's stock but otherwise the shares were widely dispersed, with the average number of shareholders approximating 25,000. As indicated, American Express stock traded regularly, witnessing active participation by investors in the market. Although Grossman's study involved a single case only and one should be cautious, therefore, in inferring far-reaching conclusions from it, his findings would seem at odds with the theory that limited liability is indispensable for a liquid stock market in which shares trade at one equilibrium price.

One may argue, however, that as American Express shares were subject to *pro rata* unlimited liability instead of joint and several liability, other shareholders' wealth levels were irrelevant to investors' appreciation of the shares as pursuant to the *pro rata* rule, any one shareholder's exposure was contingent solely upon his portion of the company's total shares outstanding. Thus share prices would have been exclusively determined by investors' expectations with respect to the prospects of the business (just as under limited liability) and would not, as under joint and several liability, have been a function of both the company's prospects and the relative wealth levels of other shareholders. Therefore, Grossman's findings summarized above may be interpreted as telling something about the stock market's response to *pro rata* liability but not on stock market behavior under a rule of joint and several shareholder liability. This view, however, would oversimplify the issue as under *pro rata* liability, too, the relative wealth levels of the shareholders may affect the appreciation of a company's shares by investors, for at least two reasons.

First, given positive costs of collection that would absorb at least a part of the amount collected, it is more likely that *pro rata* liability will be enforced against a shareholder with sufficient means to cover his proportionate share of the firm's unsettled liabilities than against an investor with little or no non-invested wealth, even if they own an equal percentage of the company's shares: it would pay creditors better to incur costs to enforce liability against a wealthy 1 percent shareholder than against a 1 percent shareholder of modest means. Similarly, the anticipated pay-off from collecting from a wealthy 1 percent shareholder may outweigh that from enforcing *pro rata* liability against a poor investor with a larger percentage shareholding. Accordingly, in reality an investor's exposure and, thus, his expected loss in the event of corporate failure may depend on the extent of his personal wealth relative to the wealth of other shareholders even if *pro rata* liability were the rule [Grossman (1995), 71]. Therefore, albeit that under this rule a shareholder will never have to bear more than his proportionate share of the company's total liabilities (as he might have to under joint and several liability), investors would have similar incentives to monitor other shareholders' wealth levels and to take the latter's wealth into account when appraising the company's shares.

Second, as Woodward [1985, 604] has noted, under any form of unlimited liability, the individual shareholders' ability to pay their share of the firm's liabilities is likely to affect the terms on which the firm will be able to obtain credit. If, for instance, under a *pro rata* liability regime, the firm has many shareholders with insufficient wealth to pay their portion in the event of failure, this would adversely affect both the amount of credit the firm could obtain and the terms on which creditors would be prepared to extend credit given that in this case, *pro rata* liability of shareholders would not provide much security to creditors. To the extent that the firm's ability to obtain credit affects its commercial prospects, therefore, the wealth levels of other shareholders would affect the value an investor will place on the company's shares, just as they would do under joint and several liability.

Given that under *pro rata* liability, as set out above, the wealth levels of the individual shareholders would continue to be relevant both to a shareholder's risk of being pursued by the corporation's creditors and to the corporation's ability to obtain credit – albeit not necessarily to the same degree as under joint and several liability –, Grossman's finding of a liquid stock market with a single market price under a *pro rata* liability rule offers indirect support for the proposition that under unlimited joint and several liability, too, a single market price for the shares in one company would prevail. The same finding must not, however, be interpreted to mean that unlimited joint and several liability would not in fact induce investors to incur significant expenses in order to monitor other shareholders' wealth, both before and after the purchase of shares, thus increasing transaction costs in the stock market compared with limited liability. It only suggests that in the particular case of American Express, *i.e.* under a *pro rata* liability rule, such additional costs did not disrupt the functioning of a liquid stock market, which in itself leaves open the possibility that even in this case, there might have been significant extra transaction costs as a result of unlimited liability.

As limited liability is not indispensable to the emergence of a single market price for the shares in a company and the functioning of a liquid stock market *per se*, how, then, does it promote free transfer of shares? It does so in four ways.

First, as described earlier, limited liability reduces the costs of exchanging shares by rendering it unnecessary for shareholders to obtain information about the wealth levels of other shareholders [Demsetz (1975), 34; Jensen and Meckling (1976), 331; Halpern, Trebilcock and Turnbull (1980), 136].

Second, because under a limited liability regime, corporate debts can adversely affect investors only to the extent of the price of their shares, limited liability lowers investors' costs with respect to examining the liabilities of the corporation [Demsetz (1975), 34]. The economics of information gathering expressed in the optimal-search rule reveal that it pays investors to expend resources in acquiring information about the firm as long as the marginal expected benefits of gathering information exceed the marginal costs. The greater is the magnitude of shareholders' maximum potential loss, the larger will be an investor's benefit from obtaining detailed information about the liabilities of the corporation and the longer it will pay him to expend resources in scrutinizing the corporation's liabilities.

Given that under a limited liability regime, the debts of the corporation can affect a shareholder only up to the value of his investment, his potential benefit from examining in great detail the liabilities of the corporation will be less and the marginal benefit of acquiring more information will sooner be exceeded by the marginal cost than under an unlimited liability regime. Thus, under a limited liability rule, investors have wealth-maximizing incentives to spend fewer resources in examining the liabilities of the corporation. By making it unnecessary for investors to examine in great detail the liabilities of the corporation, limited liability reduces the costs attending share transfers.

Third, as noted briefly in Chapter 2, with unlimited liability, investors are likely to demand restrictions on the transferability of shares [Woodward (1985), 605]. Suppose a wealthy shareholder would sell his shares in a corporation to an investor of modest means. Such a transaction would raise the probability of existing shareholders being pursued by the corporation's creditors in the event of a default, and increase the amount they might lose. For instance, if a rich shareholder sells his shares to an investor with no assets other than his shares in the firm, under joint and several liability, the other shareholders would have to make up for the part of the corporation's unpaid debts that previously would have been borne by the seller. And under *pro rata* liability, given positive costs of collection, a relatively wealthy shareholder may still face a higher risk of being pursued by the corporation's creditors than an investor of little non-invested wealth obtaining an equal percentage of the shares.

To minimize their losses in the event of corporate default, therefore, shareholders are likely to demand devices restricting the transfer of shares to investors with less wealth than the seller. It is obvious that such restrictions would impede trading. By rendering other investors' wealth levels irrelevant to a shareholder's potential loss in the event of the corporation's default, limited liability eliminates the need for restrictions on share transferability.

Fourth, unlimited liability would discourage wealthy investors from taking over poorly run firms. Investors considering the acquisition of the shares in a poorly managed company with a view to displacing its management are frequently wealthier than existing shareholders [Easterbrook and Fischel (1985), 96]. Since under an unlimited liability regime, their maximum potential loss in the event of corporate default would be higher, such investors would take more risk by becoming a shareholder than the risk borne by the existing, less wealthy shareholders. This extra risk may prevent wealthy would-be acquirers from acquiring the firm's shares even if they would be able to raise its profits.

When would-be acquirers are wealthier than existing shareholders, their anticipated extra losses in the event of a default may outweigh the extra income they may be able to obtain from more profitable employment of the firm's assets. In this event there will not be a *net* gain for the would-be acquirer from acquiring the shares. This may not be unusual if the potential acquirer is wealthy and if the default risk is high, that is, if the target firm is in trouble, and this category of firms especially would benefit from a takeover by (investors capable of appointing) superior monitors.

Under a limited liability regime, the loss in the event of corporate failure will be equal for existing shareholders and new shareholders. Therefore, gains from trade in the takeover market are now determined solely by potential acquirers' ability to obtain a higher income from the firm's assets than its existing shareholders anticipate. As under a rule of unlimited liability, by contrast, wealthy would-be acquirers would be discouraged by potentially large losses in the event of a default, the chance that investors able to appoint superior monitors will take control of a poorly run corporation will be less than under the limited liability rule. Accordingly, with unlimited liability the incentives for managers to optimize productivity and profits will be less.

Unlimited liability, then, would threaten the operation of the stock market as a mechanism encouraging effective managerial performance.

Limited Liability in the Financial Model

In the monitorial model of the corporation, limited liability economizes on the costs of intra-firm decision-making by encouraging shareholders to delegate the management of the firm to a limited number of managers. It encourages separation of management from residual risk-bearing, thereby promoting specialization. It mitigates the shirking problem among multiple shareholders by limiting the costs they may cause one another by shirking as a monitor, and by effectively reducing individual shareholders' prospective benefits from shirking. Finally, limited liability facilitates the flexible transferability of shares. In this manner it promotes the flow of shares to superior monitors, which in turn provides an incentive to managers to optimize firm productivity and profits. In all these ways, limited liability is instrumental to the effective monitoring of input behavior.

However, this is not the only function of limited liability. In addition, limited liability is considered to be important to a firm's ability to raise capital. Yet it is less obvious *how* exactly limited liability furthers the supply of capital to the firm. As said previously, there is undoubtedly some truth in the idea that limited liability promotes equity investments by risk averse investors but risk-aversion does not provide a full explanation of limited liability as a capital-raising device: with *un*limited liability risk averse investors could still supply capital in the form of loans, or take out insurance where available. Risk-aversion by investors is an *assumption* rather than a *theory* revealing how limited liability helps to raise funds for investment.

In the remainder of this chapter, we examine in some detail the significance of limited liability for attracting capital into a firm.

Cost of Capital

Under an unlimited liability regime, creditors can collect debts of the corporation from the assets of the latter and from the personal wealth of the shareholders. The risk that the corporation's assets will be insufficient to pay its debts is borne by the shareholders. In effect, shareholders bear almost the entire risk of business failure. Creditors' sole risk is that the *sum* of the assets of the corporation and shareholders' personal assets is insufficient to meet the obligations of the corporation. By reducing creditors' security to the assets of the corporation, limited liability in fact shifts the risk of corporate insolvency to the corporation's creditors.

Limited liability does not shift *all* costs of business failure to the corporation's creditors. With limited liability, shareholders continue to bear the costs of corporate failure up to the extent of their invested wealth. Creditors in turn bear the part of the corporation's debts that cannot be satisfied from the assets owned by the corporation.

Firms operated in corporate form may raise funds for investment essentially in two ways: by borrowing capital in exchange for a fixed claim on the firm's assets and cash flows which has priority over the residual claim, and by selling portions of the residual claim to investors. If the residual claimants were liable for the debts of the corporation to the full extent of their personal wealth, their losses in the event of business failure would be higher than if they enjoyed limited liability. As investors would discount the higher costs facing them in the event of failure, with unlimited liability they will presumably attach less value to the residual claim than under a limited liability rule. Consequently, the amount of money investors will be prepared to contribute to the firm in exchange for (a portion of) the residual claim will be less under a rule of unlimited liability than under a limited liability regime.

To raise the same amount of capital, the firm would have to borrow more and have to pay interest on the additional amounts borrowed. Hence, if the same capital were raised, the firm's debt-equity ratio would increase and the interest due on the extra debt would add to the firm's total interest obligations. Unlimited liability, then, would, *ceteris paribus*, change the firm's capital structure and cause additional interest obligations to arise. In contrast, with *limited* liability for shareholders, the firm could raise more capital by the sale of equity shares since investors would anticipate fewer losses in the event of a default. Thus, it would have to borrow less, which would save interest payments.

On the other hand, however, as limited liability reduces the assets from which they may obtain payment, creditors of the corporation face higher costs in the event of corporate default and thus take more risk by extending credit than under an unlimited liability regime. Under a limited liability rule, in the event of a default, creditors have to shoulder the difference between the corporation's assets and its debts themselves and cannot collect the deficit from the shareholders. Since creditors would anticipate higher costs in the event of corporate default, they are likely to charge a higher interest rate under a limited liability rule than under an unlimited liability regime: as creditors bear more risk, the risk-reflecting interest rate will be higher than if shareholders were fully liable [Meiners, Mofsky and Tollison (1979), 359-362; Posner (1992), 395]. The higher interest rate will come at the expense of returns to shareholders, and is the price shareholders pay for shifting the risk of corporate insolvency to the corporation's creditors.

In summary, limited liability improves the firm's ability to attract equity capital by limiting shareholders' losses in the event of business failure, but it raises the interest rate the firm must pay to its creditors by limiting the assets from which they may collect payment. On balance, under a limited liability regime, the corporation may need less credit as it could raise more capital from the sale of shares, but interest rates would be higher than under unlimited liability. Does this imply that the firm's total cost of capital is independent of the liability rule to which its shareholders are subject?

It does not. Such a conclusion would only be justified if the benefit limited liability generates for shareholders is merely equal to the costs it generates for creditors, and if the cost to shareholders of an unlimited liability rule equals creditors' benefit of enlarged security for payment. In that event, the cost the liability rule would impose on one party would offset the benefit to the other party and as a result, the sum of the terms on which the *joint* parties would be prepared to supply capital would not change. Under a limited liability rule, then, the extra interest that creditors charge for having less security would offset the extra amount shareholders would be willing to pay for a share when compared with unlimited liability. Under an *un*limited liability regime, the reduction in the price shareholders would be willing to pay for a share as a result of their potentially indefinite losses should the corporation become insolvent, would be offset by the lower interest rates creditors would charge.

However, if the benefit each liability rule produces for one party were to exactly offset the cost it inflicts on the other party, limited liability would not yield a net gain to either party (on the assumption that their basic attitudes to risk-bearing do not significantly differ). In that event, creditors and shareholders would *jointly* be equally well off under an unlimited liability rule. In other words, they would have no incentive to contract for limited liability (even if the transaction costs of doing so were zero), and it would be unlikely that a demand for limited liability would ever have arisen. The mere fact that the limited liability rule is prevalent in corporations therefore suggests that limited liability does produce a net benefit to both shareholders and creditors (or a net benefit to one of them sufficiently large to compensate the detriment to the other party, with at least one party being better off and without the other party being harmed after compensation is paid). Below we will examine *what* that benefit is.

To the extent that limited liability produces net gains for shareholders (net of the cost to shareholders of higher interest rates), it will promote the supply of equity capital to the corporate firm and the extra amount shareholders are prepared to pay for a share carrying limited liability will exceed (the present value of) the extra interest payable in exchange for the reduction in their anticipated default costs. The resulting higher share price then measures shareholders' gain from limited liability. Similarly, if limited liability yields a net gain to creditors (net of their anticipated higher costs in the event of a default), the interest rate differential between limited and unlimited liability would be less than the differential that could be expected solely on the basis of creditors' anticipated higher costs in the event of a default. Either way, limited liability would lower the firm's total cost of capital.

Limited Liability and Equity Capital

Limited liability relieves shareholders of any cost in excess of the amount of their investment, should the assets of the corporation become insufficient to satisfy its debts. In this way, limited liability serves as a substitute for an insurance policy protecting shareholders' non-invested wealth [Arrow (1970), 139-140]. The extra interest creditors will charge to make up for their higher costs in the event of corporate default compared with an unlimited liability regime, is the premium shareholders pay for having their non-invested wealth insured against liability for corporate debts. In a phrase of Arrow [1970, 137], "the interest rate differential is in effect a premium (...) for insurance against default, the lender being at the same time the insurer".

Investors will discount anticipated higher interest rates from the amount they are willing to pay for a share carrying limited liability, thereby pushing downward share prices and thus the amount the firm could raise from the sale of shares. However, share prices will no less reflect the fact that with limited liability, shareholders' losses in the event of corporate failure are less than with unlimited liability, and this will concurrently push share prices upward. The second effect must dominate the first, since otherwise limited liability would raise the firm's cost of capital (it would get less for its shares *and* must pay higher interest charges) and the price shareholders pay for limited liability (higher interest rates) would outweigh the benefits derived from it (fewer default costs, monitoring advantages and potential other benefits) as capitalized in share prices. In these circumstances, it would have been unlikely that demand for limited liability would have arisen.

Following the above reasoning, the capitalized value of the benefits investors derive from limited liability is likely to exceed capitalized higher interest rates so that on balance, limited liability will have an upward effect on share prices. In contrast, albeit that prices of shares carrying *un*limited liability would reflect lower interest rates, investors' potentially indefinite losses in the event of corporate failure would cause share prices to be less than if they carried limited liability.

Given that the firm could raise less funds by selling shares carrying unlimited liability, under an unlimited liability rule, investors would discount from bidding prices the interest due on the additional borrowings that would be required if the firm were to raise the same total capital under either rule governing shareholders' liability. Such additional interest obligations, although carrying lower interest rates than if shareholders enjoyed limited liability, would add to the firm's total interest obligations. Therefore, the additional interest obligations are likely to be discounted in share prices in the same manner as higher interest rates are discounted under limited liability. Which would be more important in determining share prices, the higher interest rate under a limited liability rule or the additional aggregate interest obligations under an unlimited liability rule, depends on the amounts involved. Under any rule, however, the effect on share prices will be downward.

Apart from the insurance of shareholders' non-invested wealth against liability for corporate debts, for which shareholders pay a price through less favorable credit terms, limited liability yields other benefits to investors which do not consist in the mere reallocation to creditors of the risk of corporate failure as reflected in credit terms, or which are not priced by creditors through higher interest rates or otherwise. Any benefits not priced through less favorable credit terms make up the net gain shareholders derive from limited liability, and any such "free" benefits will be reflected in the price investors are willing to pay for shares. *They* will cause share prices to be higher than under an unlimited liability regime, despite the higher interest rates, and so enhance the firm's ability to raise funds through the sale of shares.

In the first place, in addition to protecting shareholders' non-invested wealth, limited liability saves certain costs for shareholders *independently of* the reallocation of the costs of corporate insolvency which it brings about, and such cost savings will not therefore be priced through the higher interest rate charged by creditors in exchange for this reallocation.

As we have argued in our discussion of limited liability in the monitorial model of the corporation, with limited liability, shareholders will expend fewer resources on detailed involvement in the management of the firm. Moreover, as the debts of the corporation can adversely affect them only up to the extent of their investment, it is unnecessary for shareholders to monitor in great detail the corporation's liabilities. Furthermore, since the magnitude of their potential loss in the event of corporate default is independent of the wealth levels of other shareholders, limited liability eliminates the need for investors to expend resources in order to keep track of other shareholders' wealth. Finally, limited liability saves the costs of making and enforcing side-arrangements among shareholders to preclude the transfer of shares to investors with less wealth than the seller. All of these reductions in shareholders' costs increase the net return on their investment, thereby raising the value investors place on shares and enhancing the firm's ability to raise equity capital.

Secondly, limited liability produces "free" benefits to shareholders relating to the monitoring of input activity which do not consist in a bare reduction of shareholders' costs as compared with an unlimited liability regime. In our discussion of the monitorial model, we have argued that limited liability promotes effective monitoring of input performance by encouraging shareholders to entrust their investment to specialized managers and by promoting the transfer of shares to superior monitors. The more effectively inputs are monitored, the higher will be their productivity and the profits they generate, and the higher is likely to be shareholders' reward and the price they place on shares.

Thirdly, limited liability protects shareholders, free of charge, from tortious liabilities arising from the operations of the firm [Clark (1986), 9]; it shifts the risk that the corporation may be unable to pay damages for corporate torts to the tort victims, and this risk-shifting is not reflected in interest rates, nor do shareholders pay compensation for it in any other way. Tort victims by definition do not bargain with the corporation for compensation *before* being injured by the latter's operations [Posner (1976), 506]. They do not agree to expose their wealth, health, or otherwise, to the activities of the corporation in exchange for compensation reflecting the risk that the corporation's assets ultimately may prove insufficient to pay the agreed amount. Tort victims, then, are not compensated for bearing the risk of corporate insolvency through the terms of compensation, and shareholders' non-invested assets are insulated *at no charge* from the liabilities in tort generated by the business.

Liquidity of Investments

A fourth benefit investors derive from limited liability, going beyond the mere reallocation of the insolvency risk, is that limited liability facilitates liquidity of investments [Manne (1975), 514].

As we saw in Chapter 2, shareholders can liquefy their invested wealth in a particular corporation by selling their shares in exchange for cash. The operation of organized securities markets facilitated by limited liability in which shares can be readily traded, enables shareholders to liquefy investments with few transaction cost impediments. Organized securities exchanges avoid the costs of face-to-face bargaining, uniform market prices for the stock in one company economize on market participants' information costs, and so do compulsory corporate disclosure rules. Except for the cost of intermediaries (in particular, stock brokers), today's organized securities markets can be thought to resemble a Coasian environment permitting trading at (virtually) zero transaction costs. If, by contrast, the transaction costs attending stock transfers were prohibitively high, even if shares were legally transferable, no exchanges of shares for cash would take place and shareholders' invested capital would, in fact, become illiquid.

In the discussion of the monitorial model, we have described *how* limited liability reduces the transaction costs of exchanging shares, thereby effectively promoting investment liquidity. Moreover, as also described in the monitorial model, under a rule of unlimited joint and several liability, investors have risk-minimizing incentives to demand restrictions on the transfer of shares to investors of less wealth than the seller, since a shareholder's risk would go up if another shareholder were to sell his shares to an investor with less wealth than the seller: the remaining shareholders' risk of being pursued for unpaid debts of the corporation would rise, as would their potential loss in the event of a default.

Such restrictions, however, would limit the ability of the individual shareholders to liquefy their investment; they would be subject to the risk of becoming "locked in". Restrictions on the transferability of shares would reduce shareholders' ability to cash in their shares and reinvest the proceeds elsewhere. In effect, such restrictions would impose opportunity losses upon shareholders when they are precluded from shifting their invested wealth to different uses that would yield greater wealth or utility. With unlimited liability, shareholders would be subject to the risk of such opportunity losses *in addition to* shouldering the risk of infinite losses in the event of corporate insolvency. The same applies if there are no formal restrictions on share transfers but if high transaction costs would in fact preclude shareholders from liquefying their investment.

For instance, an investor may expect that the funds he has invested in a particular corporation will yield a higher return if he reinvests them in another firm. Suppose that formal restrictions on his ability to exchange his shares or high transaction costs preclude him from doing so. The difference between the investor's actual return and the return he would have earned if he had been able to shift his invested wealth to the alternative investment opportunity would then be his opportunity loss. The price investors are willing to put up for a share carrying unlimited liability will reflect the risk of sustaining opportunity losses in the future due to impediments to their ability to liquefy their investment. Limited liability, by eliminating the need for restrictions on share transfers to investors of less wealth than the seller and by reducing transaction costs in securities markets, serves to avoid such opportunity losses and so avoids the possibility that investors will discount bidding prices for such losses.

The ability to sell shares and reinvest the proceeds elsewhere is especially important to investors whose investment in a particular corporation is large in relation to their total wealth. They would be subject to the risk of suffering large opportunity losses in proportion to their total wealth if they could not easily liquefy their invested wealth. Therefore, any impediments to share transferability would discourage, in particular, investments from relatively *poor* investors. The risk of corporate failure may not as such be a serious threat to this category of investors, as wealthier shareholders are more likely to be pursued by the corporation's creditors and as high litigation costs may deter the former from seeking reimbursements from shareholders of modest means. However, the larger an investor's invested wealth as a proportion of his total wealth, the larger his potential opportunity losses in relation to his total wealth if he cannot easily shift his invested wealth in a particular corporation to more profitable investment opportunities.

By promoting investment liquidity, limited liability protects investors against opportunity losses. In this manner it encourages, in particular, investments from investors who risk large opportunity losses, *i.e.* investments from investors considering an investment which is large in relation to their total wealth. In addition, as the ability to liquefy their investment protects *all* investors against future opportunity losses, it will boost the prices that investors place on shares.

Diversification

A final benefit of limited liability for shareholders is that it permits investors to minimize their risk through diversification. In Chapter 2 we noted that shareholders can reduce their aggregate risk by holding a diversified investment portfolio, on condition that the prospects of success or failure for the various companies contained in the portfolio is not contingent on the same set of events: there must be no correlation between the returns on the separate holdings in the portfolio [Ross and Westerfield (1988), 148]. By holding a diversified portfolio, investors can diversify away firm-specific risk (but not economy-wide risk) and, consequently, achieve less variability in the total returns on their invested wealth and diminish the chance of loss, as Knight [1921, 254] already observed. They can hedge against one company's misfortune by investing in various, unrelated companies so that losses resulting from one company's misfortune will be offset by the yield on investments in other companies. In this way diversification serves to "insure" the risk of any one particular holding through pooling multiple investments, *each* with different risks attached to it [Arrow (1970), 135]. Limited liability is a prerequisite for the reduction of investment risks by diversification.

Suppose shareholders were fully liable for corporate debts. In that event an increase in the number of holdings would increase an investor's risk of losing wealth. If unlimited liability were the rule, an investor would be liable to the full extent of his wealth for the debts of each corporation in which he would own shares. Thus, he would put at risk his entire wealth with respect to each separate company in his portfolio: "If any one firm went bankrupt, an investor could lose his entire wealth" [Easterbrook and Fischel (1985), 97]. Any additional holding would add another risk of indefinite losses to the portfolio should the corporation concerned become insolvent. Unlimited liability, then, would not merely expose an investor to the risk of losing non-invested assets but it would also deprive him of the opportunity to minimize his total investment risk by holding a diversified portfolio. Rather, a risk-minimizing strategy would be to minimize the number of shareholdings [Easterbrook and Fischel (1985), 97].

Granted, with unlimited liability, investors might still diversify away firm-specific risk by supplying *loans* to different, non-related unlimited liability corporations or by investing in bonds issued by such corporations, given that debt carries limited liability. However, the risk and return features of debt substantially differ from those of equity shares, irrespective of the liability issue. Returns on debt are fixed and the probability of repayment is generally bigger for debt than for equity capital. Equity, on the other hand, offers investors the prospect of higher returns by taking more risk. Dividends on equity shares vary with the firm's success and may exceed the fixed returns on debt, and shares offer a prospect of capital gains too, which debt does not, or to a lesser extent only. Given the intrinsically different characteristics of debt, from the perspective of investors, the purchase of bonds and the provision of loans are no viable alternatives to investments in equity shares, at least not to investors who seek the investment characteristics of equity. Substituting investments in corporate debt for equity would make up a portfolio, the risk and return characteristics of which would be completely different from those of a diversified equity portfolio, or a mixed debt-equity portfolio. To investors desirous to make investments with the risk and return features of equity shares, debt investments may be complementary to, but not substitutes for, investments in equity.

Since with unlimited liability, investors would be unable to reduce their potential losses from one company's misfortune by appropriate diversification of investments in corporate equity, they would adjust their valuation of shares for the extra risk attributable to non-diversified equity holdings (or multiple holdings, each of which would carry unlimited liability). This extra risk would lower the amount investors would be willing to pay for a share, compared with an environment in which investors would be readily able to make equity investments *and* simultaneously reduce risk through diversification, that is, under a limited liability regime. Under limited liability, because of equity investors' ability to diversify away firm-specific risks, any one firm operated in corporate form could obtain a higher price for its shares (and, hence, it would have to borrow less).

The inability to reduce losses through diversification under unlimited liability would particularly harm firms' ability to attract small, passive equity investments from wealthy investors. Wealthy shareholders are probably the first to be pursued by the corporation's creditors in the event of a default. Therefore, any additional holding would raise their anticipated cost of additional capital contributions if one of the corporations in which they have invested were to become insolvent. As they would risk their entire wealth in any investment they make, irrespective of the number of shares they hold, with unlimited liability, wealthy investors would be reluctant to make small, non-controlling investments in various corporations. From this observation, Manne [1975, 513] has inferred that if unlimited liability were the rule, "small investments in corporations would tend to come only from individuals who were nearly insolvent already. Wealthy individuals would never make small investments in a corporation." To protect their wealth, wealthy investors would rather seek to control one (or a limited number of) corporation(s) in place of making a variety of small investments, or invest in corporate debt only.

One may hypothesize that reduction of risk through diversification would also be possible if shares carried unlimited liability, since in addition to shares, investors could purchase "put options" entitling them to alienate their shares, together with the accompanying liability risk, to a third party, viz. the supplier of the option, at the price stated in the option. By this theory, investors could obtain *de facto* limited liability by acquiring such put option rights, so that diversification would still be possible and risk-reflecting share prices would be more or less similar to those under statutory limited liability. However, the idea that put options could simply replace limited liability as a requisite for diversification is unsound for a variety of reasons.

First, the idea hinges on the assumption that there will always be individuals or firms offering put options of the kind and quantity required to hedge the risk of unlimited liability. This is unlikely to be the case, especially because such options would tend to originate from risk-preferring or nearly insolvent individuals only (or from firms owned by such individuals). In theory, investors or market intermediaries may establish specialized corporations (investment funds) to issue put options, for the single purpose of shifting the risk of unlimited liability to such entities. However, that would not or, at best, only partially remedy unlimited liability if the shares in the corporation issuing the put options themselves were governed by unlimited liability. Then the problem facing the organizers of the issuing entity and the intended recipients of the options would be to find investors to own such shares, or to find or create put options, or suppliers thereof, entitling the future shareholders of the cited entity to dispose of the risk of unlimited liability. Thus the specialized fund remedy would circle unlimited liability rather than eliminate it.

Second, in order to obtain *de facto* limited liability, in addition to the share price, investors would need to pay to the supplier of the desired put option a risk-commensurate price for the option, reflecting *un*limited liability. The amount payable for the option would add to the costs that investors have to incur to make an equity investment affording protection from personal liability. This is likely to have a downward effect on the price which investors would be willing to pay for a share carrying unlimited liability, as compared with the price of shares carrying statutory limited liability. Moreover, suppliers of put options for shares with unlimited liability are more expensive risk-bearers than holders of limited liability shares, since the former cannot diversify their risk given their assumption of unlimited liability. Since investors must pay the option supplier for bearing the liability risk and since the latter cannot reduce the extra risk through diversification, the combined price of the option and the share will in all likelihood exceed the price of a limited liability share. Obviously, if investors' anticipated benefit from bearing less risk were to outweigh the price of the put option right, no option transaction and consequent risk reduction would take place, and share prices would reflect full personal liability.

Third, the making and enforcement of put option contracts may absorb considerable transaction costs which could either prevent the option transaction from taking place altogether or which, if surmounted, would have a negative impact on share prices as they would raise investors' total cost of making the relevant equity investment. The making of put option contracts may be rather complicated, since the term for exercising the option to be specified in the contract (that is, the expiry date) must be more or less consistent with the anticipated term of the contracting shareholder's investment in the firm concerned, and since the exercise price of the option would now be a function, not only of certain expectations about the firm's future earnings, but also of the option supplier's estimated risk of personal liability for the time period during which the supplier is to assume the liability risk (*i.e.* the term of the option contract). Moreover, the option supplier will have loss-minimizing incentives to default on the option contract should the liability risk threaten to materialize, and this is prone to raise enforcement costs. Potentially large transaction costs would also be involved in the creation and administration of the above-mentioned specialized funds issuing put options to assume the risk of unlimited liability.

Fourth, the put option mechanism for obtaining *de facto* limited liability would only work if the law permitted investors to escape from personal liability in this manner. However, in as much as put options would be used for the purpose of shifting risk to less solvent individuals or firms, they would very much be an instrument employed to frustrate the unlimited liability rule and its underlying objective of enlarging security for creditors; the supplier of the option would act as a "straw man" who is used to insulate the more solvent shareholder from liability for corporate debts. The same would apply to specialized option-issuing funds especially created for this purpose. Legislatures and courts are rather reluctant to recognize such evasion techniques designed to thwart the purposes of the law, and may well ignore them and enforce liability on the shareholders themselves [Hansmann and Kraakman (1992), 431]. Then the option mechanism would clearly *not* be effective in limiting shareholders' risk.

Limited Liability and Debt

We have seen that lenders will charge higher interest rates on loans extended to corporations in exchange for assuming the risk of corporate insolvency. With limited liability, hence, interest rates are higher, but investors will pay more for the shares, which in turn will enable the firm to borrow less at the higher rate, the opposite being true for unlimited liability. Furthermore, parties are free to contract around statutory limited liability, and to arrive at exactly the same interest rate and other loan terms as would normally be applicable under unlimited liability.

Some authors have suggested, therefore, that the total costs of borrowing are unlikely to be affected by the liability rule to which shareholders are subject [Meiners, Mofsky and Tollison (1979); Meiners (1978), 224]. They support this proposition by a reference to the theorem developed by Coase [1960, 15-16], holding that the choice of the legal rule does not affect the allocation of resources if transaction costs are zero (on the assumption that property rights are well defined and freely transferable).

Transaction costs do exist, however, and they may well affect the allocative outcome in credit markets under different legal rules governing shareholders' liability. As we will demonstrate below, the principle of limited liability effects substantial reductions in transaction costs in credit markets. Any reduction in the transaction costs facing creditors raises their net remuneration from extending credit and so promotes the supply of credit. Creditors' gain from limited liability, then, is a higher net income due to transaction cost savings. To the extent that lower transaction costs are reflected in interest rates, a reduction in transaction costs will also favorably affect the firm's cost of borrowing and thereby benefit shareholders.

Although creditors may anticipate higher costs in the event of corporate failure under limited liability when compared with unlimited liability, these may be partially offset by lower transaction costs, causing the interest rate differential between limited and unlimited liability to be less than the differential which would exist if transaction costs under both were equal. Even though interest rates *per se* may still be higher, limited liability then brings about a *net* reduction in the firm's cost of credit, net of the interest premium payable in exchange for the shifting of insolvency risk to creditors.

How does limited liability reduce the transaction costs of contracting over loans?

First, if shareholders were fully liable for the debts of the corporation, creditors of the corporation would have to evaluate each individual shareholder's personal wealth to assess the security for repayment. The wealth levels of the individual shareholders would determine creditors' security and, thus, the terms on which the corporation may attract credit. Creditors would need to obtain information about the repayment capacity of individual shareholders in order to determine a risk-commensurate interest rate. By reducing creditors' security to the assets of the corporation, limited liability makes it unnecessary for creditors to examine the personal assets of the individual shareholders. In this way, limited liability economizes on creditors' costs of obtaining information [Clark (1986), 8-9].

Secondly, under a rule of unlimited shareholder liability, shareholders could unilaterally increase creditors' risk after they have granted credit to the corporation. For instance, if a shareholder were to use a part of his (non-invested) wealth to obtain a virtually unmarketable asset, he would decrease creditors' security. Similarly, if a wealthy shareholder would transfer his shares to an investor of less wealth, the magnitude of creditors' potential costs in the event of corporate default would go up. In either case the interest rate previously agreed may no longer compensate creditors for their actual risk. Therefore, under an unlimited liability regime, *creditors* would have incentives to demand restrictions on shareholders' freedom to dispose of their wealth and on the transferability of shares. Creditors (and not just shareholders) may, for example, demand that shareholders only alienate shares to investors with a specified minimum wealth level. Such arrangements may improve the terms on which the firm could obtain credit, but they would harm its ability to attract equity capital and lower the price investors place on equity shares [Woodward (1985), 605]. Limited liability, by rendering shareholders' capacity to repay irrelevant to the creditors of the corporation, eliminates the need for and the costs of making and enforcing side-arrangements between creditors and individual shareholders.

Thirdly, unlimited liability may not only create conflicts of interest between creditors and shareholders, but also among shareholders. The larger the personal wealth of the *joint* shareholders, the higher the creditors' security for repayment and the more favorable the terms on which the firm could obtain credit. Individual shareholders desiring low interest rates and favorable repayment terms for the corporation may wish to enter into arrangements (similar to those demanded by creditors) designed to maximize the repayment capacity of the joint shareholders [Woodward (1985), 604-605]. As noted, such arrangements may improve the firm's position in the credit market but since they would limit investors' freedom to reinvest their wealth (thereby exposing shareholders to potential opportunity losses), they would harm the firm's position in the market for equity capital.

Fourthly, under an unlimited liability regime, creditors may have to pursue various individual shareholders in order to collect the corporation's debts in the event of a default. The costs creditors would be willing to incur in order to pursue individual shareholders depend on the amount they expect to recover. In general, the larger the number of shareholders, the higher the creditors' cost of *enforcing* unlimited shareholder liability. As Manne [1975, 513] has observed, "the costs involved in assessing and collecting fractional liabilities from large numbers of small investors might frequently be greater than the anticipated recovery". Limited liability saves the cost of enforcing payment of corporate debts against individual shareholders [Clark (1986), 8-9].

Limited Liability and the Corporate Concept

In the preceding sections of this chapter, we have explored the various functions of limited liability. We observed that limited liability, *inter alia*, fosters the monitoring of input behavior by specialized managers and economizes on transaction costs in the stock market (including the market for corporate control). Limited liability is also instrumental in the operation of the corporation as a mechanism for raising capital, in particular, by reducing the transaction costs facing suppliers of equity capital and suppliers of credit, by promoting liquidity of equity investments, and by enabling investors to reduce risks through diversification. In these various regards, limited liability would seem to play an important, if not crucial, role in both the monitorial and the financial model of the corporation.

But is limited liability *necessary* to the corporation as an organizational concept? In other words, can we imagine a corporation with centralized management, residual claims divided into transferable parts and a distinct personality legally independent of its constituent human beings, but without limited liability for the residual claimants?

The analysis set out in this chapter reveals the ways in which limited liability is related to the corporate form of business organization. It does not follow, however, that limited liability is indispensable to the corporate concept and its aforementioned other features. Let us examine this a little closer.

As explained at the outset of this chapter, a corporation's legal ability to have rights and obligations of its own, independent of those of its shareholders, is conceptually different from the rule governing shareholders' liability for obligations binding the corporation. With full personal liability for the shareholders, it would still be possible for the corporation to obtain rights and to incur debts in its own name, with vicarious liability for the shareholders should the corporation fail to satisfy its obligations to creditors. Indeed, Shavell [1987, 175] has noted that relieving shareholders of personal liability is "none other than deciding against imposing vicarious liability on shareholders", without connecting such a decision to the corporation's legal entity status. The decision on the liability rule to which shareholders are subject, then, differs from the decision on whether the corporation should be entitled to act as an entity legally distinct from its shareholders.

Similarly, even with unlimited liability, shareholders may choose to entrust the day-to-day management of the corporate firm to salaried managers, particularly if they expect such managers to have a comparative advantage in running the firm, thus being capable of enhancing shareholders' revenue from the possession of the residual claim, and if the expected costs to them of managerial self-interest seeking be less than their anticipated net benefit from employing a salaried management to run the firm (see our discussion in Chapter 4 next). Depending on the number of shareholders and regardless of the liability rule, entrusting the management to salaried outsiders may also save decision-making costs relative to management by the shareholders themselves. To compare, large professional partnerships exist in which managerial tasks are performed by specialized "managing partners" or by hired managers appointed by the joint partners, despite the latter's nominally unlimited liability. (In practice, however, partners of large professional partnerships tend to incorporate themselves, thus enjoying limited liability in the same way as shareholders of a corporation. This supports the theory that limited liability is instrumental in the delegation of managerial power.)

Finally, the ability to divide the residual claim on the assets and cash flows of the corporate firm into fragmental parts and to sell such parts to investors would, in principle, also exist if the acquirers of parts of the residual claim were subject to unlimited liability. However, the demand for such fragmental parts would be less and the price investors would be prepared to pay would be lower for the reasons discussed earlier in this chapter: demand by risk averse investors would become less if not disappear, investors would have to surmount higher transaction costs, firm-specific risks could not readily be diversified away, and liquidity of investments would be threatened. Should we subscribe, therefore, to Manne's thesis [1975, 513] that "the concept of limited liability (...) flows logically from the concept of the corporation as a capital-raising mechanism"?

The answer must be negative in view of the fact that if limited liability were abolished, it would technically still be possible for corporations to raise capital by offering parts of the residual claim for sale in the capital markets. Limited liability is not a necessary condition for this capital-raising technique. It is conceded, however, that the *success* of this technique may be ascribed in great measure to the virtues of limited liability discussed in this chapter.

Limited liability, although not indispensable to the corporate concept, is clearly instrumental in taking full advantage of the corporation's abilities to raise capital and to effect specialized monitoring of input behavior. It may hence help the understanding of the dominance of the corporate concept as a form of organization for multi-member, capital-intensive businesses involving complex teams and requiring input of specialized monitoring. Without limited liability for shareholders, such businesses are rather unlikely to have the same degree of specialization in management and residual risk-bearing and the same level of capitalization through equity. They may also face both higher costs of organization, probably reflected in lower returns on equity and higher output prices, and higher costs of capital due to higher transaction costs in both equity and credit markets, equity investors' inability to reduce risks through diversification and the latter having to assume the risk that investments may prove illiquid. Without limited liability, therefore, the corporate landscape might have had quite a different outlook than it has at present and the corporate form *per se* might not have been so popular.

Notably, to the extent that limited liability facilitates separation of management and risk-bearing, if unlimited liability were the rule, there would most likely be a larger degree of shareholder participation in the management of firms operated in corporate form as would be the number of shareholder-managed firms. In addition, where the number of shareholders desirous to become involved in managerial decision-making poses a limit to the size of firms because of decision-making problems and high management costs arising as the number of shareholders increases, the average size of firms would be smaller under an unlimited liability regime than if shareholders enjoyed limited liability. Similarly, where unlimited liability would raise a firm's cost of capital and impede the aggregation of large amounts of capital for investment, firms organized under an unlimited liability rule would on average be smaller than if they had limited liability [Carr and Mathewson (1988)]. Unlimited liability limiting firm size is socially costly where it would preclude economies of scale in the production of output from being fully exploited. Moreover, in the absence of organizational substitutes suited to organize multi-member, capital-intensive businesses, the overall (*i.e.* economy-wide) degree of capitalization of productive activity would be less, meaning fewer capital-intensive businesses and less substitution of capital for labor throughout the economy and, again, threatening economies of scale. Finally, where higher transaction costs in the capital markets, higher organizational costs, higher costs of capital and fewer gains from specialized monitoring of input behavior in the firm would lead to lower profits, unlimited liability might lower the profitability of firms operated in corporate form, which in turn would discourage investment in such firms.

Carr and Mathewson [1988] have provided some empirical support to the hypothesis that with unlimited liability, firms would tend to be smaller in size than under a rule providing for limited liability of the shareholders. Using historical data on the use of limited and unlimited liability by Scottish banks in the seventeenth and eighteenth centuries (in particular, over the period between 1795 and 1879), they noted that in this era, Scotland had both banks with limited liability and banks the shareholders of which were subject to unlimited liability. There were three banks, founded over the period 1695-1746, that had been granted limited liability through a special charter from the Scottish Parliament, all other banks being subject to statutory unlimited liability. Entry to the banking industry was free until 1845, when legislation introducing severe entry restrictions was enacted, meaning that until 1845 new entrants could easily enter the banking business and compete against existing banks (if only their shareholders were prepared to accept unlimited liability). Only in 1879 was general legislation introduced which enabled all banks to obtain limited liability for their shareholders, thus effectively abolishing the previous unlimited liability rule.

Consistent with the theory, by comparing unlimited liability banks with their limited liability peers, Carr and Mathewson [1988, 775-778] found that unlimited liability had a negative impact on firm size: they report that from 1800 onwards, the average size of Scotland's limited liability banks, measured in average total assets (in pounds per bank), was almost ten times that of the unlimited liability banks. As until 1845 entry to the banking business was free, with new entrants being able to compete on the same basis as existing limited liability banks except for the liability rule, it is likely that the unlimited liability rule is of paramount importance in explaining the cited difference in average firm size.

In addition, Carr and Mathewson noted that from 1695, when the first limited liability bank was chartered, until 1845, over fifty Scottish banks failed or left banking voluntarily, whilst all three limited liability banks survived over this period. Looking solely at the period 1810-1850, for instance, the total number of banks fell from thirty-seven in 1810 to seventeen in 1850, both numbers including the limited liability banks. To the extent that survivorship in a competitive market environment, in which both depositors and investors could chose between limited and unlimited liability banks, indicates high profitability relative to competitors, these data offer indirect support for the hypothesis that the limited liability banks were more profitable than unlimited liability banks, as Carr and Mathewson conclude. This, again, would be consistent with our above-mentioned predictions on the impact of unlimited liability.

Both the data on average firm size and the authors' observations on survivorship and profitability suggest that unlimited liability placed banks at a comparative disadvantage to competitors that did enjoy limited liability. This in turn lends support to the proposition that limited liability has become dominant in large parts of the economy because of its superior abilities in the organization of business when compared with unlimited liability, that means, as a result of it being boosted by market forces.

Limited Liability in the Contractual Theory of the Corporation

In Chapter 2, we subscribed to the theory that perceives the corporation as a standard-form contract avoiding the transaction costs that private parties would otherwise have to incur in order to bring about the same arrangements through bargaining, and comprising a set of standard rules which parties would in all likelihood agree if they could bargain at zero transaction costs. The same is true for statutory limited liability.

Our discussion in this chapter suggests that limited liability is the preferred rule of both equity investors and creditors of large-scale enterprises with scattered stock ownership. If limited liability were indeed the preferred rule, in its absence, investors and creditors would have wealth-maximizing incentives to create the same through private bargaining. There are several conceivable legal instruments that they might use for this purpose.

Primarily, limited liability may be effected through direct bargains between shareholders and prospective creditors. Less cumbersome and less expensive, the corporation, on behalf of the shareholders, may stipulate in all contracts it enters into that shareholders are not liable for the obligations of the corporation (as stated in Chapter 2). Limited liability may also be achieved by including a provision to this effect in the corporation's articles of association (on the assumption that such provisions in the articles are binding upon the corporation's creditors). Indeed, prior to the coming into force of general limited liability laws, unincorporated English joint-stock companies reportedly achieved limited liability for their shareholders by including clauses to this effect, either in business contracts on a regular basis or in the articles of association [Anderson and Tollison (1983), 114; Butler (1986), 181-182].

However, none of the above-mentioned methods would suffice to effect limited liability in respect of tortious liabilities incurred by the corporation. Hypothetically, as we have noted in the preceding chapter, investors may identify potential tort victims and bargain with them for limited liability in advance of a tortious liability arising. However, the transaction costs of private bargaining would be sizeable in this scenario and may, therefore, prove prohibitive.

Using a different line of argument, Hessen [1979, 19-20] posited that if there were no statutory limited liability, non-controlling shareholders would still not be deemed to bear unlimited liability for torts generated by corporate activity. From the legal doctrine of *respondeat superior* that underlies vicarious liability rules in respect of employee behavior, he infers that, as a rule, liability for torts committed by employees is limited to superiors who are personally responsible for the selection and monitoring of the employees concerned. Accordingly, if unlimited liability for shareholders were the rule, pursuant to ordinary vicarious liability principles, it would still only be those shareholders controlling employee behavior that would face unlimited liability for corporate torts. Based on this theory, shareholders' limited liability for torts would be the rule rather than the exception, irrespective of whether shareholders *per se* would be subject to statutory unlimited liability.

From this point of view, small, passive investors would not even *need* to bargain with potential tort victims over limited liability if unlimited liability were the rule. Hence, even if private bargaining were unlikely to take place given the sizeable transaction costs, that would not raise the significant barrier to attaining limited liability which it appeared to do at the outset. In respect of small, passive shareholders, it is implicit from Hessen's approach that statutory limited liability for corporate torts only reaffirms what otherwise would have been applicable.

A major objection to Hessen's theory is that if statutory law were to impose full personal liability on the shareholders, it is likely that this liability rule would automatically take priority over vicarious liability rules in respect of torts committed by employees and the underlying *respondeat superior* doctrine. To achieve limited liability for corporate torts, then, shareholders and potential tort victims would still need to contract around the statutory unlimited liability rule and face the transaction costs of private bargaining.

Where shareholders and creditors were to surmount the hurdle of transaction costs in order to provide the former with limited liability for the corporation's obligations (either in tort or contractual), the transaction costs so incurred would raise the cost of organizing the business, including the cost of raising capital, which in turn would raise output costs (prices) and discourage investment. Where transaction costs were prohibitively high, however, it follows from Coase's theorem [1960, 15-16] that limited liability would *not* be achieved, that investors and creditors would remain faced with the less preferable unlimited liability rule, and that the benefits of limited liability discussed in this chapter would not be realized. Statutory limited liability, by avoiding the transaction costs of using private bargaining mechanisms to create limited liability, avoids such consequences and produces a rule which minimizes the effects of transaction costs on the organization of the business.

In this context, we adhere to Bainbridge's observation [1997, 865]: "Because the public corporation setting gives rise to prohibitively high transaction costs, parties cannot depend on private contracting to achieve efficient outcomes. Instead, a legally-imposed rule must function as a substitute for private bargaining." Statutory limited liability is such a substitute and ensures that the transaction costs that would otherwise thwart private bargaining over the liability rule, do not deprive investors and society at large of the virtues of limited liability. In effect, the statutory rule ensures that limited liability can operate to promote the influx of both capital for investment and specialized monitoring into the corporate firm, and facilitate the full exploitation of the other characteristics of the corporate concept, viz. legal entity status, transferability of residual claims and specialization in management and risk-bearing. For these reasons, given positive transaction costs, statutory limited liability can be considered a device which, in a phrase of Dewing [1953, 14], "for reasons of social expediency, it seems desirable to attach to the modern corporation".

PART II

THE CORPORATE DICHOTOMY: MANAGERS VERSUS SHAREHOLDERS

4. THE PROBLEM OF INTERNAL COSTS

IN THE PRECEDING chapter, we examined the various functions of limited shareholder liability. We argued that limited liability, in addition to facilitating the smooth operation of stock markets and fostering the corporate form as a capital-raising mechanism, encourages shareholders to delegate the management of the corporate firm to specialist managers. Thus limited liability promotes the centralization of managerial power: it facilitates centralized management as a method of corporate governance which, like limited liability in itself, is a prerequisite for investors' accumulation of diversified portfolios containing passive equity investments in multiple, unrelated firms.

However, as we saw in the section on principals and agents in Chapter 2, the interests of shareholders and managers are not necessarily identical. According to the contractual concept of the firm discussed in Chapter 1, the firm is viewed as "a set of contracts among factors of production, with each factor motivated by its self-interest" [Fama (1980), 289]. On the premise that both managers and shareholders are primarily interested in maximization of their personal utility or wealth, divergences of interests may result. Where such divergences exist, self-interested managers may choose to manage the corporation so as to further their personal interests and ignore those of the shareholders. In the Introduction to this book we quoted several cases suggesting that, at least in some instances, specialized managers may indeed fail to act in shareholders' best interests.

When managers neglect shareholders' interests, they impose a cost on shareholders: the corporation's profits to which the shareholders are entitled and the market value of their residual claim will usually be less than if management had concentrated exclusively on the promotion of shareholders' interests. In this respect, centralized management and the statutory principle of limited liability, by discouraging active shareholder involvement in the management of the corporate firm, may appear as a Trojan horse to the shareholders.

The benefits of managerial self-interest seeking at the sacrifice of shareholders' interests are enjoyed by the managers concerned, while its costs are borne by the shareholders in proportion to the number of shares they own, both in the form of lower profits and a lower market value of their shares. Thus, self-interested managers may unilaterally lower shareholders' returns. Therefore, managerial self-interest seeking at the expense of shareholders will reduce the attraction of the corporate form to investors and discourage investments in firms operated in corporate form. In its extreme case, the costs to investors of this type of managerial behavior may offset the benefits associated with the corporate form of organization (which were discussed in Chapter 2).

Moreover, to the extent that managerial self-interest seeking raises the costs of operating the firm and lowers investment levels, it is likely to be reflected in higher output prices to consumers and in lower levels of production. Furthermore, where corporate assets are used in the pursuit of managers' desire for personal benefit, corporate managements may disregard the demands of consumers and fail to allocate scarce resources where they are of most use to society. In all these respects managerial self-interest seeking is harmful to the public at large.

Is managerial self-interest seeking at the expense of shareholders a problem inherent in the concept of the corporation? We examine this question in the present chapter.

The Case for Managerial Shirking

Separation of Ownership and Control

The idea that managers of corporate firms may neglect the interests of the shareholders, is not a new one. It is at least as old as Adam Smith's "Wealth of the Nations" [1981], first published on March 9, 1776.

In his discussion of English joint-stock companies which enjoyed corporate features grace of a charter from Crown or Parliament and had a management separate from the suppliers of the capital stock, Smith [1981, 741] expressed skepticism about the chances of survival of firms operated in such a form, precisely because he believed that hired specialist managers (the "court of directors") would fail to promote investors' interests: "The directors of such companies (...) being the managers rather of other people's money than of their own, it cannot well be expected, that they should watch over it with the same anxious vigilance with which the partners in a private copartnery frequently watch over their own. Like the stewards of a rich man, they are apt to consider attention to small matters as not for their master's honour, and very easily give themselves a dispensation from having it. Negligence and profusion, therefore, must always prevail, more or less, in the management of the affairs of such a company."

Accordingly, Smith suggested that hired managers would lack adequate incentives to minimize the operational costs of the firm and properly exploit the firm's profitable business opportunities. Hence, they could not be expected to exert such "vigilance and attention" as would be necessary to render the firm successful in the competition ("a species of warfare") against "private adventurers" (*i.e.* investor-managed firms) [1981, 755]. From these observations, Smith inferred that firms operated as chartered joint-stock companies (*i.e.* with corporate features) whose business was directed by salaried managers and which did not possess exclusive trading privileges (monopoly rights), would be outperformed by investor-managed companies. Therefore, he envisioned little future for such firms in a competitive market environment, and even a monopoly grant would not guarantee their commercial survival: they have "very seldom succeeded without an exclusive privilege; and frequently have not succeeded with one" [1981, 741].

John Stuart Mill [1965, 139], although not *per se* unfavorable toward the corporation as a capital-raising mechanism, submitted that hired managers would be indifferent to "small gains and small losses" and, more generally, would lack "zeal". Also, John Ramsey McCulloch [1965, 361], while expressly supporting Smith's views concerning managerial "negligence and profusion" quoted above, contended that hired company managers would not infrequently act in "bad faith (...) endeavouring to advance their own interest at the expense of their employers". McCulloch [1965, 363-364] added that limited liability would seriously diminish shareholders' incentives to watch over managerial behavior so as to oppose activities detrimental to their interests, since limited liability reduces the potential cost of the corporation's failure to the shareholders [Amsler, Bartlett and Bolton (1981), 786-787].

The thesis that corporate managers may be insensitive to the interests of the shareholders has been greatly popularized by Berle and Means [1991] in their 1932 treatise on the corporation and private property. They argued that in the publicly held corporation where operations are directed by salaried managers, *ownership*, vested in the shareholders, is separated from *control* (which they denoted as "direction over the activities of a corporation" [Berle and Means (1991), 66]): the control of the corporate firm and the private wealth the shareholders have invested in it resides in the firm's management, to whose decisions the "owners" of the corporation (the shareholders) are subject. The various shareholders hold "a set of legal and factual interests" in the firm but they do not have "legal and factual powers" over it [1991, 113]. Berle and Means assumed that professional managers hence possess substantial discretionary power which they may allegedly use to operate firms in furtherance of their personal self-interests. The position of Berle and Means hinges upon the premise that the "separation of ownership from control produces a condition where the interests of owner and of ultimate manager may, and often do, diverge, and where many of the checks which formerly operated to limit the use of power disappear" [Berle and Means (1991), 7].

The Berle-Means approach is based on the observation that since the shares in publicly held corporations are typically dispersed among numerous (non-controlling) investors, individual shareholders do not have real power to discipline managers in order to have them act in the shareholders' interest. Salaried managers are thus to a great extent out of shareholders' control. Berle and Means concluded that in effect, the use of managerial discretion is largely unchecked and as a result, managers may abuse their positions to pursue personal advantage at the expense of shareholders. In other words, the shareholders are allegedly subject to exploitation by unscrupulous, self-interested company managers. Thus the conflict of interests between managers and shareholders is resolved in favor of the former, so the argument goes.

Unlike Adam Smith, however, Berle and Means were not in principle hostile toward the operation of corporations by hired managers. They believed that management by specialist managers could technically serve to improve the operation of companies, allowing the appropriate selection and development of more advanced production methods and increasing the quantities of goods and services which would become available for the satisfaction of consumer needs. In this respect management by professional managers would (or could) be beneficial to consumers. Therefore, as a remedy for managerial abuse of discretionary power Berle and Means did not propose to tighten the control of *management* by shareholders, instead they proposed the enactment of public regulation to control the activities of *corporations*. Such regulation, aimed to direct corporate behavior in the interest of society as a whole, would at the same time limit the freedom of managers to neglect shareholders' interests (and those of consumers).

The Berle-Means notion of the "separation of ownership and control" and the prospect of managerial self-interest seeking at shareholders' expense connoted with it raises a number of questions. First, as a preliminary question, are shareholders indeed the "owners" of the corporate firm? Second, to what extent are the interests of shareholders and managers different? And third, do managers really have the liberty to ignore shareholders' interests?

Risk-bearers and Managers

The contractual approach to the corporation suggests that shareholders are not properly defined as the "owners" of the corporate firm. If the corporation is conceived as being a set of contracting relationships, the concept of ownership of the corporation would appear to have little substance [Klein, Crawford and Alchian (1978), 326 fn. 54]. According to the contractual theory, "corporation" is merely the name the law gives to a particular collection of contractual arrangements, both explicit and implicit, entered into to organize a firm. What would be the sense in attaching "ownership" to this set of contracts?

The contractual concept of the corporation suggests that shareholders' rights are of a contractual nature and do not represent a proprietary interest in the corporate firm. In exchange for their respective contributions to the operations of the firm, the contracting input owners co-operating in the firm operated in corporate form receive claims to portions of the assets and cash flows of the firm. The nature and size of such claims depend on the particular contribution made. Thus, the firm, and the corporation, represents a coalition of disparate claimants to the firm's assets and cash flows. Creditors are granted a fixed claim with priority over equity claims and in general, so are workers. Shareholders receive the residual claim on the firm's assets and cash flows, the voting rights attached to the residual claim and the right to transfer the residual claim and the rights it carries. They own the *residual claim* but they do not own the corporate firm. As Demsetz [1975, 34] has put it: "What shareholders really own are their shares and not the corporation".

In principle, cooperative input owners can contract to compensate themselves for the opportunity costs of their inputs (*i.e.* the earnings in their next best alternative use) from the receipts they expect to be generated by the output they produce. Moreover, they can contract to share in a fixed ratio possible team revenues in excess of the opportunity costs of the inputs. When inputs are paid out of receipts from output, at first glance it seems unnecessary for anyone to put up wealth beforehand to compensate input owners [Fama (1980), 290]. However, total team revenues may turn out less than the opportunity costs of the joint inputs and such a difference cannot usually be predicted in advance: prices, consumer demand and other factors influencing a firm's results are inevitably subject to uncertainty of some degree. Shareholders contract to make up possible negative differences between team receipts and opportunity costs of inputs by investing, up to the size of their investment, a specified amount as equity capital on the condition that they are also given title to positive end-of-period differences between total revenues and costs. Thus, they guarantee pay-offs to other inputs in exchange for the residual claim and so assume the risk that input costs may eventually exceed total revenues (which risk is limited by the amount of their investment only). By supplying equity capital in exchange for the residual claim, shareholders provide an input like any other in the firm. In this contractual context, ownership of the corporate firm is a virtually meaningless concept [Fama (1980), 290].

If the corporation is to have an owner and if ownership is determined by the possession of the strongest claim on the corporation's assets and earnings, *creditors* may sooner be defined as the corporation's owners than shareholders, since their claim has priority over that of the shareholders and since creditors could completely wipe out the funds invested by the latter to have their claim satisfied. Secured creditors have an even stronger claim on the resources accumulated in the corporation.

The management of a corporation by hired managers rather than by shareholders is a result of specialization in risk-bearing by equity investors on the one hand and specialization in management by professional managers on the other [Alchian (1977), 144]. In Chapter 2, we identified several reasons for the separation of the functions of management and residual risk-bearing. The operation of a company by a centralized management composed of specialized managers serves to reduce the costs of intra-firm decision-making, and to cope with the shirking problem which would exist if a corporation with multiple shareholders were to be managed by its shareholders. Moreover, specialist managers may realize higher returns on shareholders' investment than the latter themselves may be able to achieve: the separation of stock ownership and management is a method of advancing investors' income by specialization of labor [Manne (1962), 402]. Also, company management by hired managers permits investors to reduce their aggregate risk by making diversified, passive investments in corporate equity.

Delegation of managerial authority by shareholders to hired managers presupposes that managers will act to further shareholders' interests. In a phrase of Demsetz [1983, 390], "it is foolish to believe that owners of valuable resources systematically relinquish control to managers who are not guided to serve their interests". But what is it exactly that shareholders desire managers to pursue?

Divergence of Interests

Wealth maximizing shareholders, of course, desire corporate managers to run the corporate firm so as to maximize stockholder wealth, *i.e.* to maximize shareholders' income from the possession of the residual claim. Wealth maximizing shareholders are sometimes said to be primarily interested in having management maximize the corporation's *profits* [Manne (1962), 402]. They will obtain such profits directly through pay-outs of dividends or indirectly in the form of capital gains, that is, through increases in the stock market value of their shares that they will earn when the shares are sold. Dividends and capital gains together make up shareholders' return on their investment.

Maximization of profits refers to the corporation's total earnings without reference to the amount of capital that shareholders have invested. Hence, the profit maximization objective may be interpreted as approving any generation of income that adds to corporate profits. However, individual shareholders will be interested in profit increases only to the extent that extra profits will increase returns on the amount they have invested. Therefore, the profit maximization objective is more accurately defined as maximization of *earnings per share* [Van Horne (1973), 3].

The profit maximization (or maximization of earnings per share) objective is sometimes interpreted as inducing management to focus on short-run gains only and to ignore long-range business planning. According to this view, profit maximizing managers tend to pursue short-run results only since such figures are reflected in the company's profits as disclosed to investors by its annual (or semi-annual or quarterly) income statements, and will neglect the exploration of and planning for future business opportunities. Accordingly, profit maximizing managers allegedly forgo long-run profit opportunities in order to achieve "quick" results.

An alternative formulation of shareholders' interest which purports to include both short-term and long-term considerations, is maximization of the value of the residual claim. The market value of shares depends on the net present value of the corporation's future profits as anticipated by investors, that means, on the corporation's prospects of future success. Therefore, managers who seek to maximize the value of the corporation's shares need to include in their decision-making the probable effects of alternative courses of action on the corporation's long-range results [Clark (1986), 18 fn. 46]. Thus, the formulation that wealth maximizing shareholders are interested in having management maximize the value of the residual claim implies that managers should attempt to maximize corporate profits for *all* accounting periods relevant to investors, including those in the long term.

As indicated above, the market price of a corporation's shares (*i.e.* the residual claim) is a function of its future earnings as anticipated by investors. Since the size of the firm's future earnings will depend on its success in meeting consumers' wants, maximization of the market value of corporate stock includes maximization of the firm's ability to meet the needs of consumers. In this regard, value maximization is not only in shareholders' interests, but also in that of consumers.

The market price of a corporation's shares represents "the focal judgment of all market participants as to what the value is of the particular firm" [Van Horne (1973), 4]. Thus, maximizing the value of a corporation's shares amounts to maximizing the value of the firm as measured by the stock market.

Managers' personal interests do not, however, naturally coincide with maximization of the value of shareholders' residual claim or maximization of stockholder wealth in general. The Berle-Means thesis that the diffusion of share ownership and the consequent absence of effective control of management allows managers to operate the corporation in their own self-interest rather than in the interests of the shareholders, suggests that there are managerial interests which are substantially opposed to those of shareholders. According to Emanuel Stein [1950, 218], corporate managements freed from effective shareholder control tend "to substitute other motives for those traditionally associated with private enterprise".

Utility maximizing managers will manage the corporation so as to maximize their personal *utility* rather than the value of the corporation's shares [Alchian (1975a)]. They are inclined to substitute aberrant managerial objectives for stockholder wealth-maximization up to the point of their utility function at which they attain maximum satisfaction. Thus, managers will search for the utility maximizing point of their utility function rather than for the point of the firm's production function which maximizes returns to shareholders [Demsetz (1983), 377]. The composition of a manager's utility function depends on the individual concerned and will usually comprise a variety of components [Machlup (1967), 19-21]. The desire for a higher pecuniary income and non-pecuniary elements (specified hereinafter) both enter a manager's utility function.

To maximize his utility, a manager may, for instance, attempt to increase his pecuniary reward at the expense of the corporation [Berle and Means (1991), 114-115]. Such attempts may result in "abuse by management of a position in which it can divert a part of the profit and income stream [generated by the corporate firm] to itself", as Berle [1962, 437] has noted. In particular, corporate managers may attempt to use corporate resources to achieve excessive salaries (bonuses, emoluments) for themselves. Monsen and Downs [1965] have reasoned that the self-interest of managers in manager-controlled firms primarily lies in maximizing the managers' lifetime income. Similarly, Berle and Means [1991, 114] suggest that in the operation of the corporation, those who are in control can "serve their own pockets better by profiting at the expense of the company than by making profits for it".

Managerial Utility Maximization

In order to divert corporate resources into their own pockets, managers may pursue various types of "get-rich-quick" strategies ("GRQ"-strategies).

The purest form of such behavior occurs when managers steal from the corporation's treasury and, possibly, disappear with the booty; that is to say, corporate management may pursue "take-the-money-and-run" strategies ("TMR-"strategies). "Take-the-money-and-run" and other forms of fraudulent behavior, once discovered, however, would hurt a manager's reputation so badly that probably no other company would be eager to hire him as a manager in the future. In effect, then, TMR (and fraud in general) would deprive managers of future opportunities to obtain personal gains from managing a company. The anticipated costs of the opportunities so lost are likely to outweigh the non-recurrent gain a manager could receive from TMR, except in those (rare) instances in which the booty would be large enough to afford the manager concerned lifetime maximum utility. Moreover, a manager's pecuniary gain from TMR or other fraud may be accompanied by non-pecuniary losses (such as liability to criminal prosecution, loss of self-esteem and becoming a social outcast), so that, in the aggregate, TMR may not bring a net improvement to the manager's utility.

Occasionally newspapers do report stories involving TMR or other forms of fraud by corporate management (for example, excessive private expenses at the company's account). But more sophisticated GRQ-strategies are available to corporate managers attempting to increase their pecuniary reward at the expense of the corporation. Usurpation of corporate opportunities by managers for themselves is generally recognized as such a strategy. Transactions between a corporation and its managers that benefit the manager(s) concerned but harm the corporation are another means by which managers can improve their personal wealth. Similarly, corporate managers may realize personal gains by making the corporation enter into transactions with another business entity which is controlled by the managers themselves or in which the latter have a significant financial interest. Such transactions may benefit corporate management but at the same time injure the interests of the corporation and its shareholders.

Additionally, managers may attempt to increase their reward in rather indirect ways. They may do so, for instance, by expanding the size of the firm's work force, since a positive relationship has been reported to exist between the amount of management's remuneration and the number of employees that managers supervise [Simon (1962); Murphy (1985); Williamson (1986), 8]. However, an increase in the number of staff without a corresponding increase in the corporation's revenues (sufficiently great to cover the extra costs of additional labor input) will, *ceteris paribus*, reduce corporate profits and returns to shareholders.

Maximization of the firm's sales [Baumol (1962); (1967)] is another objective which may appeal to corporate management, since the larger the firm's sales, the larger its cash flows, and the larger the income stream from which management may divert a part to itself to improve managerial utility. Moreover, the larger a firm's product market share, the less competition from other firms will restrain managers from operating the corporate firm in the pursuit of personal self-interests. Wealth maximizing shareholders, however, will not desire managers to *maximize* sales, but to expand sales only until the extra revenue derived from an additional unit of output (marginal revenue) equals marginal cost, that is, to expand sales up to the profit maximizing point of the firm's production function.

Another indirect way for corporate managers to improve their reward may be to maximize the growth of the firm [Marris (1964)], since both regular income and the range of opportunities for managers to pursue personal benefits at company expense tend to increase when the firm's size and scope of activities expand. Shareholders, on the other hand, will desire the firm to grow only in such measure as growth will serve to maximize stockholder wealth. Not every expansion will increase returns to shareholders. A firm may grow through investments in activities yielding a return less than the return shareholders themselves could realize if the funds associated with those investments were distributed to them. If shareholders can reinvest corporate funds in more profitable ways than corporate management does, shareholders will be better off if those funds are paid out to them (as dividends or stock repurchases) instead of being reinvested by the corporation [Jensen (1989), 66].

Furthermore, managers may attempt to secure their job and income as a manager over the long run by limiting business risks and by eschewing new ventures of which the prospects are, to some extent, uncertain [Galbraith (1967)]. Incumbent managers may expect that a reduction of the business risks and the uncertainty to which the corporate firm is subject will reduce the risk of corporate failure and thereby serve to protect their personal job and income security. However, maximization of stockholder wealth does not require managers to minimize risks but to pursue ventures with a positive net present value to the shareholders, including risky projects. Shareholders enjoying limited liability can hedge against any one project's failure by holding diversified portfolios composed of investments in various non-related companies. As *shareholders* can minimize their risk of losses by diversification, they will be interested in having management undertake even risky projects with positive net present values.

Managers may also seek to improve their utility through various forms of "on-the-job-consumption", a catch-all term referring to the use of corporate resources for a manager's personal benefit. "On-the-job-consumption" includes the taking of perquisites and fringe benefits which are not part of a manager's agreed compensation package. A manager's use of corporate resources for his personal benefit may at times appear similar to fraud, but often it is not a clear-cut question of fraud. For instance, managers may expend corporate wealth on extraordinary offices, overly luxurious furniture, acquisition of expensive art, non-productive computer software (for example, games) or superfluous hardware (to operate such games), royal class plane tickets, company airplanes, private travel, night club visits, excessive business lunches or dinners, conference holidays, expense accounts used (partly) for private purposes, use of the internet for private purposes at company expense, and other such amenities.

Moreover, a manager's utility function may contain such non-pecuniary variables as a desire for leisure, security, self-esteem, prestige, professional achievement, leadership, power or social prominence [Machlup (1967), 21; Williamson (1986), 7]. Contributions to charities from the corporation's treasury and personal relations with employees are other non-pecuniary elements from which managers may derive utility [Jensen and Meckling (1976), 312]. Accordingly, utility maximizing managers may shirk the maximization of stockholder wealth by pursuing extra leisure, by giving away corporate money or by expending corporate resources on attempts to increase their personal public prestige. Managerial strategies aimed at increasing the size of the corporation ("empire building") can not only be interpreted as an indirect way to increase management's pecuniary compensation but also as a means of increasing managers' power, prestige and social status.

Likewise, managers may improve their level of utility by taking business decisions that are motivated by their personal beliefs or convictions (for example, costly "pet projects") rather than by maximization of stockholder wealth. For instance, Stein [1950, 218] holds that hired managers tend to make decisions which reflect "management philosophy and statesmanship rather than the desire to earn and to pay in dividends as large an amount as possible". Accordingly, managers may use their positions to promote personal opinions or ambitions of whatever nature.

Williamson [1986, 7-8] argues that the above-mentioned managerial objectives are reflected in "expense preference" by corporate managers. This notion means that management does not have a neutral attitude toward costs but values certain classes of expenditures positively, such as expenditures that increase staff, managerial power or prestige, et cetera. The expenditure of corporate resources driven by managerial utility maximization may absorb a part of corporate profits as costs [Williamson (1986), 13]. Managerial "expense preference" serves to improve managerial utility but at the same time it is apt to increase corporate expenses, thereby sacrificing profits and returns to shareholders [Machlup (1967), 20].

Monitoring by Shareholders

The divergence of interests between shareholders and managers is not hidden in the obscurity of managers' minds but is perceptible to shareholders. As they will realize that utility maximizing managers may have other objectives at heart besides maximization of the value of shareholders' residual claim, one may be inclined to assume that wealth maximizing shareholders will actively monitor corporate managements in order to prevent departures from their interests. The Berle-Means line of argument, however, holds that large numbers of scattered shareholders are effectively powerless (that means, unable to influence managerial behavior if they wish to) and, hence, unlikely to ensure compliance of managerial actions with shareholder interests.

As described, Berle and Means claim that owing to the diffusion of stock ownership, management is in control of the corporate firm with few constraints from shareholders. A related observation submits that the dispersion of stock ownership over a multitude of shareholders diminishes *incentives* for individual shareholders to monitor managerial behavior, since the smaller each shareholder's proportion of a firm's total number of shares issued, the smaller the return to any one shareholder from actively seeking to influence corporate management [De Alessi (1973), 842]. Given the small relative size of his shareholding and his consequent limited voting and bargaining power, active monitoring in order to influence managers' decisions might simply not be worth its costs. Furthermore, as we saw in Chapter 3, by limiting the magnitude of shareholders' potential losses in the event of corporate failure, limited liability discourages shareholder involvement in both the actual management of the firm and in the monitoring of the hired management. The idea that shareholders not involved in the firm's management would fail to adequately monitor hired managers' performance goes back once more to Adam Smith. Smith [1981, 741] observed that the greater part of the owners of the stock in chartered joint-stock companies "seldom pretend to understand any thing of the business of the company; and (...) give themselves no trouble about it".

However, both limited liability and the dispersion of shares among multiple non-controlling shareholders do not imply that shareholders will be *indifferent* to the decisions and behavior of management. As their income from the residual claim depends on whether or not management is properly acting to maximize stockholder wealth, they do have, in principle, wealth-maximizing incentives to keep track of the way in which management runs the business. When it then turns out that management is not operating the corporate firm in the interest of the shareholders, they may either seek to displace incumbent managers or liquefy their investment by selling their shares.

Nineteenth century British economist Nassau Senior has identified three factors which in his view determine the attention shareholders will devote to the business in which they own shares [Amsler, Bartlett and Bolton (1981), 784]. Senior held that shareholders' attention to the firm depends on their knowledge about the business, the time required to monitor the operations of the firm, and the amount of their investment as a proportion of their total wealth. John Stuart Mill [1965, 140] added that faithful and effective performance ("fidelity") by managers of routine tasks and of functions which are clearly part of the managerial job can be obtained through quite limited monitoring effort by shareholders [Amsler, Bartlett and Bolton (1981), 785].

A shareholder's initial incentives to monitor management's performance are determined by the amount he has invested as a share of his total wealth rather than by the percentage he owns of the total number of shares issued by the corporation. When a shareholder's investment is large in proportion to his total wealth, his total wealth level is highly dependent on the performance of the firm. Should the firm fail, in any case he would lose a large proportion of his wealth, regardless of the percentage of the firm's total stock his investment represents. For this reason his initial incentive to monitor will be large, even if he owns only a small percentage of the total number of shares in the corporation concerned. Alchian and Woodward [1987, 122] therefore conclude that it is the absolute amount of his investment, not the proportion of the firm's total shares he owns, which determines a shareholder's incentive to monitor corporate activity: "The absolute amount, not the percentage share is pertinent in motivation. Whether a million dollar investment is 100% of an enterprise or is only 5%, it is still a million dollars at stake".

Suppose an investor has invested a large share of his total wealth in one particular firm but owns only a small percentage of the firm's shares. In this event his initial *incentive* to monitor corporate activity will be large but his actual *ability* in practice to influence managerial decision-making will probably be small. A small individual shareholder has only limited voting, including bargaining, power, and the subjects on which shareholders can vote are generally chosen by management, except for those subjects on which the law or the corporation's articles requires a shareholder vote (such as amendments of the articles of incorporation, dissolution of the corporation and election of managers or supervisory directors). Moreover, in general, shareholders are not entitled to (and, as a matter of fact, small shareholders cannot) initiate or countermand specific business decisions of the corporation's managers [Clark (1985), 56-58; (1986), 22-23]. And when stock ownership is dispersed among numerous small shareholders, individual shareholders ordinarily are unable to threaten management's position. In effect, small individual shareholders have little ability to influence managerial decision-making. As Franke [1987, 147] has observed, although a shareholder's incentive to monitor depends on "the absolute amount of wealth he has invested", his actual "monitoring opportunity set" will depend on his relative stake in the corporation.

If stock ownership is dispersed among a large number of small investors, in order to exercise effective pressure on management, individual shareholders will need to form a coalition with bargaining power vis-à-vis the management: they need to join in a coalition representing a number of shares (votes) sufficiently great to credibly threaten management with replacement if it refuses to follow particular business policies or practices desired by the shareholders. However, establishing such a coalition may be prohibitively costly: shareholders must expend resources in negotiating among themselves, in taking decisions about the actions they should take, in convincing other shareholders to cooperate against management, in collecting and disseminating information concerning managerial decisions and their desirability, et cetera. Thus, if there are many shareholders with small relative stakes, the cost to individual shareholders of influencing managerial decision-making is likely to be prohibitively high [Alchian and Woodward (1987), 122]. This reasoning suggests that effective monitoring of managers by shareholders is not so much impaired by the fact itself that small shareholders have limited individual voting and bargaining power but, rather, by the cost of combining into a coalition the individual powers residing in small, scattered shareholders.

The establishment of specialized investment funds which assemble capital from a variety of individual investors for investment in one or more selected firms or branches of industry and which so concentrate multiple small investments into one block, is one form of creating a shareholder coalition with significant bargaining (voting) power towards company managements. However, the formation, administration and effective operation of such investment funds also involves considerable organizational costs which may effectively reduce shareholders' net returns from their investment, when compared with direct investments by the shareholders in the same firms or industries, whilst the relationship between fund managers and investors is subject to similar conflicts of interests (agency costs) as the relationship between the shareholders and the management of any firm in which they invest. Thus for one conflict of interests is substituted another, that between fund managers and investors. Similarly, for one monitoring problem (the monitoring of the management of the firm in which investors' money is eventually invested) is substituted another, viz. the monitoring of the management of the investment fund.

There are two more factors that impede effective monitoring of corporate managements by the shareholders. First, as described earlier, with limited liability, shareholders can minimize their aggregate risk by holding a diversified portfolio containing multiple small investments. The more diversified an investor's portfolio, the smaller his stake in any particular firm as a proportion of his total wealth and the smaller his incentive to actively monitor the performance of the management of any particular firm in his portfolio, given the costs of trying to influence management's decisions. In addition, the smaller an investor's stake in a firm as a part of his total wealth, the lower his anticipated benefit from actively seeking to influence managerial actions. Hence, the fact that investors desirous to reduce their risk will not invest a large part of their wealth in any one firm diminishes individual investors' incentives to monitor managerial behavior. Investment funds assembling investments from large numbers of investors also tend to pursue the reduction of investors' risk through appropriate diversification and fund managers' incentives to actively monitor the performance of the managements of the firms into which they put investors' money are, therefore, diluted in a similar way, except if the fund invests in a limited number of firms only.

Second, when a corporation has multiple non-controlling shareholders, individual shareholders may gain by relying upon the efforts of others to monitor the firm's management. This is the shirking problem arising among multiple dispersed shareholders described in Chapter 2. For instance, an individual shareholder may shirk the task of obtaining and evaluating information about managerial behavior, hoping that other shareholders will do the work anyway. There is a "*free rider*" problem in that an individual shareholder may choose not to monitor the behavior of corporate managers as he may expect that others will make such monitoring efforts and that he will reap the fruits of their activity, regardless of his lack of effort [Manne (1981), 690; Clark (1986), 94]. In this way he would benefit from monitoring efforts by others without having to incur monitoring expenses himself. As a result of individual shareholders' shirking there may be too little monitoring of managers by shareholders.

In conclusion, it is not so much diffusion of stock ownership *per se* that relieves managers of effective shareholder control, as Berle and Means suggested, but, rather, the cost of forming shareholder coalitions with effective monitoring power, the dilution of monitoring incentives which is inherent in diversified holdings and the free rider problem that arises where there are multiple non-controlling shareholders. Efforts by individual shareholders to collect proxies from fellow shareholders in order to assemble scattered votes into larger voting blocks serve to overcome these hurdles to effective monitoring of management by shareholders. So do "going-private" transactions, by which large shareholders or an incumbent management group financed by outside investors buy out small shareholders so that stock ownership becomes concentrated and subsequently terminate the active trading in the corporation's shares, causing it to be no longer publicly held (for example, through de-listing the corporation's shares from organized stock exchanges).

The Case against Managerial Shirking

Constraints on Managerial Discretion

As described in Chapter 2, the divergence of interests between managers and shareholders is responsible for the existence of agency costs [Jensen and Meckling (1976), 308]. Agency costs arise when the management function is separated from the function of residual risk-bearing. They are the costs associated with managerial departures from maximization of stockholder wealth. They include the costs of obtaining managerial compliance with shareholders' interests as well as losses to shareholders (including opportunity losses) that are caused by managerial failure to act in their interest. In the words of Fama and Jensen [1983a, 304; 1983b, 327], agency costs are "the costs of structuring, monitoring, and bonding a set of contracts among agents with conflicting interests [and] the value of output lost because the costs of full enforcement of contracts exceed the benefits".

Agency costs come in addition to the managers' agreed compensation packages, thus adding to the costs of managerial salaries (and bonuses) to the firm. Agency costs raise the operational costs of the firm relative to a situation in which managerial behavior would be perfectly coherent with stockholder wealth maximization. Agency costs are borne by shareholders to the extent that they lower returns to stockholders and by consumers in so far as they are reflected in the firm's output prices. And where agency costs denote losses (including opportunity losses) ensuing from managerial failure to allocate resources to their highest value in use, that is, to uses for which consumers are prepared to pay the highest price, society is hurt since the same resources could have effected greater satisfaction of consumer demands.

Earlier, we discussed how managers may depart from maximization of shareholder wealth and what hurdles dispersed shareholders must surmount to limit such departures. But are hired specialist managers *really* at liberty to ignore shareholders' interests? Do the diffusion of stock ownership and the absence of effective shareholder monitoring really afford managers a large degree of autonomy in decision-making?

Based on the apparent inconsistency of managerial and shareholder interests, as noted previously, Adam Smith [1981, 741, 755] predicted that incorporated joint-stock companies operated by hired managers which were not endowed with monopoly privileges were likely to lose in the competition against investor-managed firms in most instances. Yet to date such an effect has not occurred. By contrast, firms operated in corporate form have come to dominate important sectors of the economy. Thus, the corporation has survived the "market test" against potential alternative forms of organization [Jensen and Meckling (1976), 357]. The success of the corporate form of organization may be construed to suggest that corporate managements may *not* have or use discretionary power to ignore shareholder interests after all. What, then, might keep utility maximizing managers from pursuing their own preferences at the sacrifice of stockholder wealth maximization?

In Chapter 2 we stated that the concept of the corporation contains several devices which serve to mitigate the agency costs originating from the separation of management and residual risk-bearing: shareholder voting rights, monitoring of managers by supervisory directors, limited liability for corporate debts and alienability of shares all serve to protect shareholders against managerial self-interest seeking. These devices are *ex post* responses to the conflict between managerial and shareholder interests; they mitigate the conflict's effects without eliminating them.

However, managers are also constrained by the operation of *markets*. Market mechanisms which curtail managerial autonomy serve to align the interests of managers and shareholders *ex ante*, that is, they provide incentives to management to act in shareholders' interest, thereby avoiding conflicts of interests and limiting agency costs. Below we look at the market forces that curb managerial departures from stockholder wealth maximization.

Product Markets and Incentive Contracts

Although dispersion of shares among multiple small investors may result in the absence of effective shareholder monitoring of managers' use of power, for the reasons previously described, it does not automatically follow that the management of such firms will be insensitive to shareholders' interests. There are several market mechanisms which place checks on managerial behavior which scattered shareholders may fail to provide, and which induce managers to use corporate resources to further shareholders' wealth-maximizing interests.

Managerial discretion is constrained in the first place by competition in the market for the firm's output. Competition in product markets compels firms to minimize costs on penalty of being driven out of business by competing firms. If a firm has higher costs than its competitors, it will have to charge higher prices for its output to make up for those extra costs and to earn a profit for its shareholders sufficiently great to attract equity. Because of such higher prices, *ceteris paribus*, in competitive markets consumers will purchase less of the firm's output and buy products supplied by other firms instead. Thus, when managerial self-interest seeking raises the firm's costs, that is, where corporate resources are wasted to benefit management, the firm's ability to compete in the market for its output will be harmed. In the end, the firm will have to shut down and managers will lose their jobs and thereby the opportunity to use their positions to obtain personal gain. A manager's professional survival, then, depends on the survival of the *firm* in its competition with other firms [Fama (1980), 288]. As Williamson [1964, 2] has concluded, in competitive product markets, persistent sacrifices of corporate resources to managers' personal self-interests inexorably leads to the firm's extinction. In this way product market competition curbs the freedom of management to operate the firm to suit itself.

Incentive contracts between the corporation and its senior management are frequently used to link the remuneration management receives to the results of the firm in the market for its output. By definition, such contracts make (a part of) a manager's income dependent on the firm's results. For instance, the contract may entitle him to a cash bonus or a salary increase if profits exceed a specified amount, to a percentage of profits beyond a fixed amount or to a share in total profits. Also, the issuance of stock options or equity shares (stock bonuses) to managers as a part of their remuneration is often used to give management a direct financial interest in maximizing the value of the corporation's shares.

John Stuart Mill [1965, 141] already referred to incentive contracting as a means of motivating hired managers to keep down the firm's costs and to exploit profitable business opportunities. By linking managerial income and wealth to corporate performance, incentive contracts aim to direct managerial behavior towards shareholders' interest. When managers, for example, are rewarded shares or stock options, they will suffer reductions in their personal wealth should they depart from maximization of the value of the corporation's shares. Therefore, they will have pecuniary incentives to behave consistently with shareholders' interest.

Jensen and Murphy [1990] have produced data indicating a positive, if small, relationship between changes in the market value of the corporation's shares and the amount of top management compensation. Their examination of the pay-performance relation for over 2,000 chief executive officers of major United States corporations spanning five decades shows that these top managers experienced average wealth changes of USD 3.25 for every USD 1,000 change in shareholder value. This finding indicates that, on average, managerial wealth is sensitive to corporate performance as measured by changes in the market value of equity shares.

Other studies have revealed positive relationships between managerial stock ownership and corporate profits. Stano [1975, 275] found that "[a]verage executive stockholdings turns out to be a highly significant and important determinant of profitability". According to his findings, firm profitability increases by a significant 1.7 percent if average executive stockholdings rise from USD 100,000 to USD 1,000,000, with a further increase of 0.5 percent if managerial stock ownership rises to USD 2,000,000. Stano concluded: "An unmistakable positive relationship between profit rates among the largest U.S. corporations and executive stock interests has emerged" [1975, 277]. These findings may be interpreted to imply that stock ownership by management will enhance managers' incentives to maximize corporate profits. Indeed, one of the conclusions of the Jensen and

Murphy study [1990, 261] cited above is that the largest performance incentives of chief executive officers come from ownership of equity shares in the corporation they manage.

Jensen and Meckling [1976] suggest that when stock ownership by management rises, managers will be less inclined to depart from maximization of the firm's stock market value as they will bear a larger part of the costs of such departures in their capacity as shareholders. According to this reasoning, managerial interests become more closely aligned with shareholders' when managerial stock ownership increases (the "convergence-of-interests" hypothesis). This hypothesis is consistent with the Berle-Means association of diffusion of stock ownership with deviations from shareholders' interest: if dispersed stock ownership leads to insensitivity of management to shareholders' interest, as Berle and Means argued, it would follow that deviations from shareholders' wealth-maximizing interests are less likely to occur as share ownership becomes more concentrated in the hands of the individuals controlling the firm.

Morck, Shleifer and Vishny [1988], however, have found that the relationship between managerial stock ownership and corporate performance as measured by the firm's market value (more precisely, by the ratio of the market value of the corporation's shares to the replacement cost of its physical assets, *i.e.* Tobin's *Q*) is not monotonic. Although they did find a significant correlation between managerial stock ownership and market valuation, according to the data they produced, this relationship is not uniformly positive. In their study of 371 large American industrial firms they found (i) a positive relationship between firm value and managerial stock ownership when top management owns between zero and 5 percent of the corporation's stock, (ii) a negative relationship when managerial stock ownership is between 5 percent and 25 percent, and (iii) a further positive relationship when top management owns over 25 percent of the stock. According to these findings, the view that larger management stakes will by definition and invariably be reflected in higher market valuation of the corporation, appears to be too simplistic.

The findings of Morck, Shleifer and Vishny confirm first, that a rise in managerial stock ownership from zero causes managerial interests to resemble more closely those of shareholders [Jensen and Warner (1988), 13]. This conclusion is implied by the fact that stock market values go up as managers become stock owners. Second, the results of the Morck-Shleifer-Vishny study suggest that at less than 5 percent and at more than 25 percent stock ownership, management will be more faithful to shareholders' interest than when management owns between 5 and 25 percent of corporate stock. A possible explanation is that with stock ownership between 5 and 25 percent, management may possess enough power to resist successfully attacks on its position. In other words, with stock ownership in the indicated range, management may be entrenched in office (the "entrenchment" hypothesis), meaning that managers can deploy corporate resources in the pursuit of objectives other than value maximization without risking their jobs and salaries (although departures from value maximization will perhaps be less than if management would *not* own stock) [Morck, Shleifer and Vishny (1988), 295].

With less than 5 percent stock ownership, by contrast, management has generally insufficient power to repulse attacks on its position. Therefore, these managers are more likely to deploy corporate resources to maximize the market value of their shares (instead of pursuing alternative objectives to increase their utility), thereby acting consistently with shareholders' interest. And with managerial stock ownership exceeding 25 percent, managers' personal pecuniary interest in maximizing share value will probably have become so large that managerial interests have become quite similar to those of shareholders. This may explain the reportedly positive correlation between market valuation and stock ownership by top management between zero and 5 percent and beyond 25 percent.

To sum up, the findings of Morck, Shleifer and Vishny can be interpreted to imply that with stock ownership in the range between 5 and 25 percent, managers may trade-off value maximization against other components of their utility function, whereas with less than 5 percent stock ownership, management will have little power to do so without risking its position and with stock ownership rising beyond 25 percent, management has little incentive to depart from value maximization. According to this interpretation, the value decline that was found with management stock ownership between 5 and 25 percent reflects entrenchment of the management team, while the reported value increases reflect convergence of interests between managers and shareholders [Jensen and Warner (1988), 12-13].

Factor Markets

Factor markets (including the market for investment capital), too, constrain managerial behavior. Firms compete against other firms for the acquisition of productive resources (raw materials, intermediate goods, capital, labor). The more corporate wealth managers divert to themselves, the less will be left in the corporation's treasury to hire or to buy inputs and the lower will be the prices the corporation can pay resource owners to attract inputs into the firm. Hence, the more corporate wealth management absorbs for itself, the greater is the likelihood that the corporation will be defeated by rival firms in their competition for scarce resources, and the less managers will have to manage.

Firms compete, *inter alia*, to attract capital for investment in the assets and operations of the business. Where managers sacrifice corporate wealth to pursue their own self-interests, comparatively low profits or a comparatively low market value of the firm's shares will signal to potential suppliers of equity capital that they may earn higher returns by investing elsewhere. In effect, the firm's ability to attract equity is harmed as investors may prefer investing in those other firms. Thus, when managers fail to operate the firm in shareholders' interest, the corporation is likely to fail in the market for equity capital. And where managers fail to raise funds to acquire productive resources, they will soon find themselves without inputs to manage, and without funds to appropriate.

Moreover, when a firm's results are poor in comparison with those of its competitors, potential suppliers of capital (equity or debt) may consider investing in that firm to be relatively risky. Consequently, investors will pay less for the corporation's stock and lenders will charge higher, risk-commensurate interest rates or not provide loans at all. Thus, if a poorly run firm were still able to attract capital, it would probably get funds less easily and on less favorable terms than its competitors of superior performance. This in turn will harm the firm's ability to compete in product markets.

A firm's performance also affects the terms on which owners of raw materials and intermediate goods would be prepared to do business. The poorer a firm's results, the less inclined input owners would be to supply inputs on credit (they may prefer immediate payment in cash) and the higher the (risk-reflecting) interest rates that trade creditors would charge. Moreover, a poorly performing firm may have difficulty in acquiring high-quality labor inputs as workers may expect higher incomes and better career opportunities from work elsewhere. The more successful a firm, the higher the wages it can pay and the better the long-term opportunities it can offer to its employees.

It follows that if managers give priority to their personal self-interests in running the firm, they will have trouble acquiring command over resources, and ultimately they may be unable to manage at all (what would management manage if investors do not supply capital, resource owners refuse to supply inputs on credit and workers prefer working elsewhere?). In effect, thus, competition for capital, labor and other inputs (including competition for favorable terms of trade) provides incentives to managers to operate the firm in shareholders' interest rather than to maximize their personal utility.

The Market for Corporate Control

In addition to competition in product markets and factor markets, managers are constrained by the threat of a takeover [Manne (1964); (1965); (1981)]. When corporate resources are not used entirely in the pursuit of stockholder wealth-maximization, the market value of the corporation's shares will ordinarily be less than it would be if management were exclusively driven by shareholders' interests. Individual shareholders dissatisfied with management's performance will sell their shares, and the market value of the corporation's shares will decline. The more shareholders sell their shares, the lower stock prices will fall. In this event the market price of the shares will come to be "an index of stockholder discontent" with incumbent management [Van Horne (1973), 4].

The greater the dissatisfaction among shareholders, the greater the downward pressure on stock market prices resulting from sales by individual shareholders. In this way, dissatisfied shareholders lower the cost of taking over the firm to outsiders. As a consequence, outside investors may observe potential private wealth improvements from acquiring all or the majority of the shares in the corporation concerned and replacing incumbent management by managers whom they expect to operate the corporation more effectively in shareholders' interests. As investors able to install superior managers (or to discipline existing managers more effectively) will expect higher future returns from possession of the corporation's shares than existing shareholders do, they will normally be prepared to pay a price for the shares higher than their value to the latter and so obtain all or the majority of the shares and thereby control of the corporate firm. This takeover mechanism is known as "the market for corporate control" [Manne (1964); (1965); (1981)]. The threat of being replaced as a result of a takeover is presumed to be a major control mechanism limiting managerial discretion to depart from stockholder wealth-maximization: the "constant pressure provided by the threat of a takeover" [Manne (1975), 516] renders deviations from shareholder wealth-maximization less attractive to corporate managements.

"Corporate control" is defined as the right to determine the management of corporate resources and it includes the right to select and to remove the corporation's top management [Jensen and Ruback (1983), 5]. The market for corporate control as a mechanism for aligning managerial behavior with shareholders' wealth-maximizing interests functions through the impact of managerial performance on the market value of a corporation's shares [Manne (1981), 690]. In the words of Van Horne [1973, 4]: "The market price [of corporate stock] serves as a performance index or report card of the firm's progress; it indicates how well management is doing in behalf of its stockholders". The market for corporate control, thus, assumes the existence of a positive relation between stock prices and management's adherence to shareholders' interests [Manne (1965), 112].

When management fails to operate the corporation in shareholders' best interests, the market price of the company's shares will reveal to outsiders the possibility of realizing wealth gains by providing improved management. Manne [1965, 112-113] distinguishes between two kinds of rewards which outsiders can earn by acquiring control of a poorly run company (that is, a company which is yielding a return to shareholders below the return that could be accomplished if it were managed more effectively in shareholders' interests). First, acquirers can take over the compensation associated with the company's top-level managerial positions. Second, and more importantly, they may realize substantial capital gains (*i.e.* increases in the market value of the company's shares) by improving the company's performance. Because of the increase in the value of the company's stock an acquirer may be able to effect, Manne [1965, 113] concludes that "the potential return from the successful takeover and revitalization of a poorly run company can be enormous".

Competition in the market for corporate control means that those bidders will acquire control of a particular firm who expect the highest private wealth gains from obtaining the right to control the use of that company's resources, that is, those who offer the highest bidding prices for its shares. The highest wealth gains are likely to be anticipated by would-be acquirers best suited for improving company performance and thereby enhancing returns to shareholders. They will most effectively eliminate managerial departures from stockholder wealth-maximization. As prospective wealth gains from superior management are reflected in bidding prices, these bidders will offer the highest price for the company's shares and so obtain control. On the assumption that higher returns to investors come from superior allocations of corporate resources to meet society's demands as expressed in the demand functions for the firm's goods and services, those bidders expecting the highest private wealth gains from obtaining corporate control will concurrently be those best able to allocate corporate resources to socially valuable uses. Thus a smoothly operating market for corporate control will benefit society as a whole.

Tender offers, usually providing the existing shareholders with the opportunity during a limited period of time to sell their shares at a more or less substantial, non-negotiable premium over the prevailing market price, have been described as an "elaborate signaling device" in the market for corporate control: they inform the shareholders that an increase in the value of the firm is attainable through improved management and that such increased value can be realized only if corporate control is placed in different hands, with the extra value attainable being capitalized in the tender offer price (in particular, in the takeover premium) and disappearing from existing shareholders when the offer expires [Cohen (1990)]. In effect, tender offers promote socially beneficial transfers of corporate control to investors capable of supplying superior management to the firm.

Empirical data relating to the market for corporate control indicate that companies which are the target of a takeover attempt almost invariably realize substantial increases in their stock market value in the period of the takeover attempt [Jensen and Ruback (1983), 10-14; Jarrell, Brickley and Netter (1988), 51-52]. The evidence also suggests that these value increases be lost if the takeover attempt fails [Jensen and Ruback (1983), 14-16]. These findings are consistent with the hypothesis that corporate control transactions serve to improve target company performance: the prospect of higher future returns to shareholders is capitalized into stock price increases prior to takeover and these value increases are lost if the takeover does not materialize, that is, if the "old" management continues to manage the firm.

Moreover, empirical data suggest that managerial actions which eliminate the possibility of a takeover are attended by a decline in the market value of the company's shares [Jensen and Ruback (1983), 38-39]. The same observation has been made in relation to managerial actions which oppose (but do not eliminate completely) potential takeovers and which are not subject to shareholder voting approval [Jarrell, Brickley and Netter (1988), 62-65]. Negative stock price reactions to defensive measures by the target company's management intended to preclude a potential takeover of corporate control, indicate that the possibility of a takeover is valued positively by investors. In other words, the fact that the firm is subject to potential corporate control transactions is associated with positive wealth gains for stockholders.

The empirical evidence summarized above confirms that the takeover mechanism supplied by the market for corporate control operates to curtail managerial departures from stockholder wealth-maximization. The finding that shareholders of target companies realize substantial capital gains in successfully completed takeover attempts, combined with the finding that shareholders of bidding companies in such takeovers on average do not lose [Jensen and Ruback (1983), 16-22; Jarrell, Brickley and Netter (1988), 53], indicates that corporate takeovers produce wealth gains, *i.e.* create value. As the gains to shareholders from takeovers do not appear to be offset by losses to other parties, Jarrell, Brickley and Netter [1988, 58] conclude that the available data confirm that corporate control transactions "reflect economically beneficial reshufflings of productive assets".

Of course, the reduction in the agency costs associated with managerial departures from stockholder wealth-maximization is not the only possible source of wealth gain generated by takeovers. Productivity advances through availability of new technology and cost reductions through economies of scale between the target firm and the acquiring firm are other potential sources of gains to takeovers. The reduction of inter-firm transaction costs, for example by organizing the relationship between an asset specialized to one particular user and that user within one firm [Klein, Crawford and Alchian (1978)], may also account for takeover gains.

Many antitrust lawyers (and economists) earn a decent living on the basis of the suspicion that corporate combinations create market power, enabling exploitation of consumers by producers through contrived scarcity and consequential high prices. This reasoning suggests that wealth gains to shareholders in takeovers may come at the expense of consumers and result from the increased market power of the target firm and the acquiring firm. However, the available empirical evidence does not support the hypothesis that wealth gains created by corporate takeovers in the market for corporate control generally tend to come from the creation of market power [Jensen and Ruback (1983), 24-25].

The Market for Managerial Labor

Managers are furthermore constrained by the market for managerial labor [Fama (1980); Alchian (1975b)]. Corporate managers compete for managerial jobs in this market. Incumbent managers face competition from rival (including would-be) managers who seek to displace them, and they themselves compete against others for new positions from which they anticipate greater utility. Competition among managers to obtain more attractive employment offers elsewhere provides incentives to managers to act consistently with shareholders' interests.

The more successfully a manager advances shareholders' interests, the greater his value to investors in corporate equity and the higher the price at which they would be prepared to hire him. Accordingly, by maximizing the value of shareholders' residual claim, managers establish favorable reputations in the market for managerial services with respect to investors and so enhance future compensation for their services in that market. As Alchian

[1975b, 504] has noted, a manager's superiority to other, competing, managers is reflected in his higher labor market value. On the other hand, when a manager *fails* to maximize the value of shareholders' residual claim, his value in the market for corporate managers (*i.e.* the rental value of his human capital) is likely to decline. In this way the market for managerial labor establishes a positive correlation between a manager's commitment to shareholders' interests and his labor market value, with deviations from maximization of stockholder wealth being reflected in the devaluation of his human capital [Fama (1980)]. It follows that managers desiring to enhance the market value of their human capital have a personal interest in maximizing stockholder wealth.

Firms have incentives to reward managers in accordance with their outside labor market value since if they pay less, existing managers may leave the firm to earn a higher compensation elsewhere. Moreover, the firm will have difficulty in hiring new skilled managers if its reward system is not responsive to the outside market value of managers' human capital. And if the firm were to pay managers *more* than their market value, that is, it simply pays too much for what it gets, this would be at the expense of shareholders' earnings from the residual claim.

Managers have incentives to maximize their labor market value in order to bid up their compensation from the corporation they manage, to increase their chances of being hired by another, better rewarding corporation, and to diminish the risk of being out-valued (*i.e.* displaced) by rivals eager to take over their present job. Thus, it pays managers to increase the rental value of their human capital by faithfully serving shareholders' interests, both to maximize their personal salaries and job security in their current positions and to attract better employment offers elsewhere.

Consistent with this theory, Gilson [1990] found that directors of U.S. corporations who resigned from the board following the corporation's bankruptcy, experienced a decrease in the number of directorships held with other companies: a sample average of 2.2 directorships reduced to an average of 1.4 over the three year period following resignation from the bankrupt firm. According to this finding, the firm's bankruptcy which may be deemed illustrative of, if not synonymous with, bad management, decreases the value of a director's human capital to other firms. Similarly, Kaplan and Reishus [1990] reported that dividend cuts have a significant negative impact on the number of new outside directorships the chief executive officers of firms cutting dividends receive thereafter, when compared with chief executive officers of firms which do not reduce dividend pay-outs.

Labor market pressure on managers to advance shareholders' interest hinges on the premise that appropriate information about managerial performance is available to the managerial labor market. The market value of a company's shares is a source of information about management's performance. The higher a corporation's share prices, the more successful management is in maximizing the value of shareholders' residual claim. When the shares in a particular company are valued low relative to the market values of the shares in competing firms, share prices signal that from the point of view of investors, this company's management is not performing as well as the management of competing companies.

As share prices depend on the net present value of anticipated future profits, the higher a company's share prices, the higher the profits investors expect management to realize in the future and, therefore, the more positive is investors' judgement with respect to management's ability to advance shareholders' interests. In this way, share prices feed information into managerial labor markets.

The information revealed in share prices relates to the firm and its management as a whole and not to the performance of *individual* members of the management. Accordingly, Fama [1980, 291-292] has argued that "the rental rates for their human capital (...) are likely to depend on the success or failure of the firm [and] the previous associations of a manager with success and failure are information about his talents". He concludes that "the success or failure of the team impacts [a manager's] future wages, and this gives the manager a stake in the success of the team". Thus, a manager's market value is dependent upon the success of the firm as a whole, which in turn induces him to enhance the performance of other inputs. This observation is consistent with the view of the firm as a team in which the marginal products of individual team members are interdependent [Alchian and Demsetz (1972)].

Managers are not only disciplined by the managerial labor market outside the firm but also by competition from other managers within the firm. As noted above, the rental value of a manager's human capital is positively related to firm performance. Since this principle applies to *any* manager in a particular firm, *all* managers within that firm have incentives to monitor each other (both top-down and bottom-up). Where one manager's shirking or incompetence negatively affects firm performance, the labor market value of other managers is likely to decline. Therefore, each manager will be concerned with the performance of other managers.

The firm's top managers have incentives to displace badly performing lower managers both to secure their own positions and to enhance their personal market value. Moreover, within a firm, high ranked managers face competition from lower ranked managers eager to displace them in order to further their own careers, income and power: "Lower managers perceive that they can gain by stepping over shirking or less competent managers above them" [Fama (1980), 293]. For this reason, lower managers may attempt to direct the attention of the superiors of their superiors in rank (ultimately the shareholders) to shirking or incompetence by higher managers. Obviously, shareholders have wealth-maximizing incentives to displace shirking or incompetent top managers (or supervisory directors entitled to remove the incumbent management).

The market for managerial labor outside and inside the firm gives corporate managers a personal interest in the operation of the corporation in order to maximize stockholder wealth. Both the need to resist competitors for their present jobs from outside and inside the firm and the desire to enhance their rental value to other potential employers [Alchian (1975b), 502] induce managers to be faithful to shareholders' interests. Managerial departures from stockholder wealth maximization are likely to decrease the value of their human capital in the outside labor market and to threaten their positions within the firm. In both respects, managers who sacrifice shareholders' interests to other goals would (or might) suffer losses, including opportunity losses.

Imperfections of the Disciplinary Mechanisms

We have identified several market mechanisms that restrict managerial discretion to depart from stockholder wealth maximization. Competition in product markets and in factor markets, incentive contracting, the market for corporate control and markets for managerial labor within and outside the firm, all operate to induce corporate managers to serve shareholders' wealth-maximizing interests by giving managers a personal interest in doing so.

However, the market mechanisms described above do not entirely bridge the gap between managers' interest in maximization of their personal utility on the one hand and stockholder wealth maximization on the other. There are several reasons why the aforesaid markets are unlikely to achieve the complete assimilation of managerial behavior with shareholder interests and these we explore below.

Limits of Competition in Product Markets

Competition in the market for the firm's output will not eliminate managerial self-interest seeking at shareholders' expense as the divergence of interests between shareholders and managers and, hence, the existence of agency costs, is inherent in *any* firm in which the management function is separate from the function of residual risk-bearing. Divergences of interests (agency costs), thus, are an economy-wide phenomenon. Therefore, they are unlikely to threaten the survival of any one particular firm except where a firm incurs excessive costs from managerial self-interest seeking, that is, where it incurs higher agency costs than its competitors do: only when the amount of managerial shirking is exceptionally large can competition from other firms threaten the firm's survival and, thereby, managerial jobs. Competition in product markets, then, will curb solely excessive aberrations by corporate managements. When the amount of agency costs is more or less equivalent among competing firms, their existence will not affect competition between these firms [Jensen and Meckling (1976), 330].

Does it follow that firms which are managed by their shareholders have a competitive advantage over firms operated by hired managers, given that in investor-managed firms there is no separation of interests between risk-bearers and managers? It does not. Indeed, shareholder-managed firms do not incur costs from the divergence of interests between shareholders and managers, but the absence of this divergence does not imply that shareholder-managers will naturally appropriate fewer corporate resources or shirk less than hired managers. As Demsetz [1983] has pointed out, shareholder-managers, too, may decide in favor of using corporate resources to provide on-the-job consumption. He maintains that like hired managers, a manager who at the same time owns the shares in the company he manages is guided by utility maximization [1983, 378]. The difference is that when *hired* managers appropriate corporate resources, shareholders are generally harmed, while *shareholder*-managers using corporate resources to provide on-the-job consumption do so to benefit themselves.

Shareholder-managers may seek to achieve on-the-job benefits instead of maximizing their earnings from the residual claim as they may expect to derive greater utility from on-the-job amenities than from extra pecuniary income consumable at home. For instance, shareholder-managers may decide in favor of on-the-job consumption as in this way they can obtain tax benefits: income from dividends is generally taxed and so may be possible capital gains a shareholder-manager may receive when selling (some or all of) his shares, but on-the-job amenities may escape taxation. Also, for example, a shareholder-manager may seek to maximize his free time subject to the constraint that his earnings from the residual claim exceed some minimum amount, as he may prefer extra leisure to overworking himself to earn extra money [Baumol (1973), 15]. Other shareholder-managers may prefer governing an ever larger-growing business empire to managing a firm that yields maximum returns on their residual claim.

Now let us assume for the sake of argument that on balance the cost to the firm of on-the-job consumption by shareholder-managers is less than the agency costs in firms operated by hired managers. It still does not follow that shareholder-managed firms have a competitive advantage over manager-operated firms. The management function will not be separated from the function of residual risk-bearing *unless* the shareholders expect that the benefits to them from this separation outweigh the agency costs generated by the resulting divergence of interests between shareholders and managers. And the mere frequency of manager-operated firms suggests that the benefits to shareholders from the management of these firms being conducted by specialist managers do outweigh agency costs.

As discussed in Chapter 2, shareholder-managed firms with multiple shareholders are burdened with high costs of decision-making and with losses from shirking by individual shareholder-managers, and they do not benefit from specialization of labor through professional managers. Moreover, if the number of shareholders is *limited*, for example, to keep down decision-making costs and to avoid shirking problems (especially where the shares in a corporation are owned by a single shareholder), the amount of equity capital available to finance business ventures will be equally limited; and the less equity capital is put up by the firm's shareholders, generally the lower the amount the firm can borrow and the higher the risk-commensurate interest rates that lenders will charge. In summary, the potential advantage of less agency costs to a shareholder-managed firm is likely to be offset by competitive disadvantages in other respects.

Limits of Incentive Contracts

Incentive contracts which link a manager's remuneration to the firm's success in its competition with other firms cause managers' interests to be more closely aligned with those of the shareholders, but they are unlikely to entirely *eliminate* conflicts of interests. We do not deny that incentive contracts can be a powerful instrument for aligning hired managers' personal interests with those of the shareholders but their ability to do so is subject to various limitations.

First, incentive contracts generally make (a part of) a manager's monetary income dependent on the financial results of the firm. However, as we have seen, a manager's utility function typically contains also *non-pecuniary* variables inconsistent with stockholder wealth-maximization (such as on-the-job perquisites, desire for leisure, or desire for social prominence). When a manager expects to derive greater utility from such non-pecuniary variables than from extra pecuniary income, the prospect of extra money from the incentive contract will not motivate him to behave consistently with shareholders' interests. For instance, when a manager values extra leisure or on-the-job amenities higher than increased monetary income consumable at home (for example, because the former are not taxed), an incentive contract providing for his financial compensation to be contingent on corporate performance will not (or will only to a limited extent) discipline him. In general, incentive contracts will only align a manager's personal interests with those of shareholders up to the point on a manager's utility function at which his marginal expected utility from extra monetary income for consumption outside the firm equals the marginal expected utility derived from increased on-the-job consumption, extra leisure and other non-pecuniary variables. Ultimately, the law of diminishing marginal utility of wealth, which dictates that individuals obtain proportionately less utility from additional increments of money as their aggregate wealth increases, will put a limit on the constraints incentive contracts could entail.

By the same law, it is not likely that a manager who receives a very substantial amount (in absolute terms) as fixed salary, independent of the firm's results, will obtain much extra utility from additional money from an incentive contract. In that case, the incentive contract would add little to his actual incentive to maximize stockholder returns. For instance, a chief executive officer who earns several million dollars as fixed income will, according to the cited law, obtain proportionately less utility from increments of wealth effected by stock options or other performance-related bonuses that are awarded to him on top of his fixed salary. Instead of being an incentive for management, such extra income contingent upon the firm's fortunes could perhaps be construed as a payment-to-performance measure that facilitates comparison in the market for managerial labor.

Second, incentive contracts primarily motivate managers to maximize their own remuneration with respect to the contract concerned, that is, for the time period or periods covered by the contract. For instance, when the contract provides that management shall have a share in corporate profits or receive a bonus in cash or a salary increase if profits exceed a specified bottom line, managers have incentives to maximize profits for the accounting periods to which the contract relates. To obtain the cited bonus or salary increase, they may increase short-term accounting profits at the expense of long-range business opportunities, *i.e.* at the expense of stockholder returns over the long run. Managers may, for example, raise short-run profits by selling corporate assets at prices in excess of their book values; although yielding an accounting profit, such asset sales may well harm the corporation's future earning power.

Furthermore, when managers are rewarded stock bonuses, they will be inclined to maximize the value of the corporation's shares by the time they intend to sell their shares. Virtually the same principle would apply when management receives stock options: managers would then have wealth-maximizing incentives to maximize share value by the time they intend to exercise their option rights. Again, managers may allocate, or attempt to allocate, corporate assets to maximize their personal income from stock bonuses or stock options rather than maximize returns to shareholders over the long run. (Yet note that as stock prices depend on the net present value of expected future profits, the prospects, in practice, for managers to push up the market value of corporate equity in the short term at the expense of the long term is probably limited.)

In brief, incentive contracts may shorten managers' time horizon, whilst wealth maximizing shareholders desire managers to take into account both the short term and the long term. To shareholders, in principle all future accounting periods are relevant, not merely the period(s) to which a manager's incentive contract relates. De Alessi [1973, 848; emphasis by the author] has noted that the accounting periods relevant to corporate managers would "roughly be limited to those occurring during his tenure in office, and this time horizon would necessarily be shorter than a shareholder's to whom *all* future accounting periods matter". Instead of reducing the difference between the time horizons of shareholders and managers, then, incentive contracts for managers may increase it.

Third, where incentive contracts create uncertain prospects of future income instead of a certain prospect on which managers could simply cash in if they meet a fixed target, for example, if managers are promised stock options or stock bonuses whose market value is subject to uncertainty, instead of a fixed cash bonus if the firm earns a stated minimum profit, these contracts discourage management from engaging the firm in risky activities with positive expected returns to the shareholders, to the extent that managers are risk averse. Risk averse managers will seek to curtail uncertainty about their own future monetary income and, therefore, prefer low- (or moderate-)

risk activities with a relatively certain outcome in terms of the expected value of their incentive contract (for instance, the value of stock options), to high-risk activities which hold out a less certain income prospect of equal expected monetary value. One can safely assume that most managers are risk averse in that, due to the diminishing marginal utility of wealth, they will derive greatest utility from the initial wealth increments yielded by an incentive contract and attach less utility to additional increments of monetary income.

Where, for instance, stock options induce managers to engage the firm in a low-risk activity which they expect will yield a relatively certain option income, instead of a high-risk venture which might yield more but which would also subject the variable part of their income to greater uncertainty, stock options would reward conservatism on the managers' part: where more risk connotes innovation, development of new products, new production techniques and (other) venturesome activities, stock options and other incentive contracts that create uncertain income prospects for corporate managers discourage exploration and exploitation of new business opportunities and encourage management to stick to the familiar. This, in turn, threatens maximization of the value of shareholders' residual claim in the long run and is detrimental to society at large in so far as innovation would bring about greater satisfaction of consumers' needs.

Fourth, a point often overlooked is that contracts which provide incentives to managers to enhance the value of shareholders' residual claim, do so at a direct cost to the shareholders. Profit sharing by management, performance related cash bonuses and salary increases for managers all absorb corporate wealth that would otherwise flow to the shareholders through the residual claim. Moreover, if new shares are issued for the purpose of granting stock bonuses or stock options to managers, the existing shareholders' residual claim on the corporate firm's assets and cash flows is typically watered down; this may lead to a decline in the market price of the firm's shares unless investors attach a higher value to managers' presumed increased incentives to serve shareholder interests than they do to the reduction of shareholders' proportionate share of the residual claim. Furthermore, if the issuance to managers of bonus shares or stock options were to come from the corporation's treasury stock (*i.e.* shares held by the corporation which issued them), it would be at the expense of potential capital gains on such treasury stock which would have been earned if the same stock had been sold to investors [Machlup (1967), 20]. Thus, in order to bring about a reduction in managerial departures from maximization of stockholder wealth, shareholders would incur other costs. Incentive contracts for corporate management yield a net benefit to shareholders only if the above-mentioned costs of such contracts are less than shareholders' increased returns from greater coherence of managerial actions and stockholder wealth maximization that the incentive contract would accomplish.

Finally, the findings of Morck, Shleifer and Vishny [1988] discussed previously suggest that when stock bonuses or options cause managerial stock ownership to rise above 5 percent (but still being less than 25 percent), such bonuses enhance management's ability to pursue objectives other than maximization of stockholder wealth. In this event the issuance of stock bonuses (options) to management would be counterproductive from the shareholders' point of view.

Incentive contracts may also be costly to society at large in so far as their effect is to lower the sum of the state's revenue from corporate income taxes and private income taxes owed by corporate managers. Incentive contracts may reduce the corporation's income tax burden if corporate expenditure on such contracts is deductible from the corporation's taxable income under the applicable corporate income tax statute. Lower tax revenue to the state from corporate income taxes will not necessarily be offset by higher private income taxes for managers, since managers' private benefits from incentive contracts (for example, certain fringe benefits) may either escape taxation or be taxed at a lower rate than corporate profits. For instance, capital gains to managers from the exercise of stock option rights and subsequent stock sales may, wholly or partially, escape taxation under the private income tax statute.

Managers may deliberately seek to evade private income tax by having regular income substituted by income components from incentive contracts that enjoy more favorable tax treatment. When incentive contracts are employed as regular income substitutes so as to evade private income taxes, they reduce total tax revenue to the state (that means, to society as a whole), even if their impact on corporate income tax levels is neutral. Lower tax revenue means that society has fewer resources for investment in public goods or for other public expenditure. Moreover, if the state were to seek compensation for tax revenue losses resulting from the operation of incentive contracts for managers by adoption of higher general tax charges, the public at large is forced to subsidize managerial income and managers' use of tax evasion techniques.

If, for instance, stock options were to have private income tax advantages to managers compared with non-performance related income, such tax advantages would not merely create incentives for managers to have regular income replaced by stock options but they would also reward short-term management horizons. As stock options connect managers' time horizons to the expiry date of the option right, tax benefits associated with option rights would promote managerial decision-making for the short term. In the Netherlands, effective 1998 legislation has been introduced which both reduces the difference in private income tax treatment between regular income and income from stock options issued by corporations and opposes the shortening of time horizons as a result of option components in managers' income. According to this legislation, which applies to option rights awarded to managers and employees alike, the actual or estimated market value of any stock option awarded by the corporation is taxed as private income once the recipient becomes entitled to exercise the option and in addition, any income from the exercise or sale of option rights within a three year period after their issuance by the corporation is also subject to private income tax. Income from the sale or exercise of option rights realized *after* three years is, as before, exempted from taxation. This legislation limits managers' tax advantage from option income (as compared with ordinary income) to capital gains ensuing from the exercise of stock option rights realized at least three years after the option right was received and, thus, encourages managers to extend the time horizon of their decision-making beyond that period.

Limits of Competition in Factor Markets

Like competition in product markets, competition among firms to attract factors of production is unlikely to prevent deviations by corporate managements from maximization of stockholder wealth. Again, we do not deny that factor markets supply constraints on managerial discretion but they are unlikely to accomplish complete coherence of managerial actions with shareholder interests.

First, as conflicts of interests between managers and shareholders are common to all firms in which the management and risk-bearing functions are separate, managerial self-interest seeking is unlikely to harm any particular firm's ability to compete in factor markets, except where the size of a firm's agency costs is excessive in comparison with those of its competitors.

Second, competition among firms to acquire funds for investment in the assets of the business does not force management to *maximize* returns to stockholders but only demands that returns be kept at a level sufficient to content investors. To obtain funds for investment, investors must be compensated at a level that is satisfactory to them [Berle and Means (1991), 301]. Accordingly, in any firm, the management may seek to produce *minimum* returns acceptable to investors rather than maximum returns [Baumol (1967)]. Once managers have kept returns at a level acceptable to shareholders they may forgo possible extra returns to shareholders in order to pursue their own self-interests. Williamson [1986, 9] has defined profits exceeding the minimum level acceptable to shareholders as "discretionary profits", indicating that beyond the acceptable level managers have discretion to trade off profits in order to increase their personal utility.

Similarly, competition for loans does not require managers to maximize the value of cash flows but only to generate enough cash to pay the interest due and to repay the loan. To attract labor, raw materials and intermediate goods into the firm, it is only required that input owners be paid enough to ensure the continued supply of such inputs. Thus, pressure from factor markets will demand managers to use corporate resources to generate cash flows large enough to compensate shareholders, creditors, workers and other suppliers of inputs; it does not, however, require them to refrain from using corporate resources to further their personal interests.

Third, corporate managements may seek to attain independence from capital markets by accumulating excessive cash balances in the corporation's treasury [Jensen (1986); (1989)]. By retaining corporate earnings instead of distributing them to shareholders, managers create a source of discretion. Retained earnings which are not necessary to finance on-going business operations represent a source of funds which may quite easily be allocated to increase managers' utility rather than to maximize stockholder wealth. Conversely, distributions of cash to shareholders would reduce the amount of resources that managers control, thereby reducing the amount of corporate wealth they may use to benefit their own self-interest. As Jensen [1989, 66] has argued, although technically they can serve a competitive purpose, large balances of retained cash "often lead to waste and inefficiency".

In particular, when excess cash is piled up in the corporation's treasury, managers may finance new projects without having to go out to the capital markets to raise funds, which implies, without having to face the scrutiny of potential purchasers of stock should the project be financed through the sale of new shares, or the scrutiny of creditors should management attempt to borrow the required amount. In other words, financing projects internally avoids the monitoring by the financial markets which would occur should the firm have to raise new funds from external sources [Jensen (1986), 323]. Accordingly, managerial refusals to disgorge corporate cash to shareholders may be conceived of as attempts to insulate management from the discipline of the capital markets. When managers use retained cash for purposes yielding a lower return to shareholders than the latter would be able to achieve themselves if the money were paid out to them, shareholder interests are clearly harmed.

Limits of the Market for Corporate Control

As we discussed, the market for corporate control is identified as a major control mechanism inducing managers to behave consistently with stockholder interests. However, the operation of this market typically involves considerable transaction costs that may preclude transfers of corporate control to investors capable of reducing managerial deviations from maximization of stockholder wealth.

First, potential purchasers of corporate control need to obtain information in respect of the corporation concerned in order to determine whether they would gain by taking over control of the firm. The internal conditions of a firm, including management's performance, are neither widely known nor easy to discover, as Williamson [1986, 226] has noted, and the costs of obtaining sufficiently specific information to evaluate performance are non-trivial. True, when a corporation's existing management fails to operate the corporate firm in a way that maximizes the value of shareholders' residual claim, share prices in the stock market will reveal to outside investors potential capital gains from taking over that company and improving company management. But share prices *per se* do not disclose in what respects incumbent managers are deviating from value maximization (that is, what exactly is management doing wrong?) and how corporate performance could be improved to increase returns to shareholders (that is, where and how should the firm be revised?). Yet such information will be of vital importance to investors (and competing management teams) considering to acquire control of a company.

Second, to obtain control of a company, would-be buyers usually have to expend resources in raising the funds needed to finance a takeover, in convincing existing shareholders that they will be better off by selling their shares at the price the would-be buyer is prepared to pay, in assembling a superior management team and in installing mechanisms to ensure lasting improved managerial performance after the takeover bid has proved successful. Moreover, in a hostile takeover attempt, the bidder will also have to incur costs to overcome opposition from the target company's incumbent management against the takeover. Resistance by incumbent management against a takeover attempt is apt to raise the bidder's costs, as such resistance may both consume resources of the target company itself (through expenditures on defensive measures, including uses of corporate resources intended to reduce the bidder's returns from taking over the firm) and force the bidder to spend additional resources in order to overcome managerial defensive tactics [Easterbrook and Fischel (1981), 1175]. All such costs may diminish net potential wealth gains from acquiring control of a particular firm, thereby reducing the probability of a takeover.

In brief, the transaction costs involved in takeovers include both the costs of acquiring information on the prospective target and the costs of effecting and implementing the desired transfer of corporate control. Costs need also be incurred in evaluating the prevailing market price of the firm's shares and in establishing an appropriate bidding price at which a takeover bid would likely be both successful and profitable to the bidder. To obtain the requisite information, a would-be bidder usually needs to hire the costly services of a variety of consultants that may include investment analysts, industry experts, specialists in corporate restructurings and corporate finance experts.

If the information reveals a potential wealth increase from assumption of control of the contemplated target firm, prior to a corporate control transaction further resources usually need be expended in preparing the takeover bid, negotiating with relevant parties such as target company management, trade unions and existing block owners, and in surmounting legal impediments (for example, antitrust legislation). This process of accomplishing the desired takeover also tends to involve the engagement of expensive consultants, for example, investment bankers, lawyers and consultants on investor and media relations.

Finally, transaction costs could also arise from litigation following, or preceding, a corporate control transaction or a takeover attempt (for example, litigation between the bidder and the target company's management or between members of the bidding coalition). The presence of such transaction costs means that the theatre of the market for corporate control is rather noisy [Scherer (1988b), 80]; it is *not* a quiet, Coasian environment in which transactions occur readily and smoothly, and the noise (the transaction costs) may absorb all or part of the pleasure (the desired private wealth improvement) which the visitors to the theatre seek to enjoy. According to Robert Smiley's estimate, based upon empirical research of takeover activity in the United States, the average per share transaction costs of a tender offer, probably the most common device to pursue a takeover attempt, amount to at least 13 percent of the market price of the shares after the offer [Smiley (1976), 30].

Only when the potential capital gains inherent in the corporation's shares are large enough to offset the transaction costs attending a takeover, *i.e.* only when share prices signal large prospective wealth gains from providing improved management, is a takeover likely to take place. Indeed, incumbent management does not have to worry about displacement until the extent of its departures from value maximization exceeds the transaction costs facing prospective bidders for the corporation's stock plus the premium over the stock's prevailing market price such bidders would need to pay the existing shareholders in order to urge a transfer of corporate control. Taking into account transaction costs only, according to the above-mentioned estimate, this means that the possibility of a tender offer will pose a credible threat of displacement to incumbent managers solely if the prevailing stock market price reveals a potential capital gain from a control transfer of approximately 13 percent or more [Smiley (1976), 30]. Consequently, the threat of a takeover is likely to prevent solely *major* departures by corporate managers from maximization of stockholder wealth: because of the costs of a takeover, managerial malfeasance must be substantial before somebody will attempt to intervene.

As Eisenberg [1979, 137] has put it, "[t]he transaction costs of takeover bids are so high (...) that it is very difficult to oust an inefficient management with a takeover bid unless the management is so enormously inefficient as to justify these enormous transaction costs. Management can, therefore, sit around inefficiently and watch the market go down, and nothing can be easily done about it." Thus managerial departures from shareholders' interests that do harm investors, though not enough to offset the transaction costs of a takeover attempt, would escape discipline by the market for corporate control. In this way the effectiveness of the market for corporate control as a mechanism for disciplining corporate managers is limited. Given the transaction costs which it involves, Scherer [1988a, 54] has properly defined the market for corporate control as no more than a "last-resort mechanism (...) for constraining managers to serve stockholder interests".

In the previous section we saw that large retained cash balances insulate managers from disciplining by financial markets by making it unnecessary for them to attract funds from outsiders to invest in new ventures. However, as is often overlooked, excessive cash balances may also pervert the operation of the market for corporate control: they enable poorly run firms with large non-disgorged cash to acquire the shares in firms with a superior management that generate greater returns to investors and to take over control of such firms, instead of the other way round [Herman (1984), 536-538].

Poor managers of firms with excessive retained cash have an incentive to take over better managed firms: they can then offer to investors in the poorly run acquirer firm, the prospect of increased returns from the more effectively operated (*i.e.* more profitable) target company and so conceal their own weak performance from the acquiring firm's shareholders. Managers may also have other self-interested motives to buy in the market for corporate control, in particular, the desire to take charge of a larger firm or conglomerate (empire building) because of the higher managerial remuneration, fringe benefits, power and social prestige which tend to be associated with managing a larger firm or group of firms. In such cases, the operation of the market for corporate control will be counterproductive from the perspective of promoting effective shareholder-interested management: contrary to conventional theory, it will be *bad* management which drives out *good* management, not the opposite – a kind of Gresham's law for managers.

Limits of the Managerial Labor Market

Like the market for corporate control, the managerial labor market also faces substantial transaction costs. In order for the competition between managers to attract better jobs elsewhere to be effective, potential outside employers need to have accurate information about the comparative ability of these managers to advance the former's interests. In other words, they must know whether manager A will serve their interests better than manager B. Similarly, for the competition between managers within a firm's internal hierarchy to be effective, shareholders who have an interest in replacing underperforming top managers with more effective lower managers must have access to information about the comparative performance of individual managers. Equally, managers desiring to outperform other managers and to maximize the rental value of their human capital must also have information about the value placed on their services and those of competing managers by both the shareholders of the firm that currently employs them and by potential outside employers.

Earlier, we have argued that stock market prices contain information about managerial performance. Where the market value of a firm's shares is high compared to that of competing enterprises, stock prices indicate that management is successful in advancing stockholder interests. However, as indicated, stock prices contain information about the performance of a firm's management *team* but they do not reveal specific information about the performance of *individual* managers. It is precisely such specific, individual information that is relevant to the operation of competitive managerial labor markets both within and outside the firm.

In general, obtaining specific information about the performance and talents of individual (would-be) managers is costly. Head-hunting agencies perform a function in disclosing such information to potential employers outside the firm. However, such information is not freely available to the players in managerial labor markets either inside or outside the firm. The cost of feeding information about individual managers' performance and abilities into managerial labor markets is a threshold to effective labor market discipline. Where such costs are prohibitive, pressure from managerial labor markets is unlikely to eliminate managerial departures from stockholder interests.

Information about a manager's human capital suffers both from an adverse selection problem and from a moral hazard problem. There is an adverse selection problem in that information regarding a manager's past performance does not necessarily provide accurate information about his ability to perform well in a new job or company. A manager may have been quite successful in his current job but a promotion to a more demanding job or to another firm may simply be a step too far. Thus, although a manager's performance record may suggest that he will be a valuable asset to another company, the task of managing that other company may turn out to be beyond his level of competency. Such adverse selection problems arise because it may, and often will, be prohibitively costly, if not completely impossible, to obtain complete and accurate *ex ante* information about a manager's ability to be successful in a new job or firm. The difficulty and cost of selecting value-maximizing managers will be encountered by any firm.

There is also a potential moral hazard problem given that following appointment a manager may change his behavior to the detriment of the shareholders of the firm. He may, for example, shirk more or appropriate a larger amount of corporate resources through on-the-job consumption than he would have done before. The very fact that he has been hired may change the manager's performance incentives, and this could invalidate the evaluations upon which the firm and its shareholders relied when they decided to hire him. Whilst the adverse selection problem cited above has its origin in the cost of assessing a manager's current (*i.e.* pre-contractual) human capital, the moral hazard problem arises because of the difficulty in obtaining accurate information about a manager's postcontractual behavior.

In particular, once a manager has achieved his "dream job" or his expected final appointment (end-of-career job), he may shirk the maximization of stockholder wealth even though he may have properly served stockholder interests in his previous appointments. He may do so because labor market discipline operates through the incorporation of a manager's *past* performance in the calculation of the rental value of his human capital, as Fama [1980, 292] has explained, and when a manager is no longer in the market for a new job, he is likely to be rather insensitive to the deterioration of his labor market value: he will not face *ex post* settling up by the labor market for deviations from stockholder interests.

Fama [1980, 296] argues that "(r)ational managerial labor markets understand any shortcomings of available mechanisms for enforcing *ex post* settling up. Assessments of *ex post* deviations from contract will be incorporated into contracts on an *ex ante* basis; for example, through an adjustment of the manager's wage". However, a manager's *actual* postcontractual deviations from stockholder interests may be larger than the anticipated size of such deviations that is reflected in the *ex ante* reduction of his contractual compensation. A contract which from an *ex ante* perspective appears to adequately incorporate future managerial shirking may prove to be inadequate *ex post*. And when a manager anticipates that the rental value of his human capital will decrease by less than the benefit to him of current on-the-job consumption, *ex post* settling up through deterioration of his labor market value will be insufficient to offset his incentive to maximize his personal utility at shareholders' expense. As *any* manager may shirk the promotion of shareholder interests once he has been hired, regardless of his past performance as reflected in the labor market value of his human capital, and as *any* potential employer will face similar difficulties in anticipating a manager's postcontractual behavior, labor market competition is unlikely to resolve the moral hazard problem.

5. THE QUEST FOR REMEDIES: MARKETS, MONITORING AND MANAGERIAL LIABILITY

OUR DISCUSSION IN Chapter 4 reveals that the various market mechanisms operating to discipline corporate managers do not perfectly align managers' utility-maximizing interests with shareholders' wealth-maximizing interests. Neither competition in product and factor markets (including capital markets), nor competition in the markets for corporate control and managerial labor, nor incentive contracts related to firm performance eliminate the conflict of interests between managers and shareholders. All of these mechanisms leave managers at least some discretion to use their positions to maximize personal utility rather than to enhance shareholder wealth.

The question posed in the introduction to the preceding chapter, namely whether managerial self-interest seeking at shareholders' expense is inherent in the concept of the corporation, must therefore be answered in the affirmative. The various disciplinary mechanisms discussed earlier *mitigate* managerial divergences from shareholders' wealth-maximizing interests but do not *eliminate* such divergences.

We reiterate that managerial departures from the maximization of the value of the residual claim do not merely represent a cost to shareholders but also to society as a whole: such departures threaten the allocation of scarce resources to their most valued uses, discourage investors from pooling investment capital in corporations, reduce the likelihood of investors exploiting the benefits of specialized management, raise the operational costs of the corporate firm, and raise the prices consumers will have to pay for the firm's output. Managerial self-interest seeking increases managers' private utility while generating extra costs (agency costs) to the firm without creating extra income to compensate, and this is reflected in lower returns to investors, fewer investments, higher prices to consumers and lower output levels.

In the present chapter we look closer into three major forces that could be promoted to remedy the problem of managers pursuing objectives irreconcilable with stockholder wealth maximization and, thus, to reduce agency costs: (i) the market, particularly the markets for managerial labor, corporate control and investment capital, (ii) the monitoring of managerial behavior by the shareholders, and (iii) a legal rule imposing personal liability on managers for deviations from shareholders' wealth-maximizing interests. On our way, we will see that it is unlikely that a single remedy could be identified capable of ensuring more or less complete coherence of managerial actions with stockholders' interests in a cost-effective manner and that, hence, the best solution might be found in an attempt to combine the merits of the alternative remedies available.

Facilitating Market Mechanisms

As a preliminary observation, when discussing possible remedies to the problem of managerial aberrations, it should be noted that the prevalence of agency costs does not in itself mean that there is a problem in corporate governance that needs to be remedied. Such a conclusion would follow only if the administrative costs of introducing measures to reduce agency costs were less than the agency cost reduction achieved and if such measures would not involve socially undesirable side-effects offsetting the benefit of less agency costs. Thus, the relevant measure of comparison is not zero or less agency costs (the "ideal" norm) but the relative costs and benefits of potential alternative arrangements devised to limit managerial deviations from value maximization [Demsetz (1969), 1; Jensen and Meckling (1976), 328; Fischel (1982), 1265]. The test of any proposed remedy, therefore, is not whether it reduces agency costs, but its test is in the proposed remedy's own costs and benefits in comparison with present arrangements.

Alternatively, one may be tempted to argue that, at least from the perspective of investors, agency costs do not pose a problem requiring remedy because investors will only incur such costs if their expected gain from having specialized managers is large enough to outweigh such costs, and because anticipated agency costs are discounted in the share prices investors pay [Jensen and Meckling (1976), 313; Fischel (1982), 1266]. According to this reasoning, investors fully understand and accept the cost of managerial self-interest seeking at their expense and treat this cost as any other cost, thus it being reflected in the price investors are willing to pay for a share. Following this theory, managerial departures from shareholders' wealth-maximizing interests would not in fact constitute an injury to the shareholders. We find this idea unconvincing for several reasons.

The theory that managers' *ex post* deviations from shareholders' interests are anticipated by investors and capitalized in share prices *ex ante*, assumes that investors have full and complete information about such future deviations. This is unlikely to be the case, for the same reasons that render it unlikely that the managerial labor market will perfectly align managers' incentives with shareholders' interests. A manager's past track record may provide some information but does not contain full information about his behavior in the future. Moreover, high transaction costs, including high search and information costs, may preclude investors from obtaining proper information about a manager's past record. There is a moral hazard problem, too, because once appointed to the job, a manager may decide to pursue his personal self-interests to a larger extent than before, and so impose larger than anticipated costs on the shareholders.

Furthermore, the argument that shareholders anticipate and accept the aberrant activities of managers overlooks the fact that investors entrust the management of the firm to hired managers or purchase shares in a corporation directed by hired managers, only *given that* there are in existence certain limitations upon managers' ability to pursue self-interests to the detriment of the shareholders. These limitations do not merely ensue from the operation of the disciplinary market forces discussed in the preceding chapter, but also from existing legal restrictions to managers' discretion to consume corporate resources in the pursuit of personal utility; we will discuss such restrictions in Chapter 6. Shareholders' investment decisions will also take into account the fact that they can protect themselves from exploitation by self-interested managers by selling their shares or by ousting the management (assuming that the shareholders' voting rights include the power to do so). Any such limitations on shareholders' potential losses from managerial self-interest seeking will also be reflected in share prices. Clark [1985, 78] acknowledges the same point, stating that "market prices in an efficient market will embody expectations, not only about managerial taking of "secret profits", but also about stockholder rights to a remedy when any particular manager is caught".

The theory that agency costs do not pose a problem as such costs are anticipated in share prices is a weak one because share prices also reflect existing remedies for reducing such costs, including legal rules. The more efficacious are such remedies, the lower the agency costs reflected in share prices and vice versa. Given the relevance of remedies, one cannot conclude merely from the assumption that agency costs are incorporated in the price of shares, that such costs do not harm shareholders. If there were no restrictions to managers' ability to use their positions and shareholders' invested wealth to maximize private utility, shareholders would have to spend larger amounts in monitoring the management to prevent such managerial departures from value maximization. The larger such monitoring expenditure and the larger shareholders' anticipated losses from managerial self-interest seeking, the lower the price any one investor will be prepared to pay for a share and the fewer funds the firm can raise through the sale of equity shares.

Finally, even if investors were to correctly anticipate agency costs and take them for granted, the level of agency costs might still be undesirable from the perspective of society. High agency costs resulting in high operational costs of firms in corporate form and entailing the adverse effects previously described, may be undesirable to society at large even if there were no injury to investors. Thus there might still be a social problem waiting to be addressed. Yet as indicated, there is a need for remedy only if a reduction in agency costs can be achieved without undesirable side-effects that absorb the social benefit of that reduction.

What legal remedies do, or may, complement, in a cost-effective manner, the market mechanisms that operate to mitigate divergences of interests between shareholders and managers?

There are various methods through which the law may seek to mitigate divergences of interests in principal-agent relationships: through conferring rights on the principal entitling him to control and discipline the agent's conduct, through regulation constraining the agent's behavior, through rules designed to feed information into market mechanisms exercising disciplinary power over the agent, through imposing liability on the agent for injury to the principal, through exit rules enabling the principal to readily opt out of the agency relationship, or through combinations of such devices. Exit rules complement other disciplining mechanisms in that they enable the principal to terminate his exposure to the agent's actions should the other mechanisms fail to properly align the agent's behavior with the principal's interests.

All such devices are reflections of contractual arrangements which might arise if the principal and the agent could bargain without transaction cost impediments. The agent no less than the principal has incentives to enter into arrangements devised to reduce the latter's costs from divergences of interests [Jensen and Meckling (1976), 308]. On the assumption that the principal would discount future departures from his interests in the agent's remuneration package, if the principal were to anticipate greater departures than the agent desired or expected to be able to realize, the agent would incur a net utility loss. In addition, if the agent *ex post* were to impose a larger cost on the principal than the latter had expected *ex ante*, the principal would have a clear incentive to dismiss the agent to avoid further losses. Finally, if the principal *ex ante* expects the would-be agent to impose indefinite costs on the principal by self-interested actions, there would be no job at all for the agent.

In the context of the relationship between shareholders and managers, the law may seek to diminish agency costs in essentially three ways: by facilitating the operation of disciplinary market forces, by strengthening shareholders' control of the management of corporate resources, thus increasing their practical ability to monitor, and by imposing personal liability on managers for losses sustained by the shareholders as a result of a manager's departures from their interests. Any such rules would establish, or enhance, incentives for managers to maximize the value of shareholders' residual claim. Let us look into the cited potential legal remedies a little closer, beginning with rules facilitating the operation of market mechanisms disciplining managers.

Rules compelling corporations to disclose periodically certain financial and performance-related information furnish the market for corporate control, the managerial labor market and factor markets with information on management's performance. (Such disclosure requirements are contained, for instance, in Section 16.20 of the Model Business Corporation Act and in Chapter 9 of the Second Book of the Dutch Civil Code, both of which provide that corporations must disclose annual financial statements, including a balance sheet and an income statement.) Compulsory disclosure rules should assure that, in Eisenberg's words [1979, 136], "reliable, comparable, and objective information (...) concerning top managements' economic performance" becomes available to market disciplinary forces.

If the disclosed figures reveal that the firm performed poorly relative to its competitors, a fall in the relative price of the firm's shares in the stock market will signal to investors that wealth gains may be realized by replacing the incumbent management through a takeover of the firm's stock. Moreover, figures revealing relatively poor performance and subsequent price depreciation in the market for the firm's shares will decrease the value of management's human capital in managerial labor markets. Such figures will also inform factor owners, including banks and other professional lenders, that extending credit to the firm in question becomes more risky and that, therefore, they should adjust interest rates or restrict credit. Similarly, disclosure of data indicating weak performance relative to that of competitors will reduce the price investors will be prepared to pay for new share issues and, thus, lower the amount the firm can raise through the sale of equity shares. This would increase the firm's cost of capital relative to that of better managed competitors, which in turn would, again, have a downward effect on the firm's stock prices. In all these ways, information disclosure requirements facilitate the operation of market mechanisms disciplining managers and inducing them to adhere to shareholders' interests.

Managers, of course, realize that disclosure of financial figures revealing relatively poor performance will have the above-mentioned effects. In order to avoid decreases in the labor market value of their human capital and in order to prevent the firm from becoming a takeover target which may cost them their job, managers have incentives to manipulate financial figures in order to make the firm's financial statements present a more favorable picture of the firm's performance than is actually the case. Legal requirements that the firm's annual balance sheet and income statement be verified by an independent auditor serve to counter such incentives. However, audit requirements would lose much of their force if the auditor were dependent upon the incumbent management for his engagement. We agree with Eisenberg [1979, 138] that the right to hire and fire the independent auditor should belong to the shareholders, for they have loss-minimizing incentives to insist on accurate, reliable data concerning firm performance. (Indeed, Section 2:393 (2) of the Dutch Civil Code, for instance, puts the body of the shareholders in charge of engaging and removing the auditor.)

Disclosure of data concerning the remuneration packages which top managers receive from the corporation also feeds information into the market mechanisms disciplining corporate management. Disclosure of such data enables outsiders to review whether the price of the top managers to the firm is justified by their performance. If the managers' performance, as measured by the performance of the firm relative to its competitors, is not worth the price they charge the firm, not only will existing shareholders have incentives to reduce the managers' remuneration or replace incumbents by less expensive substitutes but also their labor market value will be less than their current value inside the firm. If the labor market value of a manager's human capital, that is, his future income stream, falls below his current income, there will be *ex post* settling up for current excessive wages should the manager move to another firm; thus the labor market would fine him by decreasing his perspectives for future wealth improvements. Moreover, if disclosed data concerning managers' remuneration show that payments to management are excessive in relation to the firm's performance, the data will inform investors in the market for corporate control that wealth gains are available through the takeover of that firm and the displacement of the management. Finally, excessive wages will signal to capital markets that lending to or purchasing shares in the firm in question is risky as the firm uses excessive funds to pay its management rather than to finance productive activity generating income to pay creditors and shareholders. Such information would raise the firm's cost of capital, triggering a downward effect on stock prices.

Labor market discipline would be strongest if remuneration data were disclosed for individual top managers, rather than for the firm's top management collectively without individualization, for it is the value of the manager's *individual* human capital that is measured in the labor markets disciplining him. Nevertheless, Section 2:383 of the Dutch Civil Code compels corporations to disclose in the annual financial statements, rewards to the "joint present and past" members of the management board and, separately, rewards to the "joint present and past" supervisory directors, without individualization, with the express exception that disclosure is not required if it would reveal a single individual's remuneration (*i.e.* if the firm's management board consists of one manager only). To enhance the discipline of top managers by the labor market, we propose that Section 2:383 be amended to provide that corporations are to disclose the remuneration paid to the *individual* members of the management and supervisory boards in an unambiguous and clear manner (not mixing up payments to present and past functionaries). On several occasions in 1998, the Dutch Minister of Finance also publicly announced that publicly held corporations organized under Dutch law should be prepared to disclose the salaries of their individual top managers annually. In April 1999, the government announced it was to prepare new legislation to this effect; such legislation reportedly, however, would provide for disclosure only on an anonymous basis. Corporations would not be required to link the individual salaries to the names of their recipients as would be advisable from the perspective of feeding appropriate information into the market.

In addition to the disclosure requirements imposed on corporate entities, the market mechanisms disciplining managers may also be furnished with information pertaining to management's performance where shareholders have the right to inspect the administrative records of the corporation, including the accounting records. Section 16.02 of the Model Business Corporation Act confers such a right on the individual shareholders; this right does not have an equivalent in Dutch corporate law. (Instead, Dutch law confers on the shareholders the right during a shareholders' meeting to request and to receive full information on corporate affairs, except if "preponderant interests" of the corporation demand that such information be withheld from them; Section 2:107 (2) of the Civil Code.) However, shareholder inspections of corporate records may involve quite substantial transaction costs that may prevent appropriate information from becoming available to the markets.

Elaborate corporate disclosure requirements are a means to avoid such transaction costs as they render it unnecessary, or unprofitable, for individual shareholders to inspect the corporation's records. More generally, compulsory disclosure rules smooth the operation of the markets disciplining managerial behavior as they reduce the costs of collecting relevant information to the players active in these markets.

Exit Rules, Voting Rights and Market Discipline

Flexible exit rules, viz. shareholders' rights to sell their shares to any one purchaser, do not merely enable shareholders to prevent (further) injury from managers' aberrant activities by opting out of the agency relationship but such rules also enhance the operation of market mechanisms disciplining managers: dissatisfaction of shareholders with the incumbent management's performance will result in high exit numbers which in turn will drive down stock prices and cause prices to incorporate the selling shareholders' dissatisfaction with management's performance, thereby informing the market for corporate control, managerial labor markets and factor markets about shareholders' dissatisfaction.

Yet both state corporation statutes in the United States and Dutch corporate law contain or prescribe restrictions on the free transferability of shares in statutory *close* corporations (see Subchapter B of the Model Statutory Close Corporation Supplement to the Model Business Corporation Act and Section 2:195 of the Dutch Civil Code). In addition, Section 2:87 (1) of the Dutch Civil Code provides that the articles of incorporation of publicly held corporations, too, *may* place restrictions on the transferability of registered shares (not on the transferability of bearer shares), save that such restrictions may not render share transfers actually or virtually impossible.

Any restrictions on share transferability interfere with the free exit principle and its above-mentioned beneficial effects. In particular, such restrictions thwart the operation of the market for corporate control. Still, the mere survival of restrictions on share transferability suggests that they *must* have an economic rationale: wealth maximizing investors will only choose to incorporate a business in an organizational form imposing restrictions on share transfers or invest in a business operated in such a form, if they attach a positive value to such restrictions, exceeding the value they associate with free exit and with disciplining of managers by and potential wealth gains from rapidly selling in, the market for corporate control.

Our hypothesis concerning the source of the potential positive value of transfer restrictions to investors is that in corporations with transfer restrictions (usually closely held corporations, with a fairly small number of shareholders who normally also form the management), the value of any one investor's shareholding is determined in part by his relationship with the specific other shareholders of the corporation. (Indeed, that hypothesis borrows from the asset-specificity theory of the firm described in Chapter 1.) It is rational for investors to opt for an organizational form with exit restrictions if they have human capital assets complementary to their equity investment which are specialized with respect to each other, so that the value of each investor's part of the residual claim becomes mutually dependent upon his relationship with the other investors. Thus, if the individual shareholders were free to sell their shares to random buyers, they would unilaterally deprive the remaining shareholders of the relationship-specific component of the value of *their* shares (*i.e.* the quasi-rental value of their investment). Transfer restrictions are a means to preserve that value (and the resulting rents) for the remaining shareholders. Assuming that the restrictions will not fully impede a transfer, they also serve to preserve that value for shareholders desirous to exit, for the latter have wealth-maximizing incentives to overcome the given restrictions only if the price of a share transfer would capitalize the relationship-specific value of their investment.

Easterbrook and Fischel [1986, 273, 278] have associated the existence of restrictions on the alienability of shares in close corporations with a perceived need to ensure compatibility between individual investors, given that in this class of corporations, the investors usually also are the firm's managers. Transfer restrictions, then, would serve both to keep out investors whose views are incompatible with those of the existing shareholder-managers and, within the firm, to encourage agreement of interests and conduct among the latter by encouraging them to act in a cooperative manner. In addition, Easterbrook and Fischel submit that once it is agreed to distribute a part of the firm's profits as salary, rather than as dividend, to the shareholders in their capacity as managers, transfer restrictions will serve to preserve the agreed-upon division of profits. Compatibility between the various shareholder-managers would seem to be a prerequisite to the procreation and survival of relationship-specific investment value where investors have human capital assets specializing with respect to each other. The same applies to arrangements on the division of (quasi-)rents derived from such relationship-specificity. Thus, both observations cited above illustrate more the presence of relationship-specific investment value (and thus confirm our above-mentioned hypothesis), rather than offer a competitive explanation of restraints on share alienability.

For the same reason (the preservation of relationship-specific investment value), restrictions on share transfers should not and, under the aforementioned United States and Dutch corporate laws, generally do not render a transfer entirely impossible. Rigid prohibitions on sale would render equity investors in a corporation hostage to each other (a hold-up potential would be created), exposing them to the risk of post-investment opportunistic behavior by fellow investors which may destroy the relationship-specific value of each investor's shareholding. In addition, as discussed in Chapter 3, if share transfers were made impossible, any investor would risk relationship-*un*specific opportunity losses by being unable to move his invested wealth to alternative uses. Both risks would make investment unattractive and lower the value of the investment, including its relationship-specific component, to any prospective investor. Exit *prohibitions*, thus, would be counterproductive from the perspective of maintaining investment value.

The operation of a market for corporate control disciplining corporate managements, requires that, in addition to the right for shareholders to transfer their shares, voting rights are tied to shares and shareholder voting rights include the right to oust the corporation's incumbent top management and to appoint new managers (or supervisory directors, who in turn appoint a new management, as in the United States governance model). However, not only the transferability of shares but also voting rights, or their effective use by the shareholders, may be restricted. Voting rights may be restricted, in particular, in United States jurisdictions, by placing shares in a voting trust (Section 7.30 of the Model Business Corporation Act) and, under Dutch law, by technically separating rights to receive dividends and other corporate distributions (and certain other shareholder rights) from the shares to which they were originally attached, issuing such separated "dividend rights" to the original shareholders (as "bearer depositary receipts") and assigning legal title to the shares *per se*, including the voting rights attached to them, to a distinct legal entity (which is usually controlled indirectly by the management of the corporation which issued the shares). If shareholders voluntarily choose to have their voting rights restricted, that choice implies that they rely on mechanisms for inducing management to maximize the value of the residual claim other than the market for corporate control.

Such a choice is rationally understandable if the percentage of total votes which a shareholder's shares carry and, thus, that shareholder's ability to influence the management through voting, is so small that the transaction costs of using his voting right (including the costs of information gathering and the costs of forming a shareholders' coalition with bargaining power with respect to the management) would be larger than the benefit the shareholder expects from casting a vote. Similarly, Jarrell, Brickley and Netter [1988, 59] note that "[i]n general, a shareholder with a small amount of shares will not invest heavily in the voting process since a small number of shares will not generally affect the outcome regardless of how they are voted"; then it simply does not pay to bother about voting. Hence, the corporation's management may easily succeed in convincing a small shareholder that the voting right's actual value to him is zero when taking into account his ability to influence the management through voting, although the same voting right would have positive value in the market for corporate control. Moreover, the costs a small shareholder would have to incur in order to *avoid* being stripped of his voting right or to preclude the emergence of other impediments (takeover defenses) to the smooth operation of the market for corporate control in respect of the firm's shares, may be prohibitively high.

The fact that the right to vote does have a positive value in the market for corporate control, separate from the value of the residual claim on assets and cash flows to which it is attached, was first recognized by Manne [1964, 1430]. The same fact has been confirmed, *inter alia*, by the empirical study conducted by Lease, McConnell and Mikkelson [1983] and by the findings surveyed by Jarrell, Brickley and Netter [1988, 60-61]. The latter conclude from the empirical evidence that "the market generally values shares with voting power more than those without" [1988, 60]. The positive value of the right to vote is acknowledged in the listing requirements of the Amsterdam stock exchange which, albeit subject to important restrictions, confer certain rights on holders of listed non-voting dividend rights created in the manner described above to regain the voting right from the entity nominally owning the relevant share (Section 5 of Exhibit 10 to the listing rules). (Note that approximately 30 percent of the companies listed on the Amsterdam stock exchange, excluding investment funds, have non-voting dividend rights traded at the exchange.)

So far we have assumed that the shareholders' right to vote includes the right to vote on the appointment and dismissal of the corporation's top management and, thus, that this condition for operation of a market for corporate control is fulfilled. That assumption is correct with respect to United States jurisdictions following the Model Business Corporation Act, Sections 8.03 (d), 8.04 and 8.08 of which make it clear that the shareholders are entitled to elect and to remove the corporation's directors; the directors in turn appoint the officers in charge of the day-to-day management of the corporate firm.

According to Dutch corporate law, in most corporations both the members of the management board and (two-thirds or more of) the members of the supervisory board are appointed and removed by the shareholders (Sections 2:132, 2:134 (1), 2:142 (1), 2:143 and 2:144 (1) of the Dutch Civil Code).

However, there is an important exception (known in Dutch as the "*structuurregeling*"): in corporations satisfying certain statutorily defined quantitative criteria (summarized below), the right to appoint and to remove the members of the management board is mandatorily bestowed on the supervisory directors (Section 2:162 of the Civil Code). In addition, except for the supervisory directors appointed at the corporation's (or the supervisory board's) inception, in this class of corporations the supervisory directors are not appointed by the shareholders but by the existing supervisory directors as a body (Section 2:158 (2) of the Civil Code). Thus, the shareholders are deprived of the right to designate the management of the corporation; that right is statutorily shifted to the supervisory directors, and the existing supervisory directors fill in vacancies in the supervisory board through co-optation. Furthermore, the supervisory board's approval is required for many decisions of the management board (as prescribed in Section 2:164 (1) of the Civil Code), primarily concerning investment and organizational matters and the issue or repurchase of shares and bonds. This governance structure applies to over 60 percent (!) of the companies listed on the Amsterdam stock exchange, excluding listed investment funds. As a consequence of this governance structure, incumbent managers and supervisory directors are to a significant extent insulated from the discipline of the market for corporate control because someone acquiring a voting majority of the firm's shares still has no right to remove them.

In the governance structure described above, shareholders' rights to influence the composition of the supervisory board are limited to the right to make non-binding recommendations of candidates for vacancies in the supervisory board (Section 2:158 (4) Civil Code) and the right to raise objections, on narrow statutory grounds only, against the appointment of individuals whom the existing supervisory directors desire to appoint to the supervisory board (Section 2:158 (6) Civil Code). In the latter event, the supervisory board may take the issue to court in order to enforce its choice of candidate upon the shareholders and the corporation (Section 2:158 (9) Civil Code). Shareholders do not have similar, or other, rights to influence the appointment of members of the *management* board by the supervisory directors.

A corporation becomes mandatorily subject to the above-mentioned governance structure if during an uninterrupted period of three years beforehand, it has satisfied each of the following requirements (Section 2:153 (2) Civil Code): (i) stockholders' equity, inclusive of the reserves stated on the corporation's balance sheet, has amounted to NLG 25 million or more, (ii) the corporation together with its subsidiaries has employed at least one hundred employees in the Netherlands, and (iii) the corporation or a subsidiary has established a works council as prescribed by the Works Council Act (pursuant to Section 2 (1) of the Works Council Act, a corporation must have a works council if it employs either at least one hundred employees, irrespective of the number of hours they work, or at least thirty-five employees for more than one-third of the ordinary working time). As soon as a corporation meets the cited criteria, it must notify the Chamber of Commerce where it is registered (Section 2:153 (1) of the Civil Code). The governance structure under which the supervisory directors appoint both the members of the management board and the members of the supervisory board itself, will then become automatically effective three years after the date of the notification, unless the corporation has previously notified the relevant Chamber of Commerce that the aforesaid criteria are no longer fulfilled (Section 2:154 (1) of the Civil Code).

However, certain exemptions and exceptions exist (which are essentially irrelevant for the purpose of our discussion); for instance, a corporation satisfying the above-mentioned criteria is nonetheless exempt from the special governance structure if at least 50 percent of its shares are owned by another corporation which is subject to this structure, or if its sole business is that of a "holding company", *i.e.* to hold the shares in and to provide financing to affiliated corporations, provided that the majority of the corporate group's employees is employed outside the Netherlands (Section 2:153 (3) (a) and (b) of the Civil Code). In addition, the shareholders of a corporation subject to the special governance structure maintain the right to appoint and remove the members of the management board (but not those of the supervisory board, who are appointed by the existing supervisory directors as described) if, in brief, at least 50 percent of the firm's shares are owned by another corporation regardless of its governance structure and if more than 50 percent of the corporate group's employees work outside the Netherlands (Section 2:155 Civil Code). Furthermore, it is of note that corporations which are not mandatorily subject to the special governance structure may voluntarily adopt this same structure, with or without the exception according to which the management is elected by the shareholders and not by the supervisory board (Section 2:157 of the Civil Code).

In its pure form, as noted, the above-mentioned governance structure relieves managers and supervisory directors from the discipline of the market for corporate control as it denies shareholders the right to change the composition of the management and supervisory boards; thus, this governance structure largely prevents the effective operation of such a market with regard to the corporation concerned. Although in itself, it does not prevent the acquisition of the corporation's shares (or a voting majority thereof), potential buyers are unlikely to perceive wealth gains from acquiring those shares if the market value of the shares were to reveal to them that wealth gains are attainable from improved management, given that after a takeover they still lack the legal power to easily displace an existing ineffective management and take over control of the management and the affairs of the firm. Even if as a result of another corporation acquiring the majority of the shares, an exemption or exception as referred to above would apply, meaning that the right to determine the composition of the management board would no longer mandatorily have to be bestowed on the supervisory directors, in order for that right to be shifted to the shareholders, an amendment of the corporation's articles of association to this effect would be required. The incumbent management (supported by incumbent supervisory directors) may refuse to implement such an amendment so that, at least for the time being, the special governance structure would continue to apply on a "voluntary" basis (in accordance with Section 2:157 of the Civil Code) [Maeijer (1994), 516-517].

Thus, the statutory governance structure under which the members of the management board are appointed by the supervisory board, which also fills in its own vacancies, and the firm's consequent isolation from the market for corporate control, creates a rather safe haven for utility maximizing managers who fail to maximize the value of shareholders' residual claim and for like minded supervisory directors who back them. Consistent with this observation, a recent study by Dutch economists Van der Goot and Van het Kaar [1997] reports that the above-mentioned governance structure has a significant negative impact on the market value of the shares of newly listed companies on the Amsterdam stock exchange that are subject to this structure, both at the time of their initial listing and at various points in the subsequent year. This study encompassed a total of seventy-four corporations (not including investment funds) that were first listed on the Amsterdam exchange between 1983 and 1992, thirty-one of which were subject to the special governance structure (that is, 42 percent).

According to the findings of Van der Goot and Van het Kaar [1997, 501], firms endowed with the special governance structure had on average a price-earnings ratio of 11.8 at their first listing, whereas firms without showed a significantly higher average price-earnings ratio of 16.5. Moreover, the average market-to-book ratio of firms with the special structure was found to be 3.2 at first listing, with a market-to-book ratio of 7.7 (!) for other firms [1997, 501]. These values were obtained solely on the basis of a distinction between firms with the special governance structure and firms without, that is, with no regard being paid to other features that might divide these categories of firms.

Furthermore, at subsequent points in the course of one year following listing, the average stock market performance of the thirty-one firms with the special structure (measured in terms of percentage increase in stock price from the initial listing price discounted by the performance of the relevant market index) was found to be significantly worse than those of the forty-three firms without, especially when compared with firms without the special governance structure but which did have specific takeover defenses similar to those adopted by firms with the special structure on top of the latter (note, only six newly listed firms had no takeover protection at all) [Van der Goot and Van het Kaar (1997), 504]. This finding suggests that investors value the constraint on the discipline of management by the market for corporate control entailed by the special structure more negatively than that effected by specific takeover defenses. For example, six months after the date of first listing, firms without the special governance structure were found to have a market adjusted extra return of 5.3 percent as compared to firms with that structure. After one year, the extra return had even increased to an average 11.4 percent, a difference solely attributable to the special structure. Considering these figures, we are of the view that to enhance market discipline over corporate managers and supervisory directors, including those who have interests at heart irreconcilable with value maximization, it would seem to be in the interests of both the shareholders and society as a whole if Dutch corporate law returned the right to determine the composition of the management board and the supervisory board to the shareholders.

In terms of thwarting the operation of the market for corporate control, the effects of the criticized Dutch governance structure are similar to those of takeover defenses which enable incumbent top management to altogether prevent outsiders from obtaining a controlling (voting) majority of the corporation's shares. Such takeover defenses, too, relieve managers (and supervisory directors) from the discipline of the market for corporate control. Various survey studies of empirical research in the area report that shares experience a decline in market value in response to the adoption of takeover defenses by the corporation (especially if the defensive measures do not require majority voting approval by shareholders) [Jensen and Warner (1988); Jarrell, Brickley and Netter (1988); Easterbrook and Fischel (1991), 196-198]; see *supra* pages 159-160. In addition, the *rejection* by shareholders of management proposals to adopt defensive measures is reportedly accompanied by a rise in the stock market price of the firm's shares [Easterbrook and Fischel (1991), 197]. These findings confirm that in the perception of investors, managers of corporations who are subject to the threat of losing their jobs following a takeover are more likely to maximize the value of the residual claim than those who are not.

In November 1997, the Dutch government submitted a proposal to Parliament for enactment of legislation to limit the restraining effect of takeover defenses on the potentiality of corporate control transactions. According to the proposed legislation, a shareholder who owns at least 70 percent of the shares in a publicly held corporation, may petition the corporate law division of the appellate court of Amsterdam to take appropriate measures to eliminate the defenses which preclude that shareholder from obtaining active control of the management and the affairs of the company concerned. Yet a 70 percent shareholder will only be entitled to bring such a petition if he has owned the stated percentage for an uninterrupted period of at least one year prior to the petition's submission. The target corporation, that means, the incumbent management, will be given the right to object to the adoption of measures eliminating existing takeover defenses on the grounds that the intentions of the petitioner (*i.e.* the would-be acquirer of corporate control) are contrary to the interests of the firm or that the petitioner should be expected to act unreasonably or unfairly towards minority shareholders, incumbent managers, supervisory directors or the corporation itself upon seizing control of the firm. Before taking a decision on the petition and the objections raised against it, the court will have to appoint three experts to advise on the petitioner's intentions as regards future business management and future composition of the management board and the supervisory board. We support the object of the proposed legislation but we are afraid that, if adopted, it will prove all but dead wood in most cases.

The proposal breathes a rather remarkable ignorance of the notions (and the significance) of investment liquidity and opportunity costs. The proposed legislation requires a 70 percent shareholder to accept a one year lock-in period without actual control of the firm he is desiring to control before he may file a petition as described above. This lock-in period will be extended in fact by the term of the legal proceedings pertaining to the petition and last until the court has rendered its decision. During the statutory lock-in period, the shareholder may not exchange a single part of his 70 percent shareholding for cash without losing the right to bring a petition. Hence, he will be exposed to potential opportunity losses by being unable to shift all or a part of his invested wealth to alternative, more profitable investment opportunities which may show up during the lock-in term. He will also risk losses resulting from detrimental actions by the management of the target firm during that period. Temporary non-liquidity of investment and consequent opportunity losses are in addition to the purchase price of his shares in the firm concerned and so raise the cost of a takeover. Incumbent management may deliberately increase the 70 percent shareholder's opportunity costs, or utter credible threats to do so, by taking business decisions unfavorably affecting the value of the firm's shares during the lock-in period in order to raise his costs of taking over control of the firm and to attempt to fend-off the attack on their positions.

The litigation resulting from the right of the target firm's management to object in court to the petition for elimination of takeover defenses will further raise the would-be acquirer's costs, as will the court's review of the latter's intentions. The proposed legislation explicitly provides that the fees of the experts appointed by the court for the purpose of examining the petitioner's intentions, must be paid by the petitioner. All such costs will add to transaction costs in the market for corporate control as will error costs incurred if the court and the experts appointed by it, wrongly assess the intentions of the acquirer. The very notion that a court may review the intentions of a would-be acquirer of corporate control is nothing but a source of transaction costs, raising yet another hurdle to be surmounted by an investor desirous to take over control of a firm equipped with takeover defenses.

Finally, the Dutch government's proposal will not alter the special governance structure previously described under which shareholders are not entitled to elect or remove the management board and the supervisory board of certain statutorily prescribed corporations. (The proposal does, however, permit the court to eliminate that structure if it has been adopted on a voluntary basis.) Thus, for firms mandatorily subject to the cited governance regime, even if a would-be acquirer were able to have the court set aside (other) takeover defenses, he would still be subject to a governance structure in which he has no right to oust the existing management and supervisory board. As a consequence, he would be unable to take control of the management and the affairs of the business, in spite of his 70 percent share ownership. This means that the proposed new law will *not* enhance corporate control transactions in respect of firms mandatorily subject to the cited governance structure. All things considered, we are inclined to conclude that the Dutch proposal, if adopted, will establish a good example of mouthpiece legislation.

Strengthening Shareholders' Control

Is a larger say for shareholders in the management of corporate resources a desirable remedy against managerial departures from value maximization?

Suppose that shareholders had a right to interfere in corporate management so as to dictate specific managerial decisions, or that management needed the approval of the shareholders before they could have the corporation engage upon a particular course of action (for instance, enter into a transaction, make an investment). Such rules would strengthen shareholders' control of the management of the corporation, and reduce managers' discretion to allocate corporate resources so as to further their personal self-interests.

However, at the same time, they would raise the costs of corporate decision-making as shareholders would have to incur larger expenditure in monitoring intra-firm activity and market developments in order to review and to prepare for managerial decisions, and as the number of interactions necessary to take a business decision would increase. In addition, the corporation's ability to take commercial decisions in a speedy manner and to respond quickly to developments in relevant product and factor markets as and when appropriate, would suffer. Furthermore, as described in the monitorial model of the corporation discussed in Chapter 2, the shareholders have delegated the management of the firm to hired managers precisely because the latter have a comparative advantage in running the firm. Allowing shareholders to become actively involved in managerial decision-making would move management authority away from those having a comparative advantage in exercising it [McKean (1978), 89]. Finally, giving shareholders rights to interfere in corporate management would create similar shirking problems among dispersed shareholders as would arise if the shareholders themselves were to run the firm. In summary, the intended benefit of fewer divergences from value maximization would come at the expense of higher governance costs and presumably less effective corporate governance.

The above observations do not mean, of course, that *any* device designed to strengthen shareholders' control of the management of the corporation would have such effects. The search is, then, for devices that restrict managerial discretion without the above-mentioned side effects. Such a device could be, for instance, a right for a specified minority of the shareholders to call a special general meeting of shareholders in order to discuss one or more issues pertaining to the management of the corporation. (Such a right is set forth in Section 7.02 of the Model Business Corporation Act and, in a somewhat disguised form, in Section 2:110 of the Dutch Civil Code.) Additionally, the shareholders might be given the right to elect a committee of shareholders to which managers should account for contemplated business decisions on important issues, such issues to be defined in the corporation's articles of incorporation or bylaws (for example, investments exceeding a specified percentage of the worth of the firm's assets). Furthermore, a specified minority of the shareholders may be given the right to add issues to the agenda proposed by the management for the corporation's regular annual meeting of shareholders (for example, a past decision by the corporation's management with which that minority is dissatisfied or a proposal from the requisite minority for future corporate action). As the costs of invoking any of the suggested rights would ultimately come at the expense of the shareholders' return, wealth maximizing shareholders will use such rights only if the anticipated benefits (viz. the benefits from establishing extra incentives for management to be faithful to shareholders' interests) are large enough to outweigh these costs.

Earlier we referred to Jensen's observation that the retention of large amounts of cash in the corporation's treasury, limits the discipline which capital markets exercise over managers given that large retained cash balances permit managers to finance new projects without having to attract new funds from the capital markets, that is, without having to account for the project's wisdom and viability to suppliers of fresh capital [Jensen (1986), 323; (1989), 66]. We also argued that excessive cash balances may pervert the operation of the market for corporate control as they allow corporations with poor managements to take over superiorly run firms. Large cash balances increase the resources over which managers have discretion and are a source of agency costs; management may allocate excessive cash to uses which yield smaller returns to the shareholders than the latter could earn if the same amount were paid out to them. To prevent excessive retained cash balances and to enhance the disciplinary force of capital markets on management's expenditure, we propose that individual shareholders be given the right to challenge dividend proposals made by corporate management and to present rival dividend and other cash distribution proposals to the joint shareholders; the competing proposals should then be discussed and voted on during the corporation's annual meeting of shareholders.

Stock repurchase programs sponsored by corporations are a market-induced constraint on managers' ability to pile up cash within the corporation, which serves to curtail managers' independence from the capital markets. From the perspective of the enhancement of capital market disciplining, corporate stock repurchases practically are an alternative to direct distributions of cash to shareholders. Yet the income tax consequences of stock repurchases to the shareholders may be different from (and preferable to) those of direct cash pay-outs. Additionally, unlike direct cash distributions applicable to all shareholders, stock repurchase programs afford individual stockholders the choice to either maintain their shares and benefit from increased capital market discipline over corporate management, which should positively affect the market value of their shares, or to cash in on their stake of the corporation's aggregate resources and invest the proceeds elsewhere. To facilitate such programs as a means for enhancing market discipline on corporate managers, in our view, individual shareholders representing a specified minimum percentage of the corporation's total shares should be given the right to launch proposals to the joint shareholders to effect that excess cash in the corporation's treasury be used to repurchase outstanding stock.

As described in Chapter 2, the introduction of supervisory directors, too, is a mechanism for increasing managers' accountability to the shareholders, which economizes on the costs of direct monitoring by the individual shareholders and which takes advantage of specialization in monitor-monitoring. However, the supervisory directors will only perform such functions if *they* are sensitive to shareholders' wealth-maximizing interests. To tie supervisory directors to the shareholders' interests, the shareholders should not merely have the right to vote on the appointment and displacement of the supervisory directors but a specified minority of the shareholders should also have the right to nominate candidates for supervisory director positions to the joint shareholders, including the right to nominate rival candidates challenging the "official" nominees proposed on behalf of the corporation. To prevent the costs of such nominations from precluding the effective use of the nomination right, successful candidates nominated by the shareholders should have the right to reimbursement of their reasonable expenditure in the contest for a supervisory directorship out of the corporate treasury; unsuccessful candidates should not, because that would give rise to nominations solely intended to extort a payment from the corporation [Dooley (1978), 83].

Critical observers may object on the basis that, independent of reimbursements for expenses, free rider problems among multiple scattered shareholders would jeopardize the efficacy of shareholder nomination of and voting on the appointment of supervisory directors. Such problems might be avoided in part if stockholder associations (that is, coalitions assembling investors in different corporations) also be given the right to nominate candidates for one or more supervisory directorships in a corporation. In addition, it would be in the interests of the shareholders if *labor unions* be given the right to designate a supervisory director as the use of corporate resources to benefit incumbent managers rather than to generate income for the shareholders is as undesirable from the perspective of the workers as it is from that of the shareholders because it harms the firm's competitiveness in product and factor markets, makes the firm a target in the market for corporate control for takeover and subsequent restructuring, and reduces the firm's chances of survival. Therefore, with regard to opposition against the use of corporate resources to advance managers' private self-interests, the interests of the shareholders coincide with those of the workers, making them natural allies in this matter.

Managerial Liability for Shareholder Injuries

Making the agent liable for the costs of departures from the principal's interests obviously creates incentives for the agent to remain faithful to the interests of the principal and to give priority to the latter in the event of a collision with the agent's private interests. Personal liability of the agent also establishes a means for compensating the principal for the injury he would sustain should the agent nonetheless pursue personal utility at the expense of the principal. Thus, a rule imposing personal liability on the agent serves to reduce agency costs both from an *ex ante* perspective, by deterring aberrant activities of the agent, and *ex post*, by entitling the principal to compensation for residual losses.

Within the concept of the corporation, managers, as a rule, are not liable towards the shareholders or the corporation for the consequences of actions committed in the course of their employment. The above-mentioned reasoning suggests that within the shareholder-manager relationship, agency costs could be reduced if personal liability were imposed on managers for injury to the shareholders resulting from managerial departures from shareholders' wealth-maximizing interests. Personal liability would encourage managers to be faithful to the shareholders, *i.e.* to refrain from pursuing goals other than maximization of the value of their residual claim, and enable shareholders to recover residual losses ensuing from aberrant activities from the managers up to the extent of the latter's wealth. However, personal liability of managers would also create substantial costs for the shareholders and for society, both directly and indirectly.

Direct costs would arise because if they were subject to a risk of personal liability, in as far as they dislike risk, managers would not merely demand compensation for supplying their human capital to the firm but also for the liability risk borne [McKean (1978), 88]. The higher the perceived risk of personal liability, the higher the risk compensation component of managers' salaries. Managers are expensive risk bearers because unlike shareholders they cannot reduce risks through diversification: managers' potential for investing their human capital is generally limited to one or two firms and any human capital investment in another firm would raise, not reduce, their risk of becoming liable.

One may object on the basis that if the liability rule successfully creates incentives for managers to align managerial actions with shareholders' wealth-maximizing interests, as the rule is intended to do, the risk that liability will be imposed is not in practice significant: if the rule effectively induces managers to refrain from activities which may trigger liability, they will not have to fear *actual* liability. According to this theory, the wage premiums managers would demand to compensate them for the risk of personal liability would be rather small, so that the liability risk would *not* result in significantly higher salaries for managers.

However, this reasoning ignores the fact that under any liability rule, managers may fail to correctly anticipate which managerial actions will and which actions will not result in personal liability, and that under any liability rule managers may encounter substantial expenses in litigation. Courts may impose liability on the basis of an action that the defending manager considered safe at the outset. Managers will recognize such a risk and demand compensation for it in their remuneration packages. The provision of personal liability insurance at the corporation's expense could lower the amount of compensation demanded, but only at a cost: the amount of the insurance premium payable.

Moreover, any manager, including a manager who is perfectly faithful to the shareholders, may have to incur expenses in defending himself in an action for damages brought against him. Such litigation costs may well be significant as a rule providing for managerial liability creates a potential for "strike suits", primarily intended to extract a settlement from the defendant equal to the value of the nuisance the suit brings upon him. To save litigation expenses, a manager may choose to make a settlement payment rather than defend himself [Morgan (1978), 94]. Utility maximizing managers are likely to demand compensation from the corporation for any litigation-related expenditures, either *ex ante* through a higher salary or through a provision in their employment contract stipulating that the corporation will reimburse them for litigation expenses, including settlement payments, as and when they arise.

Furthermore, any liability suit, whether or not it is properly founded, may hurt a manager's reputation, thereby lowering the rental value of his human capital in the managerial labor market. The risk of loss of reputation ensuing from a rule providing for potential personal liability, too, is apt to raise the remuneration managers will demand from the corporation. Liability insurance coverage would not protect managers from reputation loss and would not therefore eliminate such compensation demands.

Apart from extra payments to management if managers were subject to a risk of personal liability, a rule providing for potential managerial liability would generate significant *indirect costs* for the shareholders and for society. First, on the assumption that certain individuals (especially risk averse persons) are unwilling to assume the risk of personal liability, such a rule would reduce the pool of managerial talent from which specialized managers may be recruited: the rule would deter able persons unwilling to bear the liability risk from becoming a manager [Eisenberg (1988), 39]. Thus, shareholders may have difficulty in finding competent managers to run the corporate firm who at the same time would assume a risk of personal liability. In effect, personal liability would impede materialization of the advantages associated with specialized management and hurt the efficacy of corporate management. In addition, if the supply of specialized managers decreases, the price of managerial services would rise, regardless even of wage premiums for the bearing of liability risk.

Second, a risk of personal liability would establish incentives for managers to allocate corporate resources so as to minimize the likelihood of liability rather than to maximize the value of shareholders' residual claim. To avoid personal liability, managers would be induced to exercise more care in preparing business decisions and to incur larger expenditure to avoid mistakes than would be desirable from the point of view of the shareholders [McKean (1978), 89]. Moreover, managers would be deterred from making investments in projects with positive net present values to the shareholders if they also expected such projects to carry a positive risk of managerial liability. Thus managers may allocate corporate resources to uses motivated by a desire to avoid liability rather than to enhance shareholder wealth and forgo investments generating positive returns to the shareholders, thereby creating opportunity losses for the shareholders. From this angle, introducing a rule subjecting managers to a risk of personal liability would give rise to problems of *over*-compliance [Chapman (1996)], with the rule's *actual* effects on managerial incentives being counterproductive when measured in terms of the rule's *desired* effect of greater consistency of managerial actions with shareholders' interests.

Note that potentially liable managers are more risk averse than shareholders with limited liability because the latter, unlike the managers, can diversify away any firm-specific risks, including the risk of errors by a firm's management, by holding a diversified investment portfolio. As Chapman [1996, 1688] has observed, shareholders will therefore be "relatively risk neutral with respect to the variable fortunes of any one corporation in their portfolio". Given that a manager's risk of personal liability, by contrast, is entirely dependent upon the specific corporation in which he has invested his human capital, managers are likely to be more risk averse than the shareholders [Fischel and Bradley (1986), 266; Chapman (1996), 1688]. Accordingly, they may pursue more cautious policies in managing the firm (for example, hire more external consultants, take out more insurance, install more intensive intra-corporate monitoring systems and so on) and adopt more defensive corporate investment strategies than would be preferable from the shareholders' perspective. Diversified shareholders, on the other hand, would want to "create incentives for managers to accept all positive net present value projects, even those that are risky" [Fischel and Bradley (1986), 266].

Third, unless the liability rule would bring about the desired reduction in agency costs and such a reduction would *not* be outweighed by the rule's direct and indirect costs to the shareholders described above, payments to compensate management for the liability risk borne and for litigation costs and opportunity losses resulting from over-cautious management would decrease returns to shareholders and, hence, the price a shareholder would be willing to pay for a share. In addition, share prices would also incorporate the litigation costs *shareholders* would need to incur to enforce personal liability on the management as and when appropriate. The consequent share price reductions would harm the firm's ability to raise capital for investment through the sale of equity shares.

Finally, any liability rule the enforcement of which would require that courts second-guess the wisdom or expediency of managerial decisions, would encounter serious implementation problems. Courts would face fact-finding problems that may be substantial and difficult to resolve given the complexity of the management of, and business decision-making processes in, large organizations. Equally important, courts are simply not educated to review the way in which the management of a corporation is conducted (a judge is not a management consultant) and, hence, they lack the skills and expertise to soundly make second-guesses of managerial decisions [Block, Barton and Radin (1987), 5; Eisenberg (1988), 39]. Thus, the prospect of wrong assessments of managerial decisions by the courts would be significant. This might not merely give rise to substantial error costs; such a prospect would also create uncertainty for managers with respect to the standards that their business decisions should fulfil. Such uncertainty would, again, promote over-cautiousness on the part of management and encourage managers to adopt overly defensive business policies.

For all these reasons, under any given rule providing for potential liability of managers, courts should not be required to conduct an in-depth review of a challenged managerial decision and the facts underlying it but should confine themselves to assessing whether the decision exceeded the margin of discretion belonging to any reasonable, rationally acting manager. A court, or a division of a court, specializing in corporate legal matters would seem better equipped to make such an assessment than non-specialized, general courts dealing with all kinds of legal problems, as the former would be able to develop greater understanding of and familiarity with business (including management) practice and customs and the dos and don'ts therein.

Given the aforementioned direct and indirect costs which a rule subjecting managers to personal liability would give rise to, we submit that the rule's intended benefit of fewer agency costs is likely to be outweighed by the costs of the rule itself. The imposition of personal liability on managers should, therefore, in our view, be strictly limited to cases of intentional misconduct by a manager constituting injury to the shareholders and the corporation, such as fraud, theft and similar wrongful conduct, and cases of appalling mismanagement, that is, mismanagement which no single reasonable manager committed to running the corporation in the best interests of the shareholders and the corporation would have considered appropriate. In such instances, the advantages of having a specialized management (in particular, management more effective and at less cost per unit of management than if the shareholders themselves were to run the firm), as discussed in Chapter 2, would not materialize and, hence, the economic rationales for having specialized managers would cease to exist. (Indeed, as we will see in Chapter 6, both United States corporate law and Dutch corporate law limit personal liability of managers towards the shareholders and the corporation largely to the cited instances.)

Proponents of more extensive managerial liability may argue that also in cases not involving intentional misconduct or clear mismanagement, personal liability could serve to create efficient incentives for managers to refrain from activities detrimental to the shareholders if the liability standard were set in accordance with the now famous negligence formula that was propounded, in a tortious liability context, by Judge Learned Hand in *United States* v. *Carroll Towing Company* [159 F.2d 169, 173 (2nd Cir. 1947)]. According to the Learned Hand formula, a person to whose conduct a particular accident is attributable, is liable for negligence if the loss caused by the accident multiplied by the probability of the accident's occurring, exceeds the burden (meaning the cost) of the precautions that he could have taken to avert it. If the same standard were applied to determine managerial liability, managers would face personal liability for losses sustained by shareholders as a result of their actions or omissions if the amount of the loss in question multiplied by the probability of its occurring, exceeded the cost of preventing the loss (including the cost of careful evaluation of business opportunities, proper preparation of business decisions, and dismissal of courses of action which would maximize managers' utility but would be unattractive from the viewpoint of maximizing the value of shareholders' residual claim). Liability advocates would submit that under this standard of liability, managers would have incentives to avoid losses for the shareholders up to the point where the benefit of making extra loss-preventive efforts (*i.e.* fewer deviations from value maximization) would be outweighed by the costs, that means, up to a socially efficient level – just as the Learned Hand formula itself is deemed to promote the taking of precautions to avoid accidents until the costs of additional precautions would exceed their social benefit in terms of lower expected accident losses.

The above reasoning, however, defies the fact that a rule providing for extended managerial liability would create costs of its own, as we extensively discussed in the preceding pages. Therefore, to assess the social desirability of such a rule, it is not sufficient to note that extended personal liability would give managers' greater incentives to refrain from activities detrimental to the shareholders, a proposition to which one could hardly disagree. Nor does it suffice to note that a liability standard set in accordance with the Learned Hand formula would induce managers to take measures assuring compliance of their actions with shareholders' interests until the costs of doing so would exceed the benefit to the shareholders. The direct and indirect costs of the rule itself must also be taken into account and we reiterate that these costs could be so substantial that they could easily outweigh the rule's intended benefit of fewer agency costs. Any analysis which judges extended liability of managers to be socially efficient solely by reason of it promoting greater coherence with shareholders' interests, including analysis acknowledging that the liability standard should be set so as to assure that managers will not seek to avert losses to shareholders beyond the point at which more precaution is not worth its cost, suffers from the fallacies of the "free lunch" and the "grass is always greener" – which were made part of the standard tools of economic analysis by Demsetz [1969, 3-4] –, as it focuses on the liability rule's benefits while essentially ignoring its costs.

The Significance of Liability Insurance

Yet proponents of extended personal liability of managers may claim that many of the adverse effects of personal liability discussed earlier would be alleviated if managers, or the corporation on their behalf, purchased liability insurance. Liability insurance would relieve them of having to bear non-diversifiable risk, which in turn would reduce the remuneration firms would have to pay risk averse managers, increase the pool of able persons from which management could be recruited, and encourage managers to take appropriate business risks. Moreover, the insurance company would monitor their behavior so as to avoid having to make payments under the insurance policy and, by doing so, ensure compliance of managers' actions with shareholders' interests [Holderness (1990), 115-116, 118]. This idea is wrong (or, at best, only partially true), however, for at least three reasons.

First, the availability of liability insurance for managers in private insurance markets is subject to significant limitations both as to scope (claims based on fraud or illegality, for instance, routinely being excluded as may be other events triggering personal liability) and as to amount (insurance policies typically stating both deductibles and maximum amounts of coverage), meaning that the ability of insurance markets to remedy the adverse effects of managers' personal liability is equally limited. Generally, on the assumption that insurance companies endeavor to maximize returns to their residual claimants just like other commercial firms, insurance will be offered only if and to the extent that insurers are able to estimate their expected payments under the insurance policy, that is, their risk. In order for insurers to calculate their risk, they must be able to identify pools consisting of non-related risks of similar kind, as both the probability of a claim against the insurance policy and its potential amount are only objectively determinable among a large number of individuals or firms that are each exposed to a similar potential loss; in insurance theory, this predictability of losses through the formation of narrowly defined risk pools is known as the "law of large numbers". Expansion of personal liability of managers beyond the areas of fraud, dishonesty and clear mismanagement to include other cases where shareholders suffered accounting or opportunity losses as a result of managers' decisions, might impair the ability of insurers to estimate their risk by creating uncertainty concerning expected pay-outs and, to some extent, by making risks interdependent. In effect, such extended liability would both reduce the amount of insurance coverage that insurance companies would be prepared to supply and raise the premiums they would charge.

This is illustrated by the widely acknowledged crisis in directors' and officers' liability insurance (D&O insurance) that struck the supply side of the market for such insurance in the United States in the mid-1980s (roughly from 1984 through 1987). The term "crisis" was used to denote the simultaneous occurrence of the following events: a reduction of the amounts covered by D&O insurance policies offered throughout the market, a rise in deductibles further reducing effective coverage, the complete withdrawal of some insurance companies from the D&O insurance market, and a substantial increase in premiums for the insurance still available. Uncertainty in the legal and business communities over how courts would apply existing legal standards determining managerial liability, in particular, whether and to what extent they would expand personal liability of directors and officers beyond the "traditional" cases of fraud and dishonesty, was identified by Romano [1989, 24-25; 1991, 68] as a principal cause of the D&O insurance crisis. Such uncertainty was most visibly entailed by the highly publicized, controversial decision of the Delaware Supreme Court in *Smith* v. *Van Gorkom* [488 A.2d 858 (Del. 1985)] that *prima facie* expanded D&O liability by holding directors liable for gross negligence because of their failure to have properly informed themselves about their company's value before deciding to support a take-over bid for their company.

Uncertainty over what courts would consider a breach of duty by a manager (an officer or a director) justifying imposition of liability and, in particular, the possibility that conduct previously considered "safe" might result in personal liability, created difficulty for insurers in predicting when they would have to make a payment under a D&O insurance policy. This difficulty arose not merely from the fact that the incidence of managerial liability became harder to predict, but also from an increase in litigation frequency probably inspired by the perceived increased prospect for obtaining a favorable liability award, or a lucrative settlement which the insurance company would typically also have to reimburse under the D&O policy. In addition, as a result of the uncertainty concerning the limits of managerial liability, the *range* of possible settlement payments most likely also increased as settlement negotiations took place in the context of this legal uncertainty which, again, made it more difficult for insurers to estimate their risk (especially when taking into account that in the United States, most liability suits settle) [Romano (1991), 60, 68]. The difficulty for insurers in predicting their expected payments under any policy that ensued from increased uncertainty over the application of the D&O liability standard by the judiciary, culminated in the above-mentioned manifestations of the insurance crisis (reduction of coverage, withdrawal from the market by some insurers, and higher premiums to compensate for uncertainty over future pay-outs).

Another reason why the extension of managerial liability, or the perception of an extension, beyond cases of fraud and clear mismanagement would impair insurers' ability to calculate their risk is that through such extension, the incidence of liability may become dependent on factors other than a manager's own conduct. In her explanation of the D&O insurance crisis of the mid-1980s, Romano [1989, 13] noted that an increase in the number of liability suits against corporate managers, as occurred during the D&O insurance crisis years, may have been partially due to general economic conditions that in themselves are independent of the defending manager's behavior: "(...) the economic environment can encourage transactions or create situations that breed litigation". She identified several such economy-wide conditions that would seem to correlate with the number of suits against managers, including, in particular, merger and acquisition activity and business failures.

Claims seeking imposition of managerial liability may be brought because of a shareholder's dissatisfaction with the management's role in relation to a merger or an acquisition in which his company was involved, either as actor or as target. Mergers and acquisitions would appear to come in waves touching upon an industry or an entire segment of the economy rather than being confined to a few individual firms. To the extent that personal liability is imposed more often as the number of mergers and acquisitions increases, more merger and acquisition activity would mean a greater risk of personal liability for managers of all firms in the relevant industry. Bankruptcy cases are another area conducive to liability suits against corporate managers as shareholders and bankruptcy trustees may attempt to recover losses from the firm's management, for instance, in an attempt to obtain payment under the D&O insurance policy. The number of corporate bankruptcies correlates with the overall state of the economy: an economic recession typically raises the probability of business failure throughout the economy, *i.e.* for all firms. Consequently, to the extent that bankruptcy encourages litigation over personal liability, if bankruptcy rates increase due to bad performance of the economy, the average incidence of D&O liability claims will increase for all firms.

Where the incidence of managerial liability is correlated with industry-wide or economy-wide developments such as those described above, liability risks become interdependent among all firms affected by these developments (for instance, among all firms in the industry that is subject to increased merger and acquisition activity). The insurance company's pay-outs under any policy would then come to depend not merely on the insured party's behavior but also on economic conditions independent thereof that would increase the probability of insured losses occurring and that would raise the insurance company's risk of loss under any policy. Where risks are correlated in this manner, it will be difficult if not impossible for insurers to calculate their expected payments under any policy. They will be unable to identify separate pools of non-related risks, so that the operation of the law of large numbers will no longer apply to the prediction of losses [Romano (1989), 15]. In this context, it should be noted that legal uncertainty over the extent of managerial liability as may ensue from uncertainty concerning the application of the liability standard by the courts, may also create interdependence of liability risks as such uncertainty would affect all insureds (meaning that the risk of personal liability being imposed would be subject to the same legal uncertainty in respect of every firm), with similar effect [Romano (1989), 25].

Where insurance companies are not readily able to estimate the risk of loss, they will either be prepared to provide limited coverage only (that means, a low maximum insured amount, high deductibles and important exclusions) or not be prepared to provide coverage at all. Moreover, given that uncertainty over future pay-outs increases the amount of loss that insurance companies must be prepared to face, to the extent that coverage is provided, they will charge premiums that may be higher than the risk perceived by potential purchasers of insurance in order to ascertain that they will meet their costs under the insurance policy [Shavell (1987), 198]. In the latter event, potential purchasers of insurance will refrain from taking out insurance or purchase less coverage as the amount of the insurance premium would outweigh their expected losses. More specifically, only high-risk agents (*i.e.* incompetent and self-centered managers) would in fact be inclined to buy insurance because premiums would exceed losses anticipated by low-risk insureds. The departure of low-risks from an insurance pool will force insurers to further contract coverage (for instance, by raising deductibles) and to raise premiums once again which will cause more exits from the pool by insureds whose risk is less than the premium charged. At the end of the day, the risk pool may completely unravel, to the effect that risks would become uninsurable [Priest (1988), 208-209].

To sum up, where extension of managerial liability would impair insurers' ability to predict losses by enhancing uncertainty over the incidence of liability and by making liability risks interdependent among various firms, the insurance coverage they will be prepared to provide will become less, which may ultimately even result in complete reluctance to provide coverage. In addition, to the extent that coverage is offered, premiums are likely to go up in order to ensure that they will cover the payments the insurance company may have to make under the insurance policy given uncertainty and correlation of risks. This, in turn, is likely both to reduce the amount of coverage that will be bought and to cause low risks to leave the insurance pool which, at its worst, again, will cause D&O liability risks to become uninsurable. To the extent that extended personal liability of managers would disrupt the D&O

insurance market as described, market provided insurance will obviously be incapable of alleviating the adverse effects associated with increased managerial liability. Where D&O insurance would become unavailable or unaffordable, hence, extended liability would result in managers having to bear more (non-diversifiable) risk, with the consequences described earlier. For instance, during the D&O insurance crisis years, United States companies reported difficulty in finding and retaining outside directors on their boards because of persons appearing to be unwilling to bear an uninsured risk of personal liability.

With respect to the area of products liability which in the mid-1980s was confronted with a similar insurance crisis, by empirically comparing the performance of products-liability insurance markets under different United States state laws, Viscusi [1990] found that the availability of liability insurance varied under different statutory regimes, with more insurance coverage being available if statutory provisions existed which rendered the liability risk less volatile by constraining liability and reducing uncertainty as to maximum exposure levels and which, thus, made it easier for insurance companies to predict risks. Viscusi's findings confirm that differences in the scope of legal liability rules have a direct, significant impact on the insurance coverage that markets will produce, as we suggested above in respect of the availability of D&O liability insurance under extended managerial liability.

Apart from capacity constraints on the part of insurance markets to produce D&O insurance, there are two more reasons why liability insurance could be no more than an incomplete means to remedy the disadvantages of extended personal liability of managers, viz. the possible divergence between managerial decisions that would be optimum from the shareholders' perspective on the one hand and courses of action preferred by insurers on the other, and the possible dilution of managers' incentives to take care in order to avoid losses, which might result from the purchase of D&O liability insurance. One of the benefits associated with D&O liability insurance, as indicated above, is that the insurance company would monitor managerial behavior in order to avoid having to pay out under the insurance policy. In effect, monitoring services provided by the insurance company purportedly would give managers incentives to act in the shareholders' interests quite similar to those that personal liability without insurance would create.

As Holderness [1990, 118-123] has pointed out, monitoring services by D&O insurers are rendered in various ways: (i) before insurance is provided, by the insurance company's investigation of the firm seeking D&O insurance for factors that might increase its exposure and by demands it may make for changes in the firm's organizational structure or business practices to reduce its risk, (ii) once the insurance has been supplied, through the terms and conditions of the insurance policy and through the denial of coverage should the firm (or the relevant director or officer) fail to comply with these terms and conditions (for instance, the policy may exclude certain managerial actions that may trigger personal liability from coverage), and (iii) after a legal action has been brought against a particular manager for imposition of personal liability, by the insurance company investigating the allegations made and demanding that the relevant individuals take remedial action where appropriate. Moreover, D&O insurers typically monitor managerial behavior when renewal of an existing policy is sought, by evaluating management's past performance and its claim record under the existing policy and by raising insurance premiums or by demanding specific behavioral or organizational changes as a condition for renewal if the outcome of the evaluation is unsatisfactory. Furthermore, D&O liability insurance is said to produce monitoring benefits in a more indirect way, viz. by encouraging managers to monitor each other's behavior where one manager's actions may result in loss of coverage for all of them, and by facilitating the recruitment of outside directors who monitor the performance of the firm's day-to-day management [Holderness (1990), 119].

However, the insurance company's motive to monitor managerial behavior and, thus, its objective in monitoring is not necessarily identical to that of the shareholders. D&O insurers monitor in order to reduce their exposure under the D&O policy, that is, to avoid claims against managers personally, whereas shareholders, as we have seen, are interested in monitoring in order to ensure that management will take actions that maximize the value of their residual claim and will abstain from activities detrimental to the attainment of this objective. This distinction is relevant particularly where shareholders and D&O liability insurers have different attitudes towards risk. Whereas, as we have also discussed, shareholders holding well-diversified portfolios will be risk neutral and will want management to undertake risky projects with positive net present values, there will be a tendency for insurance companies to be risk averse as more risk-taking by the firm means greater potential losses under the insurance policy and as catastrophic liabilities covered by the insurance could drive the insurance company out of business. Risk-aversion on the part of insurers is supported by their frequently taking out reinsurance, which they would not do if they were indifferent to the possibility of suffering losses (including potentially catastrophic losses) under any policy, given that they have already been compensated for this possibility through the premiums they charge purchasers of insurance.

Where personal liability of managers is extended, on assumption that liability insurance coverage is also extended, the insurance company's exposure under the D&O policy will increase, with the possibility of catastrophic liability also increasing. This increased exposure will increase the importance of risk-aversion on the part of the insurance company, which will deepen the gap between the shareholders' interests and those of the insurance company with respect to the actions that they would want the firm's management to undertake or to reject. To the extent that risk averse insurers would want management to behave differently than risk neutral shareholders would, monitoring by liability insurers would serve the insurance company's interests but not those of the shareholders. In other words, where extended liability promotes risk-aversion on the part of D&O insurers, monitoring by insurance companies may exacerbate rather than remedy the risk averse incentives that extended personal liability would give corporate managers and may discourage rather than encourage the firm's operation in the risk neutral way that diversified shareholders would prefer.

Finally, where the insurance company is unable, or merely partially able, to control managerial behavior, the purchase of liability insurance may distort managers' incentives in quite the opposite direction: if managers expect the losses they might cause to be more or less fully covered by their D&O liability insurance and if at the same time liability insurers have imperfect ability to influence managers' behavior, the purchase of liability insurance would dilute managers' incentives to take care in order to avoid losses (*i.e.* reduce risk) to the shareholders given that the insurance company would indemnify them anyway for losses arising from personal liability, except for possible decreases in the rental value of their human capital [Shavell (1982), 127; (1987), 195-196]. Only where insurers are able to determine managers' level of care (through direct monitoring, through the use of deductibles and exclusions, by linking premiums to managers' efforts to prevent loss, or otherwise through the terms of the insurance policy) will their incentives to take care be similar to those they would have in the absence of insurance, that is, if they (and not the insurance company) had to bear the risk of personal liability, disregarding for the moment the fact that the insurance company may pursue a greater degree of risk-aversion on the managers' part than diversified shareholders would choose (which would not substantially change the argument). It follows that where insurers are only partially able to determine managers' level of care, the purchase of full D&O insurance coverage would offset the additional incentives to act in the shareholders' interests that extended personal liability would create.

Shavell [1986, 46; 1987, 241] has explained that this effect of liability insurance is even more serious in instances where the insured's personal wealth is less than the liability he may incur. In such event, the insured's wealth being less than the amount for which he may be liable would in itself reduce his incentives to avoid losses; liability insurance coverage would further dilute these incentives if the insurer were unable to perfectly monitor the insured's level of care and link the terms of the insurance policy to it. This observation is relevant to the matter of personal liability of managers as in many instances, the amount of loss that managers may cause to the shareholders, in particular, the depreciation in the value of the latter's residual claim for which they may be responsible, will exceed managers' private wealth. Possible personal liability, then, establishes an effective threat only to the extent of managers' wealth, a threat that will be further reduced if insurance coverage is obtained and the insurer is unable to determine to some extent managers' efforts to prevent losses.

In brief, whereas active monitoring by the D&O insurance company may induce managers to take too little risk from the shareholders' point of view, the (partial) absence of such monitoring may induce them to exercise too little care to reduce risks, the latter problem being exacerbated where managers' personal wealth is less than the losses they might cause to the shareholders. Both effects are socially undesirable: the former, because it encourages loss-prevention beyond the point at which more prevention is not worth its cost and discourages investments in risky activities, the expected benefits of which to investors would outweigh their expected costs and which, therefore, would be socially beneficial to make (provided that no costs are shifted to third parties); the latter, because it encourages over-risky behavior on the part of management, *i.e.* courses of conduct which may cause losses that could have been prevented at less cost than the anticipated loss so avoided, meaning that society as a whole would be better off if more resources were dedicated to prevention activity.

6. Disciplining the Unfaithful Agent – Legal Responses to the Internal Costs Problem

IN THE TWO preceding chapters we discussed the divergence of interests between residual claimants and salaried managers. This divergence of interests is inherent in the separation of investment and management functions, one of the principal features of the multi-shareholder, publicly held corporation. Paradoxically, whilst the residual claimants entrust the management of the corporate firm to specialized managers with a view to increasing the value of the residual claim, by taking advantage of their positions to maximize personal utility such specialized managers may unilaterally appropriate at least a part of the added value resulting from specialized management.

The prevalence of managerial utility-maximizing behavior at shareholders' expense was approached essentially from a "market failure" perspective: in Chapter 4, we described when and why the relevant market mechanisms disciplining managers fail to resolve the conflict of interests observed and in Chapter 5, we discussed, from a theoretical point of view, several legal vistas that might be pursued to alleviate this problem, including the possible strengthening of these market mechanisms themselves. Now we will outline where and how in reality the law steps in to correct shortcomings in the operation of disciplinary market forces, and see whether the principal legal remedies are consistent with the economics underlying the separation of business management and residual risk-bearing as a principle of corporate organization.

For this purpose, we survey what legal remedies United States corporation law, having emanated from a common law tradition, and Dutch corporation law, having emanated from a civil law background, have developed in order to resolve the conflict of interests between shareholders and managers. We concentrate on major issues since our purpose is not primarily to describe every detail of the relevant laws but, rather, to examine whether the fundamentals of the respective legal remedies can be explained from the perspective of economic theory like the corporate form of organization to which they relate. In the same context, we attempt to compare United States legal remedies to Netherlands remedies.

The Internal Costs Problem: U.S. Law

Fiduciary Duties

As set forth in Chapter 5, there are several ways in which the law may seek to mitigate conflicts of interests between shareholders and managers: by imposing information disclosure requirements on corporations that feed information into markets disciplining managers, by bestowing monitoring rights (including voting rights) on shareholders, by providing for flexible exit rules for shareholders, by restraining managerial discretion in the management of corporate resources, and by holding managers liable for aberrant activities.

Both United States law (hereinafter, U.S. law) and Dutch law contain disclosure requirements for publicly held corporations to feed information into disciplinary market mechanisms, both U.S. law and Dutch law confer voting rights on shareholders enabling them to directly monitor the management, and both U.S. law and Dutch law allow shareholders to protect themselves from managerial self-interest seeking by selling their shares. However, both laws fundamentally differ in the manner in which they seek to control managerial behavior through legal behavior restraints and in the use of personal liability to remedy managerial departures from shareholders' interests. Therefore, our focus is on the different legal standards for aligning managerial behavior with the interests of the shareholders and on the liability rules devised to remedy aberrant activities of managers.

U.S. corporate law's prime regulatory device to mitigate managerial self-interest seeking at shareholders' expense is the concept of fiduciary duties of directors and officers of corporations. Having emanated from the common law, such fiduciary duties are now included in a large majority of state corporation acts and have thus been translated into statutory law. Although there are differences in the manner in which fiduciary duties are described in state corporation statutes and in the manner in which they are applied by courts in different state jurisdictions, the concept as such is similar throughout the United States. Below we describe the fiduciary duties concept as it is commonly understood throughout state corporation laws.

Directors, including executive directors who are at the same time officers of the corporation as well as non-executive directors, and officers who are not also directors, are subject to two fiduciary duties to the shareholders and the corporate entity, viz. the duty of loyalty and the duty of care. Components of both duties are reflected in the general standards of conduct for directors defined in Section 8.30 (a) of the Model Business Corporation Act. Section 8.30 (a) reads: "A director shall discharge his duties as a director, including his duties as a member of a committee: (1) in good faith; (2) with the care an ordinarily prudent person in a like position would exercise under similar circumstances; and (3) in a manner he reasonably believes to be in the best interests of the corporation". Section 8.42 (a) contains a similar standard of conduct for officers.

The *duty of loyalty* obliges directors and officers (hereinafter collectively referred to as managers) to give priority to the best interests of the corporation and its shareholders when a conflict may arise between the latter and their personal self-interests. In *Guth* v. *Loft, Inc.* [5 A.2d 503, 510 (Del. Ch. 1939)] the court construed the duty of loyalty to mean that a corporate manager must "refrain from doing anything that would work injury to the corporation, or (...) deprive it of profit or advantage which his skill and ability might properly bring to it, or enable it to make in the reasonable and lawful exercise of its powers".

The duty of loyalty prohibits managers from using their position as a manager to pursue personal profit or other personal advantages to the detriment of the corporation and its shareholders. Fraud, taking of corporate property, abuses of office, diversion of corporate resources to uses in which managers have an interest but for which there is not a rational business purpose, and self-interested transactions harmful to the corporation, all violate managers' duty of loyalty. So does a manager's usurpation of corporate business opportunities in the pursuit of private gain: the duty of loyalty compels managers to refrain from entering into activities competing with those of the corporation, from exploiting commercial opportunities in which the corporation has an interest, and from acquiring property if the corporation itself has an interest in acquiring that property.

In *Kullgren* v. *Navy Gas & Supply Co.* [135 P.2d 1007 (Colo. 1943)], in an exemplary definition, the court described the duty of loyalty by holding that a manager (in this case a director) "owes loyalty and allegiance to his corporation, a loyalty that is undivided and an allegiance that is influenced in action by no consideration other than the welfare of his corporation". The court continued: "He [the manager] is held in official action, to the extreme measure of candor, unselfishness, and good faith. Those principles are rigid, essential and salutary".

The *duty of care* prescribes that managers should dedicate to the management of the corporation that level of care, effort, skill, judgment and diligence that a reasonably prudent person would exercise in similar circumstances [Clark (1986), 123]. For instance, in *Graham* v. *Allis-Chalmers Manufacturing Co.* [188 A.2d 125, 130 (Del. 1963)], the court stated that "in managing the corporate affairs [directors] are bound to use that amount of care which ordinarily prudent men would use in similar circumstances". As early as 1891, the U.S. Supreme Court had ruled, in *Briggs* v. *Spaulding* [141 U.S. 132, 152], that directors must act in the same manner as would "ordinarily prudent and diligent men (...) under similar circumstances, and in determining that (...) the usages of business should be taken into account".

The duty of care in any event requires that managers "give the corporate entity the benefit of their best judgment and care", as the court in *Great Western United Corp.* v. *Great Western Producers Coop.* noted [588 P.2d 380, 382 (Colo. 1978)]. To this end they must make business decisions in a conscious and rational manner, giving due consideration to the relevant facts and the needs of the business [*Hoye* v. *Meek*, 795 F.2d 893 (10th Cir. 1986); *DePinto* v. *Provident Security Life Ins. Co.*, 374 F.2d 37 (9th Cir. 1967)], they must genuinely endeavor to properly perform the tasks and responsibilities assigned to them [*Francis* v. *United Jersey Bank*, 432 A.2d 814 (N.J. 1981); *Heit* v. *Bixby*, 276 F.Supp. 217 (E.D. Mo. 1967)], and they must assure themselves that they are reasonably informed of the relevant material facts before deciding what action shall be taken in a particular matter [*Smith* v. *Van Gorkom*, 488 A.2d 858 (Del. 1985); *Hanson Trust PLC* v. *ML SCM Acquisition Inc.*, 781 F.2d 264 (2d Cir. 1986)]. The obligation to be reasonably informed which is entailed by the duty of care, may be construed to include a duty for board members "to attempt in good faith to assure" that the corporation has an internal information and reporting system designed to provide to senior management and to the board itself timely, accurate information concerning the corporation's affairs, as the court of *In re Caremark International Inc.* [698 A.2d 959, 970 (Del.Ch. 1996)] decided.

In a number of states, courts have applied a somewhat stricter standard of conduct, requiring managers to use the degree of care that ordinarily prudent men would exercise in conducting their *own* affairs. The standard for determining what level of care is appropriate then is not so much the care required in similar circumstances but, rather, the degree of care a reasonable man would exercise in relation to his personal affairs. For instance, in *Dykema* v. *Muskegon Piston Ring Co.* [82 N.W.2d 467, 471 (Mich. 1957)] the court demanded "that care which every man of common prudence takes in regard to his own affairs", whilst the court in *FMA Acceptance Co.* v. *Leatherby Insurance Co.* [594 P.2d 1332, 1334 (Utah 1979)] required "such attention [care] as an ordinarily discreet business man would give to *his own concerns* under similar circumstances" (emphasis added). However, the substantive meaning of the cited distinction and the material effect thereof on judicial decisions, if there is any effect at all, does not appear to be significant and, thus, the distinction itself would seem predominantly a matter of semantics.

Shareholders' Derivative Suit

The fiduciary duties described above reduce managers' freedom of action. The duty of loyalty prohibits managers from allocating corporate resources, including their own human capital, for purposes conflicting with shareholders' interests, and from usurping corporate opportunities. The duty of care obliges managers to deploy their skill, effort and so on, so as to further the best interests of the corporation and the shareholders rather than their personal self-interests. Both duties operate to align managerial behavior with the interests of the shareholders, and in this manner they serve to reduce agency costs.

In the absence of fiduciary duties, managers would have fewer restraints on the use of their superior knowledge and information about the business for the maximization of their own utility. Shareholders would then have loss-minimizing incentives to monitor in detail managerial behavior and, consequently, to spend extensive resources in gathering and evaluating information on the performance of the cooperative inputs in the firm in order to find out whether the management was doing a proper job. Specialized managers running the firm can obtain such information at less cost than shareholders, since they are specialists in acquiring and interpreting information on input behavior in team productive processes. Indeed, they are hired precisely because of their superior ability to do so. The fiduciary duties of loyalty and care, by tying in managers with shareholders' interests, are a legal device for lowering shareholders' costs of monitoring and information gathering and, thus, for economizing on the operational costs of the corporate form.

The efficacy of the fiduciary concept requires that the duty of loyalty and the duty of care can effectively be enforced on corporate managers. To this end state corporation laws entitle shareholders to institute, on behalf of the corporation, legal action against managers through a derivative suit. A derivative suit is an action brought by a shareholder in the right of the corporation in order to claim damages for an injury sustained by the corporation, or to seek injunctive relief. To make it clear that the action is brought in the right of the corporation and not in that of the individual shareholder, Section 7.41 (2) of the Model Business Corporation Act provides that the shareholder-plaintiff must use the derivative proceeding so as to "fairly and adequately [represent] the interests of the corporation in enforcing the right of the corporation".

Shareholders may institute derivative proceedings to impose personal liability on corporate managers on the basis of a breach of their fiduciary duties. If a claim for damages raised in a derivative suit against one or more managers is awarded, the manager(s) concerned must compensate the *corporation* for the injury sustained by it as a result of their breach of duty. The compensation paid into the corporation's treasury will benefit shareholders through their residual claim and so indirectly indemnify them for losses resulting from the manager's failure to observe the duty of care or the duty of loyalty. Shareholders' rights to bring derivative proceedings and the liability rule imposing personal liability on managers for breaches of fiduciary duty complement the fiduciary concept: they deter managers from failing to exercise the requisite care and from disloyally letting their personal self-interests prevail over shareholder and corporate interests, and they entitle shareholders to compensation, via their residual claim on the corporation's assets and cash flows, should managers nonetheless shirk their duties.

In addition to the right to institute derivative proceedings, state jurisdictions recognize a right for shareholders to bring direct personal actions against corporate managers. In such a direct action, which is instituted by a shareholder in his own right or in the right of the class to which he belongs, not on behalf of the corporation, the shareholder may seek damages payable to himself (or to the class he represents) rather than to the corporation. However, the right to bring a direct suit against a manager is generally restricted to alleged violations of shareholders' individual rights and consequent personal injury sustained by the shareholder (or the class) in question in his individual capacity, distinct from injury suffered by the corporation. When managers violate their duty of care or their duty of loyalty, the injury is primarily done to the corporation and affects shareholders only indirectly, through their residual claim. Therefore, to redress injury resulting from managerial violations of fiduciary duties, a derivative suit instituted on the corporation's behalf, and not a direct personal action is the appropriate legal means [Clark (1986), 662-663].

If, on the basis of the fiduciary principles, shareholders were able to challenge in court virtually every managerial action they felt uncomfortable with, managers' perceived risk of personal liability would be significant and high litigation costs would result. As discussed in Chapter 5, managers would demand compensation for both anticipated litigation expenses and the risk of personal liability through higher salaries or otherwise, whilst shareholders would discount at least future litigation costs from the amount they would be willing to pay for a share. (Only *successful* shareholder-plaintiffs are entitled to recover reasonable expenses from the corporation, as we fuller discuss below, and any such recovery would absorb corporate resources, which would also be discounted from stock prices.) Eventually, more expensive management remuneration packages and high litigation costs may offset the benefit of fewer agency costs which the fiduciary concept and shareholders' right to bring derivative proceedings should bring about.

Moreover, as also noted in Chapter 5, if managers were in fear of litigation in relation to every decision they made, they would spend more resources in studying, preparing and obtaining information about contemplated business decisions, even beyond the point at which the benefit to shareholders of such additional expenditures is outweighed by the cost. In addition, to protect themselves from personal liability, managers would be induced to avoid investments in commercially risky projects, even if such investments would have positive net present values to the shareholders. Shareholders would then suffer opportunity losses. In other words, if there were a substantial opportunity for dissatisfied shareholders to successfully sue the management, managers would be inclined to exercise too much care (they would be "over-deterred") and to deploy corporate resources to avoid personal liability rather than to maximize shareholders' wealth. On balance, therefore, the prospect of liability suits relating to breach of fiduciary duty may produce a net *negative* effect on the value of shareholders' residual claim instead of enhancing stockholder wealth.

One answer to this problem is the requirement commonly found in state corporation laws that shareholders desirous to bring a derivative suit must first request the corporation itself, that means, its board of directors, under whose authority all corporate powers are exercised (Section 8.01 (b) of the Model Business Corporation Act), to take suitable corrective measures. Shareholders may demand that the directors either cause the corporation to bring an action for damages against the managers who allegedly injured the corporation by breaching fiduciary duties, or take other appropriate corrective measures. The demand requirement is defined, for example, in Section 7.42 (a) of the Model Business Corporation Act where it states that a shareholder may not commence derivative proceedings unless "a written demand has been made upon the corporation to take suitable action". Section 7.42 (b) adds that once the demand has been made, the shareholder must observe a ninety day waiting period during which the corporation itself may take corrective action, unless the corporation rejects the demand within that period or unless "irreparable injury to the corporation" would result if commencement of the derivative action were to be postponed by those ninety days.

The demand requirement does not usually preclude shareholders from bringing a derivative suit if corporate management refuses to take suitable action as demanded. In particular, if the directors refuse to take legal action against the alleged wrongdoers, shareholders can nonetheless pursue a derivative action on behalf of the corporation if they establish facts indicating that the directors were personally involved or interested in the situation shareholders seek to remedy, or that their refusal to take the action demanded was motivated by bad faith [Clark (1986), 644]. Accordingly, directors who allegedly violated their fiduciary duties will usually be unable to preclude derivative proceedings themselves. Moreover, even if due observance of the demand requirement would not have caused "irreparable injury" to the corporation, courts frequently excuse demand if shareholders could reasonably have assumed that making a demand on the corporation would not have led to the desired corrective action, especially if the management is dominated or controlled by the individuals against which shareholders' complaints are directed. In practice, therefore, the demand requirement is not a significant restraint on shareholders' ability to bring liability suits against corporate managers.

The principal, and more important, response of U.S. corporate law to the above-mentioned adverse effects of liability suits against corporate managements is the *business judgment rule*. The business judgment rule is a common law device reducing managers' exposure to the risk of personal liability largely to clear-cut, unambiguous cases of neglect of duty, including managerial self-interest seeking at shareholders' expense in as far as such behavior is outlawed by the standards of care and loyalty.

The Business Judgment Rule

The business judgment rule in essence establishes that courts will not second-guess management's purely business judgments and will not hold managers liable for mistakes in business judgment on the sole basis that their decisions have proven errors, save in certain exceptional instances. The business judgment rule may be understood as the corporate legal counterpart of the concept of judicial self-restraint in U.S. constitutional law. Whilst, according to the latter concept, the judiciary is not concerned with the wisdom and expediency of a challenged legislative act, the business judgment rule precludes the courts from second-guessing the wisdom of managerial acts.

Under the business judgment rule, managers are not liable for losses resulting from unwise or inexpedient business decisions, even if a reasonable person would not have made the same judgment, provided "the judgment was made in good faith and on due inquiry and had a rational basis", as Eisenberg [1988, 38-39] has stated. The court in *In re Caremark International Inc.* [698 A.2d 959, 967, 968 (Del.Ch. 1996)] expressly ruled that a judge or a jury in hindsight believing a particular board decision to be "substantively wrong", "stupid", "egregious" or "irrational", provides no ground for personal liability of a director, by virtue of the operation of the business judgment rule, so long as the process employed in arriving at that decision was "either rational or employed in a good faith effort to advance corporate interests". Thus, the court concluded, "the business judgment rule is process oriented and informed by a deep respect for all good faith board decisions".

The rule in fact comprises a judicial presumption that in making business decisions, managers have duly complied with the fiduciary duties resting upon them, unless the facts of the case demonstrate otherwise. Accordingly, the business judgment rule is often referred to as a judicial *presumption of regularity* [Block, Barton and Radin (1987), 7], for it "presupposes that reasonable diligence lies behind the judgment in question", as Clark [1986, 124] has put it. In *Sinclair Oil Corp.* v. *Levien* [280 A.2d 717, 720 (Del. 1971)] this presumption has been phrased as follows: "A board of directors enjoys a presumption of sound business judgment, and its decisions will not be disturbed if they can be attributed to any rational business purpose. A court under such circumstances will not substitute its own notions of what is or is not sound business judgment". In *Aronson* v. *Lewis* [473 A.2d 805, 812 (Del. 1984)] the business judgment rule has subsequently been refined as "a presumption that in making a business decision, the directors of a corporation [have] acted on an informed basis, in good faith and in the honest belief that the action taken was in the best interests of the company".

Section 4.01 (c) of the Principles of Corporate Governance: Analysis and Recommendations (1994), prepared by the American Law Institute, contains the following definition of the rule, summarizing the existing case law: "A director or officer who makes a business judgment in good faith fulfills [his] duty [of care] (...) if the director or officer: (1) is not [privately] interested in the subject of the business judgment; (2) is informed with respect to the subject of the business judgment to the extent the director or officer reasonably believes to be appropriate under the circumstances; and (3) rationally believes that the business judgment is in the best interests of the corporation."

The business judgment rule does not subject managers to new substantive standards of conduct other than those already embodied in the duty of loyalty and the duty of care. Rather, by preventing the courts from second-guessing mere business judgments, it provides corporate managers with substantive protection from personal liability and relaxes the restraining effect of the cited duties on their discretion to make business decisions.

The business judgment rule is foremost a *procedural* tool applied by the courts when enforcement is sought of managers' fiduciary duties, in particular, when managers are alleged to have injured the corporation by a breach of duty. It is a means by which courts will review managerial decisions which have received complaint, and on the basis of which they may dismiss ill-based claims for damages or injunctive relief. Moreover, the business judgment rule imposes on the shareholder-plaintiff the onus of proving that in a particular case the managers were not justified in acting as they did: shareholders seeking relief against managerial actions must rebut the presumption that the action concerned was within the scope of managers' reasonable business judgment as protected by the business judgment rule [Block, Barton and Radin (1987), 9-10].

Within the business judgment rule, five component parts can be distinguished, and managers enjoy the protection of the rule only if all five elements have been fulfilled [Block, Barton and Radin (1987), 9-17]. If a managerial decision is challenged, the courts will (or should) confine themselves to the examination of whether these five elements are present.

First, there must be a business decision, meaning that the rule does not insulate managers from complaints that they failed to take action if there was no conscious decision not to act. Indeed, in *Aronson* v. *Lewis* [473 A.2d 805, 813 (Del. 1984)] the court found that the business judgment rule "has no role [to play] where [managers] have either abdicated their functions, or absent a conscious decision, failed to act" when action would have been appropriate.

Second, the rule solely protects decisions in which managers did not have a personal self-interest. As described earlier, the duty of loyalty prohibits acts of self-dealing detrimental to the corporation, appropriation of corporate opportunities and other actions intended to bring personal benefit to the manager concerned at the corporation's expense. Departures from managers' duty of loyalty are not shielded by the business judgment rule.

Third, from the duty of care principle it follows that only those managers are protected who have exercised due care both to obtain and to consider appropriate information prior to taking the business decision concerned. Consequently, to enjoy the protection of the business judgment rule, they must have attempted to assure themselves that sufficient information to reach an informed business judgment had come to their attention in a timely manner [*In re Caremark International Inc.*, 698 A.2d 959, 970 (Del.Ch. 1996)]. Uninformed decisions, based on intuition and purported commercial feeling rather than on material information concerning the relevant facts, fall outside the scope of the business judgment rule, as was established in *Smith* v. *Van Gorkom* [488 A.2d 858 (Del. 1985)]. In that case, the court ruled that the business judgment rule does not protect directors who made an "unintelligent or unadvised judgment" after failing to acquaint themselves, prior to making the business decision concerned (relating to a takeover bid for their company), with "all material information reasonably available to them" [488 A.2d 858, 872 (Del. 1985)].

Fourth, only business decisions taken in good faith, that is, honestly intended and believed to further the interests of the corporation and its shareholders, are protected. Decisions not motivated by a genuine desire to promote these interests, including, for example, fraudulent decisions, fall outside the realm of the business judgment rule.

Fifth, the rule does not protect abuses of managers' discretionary power, including decisions resulting in a waste of corporate resources, such as a decision to have the corporation enter into a transaction which "fall[s] short of intentional or inferred fraudulent misconduct" but which nonetheless is so disadvantageous to the corporation that no rational business judgment could sustain that decision, as the court in *Gimbel* v. *The Signal Companies, Inc.* [316 A.2d 599, 610 (Del. Ch. 1974)] considered. Abuse of discretion will frequently concur with, but does not require, bad faith: decisions honestly taken to benefit the corporation and the shareholders but in reality so grossly unfavorable to them that no rationally acting person would have taken that decision, may be considered an abuse of discretionary power by the management.

The business judgment rule presumes that managerial actions duly satisfy all five requirements described above. Shareholders seeking relief against a particular managerial action must establish facts demonstrating that at least one element of the rule has not been satisfied. If, for instance, a shareholder demonstrates that a particular decision was solely driven by a manager's personal self-interest, that a manager failed to properly inform himself of the relevant facts prior to making a business judgment, or that his action was tantamount to fraud, the business judgment rule will not shield managers from personal liability.

To sum up, managerial inactivity, self-dealing at the expense of the corporation, usurpation of corporate opportunities, failure to exercise due care in preparing business decisions, bad faith, fraudulent behavior, waste of corporate resources and (other) abuses of discretionary power are not protected by the business judgment rule. In such instances, shareholders may institute a derivative action against managers to hold them personally liable for damages payable to the corporation. As regards the duty of loyalty, any disloyal behavior through which managers pursue personal gain to the detriment of the corporation falls outside the protection of the business judgment rule. As regards the duty of care, a risk of personal liability only exists if managers have evidently acted negligently, not merely mistakenly, in one of the manners described above, and personal liability is most likely to be imposed in instances of conscious misconduct or gross negligence.

In effect, the business judgment rule largely limits the threat of personal liability to cases of disloyalty and striking mismanagement, and insulates managers from liability for business decisions which were properly prepared, made in good faith, rationally defendable and honestly believed to be in the best interests of the corporation and its shareholders. In this manner the rule protects managers from "substantive second guessing by ill-equipped judges or juries, which would, in the long-run, be injurious to investor interests", as the court in *In re Caremark International Inc.* [698 A.2d 959, 967 (Del.Ch. 1996)] considered, thus providing them with the requisite discretion to run the business so as to enhance shareholders' wealth, while at the same time deterring departures from that objective. Indeed, shareholders' benefit from management by specialized managers is greatest where managers have both discretion and incentives to use their skills so as to direct productive resources in the firm in the interest of the shareholders, and where they are not discouraged by potential personal liability from making decisions which, judging *ex ante*, they may rationally expect to be beneficial to the shareholders (but which in the end, with hindsight, might fail to yield the expected result). This rationale underlying the business judgment rule was clearly understood by the court in *Financial Industrial Fund, Inc.* v. *McDonnell Douglas Corp.* [474 F.2d 514, 518 (10th Cir. 1973)], which found that "in order to make the corporation function effectively, those having management responsibility must have the freedom to make in good faith the many necessary decisions quickly and finally without the impairment of having to be liable for an honest error in judgment".

On the other hand, the instances in which the business judgment rule does not shield managers from personal liability typically involve cases in which, from an *ex ante* perspective, the cost to shareholders of management's behavior outweighs shareholders' prospective benefit from having the firm run by specialized managers. Such behavior would threaten the whole concept of centralized management as it would force shareholders into extensive and costly monitoring to prevent net losses from employing specialized managers, and this explains the limitations to the protection managers may obtain from the business judgment rule. In both regards, the business judgment rule is instrumental to the concept of centralized management in corporations.

Efficacy of Derivative Litigation

Shareholders' derivative action to enforce managers' duties of loyalty and care complements market disciplinary forces, incentive contracting and monitoring by shareholders on the basis of their voting rights, as a mechanism for aligning managerial behavior with investor interests. The right to bring a derivative action provides shareholders with a monitoring instrument in addition to their voting rights: it enables them to monitor corporate managements through the court room, and to make use of a public institution, the judiciary, to enforce managers' private duties towards the shareholders and the corporation.

As discussed in Chapter 4, effective monitoring by scattered individual shareholders is threatened as the cost of monitoring managerial behavior (including the cost of obtaining the requisite information about value maximizing policies, the cost of detecting managerial actions contrary to shareholders' interests and the cost of forming powerful coalitions with fellow investors to enforce desired management actions) may exceed an individual shareholder's anticipated benefit from incurring such costs. In particular, if a shareholder owns only a small percentage of the total shares, both his ability to influence managerial behavior through active monitoring and his anticipated benefit from monitoring efforts will be small, so that the aforesaid costs of monitoring may well be prohibitively high. In these circumstances, it would be perfectly rational for individual shareholders to abstain from actively monitoring managerial performance.

The same factors would discourage individual shareholders from bringing a derivative action against managers to obtain compensation for and on behalf of the corporation for an injury sustained by the latter resulting from managers' violation of fiduciary duties: if a shareholder owns only a small percentage of the shares, his proportionate share of the compensation paid to the corporation would be equally small and probably smaller than the expenses he would need to incur to bring the action. Moreover, given such expenses and given the inevitable uncertainty, present in any suit, with respect to the court's decision (and the potential attainment of a profitable settlement), individual shareholders would have incentives to rely upon others to bring the action. To avoid such free rider problems and, thus, to enhance the effectiveness of the derivative suit as a monitoring instrument, case law has entitled shareholder-plaintiffs in derivative proceedings to recover litigation expenses (including attorneys' fees) from the corporation if the action constituted a "substantial benefit" to the corporation.

A "substantial benefit" is present if the action resulted in a judgment or an amicable settlement or in corrective action in fact by the defending managers which accomplished "a result which corrects or prevents an abuse which would be prejudicial to the rights and interests of the corporation or affect the enjoyment or protection of an essential right to the stockholder's interest", as the court in *Bosch* v. *Meeker Cooperative Light & Power Association* [101 N.W.2d 423, 427 (Minn. 1960)] decided. A "substantial benefit" may exist, for instance, if the defending manager(s) were ordered to pay damages to the corporation, or if the relevant judgment or settlement conferred non-pecuniary relief on the corporation satisfying the aforesaid test. The "substantial benefit" rule reduces individual shareholders' cost of bringing a meritorious action based on violation of managers' fiduciary duties and, in consequence, increases the probability that the anticipated benefit to an individual shareholder from bringing such an action will outweigh his expected cost.

Yet some scholars, based on empirical data, have questioned the efficacy of shareholders' right to bring a derivative action as a means of assuring that managers govern the corporate firm in the interest of the shareholders. Fischel and Bradley [1986] have examined changes in the market price of the shares of corporations in whose name shareholders have brought derivative proceedings to impose personal liability on incumbent managers. They examined stock price reactions following the dismissal of the derivative suit by the court for which the action had been instituted, for a sample of firms listed on the American or New York Stock Exchanges. The judicial decisions included in their study were rendered between July 2, 1962 and December 31, 1983.

Fischel and Bradley begin from the assumption that if derivative suits serve the interests of the shareholders as they purport to do, that is, if they serve to reduce agency costs, the market price of the firm's shares should fall if the court dismisses the suit. In their own words, the court's termination of a derivative action might signal to the market "the court's unwillingness or inability to prevent the firm's management from expropriating the wealth of the firm's equityholders" [1986, 278]. As a consequence, the market price of the firm's shares should decrease "by the discounted value of the increase in agency costs arising from the increased discretion that the court's decision gives the firm's management" [1986, 279]. However, in reality they did *not* find statistically significant negative stock price reactions to the termination of derivative actions. From this finding they conclude that investors do not attach significant positive value to derivative actions and that, therefore, potential personal liability of managers is relatively unimportant in aligning managerial incentives with shareholders' interests.

The reported absence of significant negative stock price reactions to the termination of derivative proceedings does not, in our view, justify such a far-reaching conclusion. First, on the (realistic) assumption that courts will tend to dismiss primarily non-meritorious actions, the continuation of a dismissed action would probably not have yielded a net benefit to the corporation and the shareholders. Thus, if the action was non-meritorious, that is, if the defending functionaries had not committed a more or less serious wrong the action could redress, there is no reason why investors should attach positive value to the action's continuation and negative value to its dismissal. The absence of a significant decrease in stock prices in response to the suit's dismissal by the court then reflects the absence of merit in the action, not a value judgment by investors on the mere *possibility* of holding managers liable for breach of fiduciary duty.

Second, regardless of the action's merit, investors may have correctly anticipated its dismissal by the court. Such anticipation would be incorporated in stock prices prior to the suit's actual termination, so that the court's decision would not reveal any "new" information to the market to which stock prices should or might respond. As Goetz [1986, 346] has noted, if investors' expectation of a dismissal has been incorporated into the stock's evaluation in the manner described, "there would be no reason to anticipate any market reaction at all" to the actual dismissal. Fischel and Bradley [1986, 278] have attempted to wave such a criticism away by assuming that market participants had not fully anticipated the judicial decisions on dismissal included in their study. This assumption, however, is at odds with standard economic theory relating to the operation of securities markets which holds that investors' expectations about the future are capitalized in current stock prices and in addition, it would seem hard to reconcile with the very purpose of their study, *i.e.* the examination of stock market reactions in a real world context, meaning on the basis of information actually available to market participants. In fact, the assumption they have made is basically the crux of the question they seek to answer.

Third, alleged violations of managers' fiduciary duties and derivative proceedings based upon such alleged violations are firm-specific events, and so is the termination of a derivative action against a firm's management. On the assumption that most investors hold diversified investment portfolios in order to avoid bearing firm-specific risk, the dismissal of a derivative suit brought in the name of any particular firm in his portfolio is unlikely to have a significant impact on an investor's appreciation of that firm's shares in so far as the dismissal would increase his risk of wealth reductions as a result of self-interest seeking by the firm's management. Given diversification and investors' consequent relative insensitivity to firm-specific risk, market prices would not need to decline following the suit's dismissal to compensate investors for such additional firm-specific risk [Demsetz (1986), 353]. Fischel and Bradley have failed to take into account such effects of diversification on stock price responses to the termination of derivative proceedings and on the interpretation of perceived (non)responses.

Another study that questions the efficacy of shareholders' derivative suit (and direct class actions) in reducing agency costs has been conducted by Romano [1991]. She examined shareholder litigation (including both derivative and class actions) in respect of a sample of 535 publicly held corporations traded on the New York Stock Exchange or in the NASDAQ system over a period from the late 1960s through 1987. Important findings of her study are: only 19 percent of the firms in the sample experienced a shareholder suit in the investigated period, approximately 65 percent of these suits were settled amicably, only half of the settlements involved a monetary recovery, 30 percent of all settlements afforded non-pecuniary structural relief (such as changes in corporate governance arrangements), only 5 percent of the settlements involved both a monetary recovery and structural relief, and in the one-third of cases which did not settle, court decisions in favor of the shareholder-plaintiff were extremely rare. Furthermore, Romano found that in settlements involving monetary recovery which could be valued, the average recovery amounted to 1.3 percent of firm assets (or USD 9 million), with substantial variation in the actual settlement amounts (ranging from USD 226,000 to USD 118 million), and that the per share value of monetary recovery in derivative actions was small (USD 0.18 on average, or approximately 2 percent of the stock market price on the day prior to the filing of the lawsuit). She concluded that shareholder litigation is an infrequent occurrence for the publicly held corporation and that with the majority of shareholder suits settling, settlements provided only minimal compensation.

Romano [1991, 84] maintains that the data summarized above support the conclusion that "shareholder litigation is a weak, if not ineffective, instrument of corporate governance". While not quarreling with the empirical findings, we are unconvinced that they prove that the shareholders' right to bring a lawsuit is ineffective in aligning managers' incentives with shareholders' interests. Even if the number of and the actual relief obtained in shareholder initiated legal actions may be small, the *right* to bring such an action may in itself still be important. As Romano [1991, 60] herself has acknowledged, the fact that the majority of shareholder actions settle does not provide useful information about the effectiveness of shareholder litigation, since in this respect they are no different from other civil lawsuits. Little can be drawn from the reported infrequency of shareholder suits either, since this finding might also be interpreted to confirm the success of the business judgment rule in discouraging shareholders from engaging in frivolous, non-meritorious litigation.

The limited financial recoveries observed might also be attributed to the operation of the business judgment rule, which mitigates the scope of potential personal liability and which is, therefore, likely to have a negative impact on settlement amounts, and furthermore, possibly, to the unknown facts of the individual cases and wrongdoings concerned. More fundamentally, the Romano study (and the Fischel and Bradley study as well) assesses the efficacy of shareholder actions predominantly on the basis of the compensatory benefits (pecuniary recovery and structural relief) such actions produced (or could have produced, in the Fischel and Bradley study) for the corporations included in the study. However, after-the-fact compensation for injury sustained by the corporation as a result of managerial malfeasance is not the only goal of, and not the only potential benefit from, shareholders' right to bring a derivative proceeding.

Shareholders' right to bring a derivative action against managers for violations of fiduciary duties also serves to *deter* such violations, that means, to create *ex ante* incentives for managers to observe the duties of loyalty and care. (Remarkably, Fischel and Bradley [1986, 261] have acknowledged generally that liability rules "create incentives to engage in socially desirable conduct".) The more effectively violations of managers' fiduciary duties are deterred, the fewer the actual violations and the lower the demand for compensation of injuries resulting from such violations will be. The infrequency of shareholder suits and the minimal compensatory benefits reported by Romano may be viewed as an indication of a substantial deterrent effect of shareholders' right to sue corporate managements. The principal benefit of that right would then lie in deterring managerial malfeasance, not in providing compensation for injury caused by it. In any event, Romano's findings summarized above do not provide evidence *rejecting* the deterrent effect of shareholder litigation. Any conclusion concerning the effectiveness of such litigation as an instrument for reducing agency costs should, in our view, appraise its deterrence rationale and effect no less than observed compensatory effects. Romano [1991, 85] recognizes this but refers to the virtual impossibility of measuring a general deterrent effect of shareholder suits on managerial behavior. (Measuring a specific deterrent effect of shareholder litigation on the management of firms that have experienced shareholder suits, however, might well be possible. Such an examination would require a comparison of the performance of firms which did experience such litigation with the performance of firms that did not, during the period directly after the litigation had ended through a judgment, a settlement, or otherwise (not after a lawsuit was filed because the suit's filing, the anticipated outcome of the suit and the underlying facts might already have been evaluated by investors and reflected in stock prices.) If then the firms which had undergone litigation were to show abnormal stock price increases compared with the firms with no previous lawsuits, *ceteris paribus*, a specific deterrent effect (less agency costs) might be inferred. However, neither the Romano study nor the Fischel and Bradley study contains such data.)

The deterrent role of potential shareholder suits to redress managerial violations of fiduciary duties also provides an alternative explanation of the absence of statistically significant stock price reactions to the termination of a derivative action which was reported by Fischel and Bradley. The general deterrent effect of shareholders' right to bring an action on behalf of the corporation against one or more managers applies to all corporations alike, and will therefore be reflected in the market's evaluation of any corporation's stock. If general deterrence (and not compensation) is the principal benefit of that right, dismissal of a derivative suit (meaning that no compensatory benefit will be realized) is relatively irrelevant to investors' appraisal of the shares in the corporation concerned; it does not alter the perceived general deterrent effect on corporate managements which is capitalized in share prices. In addition, as the Reporter's Note at the outset of Part VII, Chapter 1, of the American Law Institute's Principles of Corporate Governance indicates, even if empirical data were to reveal a significant negative stock price reaction to the dismissal of a derivative action, such a reaction would still not reveal, or alter, beneficial deterrent effects of the action on *all* corporate managements; hence, such a finding would not justify the conclusion that derivative litigation is generally ineffective in deterring managerial malfeasance.

The deterrence benefit of shareholder derivative litigation has been recognized in case law. In this context, the above-mentioned Reporter's Note refers to the judicial decisions in *Diamond* v. *Oreamuno* [24 N.Y.2d 494, 498 (1969)] and *Mills* v. *Electric Auto-Lite Co.* [396 U.S. 375, 396 (1970)]. In the first case, the court considered that "the function of such an action (...) is not merely to compensate the plaintiff for wrongs committed by the defendant but (...) to prevent them, by removing from agents and trustees all inducement to attempt dealing for their own benefit in matters which they have undertaken for others". In the second case, the United States Supreme Court recognized that plaintiffs in shareholder litigation may have "rendered a substantial service to the corporation and its shareholders" even though "it may be impossible to assign monetary value to the benefit". Deterrence of managerial self-interest seeking at shareholders' expense may, on its own merits, constitute the primary social benefit of shareholder litigation, as these court decisions suggest, regardless of potential compensatory benefits, with the business judgment rule discouraging non-meritorious actions. From this angle, empirical studies questioning the efficacy of such litigation on the basis of a perceived lack of compensatory benefits address, at best, only part of the issue.

The Internal Costs Problem: Dutch Law

Corporate Interest versus Shareholder Interests

Under U.S. corporate law, a business corporation is first and foremost conceived of as a vehicle for generating shareholder wealth. The court in *Dodge* v. *Ford Motor Co.* [204 Mich. 459, 507, 170 N.W. 668, 684 (1919)], in a seminal formulation, phrased the concept as follows: "A business corporation is organized and carried on primarily for the profit of the stockholders. The powers of the directors are to be employed for that end. The discretion of directors is to be exercised in the choice of means to attain that end, and does not extend to a change in the end itself (...)".

The same concept is reflected in Section 2.01 (a) of the American Law Institute's Principles of Corporate Governance: Analysis and Recommendations, stating that "(...) a corporation should have as its objective the conduct of business activities with a view to enhancing corporate profit and shareholder gain". True, it is increasingly being recognized in case law, by commentators and in state corporation statutes, that corporate managements should have the discretion to utilize corporate resources so as to benefit widely acknowledged public interests, even at the sacrifice of some profit. This view is endorsed by Section 3.02 (13) of the Model Business Corporation Act, according to which a corporation (meaning its board of directors) has the power "to make donations for the public welfare or for charitable, scientific, or educational purposes", unless its articles of incorporation provide otherwise. Similarly, Section 2.01 (b) (3) of the Principles of Corporate Governance provides that the corporation, in the conduct of its business, may "devote a reasonable amount of resources to public welfare, humanitarian, educational, and philanthropic purposes". However, the right to devote corporate resources to such public interest purposes does not fundamentally change the concept of the corporation as an instrument to earn profit for its shareholders.

First, the aforesaid right pertains to the *use* that is made of corporate earnings, that means, profit spending. It does not alter or prejudice the generation of profit and shareholder gain as an end in itself and as the guiding principle for corporate management in running the business. Secondly, the utilization of corporate resources for public welfare, humanitarian and similar purposes is subject to a limit of reasonableness as developed in case law. Important factors in determining what is "reasonable", are: whether the manner of utilization of corporate resources is somehow related to the corporation's business, whether the corporation itself derives a direct or indirect benefit from the resource use concerned, and whether the particular use (and the amount involved) is customary for a corporation of that kind. The corporation's financial condition, too, bears upon what is reasonable. Furthermore, the particular use of corporate resources must not be "(...) so "remote and fanciful" as to excite the opposition of shareholders whose property is being used", as Garrett [1967, 297] has stated. The test of reasonableness illustrates that management's power to favor public and charitable interests, as opposed to shareholder interests, is *not* a substitute for, but is in addition to and independent of management's commission to pursue corporate profit and shareholder gain.

Consistent with the view of the corporation as a wealth producing vehicle for the shareholders, directors and officers owe the fiduciary duties of loyalty and care described above to both the corporation *and* the shareholders [Block, Barton and Radin (1987), 1]. As the court in *Alpert* v. *28 Williams St. Corp.* [63 N.Y.2d 557, 568 (1984)] noted: "[T]hey have an obligation *to all shareholders* to adhere to fiduciary standards of conduct and to exercise their responsibilities in good faith when undertaking any corporate action" (emphasis added).

From the perspective of managers' fiduciary duties, there is no difference between the corporation and the shareholders. As the corporation is to be operated for the benefit of the shareholders, the interests of the corporation are presumed identical to the wealth-maximizing interests of the shareholders. For the same reason, managers owe identical fiduciary duties to the corporation and the shareholders.

In Dutch corporate law, by contrast, shareholder interests are distinguished from the interests of the corporation, and it is the latter which managers are to serve. Before looking into this a little further, let us briefly summarize the governance structure of corporations according to Dutch corporate law that was described in Chapter 2.

Whereas U.S. state corporation statutes provide for the board of directors to be the corporation's single governance body, under the direction of which the business and affairs of the corporation are to be managed and which usually appoints the officers, Dutch corporate law provides for a two-tier governance structure consisting of a "management board" and a "supervisory board". The firm's day-to-day management is conducted by the management board, whilst the supervisory board monitors (supervises) the performance of the management board and the firm in general. Both the members of the management board and the members of the supervisory board are bound to exercise their respective powers in the interests of the corporation (Sections 2:9 and 2:140 (2) of the Civil Code).

The members of the management board (hereinafter, the managers), to whom we confine ourselves, are obliged *towards the corporate entity* to properly perform the tasks and responsibilities assigned to them (Section 2:9 of the Civil Code). From this obligation it is inferred that in making decisions, managers must not merely take into account shareholders' wealth-maximizing interests, but that they must take the interests of the corporation *itself* (the "corporate interest", in Dutch the "*vennootschappelijk belang*") as their directing standard in running the corporate firm. The underlying presumption is that since the corporation is an entity legally distinct from the shareholders, it should also have interests of its own, distinct from those of the shareholders.

What are the distinct interests of the corporation that should guide the managers? One leading commentator has defined the corporate interest as the interest of the corporation in its own prosperity, progress and continuity, with a view to the attainment of the objective for which the corporation has been organized as stated in the articles of incorporation [Maeijer (1964), 6; (1994), 366]. (Dutch law requires that the articles of incorporation state the purpose of the corporation (Section 2:66 of the Civil Code). According to the Model Business Corporation Act (Section 2.02 (b)), by contrast, such a provision is merely optional: the articles may, but are not obliged to, set forth the specific purpose or purposes for which the corporation is organized. Pursuant to Section 3.01 (a), if the articles do not define a narrower purpose every corporation will have "the purpose of engaging in any lawful business".)

Another commentator has construed the notion of corporate interest to mean the outcome of a balancing process in which the interests of the various persons involved in or affected by the activities of the corporation are to be considered [Van der Grinten (1992), 406-407]. Viewed from this angle, the corporate interest concept is a clear reflection of the nexus-of-contracts theory of the corporation referred to in Chapter 2, since it recognizes the variety of private interests inherent in the corporation. *Whose* interests should be balanced in determining the corporate interest depends on the persons involved in or affected by the corporation in question in each particular case. In both approaches, shareholders' interests are only one factor which managers should consider in the making of business decisions. Other factors include, in particular, the interests of the corporation's employees and creditors [Sanders and Westbroek (1994), 245].

"Corporate interest" must not be construed to add promotion of public (charitable, humanitarian) interests to the enhancement of shareholder gain. Neither does it refer to the sum of shareholders' interests and the interests of all kinds of outsiders who might potentially be touched, directly or indirectly, by the corporation's activities. Instead, the notion aims to preclude a single managerial focus on the shareholders and to compel management to consider in addition, in relation to the viability and prosperous operation of the firm itself, the interests of other human agents who enable the operation of the firm organized in corporate form. The corporate interest *may* coincide with the wealth-maximizing interests of the shareholders but depending on the circumstances it may also have different connotations, given that its scope is broader. In the latter event, managers must give priority to the interests of the corporation over those of the shareholders. In *Doetinchemse IJzergieterij et al.* v. *Uitgevers Maatschappij C. Misset* [NJ 1949, 465 (HR 1949)] (a case involving supervisory directors but the principle also applies to the members of the management board), the Supreme Court expressly acknowledged that if there is a collision with shareholders' interests, the corporate interest should always prevail.

In summary, under Dutch corporate law, the notion of corporate interest has a life and a meaning of its own in the same way and to the same extent that the corporation itself lives a life of its own, distinct from the shareholders. The meaning of corporate interest is liable to vary between different corporations depending on the nature of each corporation's activities, the persons they affect, the commercial environment in which the corporation operates and the objective stated in its articles, and it is not identical to or a mere derivative of the interests of any particular human beings, including the shareholders.

Managers are to serve the corporate interest rather than the interests of the shareholders since according to the Dutch concept of the corporate form, essentially differently from the U.S. model, they do not stand in a fiduciary relation to the shareholders. Their dos and don'ts, therefore, are not defined by or deduced from a fiduciary relationship with the shareholders. Instead, it is the managers' *function* within the organizational framework of the corporation that *per se* determines their responsibilities and behavioral constraints. The managers' function in the legal structure of the corporation is to run the corporate firm (Section 2:129 of the Civil Code), with the power, authority and obligation to do so residing in that function. Managers' obligation to exercise their power and authority in the best interests of the corporation is based on this conceptual role.

The fact that managers are to serve the corporation rather than the shareholders does not give them license to sacrifice shareholder wealth in the pursuit of personal self-interests. Whereas in U.S. corporate law, fiduciary duties restrain managers' discretion, in Dutch law they are subject to the legal behavioral constraint compelling them to use their positions to further the interests of the corporation. From the perspective of discouraging the use of corporate resources for purposes of managerial self-interest seeking, managers' obligation to serve the corporate interest performs a similar role to the behavioral constraints established by managers' fiduciary duties in U.S. law. Allocations of corporate resources primarily motivated by managers' personal self-interests, independent of corporate interests, are prone to involve a departure from both the interest of the corporation and the shareholders' wealth-maximizing interests. In this respect, managers' obligation to promote the corporate interest serves to protect the shareholders too.

The Rescission Remedy

As we saw earlier, according to U.S. law, shareholders may sue directors and officers in a derivative action for violation of their fiduciary duties. Dutch law does *not* entitle shareholders to commence derivative proceedings on behalf of the corporation against managers who have acted against the corporate interest.

However, as we elaborate below, to prevent the corporation or themselves incurring injury from managerial decisions, shareholders may in their own right seek rescission of "unreasonable and unfair" decisions of the management board, including decisions which are irreconcilable with the interests of the corporation. In addition, as we will see in the next section, managers may become subject to personal liability for damage sustained by the corporation as a result of their improper performance.

Shareholders may institute an action against the corporation to obtain a court ruling rescinding a particular management decision on the basis of Sections 2:8 (1), 2:15 (1) (b) and 2:15 (3) (a) of the Dutch Civil Code.

Pursuant to Section 2:8 (1), the corporation and the persons involved in its constituent bodies (shareholders, managers and supervisory directors) must act towards one another in conformity with the principles of reasonableness and fairness. A management decision that sacrifices corporate interests for the managers' personal benefit is prone to be unreasonable and unfair towards the corporation and, in so far as shareholder interests are harmed, also towards the shareholders. Generally, Maeijer [1994, 367] notes that management decisions solely intended to serve purposes other than the corporation's interests violate the principles of reasonableness and fairness.

Pursuant to Sections 2:15 (1) (b) and 2:15 (3) (a), a shareholder may demand that the court rescind an unreasonable and unfair management decision, provided that the shareholder concerned has a reasonable interest in management's alleged violation of reasonableness and fairness in the case concerned. On the basis of the same sections, shareholders may also seek injunctive relief in order to prevent the implementation of a decision whose rescission they desire.

Shareholders' right to seek rescission of allegedly unreasonable managerial decisions is limited in several ways. The right solely applies to decisions of the management *board*, not to decisions by individual managers (Section 15 (1)). The right must be exercised within one year of the decision being made public or becoming known to the shareholder-plaintiff (Section 15 (5)). The right itself does not serve to restrain managerial actions that are *not* based on decisions of the management board. Finally, as indicated above, shareholders that do not have a reasonable interest in the violation complained of may not demand rescission (Section 15 (3) (a)). For instance, a shareholder who voted in favor of a particular policy in the shareholders' meeting may not subsequently demand rescission of a management decision intended to implement, and complying with, that policy.

Shareholders' right to demand rescission of a management decision is not confined to decisions violating corporate interest but extends to any unreasonable and unfair decisions. At least in theory, shareholders may also attack decisions that in themselves serve the corporate interest but which are unreasonable and unfair from the point of view of a particular shareholder's *own* interests. However, such attacks will only rarely be successful, given that managers *ought* to be guided by the interests of the corporation and ought to give priority to the latter in the event of a conflict with shareholders' interests. If a management decision is tenable in view of the corporation's best interests, a cause for rescission may exist only if nonetheless under the circumstances the decision was so manifestly unfair to the shareholder-plaintiff that the management board could not in all reasonableness have decided as it did it, that is, only in the most unusual cases.

The Liability Remedy

In addition to the rescission remedy available to shareholders, managers may become subject to personal liability *to the corporate entity*, on the basis of Section 2:9 of the Civil Code, if they fail to properly perform their job. For a successful liability action, it is a prerequisite that the corporation has suffered damage as a result of management's allegedly inadequate performance. This damage requirement does not apply to a rescission action, although a management decision is more likely to be deemed unreasonable and unfair and, hence, liable to rescission, if its implementation would (or already did) result in injury to the corporation.

In *Staleman and Richelle* v. *Van de Ven Automobielbedrijf et al.* [NJ 1997, 360 (HR 1997)], the Supreme Court decided that the standard of culpability for the imposition of liability on a manager is gross negligence. Thus, managers do not have to fear personal liability for pure mistakes committed in the course of running the firm, even if such mistakes are due to ordinary negligence. The risk of liability is limited to instances in which they grossly neglect their functions and responsibilities towards the corporation, that is, cases of clear mismanagement. Mistakes in business judgment falling below the gross negligence standard are for the account and risk of the corporation and the joint shareholders. In practice, the gross negligence standard provides managers with similar protection from personal liability as the business judgment rule does under U.S. law.

Whether or not there has been gross negligence on the part of a manager depends on the facts of the individual case concerned. In *Staleman and Richelle* v. *Van de Ven Automobielbedrijf et al.*, the Supreme Court noted that in determining whether there has been gross negligence, a court should consider, *inter alia*, the nature of the corporation's activities, the business risk generally involved in such activities, the allocation of tasks within the management board, the existence of intra-corporate guidelines for the management, the information which the defending manager possessed or should have possessed at the time he made the decision or performed the action in question, and the discernment and prudence which should be expected of a competent manager diligently performing his job.

The gross negligence requirement may be satisfied by individual managers or by the management board collectively. If only an individual manager (*i.e.*, one particular board member) acted in gross negligence, liability may be imposed upon him but not on the other board members [Van der Grinten (1992), 457-458]. By contrast, if the corporation is found to have been improperly managed by the management *board* in a grossly negligent manner, the board members will be jointly and severally liable for the injury sustained by the corporation. However, an individual board member may then relieve himself of liability by demonstrating that not only was *he* not to blame for the board's improper performance but that he also had endeavored to *prevent* injury to the corporation.

Although the wording is different, the behavioral standards reviewed in the context of the gross negligence test in Dutch law resemble those comprised by the duty of care regarding managers set out in U.S. corporate law. Section 4.01 (a) of the Principles of Corporate Governance: Analysis and Recommendations, defining the duty of care, provides that directors and officers are to perform their functions "in good faith, in a manner that he or she reasonably believes to be in the best interests of the corporation, and with the care that an ordinarily prudent person would reasonably be expected to exercise in a like position and under similar circumstances". A manager who acts accordingly will also satisfy performance requirements under Dutch law, and will therefore not become subject to personal liability pursuant to Section 2:9 of the Civil Code.

Manifest departures from corporate interests may well qualify as gross negligence towards the corporation and therefore subject management to personal liability. Thus, the allocation of corporate resources to uses solely motivated by managers' personal self-interests at the sacrifice of corporate income, may lead to imposition of personal liability. For instance, liability may be imposed for embezzlement of corporate funds or self-dealing to the detriment of the corporation, or if managers choose leisure instead of properly preparing investment decisions or exploiting the corporation's commercial opportunities. In any event, however, the gross negligence culpability test must be satisfied, meaning that relatively insignificant departures from corporate interests are unlikely to result in personal liability.

As in a derivative suit under U.S. law, if liability is imposed, managers must pay damages to the corporation; they must then repair the damage that the corporation has sustained as a consequence of their grossly negligent improper decisions or actions. However, no liability for damages will exist if the relevant manager was previously discharged from liability, for example, upon his leaving office or upon the adoption or approval of the corporation's annual financial report by the shareholders, provided the facts on which liability could be based were made available prior to discharge; facts not disclosed are deemed to have been excluded from the discharge granted.

A liability suit based on a manager's allegedly improper performance must be brought by the corporation since it concerns the manager's obligations towards the corporation [Van der Grinten (1992), 458; Maeijer (1994), 416]. It is then for the corporation-plaintiff to demonstrate gross negligence and to establish the damage the corporation has suffered due to management's improper performance. (In the event of the corporation's bankruptcy, the trustee appointed by the court may also commence a liability action against managers. An action brought by the trustee will, in our view, ordinarily be intended for the benefit of the creditors rather than that of the corporation or the shareholders; therefore, we will not discuss this possibility further.)

Unlike the situation under U.S. law, as stated at the outset of the preceding section, shareholders are *not* entitled to bring a derivative action against a manager in the name of the corporation to redress an injury allegedly inflicted on the latter. However, the shareholders may adopt a resolution by which it is decided that the corporation itself should bring an action for damages against one or more managers. Such a decision, which is binding on the corporation, may also be made by the supervisory board, or by the management board itself.

If the action is directed against a former manager, the aforesaid decision is to be implemented by the present management board, which will represent the corporation in the action as usual (Section 2:130 of the Civil Code). However, if the target is an incumbent manager, the corporation will be represented by the supervisory board which will bring the action on the corporation's behalf, unless the articles of incorporation provide otherwise and unless the shareholders designate another person (for example, a shareholder) to represent the corporation (Section 2:146 of the Civil Code). Also if the corporation does not have a supervisory board, the shareholders may designate a person to bring the action on behalf of the corporation [Maeijer (1994), 375]. Like the derivative suit in U.S. law, the right of the supervisory board to bring an action against an incumbent manager and the right of the shareholders to designate another person to bring such an action, are intended to remedy the conflict of interests which would arise if incumbent managers were to bring an action against themselves on behalf of the corporation, and to avoid frustration of such an action by the incumbent managers. (In practice, however, if grounds exist for bringing an action for damages against an incumbent manager, such a manager is usually dismissed, with a potential subsequent liability suit being brought by the remaining or the succeeding managers, or by the trustee in the event of bankruptcy.)

Prima facie incumbent managers can avoid personal liability towards the corporation if the latter does not have a supervisory board capable of bringing an action (or if the supervisory board refuses to bring the action) and at the same time, only a minority of the shareholders is of the opinion that one or more managers have acted in gross negligence towards the corporation and should be held liable for the injury the corporation has sustained. For instance, if the management controls the majority of the shares in a corporation which does not have a supervisory board, the minority shareholders will be unable to oblige the joint shareholders to designate a representative to bring an action for damages against incumbent managers on behalf of the corporation. As a consequence, on the face of it, management may therefore neglect the interests of the corporation without having to fear personal liability.

However, in such an event the minority shareholders may, in our view, sue the corporation, and the members of the management board personally, to obtain a court order compelling the corporation to bring an action for damages against one or more incumbent managers. Maeijer [1995, 1346 (1)] apparently holds the same opinion. Such a shareholder action should be based on the reasonableness and fairness principles which the corporate entity, as well as the managers, are to observe vis-à-vis the shareholders pursuant to Section 2:8 (1) of the Civil Code. Accordingly, the shareholder-plaintiffs in the action should demonstrate to the court that they would be treated unreasonably and unfairly if no liability action were brought against a particular manager on behalf of the corporation. To this end, they must submit facts to the court indicative of grossly negligent improper performance on the part of the manager(s) against whom they desire the liability action to be brought.

In addition, based on Section 2:345 (1) of the Civil Code, shareholders satisfying certain quantitative criteria (set forth in Section 2:346 (b)) may request the appellate court in Amsterdam, which is statutorily designated for this purpose, to order an official inquiry into the management and affairs of the corporation. If such an inquiry reveals facts indicating mismanagement, the shareholders may subsequently take the action described above. The appellate court may not itself impose liability upon a manager in the course of the inquiry proceedings but, at the shareholder-plaintiff's request, it may order other corrective measures including, *inter alia*, the dismissal or suspension of one or more managers and the rescission of management decisions (Sections 2:349 (a) and 2:356 Civil Code).

Actions for Damages by Shareholders

Are shareholders also entitled to bring personal actions against managers to seek damages payable not to the corporation, but to the shareholder-plaintiff personally?

In *Poot* v. *ABP* [NJ 1995, 288 (HR 1994)], the Supreme Court ruled that a shareholder is not entitled to damages from a third party wrongdoer if the injury in respect of which the redress is sought has been sustained by the corporation, affecting the shareholder only indirectly via (a decrease in) the value of his shares. In that event, the Court held, it is solely for the corporation to seek redress, since the wrong complained of was committed against the *corporation*; damages paid to the corporation will make good the decrease in the value of the shares so that in addition to the corporation itself, the shareholders will also be compensated.

Gross negligence by a manager in the performance of his managerial functions, *i.e.* in his professional capacity, may constitute an injury to the corporation and ordinarily affects the shareholders only indirectly; consequent wealth losses by the shareholders are derivatives from the damage sustained by the corporation. Therefore, based on the Supreme Court's reasoning in *Poot* v. *ABP*, only the corporation will be entitled to claim damages from the relevant manager.

A shareholder may bring a personal action against a manager only to redress an injury affecting him in his individual capacity [Van der Grinten (1992), 459], that is, other than through a decrease in the value of his shares resulting from an injury to the corporation. If the injury is sustained primarily by the latter, the manager owes damages to the corporation and not to the individual shareholders [Maeijer (1994), 416], and liability to pay such damages may be enforced by the corporation only (as described in the preceding section). The distinction between actions to redress corporate injury and actions to redress individual injury is similar to the distinction between derivative actions and direct actions in U.S. law: a derivative action is brought in the right of the corporation for an injury to the corporation, with damages payable to the latter, whereas a direct action is brought by a shareholder in his own right (or in the right of the class to which he belongs) for an injury to the shareholder in his individual capacity, with damages payable to the shareholder(s). (This distinction is expressly acknowledged in Sections 7.01 (a) and 7.01 (b), respectively, of the Principles of Corporate Governance: Analysis and Recommendations.)

In *Kip and Sloetjes* v. *Rabobank* [NJ 1997, 662 (HR 1997)], a case involving a claim for damages by shareholders against a third party on the basis of an alleged wrong to the shareholders in their own right which had allegedly forced them to sell their shares at a very disadvantageous price, the Supreme Court affirmed shareholders' right in principle to claim damages for an individual injury. The Court considered, *inter alia*, that in the case concerned, payment of damages to the corporation would *not* repair the shareholders' alleged injury (viz. the loss resulting from the sale of their shares).

Cases not consisting of a wrong primarily affecting the corporation in which individual shareholders may successfully bring an action for damages against a manager, on the basis of an alleged wrong directly affecting them, are extremely rare. They are limited to instances in which the shareholder's damage is not a mere derivative of an injury sustained by the corporation, and such cases therefore require a wrong to the individual shareholder independent of any wrongdoing towards the corporation [Maeijer (1995), 1346 (2)]. Whereas an action for damages brought by the corporation will be based on a manager's allegedly grossly negligent performance of his managerial functions, as discussed above, an action for damages brought by an individual shareholder will ordinarily be based on an alleged tort committed towards the shareholder-plaintiff.

A manager may become subject to tortious liability, for instance, if he has violated his obligation pursuant to Section 2:8 of the Civil Code to observe the principles of reasonableness and fairness towards the shareholder-plaintiff [Van der Grinten (1992), 407], for example, by taking a decision or performing an action solely or predominantly intended to injure the shareholder-plaintiff. However, as we discussed in relation to the potential rescission of management decisions, a departure from shareholders' wealth-maximizing interests will not in itself be deemed unreasonable and unfair. Accordingly, the mere fact that managers may have given priority to corporate interests at the sacrifice of shareholder interests, will not *ipso facto* render them susceptible to tortious liability.

If individual shareholders were entitled to claim damages for managerial actions causing injury to the corporation and affecting shareholders only indirectly, through decreases in the value of their shares or through dividend cuts (or both), a far greater number of suits would be necessary to redress the same damage than if the right to claim damages were concentrated in and reserved for the corporation. Both the Dutch rule that only the corporation may demand compensation for an injury sustained by it and the U.S. rule that shareholder actions against managers seeking relief for such an injury be brought in the right of the corporation, serve to avoid numerous suits for damages by individual shareholders and, thus, economize on the costs of enforcing managerial liability. In essence, these rules serve to exploit the transaction cost advantages associated with having the corporation operate as an entity distinct from the shareholders: as it is the *entity* which has encountered the basic injury complained of, minimum transaction costs requires that also the redress action is brought by or on behalf of that entity.

The right for shareholders to bring a derivative action in the name of the corporation in order to redress an injury to the latter, will enter into Dutch law if the proposal for a fifth European directive on company law, dated August 19, 1983, be adopted by the Council of the European Union. According to Section 16 of this proposal, the member states of the European Union will have to enact implementing legislation providing that proceedings to enforce liability of members of the management board (and the supervisory board) for damage sustained by the corporation may be commenced "on behalf of and also in the name of the company by one or more shareholders: (a) who hold shares of a certain nominal value or accounting par value which the Member States shall not require to be greater than 5 percent of the subscribed capital; or (b) who hold shares of a certain nominal or accounting par value which the Member States shall not require to be greater than 100,000 ECU. This figure may vary up to not more than 10 percent for purposes of conversion into national currency". The proposal for a fifth directive on company law, including the proposed right for shareholders to bring derivative proceedings, applies to publicly held corporations only.

The introduction of a derivative action for shareholders in Dutch corporate law will make it simpler for shareholders to enforce liability on managers for an injury to the corporation. They will no longer depend on supervisory directors to bring an action for damages or on a majority of the shareholders deciding that such an action be brought, or on a court order compelling the corporation to bring the action if fellow shareholders and the supervisory board refuse to cooperate for that purpose. In effect, managers' incentives to perform managerial functions properly may well be strengthened, whilst the quantitative hurdle a shareholder desirous to commence a derivative action must surmount will discourage both frivolous and vexatious suits compelling managers to incur litigation expenses without cause. In addition, the proposal for the fifth directive does not, in our view, provide for a relaxation of the gross negligence standard for liability of managers. Thus, the adverse effects of excessive personal liability discussed earlier would probably be avoided.

The only substantive change from current Dutch law contained in the proposal (in Sections 14 (5) and 18 (1)) which might affect the imposition of managerial liability, is that the legal effect of a discharge from liability accorded to a corporate manager by the shareholders would be restricted and thus be less likely to exempt managers from potential personal liability. However, a corresponding change in Dutch legislation is unlikely in practice to have a significant effect on the incidence of managerial liability in view of the fact that acts which at present may give rise to personal liability of managers are frequently not disclosed when discharge is given. Such acts are therefore ordinarily deemed to be excluded from the scope of the discharge (based on the Supreme Court's ancient decision in *Deen* v. *Perlak*, NJ 1921, 737 (HR 1921)), and may still lead to imposition of managerial liability.

Having arrived at the end of our survey of the behavior constraints and liability rules operating to align managers' incentives with shareholders' wealth-maximizing interests under U.S. law and Dutch law, let us briefly recapitulate. Under U.S. corporate law, managers' discretion to use corporate resources in the pursuit of personal utility is restrained by the duties of loyalty and care owed to both the corporation and the shareholders. Under Dutch law, a similar role is played by the principle of managers' obligation to serve the corporate interest, a legal notion establishing that managers should direct the corporate firm so as to further the distinct interests of the corporation.

According to both U.S. law and Dutch law, managers are not liable for injury to the corporation resulting from honest mistakes in their business judgment. Under U.S. law, managers are protected from rigorous liability by the business judgment rule, a judicial presumption that their judgment in a particular matter had a rational business purpose and was made on an informed basis, in the honest belief that it was in the best interests of the corporation. Under Dutch law, managers obtain similar protection from the gross negligence standard of culpability for the imposition of liability, as a result of which they face liability in cases of clear mismanagement only.

In summary, the legal concepts applied are different but the results are similar. The legal restrictions against imposing personal liability as a means to discipline corporate managers in both U.S. and Dutch law are consistent with our observation in Chapter 5, that the liability remedy is accompanied by costly side-effects and that, therefore, the social costs of extensive managerial liability may well outweigh the benefits.

PART III

LIMITED LIABILITY AND ORGANIZATIONAL BEHAVIOR

7. The Problem of External Costs

IN PART II OF this book, we addressed the problem of managerial self-interest seeking at shareholders' expense. However, the divergence of interests between utility maximizing managers and shareholders interested in value maximization is not the only conflict of interests bearing on the corporate firm. As Knight [1921, 254] noticed, apart from the corporation's "internal problems", viz. "the protection of its various types of members and adherents against each other's predatory propensities", there is also "the external problem of safeguarding the public interests against exploitation by the corporation as a unit".

In Chapter 4 we noted that when self-interested managers use corporate assets to maximize private utility instead of shareholder wealth, they act detrimentally to both shareholders' and society's interests. We described several market mechanisms that operate to discourage managerial departures from shareholder interests. Although, for the reasons discussed in Chapter 4, such mechanisms are unlikely to ensure complete coherence of managerial actions and shareholders' wealth-maximizing interests, they do provide certain incentives to management to operate the corporate firm in the interest of the shareholders. However, also when management runs the corporation entirely in the interest of the shareholders, society will be harmed if managers maximize shareholders' earnings from the residual claim at the expense of other members of society. The possibility that shareholders, or managers acting to maximize shareholder wealth, may pursue wealth gains at the expense of society at large is what Knight meant by the problem of exploitation of the public interest by the corporate entity.

In Chapter 3 we saw that the statutory principle of limited liability places a limit on shareholders' potential losses from corporate activities. As the losses shareholders may suffer from the operations of the corporate firm are limited to the amount of their investment, they will desire that management undertake projects with positive net present values to shareholders, even though the total social costs of the relevant project in the event of failure may be well in excess of the amount shareholders have invested. If in the end the corporation's liabilities to third parties outside the firm were to exceed the amount shareholders have invested in corporate assets, costs are shifted to such third parties. Recall from our discussion at the outset of Chapter 3 that social efficiency in corporate decision-making requires that the marginal benefits which a contemplated activity is expected to produce for the shareholders are equated with the activity's marginal anticipated costs to society as a whole. Limited liability interferes with this principle where it allows shareholders and managers acting in their interest to ignore a part of the activity's expected social costs, namely that part which exceeds the amount of shareholders' investment.

Where a corporation engages in activities that might cause losses which cannot be satisfied from its assets, limited liability imposes the risk that the assets will prove insufficient to cover the corporation's losses and thus the risk of corporate insolvency, on other members of society, viz. the corporation's creditors. Their risk equals the probability that the corporation will become unable to meet its liabilities times the amount they could lose in that event. More precisely, creditors' risk is calculated by adding up the products of each possible loss they might suffer multiplied by its probability. For instance, if the corporation's total assets at any time amount to USD 10,000 and if there is a 2 percent chance that its activities will generate total liabilities of USD 15,000 and a 3 percent probability of liabilities amounting to USD 18,000, creditors' risk is 0.02 x (USD 15,000 – USD 10,000 =) USD 5,000 + 0.03 x (USD 18,000 – USD 10,000 =) USD 8,000 = USD 100 + USD 240 = USD 340. On the assumption that under a rule of unlimited shareholder liability, they could have recovered the corporation's liabilities entirely from its shareholders, this amount reflects the risk which limited liability shifts to the creditors.

As our example illustrates, the losses that creditors would suffer should the corporation become insolvent are reflected in the risk they bear prior to insolvency. Creditors' risk at a particular point in time indicates their *expected* losses (in the example, USD 340) at that point (as opposed to *actual* losses, which they would only suffer should the corporation become insolvent and which will be zero if the corporation properly pays its debts). Greater losses *ex post*, in the event of a shortfall of the corporation's assets over its liabilities, are reflected in greater risk *ex ante*. Actual losses and risk, then, are two sides of the same coin.

In the present chapter we examine whether the corporate feature of limited liability for shareholders permits the more or less systematic shifting of business risk and, in the event of the corporation's insolvency, a part of the actual costs of corporate activities to third parties. In other words, does limited liability subsidize in either way corporate shareholders at the expense of other members of society?

The Case for External Costs

External Costs

Corporations may impose costs on third parties (denoting any parties other than shareholders and managers) in various ways. Evidently, the corporation may fail to meet its contractual obligations, thus causing financial harm to the party or parties with which the contract was concluded. For example, it may fail to repay a bank loan or to pay the agreed interest, thus injuring the lender. Moreover, the corporation may cause personal injury or property damage to third parties through torts generated by its operations. Labor accidents causing injury to workers in the corporate firm may also be regarded as a cost of corporate activity. Furthermore, third parties may suffer harm from corporate activity which does not classify as a tort or a breach of contract but which does adversely affect them. For instance, environmental pollution from industrial activities will not frequently establish a tort or a breach of contract, although it may well reduce other people's welfare (utility).

When victims of corporate actions are not adequately compensated, in effect they bear a part of the costs of the activity concerned. In fact, uncompensated victims of corporate activities contribute inputs, at no charge, to the activity concerned. Where the corporation fails to repay a bank loan or to pay the agreed interest rate on the loan, the bank is effectively forced to donate money to the firm. Similarly, a trade creditor supplying raw materials for which the firm eventually fails to pay effectively contributes inputs free of charge. And somebody sustaining property damage or bodily harm as a result of a tort generated by the business who is not properly compensated, is effectively forced to donate property or welfare to the corporate firm. As a result, the production function of the corporate firm will include some inputs for which it has not paid, *i.e.* inputs which have been appropriated from other members of society.

In consequence, the firm's level of output is prone to be inconsistent with the social costs associated with the production of the output concerned, especially (but not necessarily) if the firm operates at the point on its production function which maximizes returns to shareholders: the firm will simply produce too much output relative to the social costs of the inputs used.

In standard economic terminology, to the extent that third parties bear a significant portion of the costs of the firm's operations and, therefore, such costs are ignored in corporate decision-making, the firm will pursue a pattern of activity at which marginal social costs exceed marginal social benefits, meaning that society as a whole would be better off if the firm adjusted its operations to the point where marginal social costs equal marginal social benefits (provided that the social cost of making the adjustment is less than the added benefit obtained).

There are various legal methods for effecting that corporate production functions will include only those inputs the corporation has properly paid for, so that no costs are shifted to third parties and management is induced to equate marginal anticipated social costs with marginal anticipated benefits to the shareholders when making decisions in respect of the firm's productive activity. *Direct regulation* of productive activity and business conduct, for instance, the prohibition of certain hazardous production processes susceptible of generating great harm to other members of society, may be enacted in order to altogether avoid the appropriation of free inputs from third parties by the firm, thus aiming to reduce to zero, the amount of costs borne by third parties in respect of the regulated activity.

Establishment of *property rights* to scarce resources specifying who is entitled to determine the use of a productive resource will ordinarily enable the "owner" of the property right to obtain an injunction from a court enjoining the appropriation of the resource concerned so that it will not be included in the firm's production function. Moreover, property rights serve to foster negotiated voluntary arrangements guided by the market mechanism by which the firm agrees to remunerate the property right's owner in exchange for the right to utilize the resource to which the property right is attached; accordingly, given the agreed remuneration, no cost is shifted.

Imposition of *corrective taxes* or levies on firms that engage in activities which may impose costs on parties outside the firm is another means to oppose such cost-shifting. By appropriately taxing firms engaging in such activities, management is induced to include costs imposed on others in corporate cost-benefit calculations and accordingly, to adjust the firm's level of activity (output) to the point where marginal social costs and marginal social benefits are equal.

Finally, *liability rules* may be established which entitle third parties to compensation from the corporation for losses imposed upon them as a result of corporate activity. Liability rules serve both to prevent (*i.e.* to deter) actions that would inflict personal injury or property damage upon others and to allocate the risk of unprevented actions that do injure others. The effective operation of such rules forces the corporation to face the full social costs of its activities, at least to the extent that third parties will in fact be able to recover any losses they sustained by enforcing the liability rule against the corporation.

All of the aforementioned techniques have found their place in the law and regulation of productive activity and each of them has its limitations, depending on the particularities of the activity and the situation in question. Which one, or which combination, is preferable, therefore, will always depend on an evaluation of the relative advantages and disadvantages of the cited methods in the situation under review.

The costs of corporate activity that are borne by other members of society and not by the corporation itself (meaning its shareholders, through their residual claim), are defined as *external costs*. External costs exist whenever third parties are not, or are not entirely, compensated for the costs imposed on them as a result of corporate activity. External costs may include, *inter alia*, the cost to trade creditors of resources they have supplied for which the firm fails to pay, the cost to lenders of loans not repaid and unpaid interest, and the cost to tort victims of property damage or personal injury in respect of which they are not compensated through damages. As indicated above, when corporate management disregards, in whole or in part, the external costs of an activity, too much of the activity will be undertaken relative to its total cost to society. Thus, society will be harmed to the extent that valuable resources are allocated to uses that do not reflect their full social costs.

Similarly, when in its decision-making, management ignores the eventuality that the firm's activities may cause losses to others which it might be unable to repair, and the magnitude of such losses, management will be inclined to engage the firm to a socially excessive extent in activities that at the end of the day, may result in the externalization of costs, that means, activities which expose third parties to the *risk* of suffering uncompensated losses. Moreover, if such risk is ignored in corporate decision-making, once the firm has engaged in some risky activity, it may fail to prevent losses that it could have prevented efficiently, in other words, at a cost less than the reduction in expected losses that could have been accomplished. In either way, the firm's level of risk-taking would be socially inadequate.

Friedman [1970, 32] has advocated the proposition that "[t]he social responsibility of business is to increase its profits". Indeed, corporate managers seeking to raise profits (or, more generally, to maximize stockholder wealth) will allocate scarce resources to those uses for which consumer demand, measured by consumers' willingness to pay, is highest. In this regard, profit (or value) maximization is consistent with the interests of consumers. But the interests of society also require that corporate managers incorporate in their decision-making the anticipated external costs of corporate activities: only when the costs of its activities to third parties are reflected in corporate decision-making will the corporation's allocation of resources correspond to its full costs to society and, thus, be socially efficient. The external costs issue is ignored in Friedman's statement quoted above, which will only be accurate if amended to read: "(...) provided that no uncompensated costs are imposed on third parties".

In the absence of negotiated voluntary agreements devised to cope with external cost problems, whether or not third parties will be compensated for costs imposed upon them by actions of the corporation (for example, losses resulting from the latter's failure to meet contractual obligations, property damage, or bodily harm), depends first on the formulation of legal rights, in particular, the formulation of liability rules: do victims of corporate activity have a legal right to compensation? In a world without transaction costs, the initial definition of rights would be irrelevant to the payment of compensation, as parties would negotiate the utility-maximizing solution irrespective of the choice of legal rule [Coase (1960)]. However, as we discussed at the outset of Chapter 2, transaction costs do exist and they may prevent the utility-maximizing outcome from being reached. Whether existing legal rules are appropriate for holding the corporation liable for costs imposed on third parties, is a question beyond the scope of this book. In the discussion to follow we assume that victims of injury resulting from corporate actions are protected by legal rights (liability rules) entitling them to compensation from the corporation for costs imposed on them by corporate activity (including breaches of contract, torts, and other injury in respect of which a right to receive compensation exists).

However, whether they will *in reality* receive such compensation depends on the corporation's capacity to pay, in other words, it depends ultimately on the value of the assets of the business. If the corporation has insufficient assets to cover the liabilities in tort generated by its activities, the effectiveness of the rule imposing tortious liability is threatened, both as a compensatory mechanism and as a means for inducing management to incorporate in its decision-making the losses that corporate tortious behavior may cause to other members of society. Given that it cannot forfeit *more* than the money value of its assets if ordered to pay damages, any liability exceeding the corporation's assets makes sense only *equal to* the value of these assets, both as a deterrent and with a view to repairing tort victims' losses. Thus, in either respect, the effectiveness of the liability rule is positively correlated with the magnitude of the assets available for the payment of damages. The same observations apply, of course, with respect to corporate liability to pay damages for breach of contractual obligations.

Generally, an injurer who is unable to fully meet his liability to pay damages is "judgment proof" as he is effectively secured from enforcement of court judgments imposing such liability, to the extent that his assets fall short of his liability. Accordingly, the frustration, wholly or partially, of legal liability rules as a means for the remedy of external costs by the injurer's inability to pay, is known as the "judgment proof problem", a term popularized by Shavell [1986]. In the context of corporations, this means that liability rules establish an effective penalty only up to the value of the corporation's assets, as losses sustained by third parties for which they are entitled to damages exceeding corporate assets will affect the corporation (*i.e.* its residual claimants) only equal to these assets.

One response to the judgment proof problem is the enactment of administrative regulation immediately opposing the devolution of costs on third parties (a possibility already mentioned above as a means for preventing externalization of costs), for example, the enactment of compulsory safety standards for production processes intended to preclude excessive tortious liability from arising [Shavell (1984)]. Indeed, where firms have limited assets relative to the liabilities their activities might entail, such direct regulation of productive activity may serve as an alternative to, or as a complement of, a liability rule. However, the introduction of direct regulation such as safety regulation always requires that the regulatory authority either has adequate information about the externality-generating activity it addresses or that it is prepared to spend more or less substantial resources for the purpose of obtaining such information. Moreover, the enactment and enforcement of appropriate regulation is itself socially costly, not merely because of development and enforcement costs and the costs of public decision-making it entails but also because of the opportunity costs associated with forgone benefits from productive activity that is not undertaken due to the regulation which, if it had been undertaken, would in practice not have resulted in liability exceeding corporate assets. Finally, administrative regulation of productive activity (safety) would not solve the problem of external losses arising from corporate activities that would be undertaken notwithstanding the regulation given that the expected returns from the activity outweighed its expected private costs to the firm and its shareholders. If the regulation were a *substitute* for liability to pay damages, corporate decision-makers would have socially excessive incentives to engage the firm in activities that might injure others as the corporation would not pay at all for losses caused to other members of society [Shavell (1986), 55]; and if it were *complementary* to a liability rule, they would have similar incentives to the extent that the anticipated damages to be paid would exceed the value of the corporation's assets.

Another response to corporate inability to pay could be the appropriate definition of liability rules so as to optimize potential injurers' incentives to exercise care (*i.e.* to take preventive measures such as the use of safety devices in order to avoid external losses). In relation to catastrophic accidents causing many victims and aggregate losses greatly exceeding the injurer's wealth, Landes and Posner [1987, 256-272] have suggested that a negligence rule would be preferable to strict liability to oppose such accidents as the negligence standard would directly connect the liability risk to the potential injurer's cost of preventing the accident, by relieving him of any liability if he exercised due care to avert it. If the cost of prevention is less than the potential injurer's wealth, therefore, he will be induced to invest a part of his wealth in order to prevent the accident from occurring rather than face liability to the full extent of his wealth [1987, 257]. With strict liability, in contrast, he would not have similar incentives to take care as he would still risk the full extent of his wealth no matter how much care he exercised. In other words, under a negligence rule, the potential injurer could escape liability for damages altogether by increasing his level of care beyond the negligence standard; with strict liability, however, increasing the level of care would merely *reduce* the probability of losing his entire wealth and, thus, reduce *expected* damages payable but he would still forfeit his entire wealth if a catastrophic accident occurred. Therefore, the returns to the potential injurer from investing additionally in care, will tend to be less under strict liability than under a negligence rule [1987, 259].

However, like safety regulation, the establishment of appropriate incentives to take care would in itself not solve the problem that given the corporation's limited ability to pay damages, corporate decision-makers may engage it to too great an extent in activities that could cause injury to others, that is, to a point at which the activity's marginal anticipated social costs exceed marginal social benefits. As a rule, the magnitude of third party losses that an activity may occasion does not merely depend on the level of care potential injurers exercise in order to prevent such losses but also on the extent to which the activity is undertaken. Potential injurers' incentives to take care at a given level of activity are different from the incentives that determine their choice of the activity level *per se*. Generally, strict liability will induce potential injurers' to pursue a lower level of activity than a negligence rule would, given that under a negligence rule, they do not have to bear the losses their activity imposes on others if they act with due care, meaning that the activity level will be irrelevant to their expected costs of having to pay damages as long as due care is exercised; under strict liability, in contrast, they would have to pay for any loss inflicted on third parties, regardless of their level of care [Shavell (1987), 23-25]. With strict liability, therefore, potential injurers' expected damages are normally higher than under a negligence rule and their incentives to engage in the activity concerned will be correspondingly lower. Which rule is preferable, strict liability because of its greater impact on activity levels or negligence because of its presumed greater effect on incentives to exercise care to prevent losses exhausting the injurer's assets, will depend on the relative importance of each factor to the incidence and magnitude of external loss.

The Role of Limited Liability

Limited liability renders the corporation's residual claimants judgment proof in respect of the tortious and contractual liabilities incurred by the corporation as it releases them from the operation of the legal liability rules to which the former is subject. Thus it limits the effectiveness of such rules, both to provide compensation for injury resulting from corporate activity and as a means to prevent such injury by establishing appropriate loss-preventing incentives, to the value of the residual claimants' investment in the corporation's assets, since any judgment imposing corporate liability may only be enforced against these assets. How then does limited liability for shareholders relate to the externalization of costs by the corporation?

It does so in two ways.

First, limited liability *directly* shifts costs to third parties in the event of corporate insolvency. Under a rule of *un*limited liability, the shareholders would have to make up for the unpaid debts of the corporation. As we saw in Chapter 3, limited liability, on the other hand, imposes on the corporation's creditors the costs of corporate insolvency: should the corporation fail to pay its debts, the unpaid amounts are borne by the creditors. Limited liability shifts costs to creditors where it keeps them from collecting their unpaid claims on the corporation from shareholders' non-invested assets. Said differently, it allocates to creditors the risk of the corporation's inability to pay and relieves shareholders of any such risk once they have fully paid up the subscription price of their shares, shareholders' risk thus being confined to the risk of losing the value of their investment. This is the essence of limited liability as a risk-sharing arrangement between shareholders and creditors. The relative size of each party's risk pursuant to this arrangement, *i.e.* each party's portion of total losses should the corporation fail, is determined by the amount that shareholders have committed to the assets of the business in relation to the corporation's total debt. The lesser the value of the corporation's assets relative to its obligations to creditors, that means, the less its ability to pay, the more the risk that is shifted to the creditors and the greater will be their losses if the corporation fails.

Second, limited liability encourages corporate activities that may impose significant losses on third parties such as trade creditors, lenders and tort victims by diluting corporate decision-makers' incentives to pay regard to the effects of corporate activities on third parties, including the risk that the latter will eventually find themselves unable to enforce tortious and contractual liabilities generated by the firm for lack of assets. The shareholders being judgment proof in respect of the liabilities incurred by the corporation as a result of the limited liability rule renders them rationally insensitive to corporate liabilities exceeding the value of their investment. Because of the limited liability principle, if a particular venture becomes a success, shareholders will capture the entire reward, whilst they will bear only part of the loss in the event of a default. In effect, as we saw at the outset of Chapter 3, limited liability places a ceiling on the losses which may result from the firm's operations that are relevant to corporate decision-making: given limited liability, potential losses exceeding the amount of their invested wealth are irrelevant to the shareholders. Hence, whenever shareholders anticipate positive net returns from a contemplated corporate activity, they will desire that the corporation undertakes the activity concerned, regardless of the liabilities to third parties in excess of their investment which it may entail.

In other words, if from an *ex ante* perspective a venture is expected to generate positive wealth effects for the shareholders, although *ex post* the corporation's assets may be insufficient to offset its costs to third parties, shareholders have wealth-maximizing incentives to desire that the activity go ahead. Accordingly, the possibility of shifting a part of the costs of failure to third parties promotes projects with anticipated positive wealth gains for shareholders but with potentially large losses for other members of society in the event of failure. As the amount shareholders can lose is limited to the amount of their investment, corporate decision-makers acting in shareholders' interests will be induced to ignore possible third party costs in excess of shareholders' investment, which runs contrary to the concept that the full social costs of a contemplated activity should be considered in order to achieve social efficiency in corporate conduct. For instance, they may decide in favor of investing in a factory that causes pollution if the investment is anticipated to yield an attractive return to shareholders, although the anticipated clean-up costs of environmental spills may well exceed the corporation's financial ability.

On the other hand, if corporate managers forgo profitable investment opportunities which would expose third parties to potentially large losses (for instance, if they were to decide against investing in the above-mentioned factory because of possible environmental costs), their behavior may be understood as a departure from maximization of shareholder wealth. Consequently, as we saw in Chapter 4, the rental value of a manager's human capital in the outside labor market may deteriorate, thereby injuring his ability to attract better employment offers elsewhere. Also, outsiders may observe possible wealth gains from bidding on the stock market in order to acquire control of the company, firing or disciplining incumbent managers and deciding in favor of the project previously rejected (*i.e.* build the factory that causes pollution although the corporation will probably be unable to pay for future clean-up costs). In this way market mechanisms may punish managers whose business decisions do take into account the costs of corporate activities to third parties, that is, those who *would* take decisions reflecting their full costs to society as a whole.

The observation that with limited liability, wealth maximizing shareholders will want managers to ignore potential losses exceeding shareholders' invested wealth whereas such losses are relevant from a social efficiency perspective, should not be misinterpreted to imply that for corporate decision-making to be socially efficient, management should reject each possible activity that one day might cause losses to third parties in excess of the corporation's assets (*i.e.* that might externalize costs). Rather, given that the actual success or failure of a contemplated activity is invariably subject to some degree of uncertainty, management should abstain from engaging the firm in activities that would cause *expected* losses to shareholders and creditors jointly in excess of the activity's expected benefits to the shareholders (which would mean that the activity's anticipated social costs outweighed its expected benefits). *Potential* losses will be relevant to corporate decision-making because in order to determine the *expected* losses entailed by an activity, each potential loss must be multiplied by the probability of its occurring (following which the resulting values must be totaled). Whether the expected amounts will in fact materialize depends, of course, on the activity's actual results. From the point of view of social efficiency, if expected losses to society in full are less than expected returns to the shareholders, it is desirable that the activity in question be undertaken (even though *potential* losses may outweigh corporate assets and even though at the end of the day, the corporation may prove unable to remedy the *actual* losses imposed on third parties) [Shavell

(1986), 58 fn. 32; (1987), 169]. If, in contrast, expected losses to shareholders and creditors jointly in the event of failure exceed the expected benefits to the shareholders in the event of success, the engagement of the corporation in the activity concerned would be socially inefficient.

Where corporate decision-makers ignore potential losses inasmuch as they exceed shareholders' invested wealth, their estimate of the activity's expected social costs will be too low and in consequence, they will raise the risk to which creditors are exposed and increase their actual losses should the corporation become unable to satisfy its payment obligations, in comparison with the situation where the activity's expected full social costs had been taken into account. More specifically, shareholders and managers acting in their interests more or less systematically ignoring potential losses exceeding shareholders' invested wealth, will affect corporate decision-making in at least three ways (as Shavell's more general discussion of the judgment proof problem suggests [Shavell (1986), 45-58]).

In the first place, the level of activities that could cause losses in excess of the value of the corporation's assets would be higher than if the full extent of such losses were considered: as limited liability promotes projects with positive net present values to the shareholders regardless of whether the project's liabilities might exhaust the corporation's assets, there will be a tendency for corporate decision-makers to engage the firm in a socially excessive level of risky activity, that is, to take business risks at which marginal expected social costs exceed marginal expected benefits to the shareholders (as is further illustrated by an accounting example in the next section). In this way, limited liability for shareholders may be considered to induce managers to pursue over-risky business ventures and investments. Devra Golbe [1988] has demonstrated that the tendency for firms to pursue risky projects and, thus, the probability of marginal expected social losses outweighing marginal anticipated returns to the shareholders, may be even greater if the firm is approaching bankruptcy: given that limited liability guarantees that their shares will never be worth less than zero and normally, the shares will be approaching this minimum value if bankruptcy is near, increasing the riskiness of the firm's operating returns may produce large anticipated wealth gains for the shareholders, net of their possible (and expected) losses, from increases in the value of their shares, on which they will cash in if the risky project pays off and the firm remains in business, at the expense of higher expected losses to the firm's creditors. As suggested by Golbe [1988, 79], this dual effect of increasing risk could foster the formation of coalitions consisting of shareholders and lenders willing to cooperate with the firm and with each other to avoid bankruptcy, the latter to avoid loss, the former to secure their expected gain from the firm's continuation.

Secondly, at a given level of activity, corporate decision-makers' incentives to take care in order to avoid losses may be insufficient as because of the limited liability principle, the shareholders have no incentive to invest in precautionary measures meant to prevent losses *exceeding* their investment (which they will treat as imposing on them a loss only equal to their investment). Given limited liability, the amount of loss which the shareholders consider worth preventing may be less than the expected total losses associated with the firm's activities, and their investments in care (*i.e.* loss prevention) will be proportionately less. Therefore, the corporation may fail to reduce the probability or the magnitude, or both, of the losses its activities might cause to others (including losses exceeding the firm's assets) to the socially efficient point at which the marginal social costs of prevention activity equal the marginal social benefit in terms of lower expected losses. To phrase differently, by not exercising care to prevent losses exceeding shareholders' invested wealth, the firm may fail to raise the level of care as long as the reduction in the risk of loss that extra care would accomplish exceeds the increment to the costs of exercising care.

Similarly, incentives to have the corporation purchase liability insurance are diluted given that the insurance coverage desirable from the shareholders' perspective is determined by their own maximum possible loss rather than by the full extent of the liabilities the firm's activities may cause. As the amount shareholders may lose is limited to the value of a corporation's assets, it does not pay them to have the corporation take out insurance beyond this value, even though its activities may generate far greater liabilities (for example, arising from torts attributable to the corporation). In consequence, it will be a rational decision for corporate decision-makers to confine the corporation's liability insurance to the value of its assets: if more insurance were obtained, the shareholders would pay, through the insurance premiums, for losses from which limited liability had already released them. In this way, limited liability may adversely affect third parties' ability to obtain compensation through the corporation's insurance policy for harm imposed on them by its activities. In addition, where insurers' potential exposure would be less as a result of firms purchasing less insurance coverage than under unlimited shareholder liability, insurance companies' incentives to actively monitor corporate activity with a view to preventing losses (for instance, through demanding additional safety devices) would be adversely affected as well, since their expected return on monitoring expenditures decreases as they have less exposure under the insurance policy.

According to the reasoning described above, the downside of limited liability is not so much that it precludes creditors from collecting their claims against the corporation out of the shareholders' non-invested wealth but, rather, that limited liability creates perverse incentives to take business decisions which systematically disregard the potential costs of corporate activities to third parties in excess of shareholders' investment. Thus limited liability creates incentives for underinvestment in loss-prevention and the purchase of liability insurance, and for excessive allocation of scarce resources to hazardous economic activities or, generally, to activities involving potentially large social costs [Halpern, Trebilcock and Turnbull (1980), 126]. As a result, third parties will be exposed to greater risk of suffering losses from the corporation's actions, and to greater actual losses in the event of a default, than they would have been if management had taken into consideration such losses up to the full extent of shareholders' wealth (*i.e.* including shareholders' non-invested assets).

Limited Liability and Investment Decisions

If the amount shareholders have invested in the assets of the corporation turns out to be insufficient to pay its liabilities, losses are imposed on the corporation's creditors. Where limited liability actually keeps the shareholders from having to pay for such losses, that is, in the event of corporate default, the limited liability rule effectively shifts costs to creditors. And where limited liability induces corporate managements to take into account in their decision-making less than the anticipated costs of corporate activities to other members of society, limited liability encourages business decisions and behavior patterns that would result in the shifting of costs if the corporation fails and, thus, raises the probability of third parties having to bear losses as a result of corporate activity. This is the core of the argument which states that limited liability externalizes risk.

This potential effect of limited liability was already indicated by nineteenth-century political economist John Ramsey McCulloch [1965, 363-364], when he argued that limited liability would induce men "to engage in desperate adventures". McCulloch believed that such over-risky activities were the inevitable result of limited liability disconnecting the decision to undertake a venture from bearing responsibility for the full consequences (including the costs of possible failure) of that decision [Amsler, Bartlett and Bolton (1981), 787].

In his discussion of limited liability, Landers [1975; 1976], too, suggests that limited liability externalizes business risk. Through the statutory principle of limited liability combined with low capitalization requirements, he submits, "the law has, to a large extent, placed the costs of promoting new businesses on the creditors of the corporation and, through them, on the public as a whole" [1975, 593]. Ignoring the significance of limited liability to the separation of management and residual risk-bearing in the corporate firm and limited liability's other functions as discussed in Chapter 3, Landers [1975, 618] regards the shifting of risk as the very origin of the limited liability principle: "(...) it is relatively clear that the doctrine of limited liability was envisioned as a protection for individuals who invested in business enterprises. Insofar as the corporation itself could not pay its debts, society at large was to bear the costs of the corporate enterprise". From a similar perspective but with a more negative undertone, Otto Kahn-Freund [1944, 54] advocated that limited liability has "often become a means of evading liabilities and of concealing the real interests behind the business".

Let us now illustrate the impact of limited liability on investment decisions by a simple accounting example. Imagine a corporation which has raised 4 million U.S. dollars in equity capital from its shareholders and whose management is considering investing the entire amount in a chemicals manufacturing plant. Suppose that if the corporation were to invest the amount put up by its shareholders in constructing and operating such a plant over a ten year period, there would be a 65 percent chance that the corporation would earn aggregate profits of USD 7 million, a 20 percent chance of a combined profit of USD 12 million and a 10 percent chance of an aggregate USD 2 million loss for the ten year term (all amounts being discounted to present values on the date of the investment). Suppose further that there would be a 5 percent probability that at one point during the relevant period the corporation would incur a catastrophic loss of USD 120 million, for instance, as a result of an explosion generating massive liabilities in tort. Ignoring, for argument's sake, changes in the investment value (the market value of the plant), on balance the expected return to shareholders, net of expected losses, would be USD 750,000 positive over the full ten year period (0.65 x USD 7,000,000 + 0.20 x USD 12,000,000 – 0.10 x USD 2,000,000 – 0.05 x USD 120,000,000), if the full potential tortious liability of USD 120 million is taken into consideration. That means, shareholders would earn a return of USD 75,000 per annum, amounting to a return on equity rate of 1.875 percent a year.

This return rate would render the investment clearly unattractive to investors, given that the yield on (virtually) risk-free government bonds (for example, United States Treasury bonds) tends to be well above 1.875 percent per annum, so that they would be unlikely to support a management decision in favor of making the investment concerned. The investment in the contemplated chemicals manufacturing plant would also be disadvantageous from the perspective of society as a whole: the relatively low rate of return on invested capital, compared to returns on alternative investment possibilities (such as government bonds), signals that the same resources are valued higher by society if allocated to a different use.

Now take into account the liability rule to which the shareholders are subject. If they were subject to unlimited liability, the relevant cost-benefit calculation desired by the shareholders would follow the pattern set forth above. As they would lose their entire non-invested wealth, the full expected tortious liability (a 5 percent chance of USD 120 million) would be relevant as a cost (subject to the amount of shareholders' total non-invested wealth only). But if the shareholders, by contrast, enjoy limited liability, the calculation (and the resulting investment decision) would be completely different: instead of USD 120 million, shareholders would wish the potential tortious liability be taken into account only up to the value of their investment, *i.e.* USD 4 million, being their maximum loss. Adjusted accordingly, over a ten year period on balance, the expected net returns to shareholders on the investment in the above-mentioned chemicals plant would now be USD 6,550,000 positive (0.65 x USD 7,000,000 + 0.20 x USD 12,000,000 – 0.10 x USD 2,000,000 – 0.05 x USD 4,000,000), which equals a return rate of USD 655,000 per annum and an annual return on equity rate of 16.375 percent. This return is clearly more attractive to investors than the return in our previous calculation (and higher than the usual yield on government bonds) and is therefore likely to lead to a positive investment decision, although the social costs of the plant (the expected liability in tort) are unchanged.

As our example illustrates, limited liability inducing investors (and managers acting in their interests) to ignore potential third party losses beyond the value of their investment is not an isolated datum. The more fundamental issue is that as a consequence of external costs being ignored in the making of investment decisions, limited liability leads to a use of socially valuable resources different to that which would be chosen if the investment's full anticipated social costs were taken into consideration. If full social costs are taken into account, a different use of resources having greater regard for the interests of third parties would result, which would expose other members of society to less hazard and reflect greater concern for their welfare (for instance, carry fewer tort risks), which would not, or to a lesser degree, pursue stockholder wealth maximization through actual or potential wealth transfers from the corporation's creditors, and which would result in smaller losses to third parties in the event of the corporation's default – that means, a use of resources more consistent with its actual cost to society as a whole. Thus, the partial ignorance of an activity's social costs provoked by limited liability shatters the logic that consumers' willingness to pay alone compels firms to allocate society's scarce resources to the uses that are valued highest by society as a whole.

The Case against External Costs

The idea that limited liability externalizes risk to the corporation's creditors is based on the premise that creditors are not compensated for the extra costs they would bear in the event of a default in comparison with their costs under unlimited shareholder liability. Several scholars have questioned this premise.

Manne [1975, 514], for instance, has argued that the risk of corporate insolvency is generally understood by the corporation's creditors and treated by them as any other cost. In addition he points out that mandatory disclosure of corporate financial data serves to inform creditors about the magnitude of this cost. These observations suggest that limited liability does *not* shift uncompensated business risks to the corporation's creditors as the risk of corporate insolvency is voluntarily assumed by the latter, and likely to be reflected in the interest rates they charge the corporation.

For the same reason, Posner [1976] has submitted that the limited liability principle does not disadvantage creditors. Posner assumes that creditors are fully aware that under limited shareholder liability, the costs of corporate insolvency will lie with them. Therefore, he maintains, they will make up for the extra loss they would suffer in the event of the corporation's default by insisting upon interest rates higher than those they would charge if the liability rule permitted them to recover their unsatisfied claims from shareholders' non-invested wealth. The interest rate creditors will charge, then, is not merely compensation for the provision of credit but also for the bearing of the risk that the corporation's assets will prove insufficient to repay the amount extended [1976, 501]. By this theory, creditors are compensated *ex ante* for their higher costs *ex post* should the corporation become insolvent: "[Creditors are] fully compensated by the higher interest rate that the corporation must pay by virtue of enjoying limited liability" [1976, 503].

Thus the interest rate charged will compensate creditors for shouldering the risk of corporate insolvency, regardless of whether this risk will ever materialize. In estimating the default risk and in setting a risk-commensurate interest rate, creditors may take advantage of the information on companies' creditworthiness which is available from specialized rating agencies, in addition to information disclosed by the corporation itself. But creditors may also actively seek to reduce the amount of risk shifted to them, which in turn will reduce the risk-reflecting interest rate. By reducing their risk of non-payment, creditors would reduce their actual costs should the corporation become insolvent. For this purpose they may demand, for instance, that the corporation effects the encumbrance of certain assets as security for the fulfillment of its payment obligations to them. Moreover, creditors may insist upon a contract provision compelling the corporation to provide additional security in the future at the creditor's first request. Such a provision would permit creditors to stabilize their risk if the corporation were to undertake business ventures that would increase the risk of non-payment.

Furthermore, creditors may reduce their expected loss in the event of corporate default by requiring that the corporation's shareholders personally guarantee the payment of the corporation's debts. Similarly, they may demand that individual shareholders supply collateral (*i.e.* non-invested wealth) for the payment of corporate debts. By such means, creditors may effectively contract around the statutory principle of limited liability.

In conclusion, according to the reasoning stated above, as creditors are free to charge risk-commensurate interest rates and to adjust other contract terms to the limited liability rule, limited liability is unlikely to transfer uncompensated business risks to creditors of the corporation. Since creditors may mitigate their loss in the event of corporate default through various contractual devices as indicated above and since they are compensated *ex ante* through higher interest rates for the (remaining) costs of corporate insolvency which limited liability shifts to them, there is, so the argument goes, no externality [Posner (1976), 503; (1992), 395].

The question of whether limited liability externalizes the risk of corporate insolvency to creditors is similar to the question of whether liability insurance allows potential injurers to externalize the costs of accidents. With liability insurance, potential injurers generally have less reason to avoid accidents than if they were to pay from their own pockets the costs of accidents attributable to them. The same applies to corporate attitudes to business failure when shareholders have limited liability. It should be noted, however, that liability insurance for potential injurers does not externalize the risk of accidents where victims of extra accidents which may occur as a result of potential injurers' decreased incentives to avoid accidents, are fully compensated out of the liability insurance and where liability insurers are compensated *ex ante*, through insurance premiums, for the payments they make to the beneficiaries of the insurance policies. If an insurer agrees to bear the liability risk and if victims of accidents are fully compensated, there is no externality [Shavell (1982); Landes and Posner (1987), 13].

By requiring creditors to assume part of the risk of business failure, the statutory principle of limited liability creates a form of non-market insurance of shareholders' non-invested wealth, as Arrow [1970, 139-140] has observed. From this angle, creditors (the "insurers") provide insurance of the non-invested assets of the shareholders (the "victims") against the risk of corporate failure (the "accident"). The insurance premium paid is the differential between the interest rate creditors charge under limited liability for shareholders and the rate they would charge if they could collect corporate debts from both the assets of the corporation and shareholders' non-invested assets. Accordingly, creditors' costs (as insurers of shareholders' personal wealth) in the event of corporate failure (corporate insolvency being the insured risk) may be larger with limited shareholder liability but so are their (pre-insolvency) revenues as insurers. Where creditors agree to "insure" shareholders' liability for corporate debts in this way, there is no externality. And where creditors were to reduce the insurance coverage they provide, for example, by demanding personal guarantees from shareholders for debts of the corporation, the insurance premium they could charge as a part of the interest rate would be proportionally lower.

To constrain the risk that the corporation's assets will be insufficient to pay its debts, creditors frequently use instruments similar to those used by liability insurers. First, creditors may incorporate into loan contracts clauses designed to prevent behavior that would increase the probability of realization of their risk (*i.e.* non-payment of their claims), just as insurers do. Contractual restrictions on the corporation's ability to alienate assets at less than their market value and limitations on the pay-out of dividends may be viewed as such preventive arrangements. Second, creditors may reduce their aggregate risk of non-payment by pooling risks, that is, by supplying a large number of small loans to different borrowers rather than a few large ones. In the same way, liability insurers choose to insure numerous potential liabilities, each of which may result in a relatively small exposure for the insurer. And third, just like insurers, creditors may relieve themselves of some or all of their risk by reinsuring the risk of non-payment of their claim, for example, through selling their claim at a discount in exchange for immediate cash or by taking out credit insurance where available.

Let us assume for the moment that creditors are indeed compensated *ex ante*, as reasoned above, for the extra loss they would suffer in the event of corporate insolvency. How will such compensation affect corporate decision-making?

As the corporation must now pay, through higher interest rates and less favorable contract terms, for the risk that is shifted to creditors, corporate managements are induced to take into account the full risk that the corporation's assets may become insufficient to pay off its creditors: when the corporation is to pay for shifting the costs of future insolvency to creditors, these costs *are* relevant to calculating the net anticipated private gain to corporate shareholders from a contemplated activity. As a result, the corporation will now engage in activities of which the risk that they will lead to corporate insolvency is consistent with the expected losses to shareholders and creditors jointly, that is, with the activity's anticipated *social* costs.

As mentioned at the beginning of this chapter, the risk that the corporation will default in the future represents a current cost to creditors equal to the probability of corporate insolvency times creditors' potential loss in the event of default. When this cost is reflected in interest rates (and other contract terms) facing the corporation, it will almost unavoidably be taken into account in corporate cost-benefit calculations. Accordingly, management will select activities carrying the level of default risk at which marginal anticipated benefits to corporate shareholders from the activity concerned equal marginal social costs [Easterbrook and Fischel (1985), 107]. Thus, although total losses to creditors in the event of corporate insolvency may still be higher than with unlimited shareholder liability, the amount of risk shifted to creditors will not exceed the amount for which the corporation has compensated them (as would be the case if creditors were not properly compensated for bearing the risk of insolvency).

Where creditors are compensated *ex ante* for bearing the risk that the corporation's assets may be insufficient to pay off its debts, the corporation will choose activities which maximize anticipated stockholder returns taking into consideration the expected costs of a default to shareholders *and* to creditors. Similarly, once the corporation has engaged in an activity that may cause losses in excess of corporate assets, the level of care it will exercise to prevent losses and the amount of insurance it will take out, will correspond to expected social losses instead of only to shareholders' expected private losses. Consequently, the total degree of corporate risk-taking will be commensurate with its social costs and hence, socially efficient; there will be no "excessive" risk-taking by the corporation.

Flaws in the Compensation Argument

Involuntary Creditors

The theory that creditors are compensated for the risk limited liability shifts to them assumes that creditors negotiate *ex ante* to obtain compensation for the loss they may suffer later owing to shareholders' non-liability for the debts of the corporation. Such negotiations in turn require that creditors *voluntarily* provide credit. Indeed, when a bank grants a loan or when a supplier of inputs sells on credit, it is their voluntary decision to do so. But not all credit is given voluntarily. Corporations may have two categories of creditors who have not consented to giving credit.

First, there are creditors whose extension of credit, and the applicable rates, is prescribed by public regulation. These statutory creditors include the tax authorities and public agencies authorized to collect amounts payable under social security laws. Tax rates and social security premiums are fixed by statute law and their magnitude is independent of the risk that a particular debtor-corporation may default. Unlike lenders and trade creditors, tax authorities and social security agencies do not negotiate *ex ante* with a particular corporation to set a rate reflecting the risk of that corporation's insolvency. Thus, the amount of taxes and social security premiums a corporation is to pay will not incorporate a premium to make up for the insolvency risk of that corporation.

Statutory rights of preference for, for example, the tax authorities over other creditors in the event of bankruptcy, establish an *ex post* remedy for the state treasury's inability to bargain for *ex ante* compensation for the insolvency risk. However, such preferential rights do not alter the fact itself that no compensation for the insolvency risk shifted by limited liability is agreed, and that the state treasury is unable to bargain *ex ante* for protection against that risk or for adjustment of tax rates to the corporation's risk of insolvency. Statutory rights of preference are primarily a means for after-the-fact loss *reduction* rather than an instrument for loss *avoidance* as they come into play only after the insolvency risk has materialized. They do not preclude the uncompensated transfer of business risk in itself which *ex ante* negotiations, in contrast, would serve to avoid.

The charging of advance levies is a means to altogether avoid the shifting of risk to the state treasury or social security agencies. In that event, the charging authority does not become a creditor at all and, hence, does not assume the risk of corporate insolvency in respect of the amount levied in advance so that it is not affected by the rule governing shareholders' liability.

A second category of involuntary creditors consists of victims of torts generated by the corporation's activities. They are creditors by virtue of their right to receive damages once the corporation's liability in tort has been established. A tort constitutes a transaction by which the victim is *forced* to contribute to the activities of the tortfeasor. The damage to a tort victim's property, personal health or otherwise is an input to the corporation's activities, just like labor, capital and raw materials. The single, yet fundamental, difference is that tort victims have not agreed to supply their property, health or otherwise as an input to the corporation. In other words, they have not consented to being injured by the corporation's activities. A bank loan or a contract for the supply of raw materials requires bilateral agreement between the supplier and the corporation. Tort victims' damage, in contrast, is the result of a unilateral action of the corporation, with their compensation being determined *ex post*.

Potential tort victims are not merely subject to the risk of suffering injury but also to the risk that eventually the corporation will be unable to satisfy their claims for damages. As no bilateral negotiations take place in advance, potential victims of corporate torts will not be compensated for bearing the risk that the corporation's assets may be insufficient to cover its liabilities in tort [Posner (1976), 506; (1992), 396]. Limited liability, then, permits the shifting of uncompensated business risks to the corporation's involuntary creditors.

As the corporation does not have to pay a premium to involuntary creditors for bearing the risk that their claims may exceed the value of the corporation's assets, potential liabilities to involuntary creditors in excess of corporate assets are irrelevant to the corporation's cost-benefit calculations. Hence, potential losses to involuntary creditors that it may be unable to pay, will not be taken into account in corporate decisions relating to whether or not a particular project should be undertaken or to how much the corporation should invest in order to prevent losses to other members of society. Therefore, with limited shareholder liability, corporate management is likely to decide in favor of undertaking projects which may generate tortious liabilities well exceeding the value of the corporation's assets if only they have a positive net present value to its shareholders. In this way limited liability promotes externalization of costs to involuntary creditors.

Management's decision would probably be different if the corporation were to compensate potential tort victims for bearing the risk that the corporation may default on its liabilities in tort. In that event future tortious liabilities exceeding corporate assets would be a current cost to the corporation, represented by the risk premium it must pay, and would therefore become relevant to the calculation of shareholders' net expected private gain from a particular project. The higher the tortious liabilities a project may generate, the higher this cost would be, and the less likely it is that the project would have a positive net present value to shareholders. However, as involuntary creditors are not *in fact* compensated for the risk imposed upon them and as their losses in the event of a default are therefore irrelevant to the corporation's cost-benefit calculations, the risk the corporation will take is likely to be too great in relation to the costs its activities may impose on this class of creditors.

Clark [1986, 10] argues that the externalization of risk to tort victims by the limited liability rule is chiefly a "theoretical problem", as so far excessive liabilities in tort have caused very few large, publicly held corporations to go bankrupt. This observation, however, understates the problem. The problem is not so much that with limited shareholder liability, some of the costs of corporate activities may be borne by the corporation's involuntary creditors in the event of corporate failure (as they cannot collect their unpaid claims from shareholders' personal assets) but, rather, that these creditors are not compensated for the risk that the corporation's assets may be insufficient to satisfy their claims. Therefore, corporations' incentives to reduce risks, that is, to lower the probability or the magnitude of the losses that their activities may impose on others, will be diluted to the effect that they will systematically take greater business risks than they would if they had to pay compensation to involuntary creditors for the risk of non-payment of their claims.

As a consequence, corporations are apt to follow behavior patterns – which can range from their engagement to a socially excessive extent in activities that may cause losses exceeding corporate assets and the exercise of inadequate care to prevent losses at a given level of activity, to the purchase of insufficient liability insurance coverage – that are inconsistent with the anticipated social costs associated with their activities and that, therefore, may be regarded as socially undesirable regardless of whether or not at the end of the day, the corporation will be in default. Also, if a default would occur in fact, given the greater risks taken, the *sum* of the corporation's unpaid debts will most likely be higher than if the corporation had to pay its involuntary creditors for the default risk imposed upon them.

It is true, of course, that the dilution of incentives to reduce risks that is entailed by the limited liability rule, is most significant where there is a significant probability of losses exceeding corporate assets given that in the absence of such a probability (for instance, if the value of the corporation's would not in fact release the shareholders from risk and, hence, would not allow them to shift risk to parties outside the firm. However, one may not conclude from this observation that limited liability will lead to a dulling of incentives solely with respect to firms with modest assets. Even firms with substantial assets may engage in activities which may cause losses exceeding their ability to pay (for instance, they may engage in hazardous production processes that could cause catastrophic injury in the event of a breakdown, or they may manufacture products that might give rise to mass tort claims in the event of a manufacturing defect) [Shavell (1987), 168].

Perhaps more importantly, firms with substantial assets may deliberately incur substantial liabilities to voluntary creditors (for instance, by contracting bank loans in order to acquire capital for new investment, to obtain cash for distribution to the shareholders, or to enhance the monitoring of management by the capital markets). This would raise the firm's total debt burden (and, *ceteris paribus*, its debt-equity ratio) which in turn would raise the probability of total liabilities to voluntary and involuntary creditors collectively exceeding the corporation's ability to pay. In this event, despite the presence of substantial assets in the firm, limited liability will tend to dilute the corporation's incentives to avoid losses inasmuch as anticipated losses exceed corporate assets. Note that even where the probability of losses exceeding corporate assets is rather small, for instance, if there is a slight chance of a catastrophic event triggering enormous liabilities in tort, incentives may be diluted with respect to the reduction of the chance or the possible magnitude of such a catastrophic loss as, given limited liability, the greater part of the loss would be borne by the corporation's creditors anyway and as, therefore, this part would not be worth preventing from the shareholders' perspective.

Voluntary Creditors

With limited liability for shareholders, involuntary creditors and voluntary creditors each bear a part of the risk of corporate insolvency. Whilst involuntary creditors are not compensated for bearing this risk, voluntary creditors are, so the theory goes. But will money lenders and trade creditors, in reality, raise the risk-free rate on credit by a premium that reflects the risk of corporate insolvency?

In a world with zero transaction costs in which complete information about insolvency risks is available at no cost, indeed they would. In such a world, would-be creditors could readily make themselves acquainted with the corporation's capacity to pay, bearing in mind the risk of corporate assets would-be creditors could readily make themselves acquainted with the corporation's capacity to pay, bearing in mind the risk of corporate assets falling short of the corporation's obligations. Moreover, as negotiations would be cost free, no barriers would exist to creditors negotiating risk-commensurate interest rates. In this Coasian world, individual credit arrangements would not be affected by the statutory rule governing shareholders' liability. Negotiations between corporate borrowers and creditors would in any event result in *ex ante* payment of risk premiums accurately reflecting the underlying insolvency risk.

If transaction costs were zero, parties would simply negotiate until they eventually arrived at an arrangement under which the terms on which investors in corporate equity were prepared to borrow equaled the terms on which creditors were prepared to provide credit. This equilibrium arrangement would be independent of the statutory liability regime. If shareholders preferred having a low interest rate to enduring less risk, the credit arrangement would provide for unlimited liability. On the other hand, if they chose to have their non-invested assets insulated from liability, the arrangement would offer limited liability to investors at the price of a higher interest rate [Meiners (1978), 224; Meiners, Mofsky and Tollison (1979); Anderson and Tollison (1983), 114-115].

However, there are several reasons why, in the real, non-Coasian world, not only *in*voluntary creditors but also *voluntary* creditors are rather unlikely to obtain adequate compensation for the risk of corporate insolvency which limited liability imposes upon them. First, statutory restrictions may exist which prevent creditors from obtaining risk-reflecting interest premiums. There may be statutory control of interest rates, either in the form of interest ceilings or in the form of fixed interest percentages. Such regulation would obviously limit the ability of creditors to charge risk-commensurate interest rates.

Second, prospective creditors' ability to charge compensation for the risk of non-payment is dependent upon the information they have about the corporation's capacity to pay. To assess the risk of a default, creditors require, in particular, "accurate information about the existing and expected assets and liabilities of the borrowing corporation (...)", as Posner [1976, 508] acknowledges. Such information is not freely available. Reliable information about the insolvency risk may be hard to obtain and in any event there is a real cost to acquiring such information. This cost will tend to become higher as more accurate information is sought. Prohibitive costs of information gathering may keep creditors from charging risk-commensurate premiums.

Mandatory disclosure of corporate financial data does not merely feed information into market mechanisms disciplining managers, it also serves to reduce creditors' and would-be creditors' costs of gathering information about corporate ability to pay. However, a corporation's disclosed financial statements merely reveal information about the past. They do not normally inform a creditor about the actual risk of default as at the date at which he contracts with that corporation. Moreover, the balance sheet and income statement of a corporation may fail to disclose certain data relevant to the assessment of its capacity to pay. For instance, a corporation may have issued guarantees for the payment of debts incurred by companies affiliated to it. Such guarantees may not be shown in its financial statements, although they could cause the issuing corporation to run into serious financial trouble if the company to which the guarantee relates were to default. When a creditor is unaware of such a guarantee or of other information relevant to assessing a corporation's capacity to pay, the risk premium he demands is unlikely to accord with the true risk of non-payment.

Third, the costs of negotiating compensation for the default risk may be prohibitive (even when a creditor has more or less reliable information), especially when those costs are large relative to the creditor's anticipated return from the transaction concerned. Similarly, high negotiation costs may stand in the way of a contractual modification of the statutory limited liability rule, even if, in the absence of transaction costs, the creditor and the corporation's shareholders chose to reduce the former's exposure by extending shareholders' liability in exchange for a lower interest rate.

The larger the stake involved, the greater the probability that a creditor will be prepared to incur substantial information and negotiation costs to achieve an arrangement which properly compensates him for the risk of non-payment, and which at the same time creates a risk-return relationship in accordance with that creditor's preferences. For instance, for a bank considering the extension of a large loan, it probably pays to surmount high transaction costs in order to set a risk-reflecting interest rate, and to adjust the limited liability rule should the bank desire to reduce its risk. But for a small trade creditor, transaction costs are rather more likely to be prohibitive. Thus the existence of positive information and negotiation costs provides a possible explanation of why large creditors more often than relatively small creditors, devote resources to negotiating a deviation from the limited liability rule: the larger the amount of credit supplied, the greater the likelihood that it will pay a prospective creditor to expend resources in negotiating a shareholders' guarantee providing him with additional security for payment.

Fourth, competition among would-be creditors may enhance

uncompensated transfers of business risk from corporate borrowers to creditors. For instance, if there are many potential suppliers of a particular input who are willing to sell it on credit, to stay in business any one of them may have to settle for a price incorporating a lower premium than the premium which would make up for the actual risk of non-payment. Similarly, if there are many would-be money lenders relative to the amount of credit demanded, competition among them is likely to drive interest rates down. Market interest rates may then force individual lenders to accept a lower interest rate on a loan than the rate that would compensate them for the risk that the corporate borrower will fail to repay it. In brief, in a competitive market, the struggle for commercial survival may preclude creditors from obtaining proper compensation for the risk of corporate insolvency.

Fifth, possibly, but not necessarily, as a result of competition among would-be creditors, bargaining power may be unequally divided between would-be creditors and the corporation [Clark (1986), 76]. The corporation may have greater bargaining power, for example, if it already has substantial credit outstanding which is due to the creditor concerned, it may threaten to default unless new credit is extended on favorable terms. The greater the corporation's relative bargaining power, the lower the probability that creditors are able to obtain risk-commensurate interest and other credit terms.

Sixth, the risk of insolvency may change as time passes [Posner (1976), 503]. Suppose a creditor is able to charge compensation for the debtor's default risk when the credit arrangement is negotiated. This compensation may still not reflect his actual risk should the anticipated risk of insolvency increase afterwards. Credit terms are negotiated on the basis of information available when the credit arrangement is made. Accordingly, the terms of the arrangement are based on the default risk as it is estimated at that time [Posner (1992), 395]. However, the risk of insolvency may increase after the credit terms have been agreed upon. In that event the agreed compensation may prove to be too little to compensate the creditor for the actual risk of default.

One may object on the basis that creditors will anticipate such *ex post* changes in the default risk so that they will be reflected in the terms of the arrangement [Posner (1976), 503-504]. Indeed, loan agreements entered into by banks frequently include a provision entitling the bank to demand additional security from the borrower after execution of the agreement, thereby protecting the bank against future increases in the risk attached to the loan. The amortization of loans (meaning the repayment of the amount outstanding in regular periodic amounts throughout the loan term as opposed to a single lump sum payment at the end) is another way of protecting lenders against future increases in the risk of non-payment. Nevertheless, increases in the default risk after the terms of the credit arrangement have been agreed upon are hard to predict and to quantify at the outset. Where creditors have not anticipated such future changes of the default risk and where credit terms have not been set accordingly, creditors will not be compensated properly for the added risk if the risk attached to the loan increases.

Risk-shifting Strategies

For the reasons discussed above, in a world with positive transaction costs, limited liability permits the uncompensated transfer of business risks to involuntary as well as to voluntary creditors: creditors from either category may not receive adequate compensation for shouldering the risk of corporate insolvency. In effect, limited liability creates an opportunity for shareholders (and managers driven by shareholders' interests) to pursue benefits for shareholders at the expense of creditors. Corporate managements may exploit this opportunity through a number of risk-shifting strategies.

In the first place, as is apparent from our discussion of the impact of limited liability on investment decisions, managers may deliberately have the corporation engage in ventures with a positive net present value to shareholders but with a high default risk. In this way they can exploit risky projects, the benefits of which will flow to the shareholders but the costs of which in the event of failure will mainly be borne by the creditors. Where creditors are not adequately compensated for bearing an activity's default risk, they in fact provide a subsidy to shareholders equal to creditors' estimated default costs (*i.e.* the probability of failure multiplied by creditors' loss in that event). The larger a project's chance of failure and the greater the loss it may cause to creditors, the greater their subsidy to shareholders.

Increasing the probability of default after the corporation has obtained credit is a related strategy through which shareholders may shift risks to creditors. By deliberately increasing the default risk after the terms of the credit arrangement are set, the corporation unilaterally amends the arrangement to the detriment of creditors. In particular, corporate managers backed by shareholders may increase the default risk by raising the debt-equity ratio after a credit arrangement has been agreed upon [Posner (1976), 504; (1992), 395]. The higher a corporation's indebtedness, the higher the risk that it cannot fulfil its obligations in case of business adversities.

Managers may increase the debt-equity ratio, for instance, by selling assets of the business and distributing the proceeds to the shareholders.

Alternatively, they may alienate assets owned by the corporation to shareholders at less than their market value. Moreover, managers may burden the corporation with additional loans. A corporation's risk of defaulting on a loan and the amount creditors may lose may also be increased by the withdrawal of funds from the corporate treasury in the pursuit of shareholders' personal needs, for example, by using a loan granted to the corporation to purchase goods for consumption by its shareholders. In each of these events, creditors' security for payment is reduced after the credit arrangement is made.

Undercapitalization of the corporation is probably the most straightforward means by which corporate managers can exploit the limited liability principle at the expense of creditors. The term "undercapitalization" is usually, albeit somewhat imprecisely, applied to indicate that a corporation has been furnished with inadequate assets to cover the reasonably foreseeable liabilities which its operations might entail. In particular, undercapitalization is deemed to be present when the marketable value of the assets owned by the corporation is too low to cover the probable liabilities incident to the business. The fewer assets a corporation has in relation to the liabilities it may generate, the greater will be creditors' losses in the event of failure. Accordingly, the lower a corporation's level of capitalization (*i.e.* the value of its assets), the greater the cost externalized to creditors if they are not properly compensated *ex ante* for the risk of non-payment. Limited liability induces corporate managers to undercapitalize the corporation in order to shift the greater part of the costs of failure to creditors and, prior to failure, to maximize the subsidy provided by creditors to shareholders through the bearing of business risk. Therefore, undercapitalization is not an isolated problem but largely a consequence of the incentives to externalize risk to which statutory limited liability gives rise.

Legal capitalization requirements provide some protection to creditors against trading with undercapitalized corporations, but only to a limited extent. Statutory provisions may prescribe a specified minimum initial capital for a firm to obtain a certificate of incorporation (as is the case, for instance, in the Netherlands but is nowadays uncommon in the United States; see Chapter 9 *infra*). However, once the certificate of incorporation has been issued, the minimum initial level of capital may not be maintained in the assets of the business or the corporation may, deliberately or not, incur liabilities well exceeding the prescribed minimum capital. In addition to initial capitalization requirements, business corporation statutes may provide that during their existence corporations must maintain certain minimum financial reserves. However, such requirements still allow scope for corporate management and shareholders to engage the corporation in activities, the probable costs of failure of which may exceed the prescribed reserves. Moreover, the firm may simply fail to maintain the prescribed reserves and so deny creditors the protection they should be awarded. In either event, corporation statutes typically continue to grant limited liability to the shareholders.

Statutory capitalization requirements oppose externalization of risk in as far as they increase the amount that corporate decision-makers will take into account as relevant losses when deciding whether to engage the firm in a particular activity and when determining the level of care following the engagement in that activity: the more invested wealth shareholders have at stake, other things equal, the greater the proportion of the total social costs the activity may generate which will be relevant to the shareholders as private costs. As a consequence, the greater the capital invested, the less will be shareholders' incentives to engage the firm in activities that might cause losses exceeding corporate assets and, thus, the smaller the probability that it will externalize risk. Moreover, the more capital is maintained in the assets of the business, the smaller the probability that at the end of the day creditors will come to suffer unrecoverable losses. However, it is important to note that legal capitalization requirements do not as such eliminate the incentives to externalize risk entailed by the limited liability rule since under a limited liability regime, shareholders and managers acting in their interests will at any prescribed capital level have wealth-maximizing incentives to pursue ventures with positive net present values, irrespective of the possibility of losses exceeding the corporation's capital. Thus, capitalization requirements will provide too little deterrence where shareholders' expected private benefits from an activity are outweighed by its expected social costs but are still greater than the prescribed capital times the probability of a loss (*i.e.* where shareholders' expected private costs are less than expected social costs). If, for instance, shareholders expect a benefit of USD 100 at an 80 percent chance, with a 20 percent chance that the activity in question will cause total losses of USD 1,000 and with a capital requirement of USD 250, they will desire that the activity go ahead: their expected benefit of 0.80 x USD 100 = USD 80 is less than the expected social costs of 0.20 x USD 1,000 = USD 200 but still greater than their expected private loss of 0.20 x USD 250 = USD 50.

There is a second, perhaps more fundamental negative aspect to, in particular, minimum initial capitalization requirements that demand a certain amount of capital to be invested in the business as a condition for permission to incorporate. This is that they exclude from doing business as a corporation any party that is unable to put up the requisite minimum amount, including parties that would not engage the firm in activities which may cause losses in that amount and parties that would be able and willing to make an investment sufficient to cover expected losses less than the prescribed minimum. As Shavell [1986, 54; 1987, 169] has explained, a requirement that potential injurers have some minimum level of assets before they be allowed to engage in a particular activity requires them to have assets sufficient to compensate either all or a certain portion of the actual losses they may cause. However, it is socially beneficial that the activity is permitted not if the injurer is able to pay *actual* losses but if *expected* social costs are less than the expected benefits from the activity (or, more precisely, if at the margin they are equal) [Shavell (1987), 169].

For instance, if a 5 percent chance exists that an activity would cause total losses of USD 100,000 and a 95 percent chance that it would not cause losses at all, its *expected* loss is only USD 5,000 and whenever expected benefits exceed this amount, engaging in the activity will be socially desirable despite the fact that *actual* losses may be twenty times higher. Any party willing to put up USD 5,000 will be induced to take into consideration the activity's full expected social costs (as they equal his expected private loss) when determining the activity level and the amount of care he will exercise and should, therefore, be permitted to engage in the activity. Accordingly, it is socially desirable that a contemplated activity, the expected social costs of which are less than the acting party's expected benefits will go ahead if that party has assets equaling expected social costs, even though in the event of failure the activity might result in *actual* losses exceeding his assets. For the same reason, any firm with sufficient assets to pay the *expected* losses resulting from its activities ought to be permitted to incorporate even though it may be unable to pay actual losses. The problem with minimum capitalization requirements, then, is that they deny access to the corporate form to firms able to pay expected losses where such requirements demand that resources be put up to make good actual losses in excess of expected losses. Returning to our example, a requirement that parties put up more than USD 5,000 to pay future liability awards would simply exclude some parties whose actions would have been socially efficient had they been permitted to engage in the activity concerned (namely, those willing to pay USD 5,000 expected losses but not USD 100,000).

To sum up, a requirement that firms have some minimum initial level of capital as a condition for being permitted to do business as a corporation would under-deter to the extent that it would still allow firms to engage in activities, the expected social costs of which exceed the prescribed minimum, and it would over-deter to the extent that it would exclude the use of the corporate form from parties willing and able to pay expected losses that are below the minimum level. As the undercapitalization problem is largely a consequence of the incentives to externalize risk that arise from limited liability, it would probably be tackled more effectively by rules aimed at mitigating such incentives than by the direct regulation of a corporation's level of capital.

Undercapitalization is frequently associated with the establishment by a wealthy parent corporation of subsidiaries with low capitalization levels. By organizing different parts of a business in separate corporations, the assets from which creditors can enforce their claims are limited to the assets of the part of the business from which the claim concerned has arisen. In this way, limited liability insulates parts of the business from liabilities generated by other parts, although the activities of affiliated corporations may be related or even interdependent. By virtue of each individual corporation enjoying limited liability, the use of subsidiaries enables the shareholders of the parent corporation to limit their potential losses from any subsidiary's default to a *part* of the assets over which they ultimately have the residual claim (through their shares in the parent).

Thus, limited liability does not merely limit investors' risk to the amount of their investment, it also enables them to further reduce their risk to a part of that investment. *Creditors'* risk will rise proportionately to the reduction of shareholders' risk, that is, proportionately to the reduction in the assets from which they may recover their claims. Accordingly, limited liability enables the use of subsidiary corporations to shift risks to creditors. The use of subsidiary corporations is particularly appealing to investors when it enables them to dispose of much of the risk associated with projects with uncertain prospects of success or that are capable of generating large liabilities: by organizing such projects in a separate corporation, investors can isolate high-risk activities from the rest of the business and place the risk (cost) of their fortune or misfortune in great measure on creditors.

8. Extended Liability and Other Possible Remedies

LIMITED LIABILITY MOTIVATES shareholders and managers acting in their interests to ignore in their decision-making the social costs of corporate activities that exceed the value of the corporation's assets. As a result, the corporation's incentives to reduce risks will be diluted, causing it to engage to a socially excessive extent in activities that may entail losses in excess of corporate assets, to take inadequate care to prevent losses to others at a given level of activity, and to take out too little liability insurance coverage.

In Chapter 7, we argued that both involuntary and voluntary creditors are unlikely to obtain full compensation for bearing the risk that the corporation's assets ultimately prove insufficient to pay off its debts. *Involuntary* creditors, such as tort victims and tax authorities, are simply unable to negotiate compensation for the default risk which limited liability imposes upon them. *Voluntary* creditors, including both lenders and trade creditors, have to overcome significant transaction costs to obtain such *ex ante* compensation. In addition, they may not have sufficient information to assess the *ex ante* default risk correctly. Moreover, the corporation may unilaterally increase the risk of insolvency after a premium to compensate voluntary creditors for bearing the default risk has been agreed.

In effect, the limited liability principle is liable to externalize business risks to the corporation's creditors. As a consequence, the risk of loss to which creditors are exposed and their actual loss in the event of a default will be higher than it would be if the corporation were to include in its business decisions the anticipated costs of its activities to creditors, through risk-commensurate premiums payable to the latter. The problem of uncompensated transfers of business risk is exacerbated, in particular, by undercapitalization of the corporation and by its use of undercapitalized subsidiaries.

The externality problem entailed by limited liability indicates a conflict of interests between the corporation and its wealth maximizing shareholders on the one hand and other members of society on the other, which is not resolved through private bargaining in the market place. In the present chapter we discuss several possible remedies that, at least in theory, may help to narrow this conflict by correcting the inefficient incentives created by limited liability and, thus, opposing the shifting of uncompensated risk to parties external to the corporation. First we discuss the possibility of extending shareholders' liability, following which we address other possible remedies, including an insurance requirement complementing the present limited liability rule and the establishment of a fund to be sponsored by corporations from which unpaid creditors may obtain compensation in the event of corporate insolvency.

The Social Costs of Unlimited Liability

As described previously, socially efficient decision-making requires that the corporation equate the marginal anticipated benefits of a contemplated activity (*i.e.* the expected proceeds for shareholders if the venture becomes a success) to its marginal anticipated social costs (including losses to shareholders, voluntary and involuntary creditors in the event of failure). Limited liability interferes with this principle as it renders losses to creditors exceeding the marketable value of corporate assets irrelevant to corporate decision-making. In effect, the limited liability rule allows shareholders to pursue personal gain potentially at the expense of other members of society. Should limited liability for shareholders as a statutory principle therefore be abolished?

Unlimited liability for shareholders would undoubtedly induce corporations to consider the perceived social costs of corporate activities up to the combined value of shareholders' invested wealth and the value of their non-invested assets. As under an unlimited liability rule, creditors can recover a corporation's unpaid debts from shareholders' non-invested wealth, corporate decision-making would now pay regard to potential losses to creditors exceeding corporate assets, up to the size of shareholders' personal assets. Accordingly, corporate managers would select that level of risk at which marginal anticipated benefits to shareholders in the event of success equal marginal anticipated costs to shareholders and creditors jointly in the event of failure. In this manner, unlimited liability would encourage corporations to pursue socially efficient courses of action.

However, apart from the benefit of promoting greater consistency of corporate activities with their actual social costs, unlimited liability would also generate costs to society. Abolition of the statutory limited liability rule in favor of an unlimited liability regime would be desirable only if the above-mentioned benefit of unlimited liability were to exceed its disadvantages compared with the existing limited liability rule.

The economic functions of limited liability were described in Chapter 3. The social costs of introducing unlimited liability can in great measure be inferred from that discussion. Below we review the main effects of a change to unlimited liability on the monitoring of the corporate firm and on the corporation as a capital-raising device.

Unlimited liability would thoroughly upset the monitorial model of the corporation. Given that under unlimited liability, managerial decisions may ruin a shareholder, shareholders would have risk-minimizing incentives to demand detailed involvement in the firm's management. In other words, with unlimited liability, centralization of decision-making authority with a specialized management would be a less rational decision for shareholders to make than it is under a limited liability regime. Active shareholder involvement in managerial decision-making does not merely imply that more resources will be absorbed in running the firm but, more fundamentally, it entails that the advantages associated with separation of the respective functions of operational management and residual risk-bearing will not be exploited. Thus, the degree of specialization in management would be less and as a consequence, production processes would forgo the greater ability and dexterity of management by specialist managers at a lower per-unit cost. In addition, where the higher costs of intra-firm decision-making were to absorb prospective gains to factor owners from cooperative production, team production would not be organized at all.

As indicated above, as with unlimited liability they bear more risk than with limited liability, shareholders would have increased incentives to monitor the behavior of cooperative production factors in the firm. The aggregate amount of resources shareholders are likely to spend in monitoring input behavior would therefore be larger. However, *individual* shareholders will have a stronger temptation to rely upon others to monitor productive activity in order to avoid such larger monitoring expenditures. In this way unlimited liability would add to the free rider problem which exists among a multitude of non-controlling shareholders.

Furthermore, as set out in Chapter 3, a rule of unlimited liability (in particular, a rule of joint and several liability) would induce shareholders to expend resources in monitoring the relative wealth of other shareholders as any shareholder's risk of becoming liable for corporate debts would depend on the value of his fellow shareholders' non-invested assets in relation to his own wealth. For the same reason, unlimited liability would raise the transaction costs associated with share transfers: to assess the risk he would take by acquiring shares and to determine whether he would gain from purchasing at the prevailing market price, a prospective investor would have to examine the relative wealth levels of the existing shareholders in addition to the firm's earning potential and liabilities.

Unlimited liability would not only threaten the transferability of shares by raising transaction costs, but also by inducing investors to demand restrictions on share transfers to purchasers of less wealth than the seller. High transaction costs as well as restrictions on share transferability would diminish the prospect of share transfers to superior monitors or to investors able to effect wealth gains by displacing ineffective managers, thereby threatening the operation of the stock market as a mechanism which compels managers to deploy resources to their most valuable uses.

It is often overlooked that unlimited liability may also have different tax effects upon investors when compared with limited liability. With *un*limited liability, in the event of corporate bankruptcy, every personally liable shareholder's proportional stake in the corporation's unsettled debts may qualify as a deductible loss for that shareholder's taxable income and so reduce his private income tax obligation. In this case, there would be a tax subsidy on the corporation's deficit favoring shareholders, consisting of personal income tax savings, that is, a wealth transfer from the state treasury to investors, equal to a part of the deficit. With *limited* liability, however, shareholders' ability to deduct investment losses from their taxable private income is largely limited to depreciation deductions based on capital losses on the value of their shares. If, as a result of the corporation's bankruptcy, his shares become worthless, a shareholder may have an income tax deduction for the lost value of the shares but not for a proportionate stake in the total debt which has accumulated in the corporate entity.

Although the implications of the above-mentioned tax difference with respect to shareholders' behavior are not without ambiguity, it may not be construed to imply that with unlimited liability, shareholders have tax-motivated incentives to let a firm burdened with debts go down as their more favorable tax position would by no means offset their losses from personal liability; by contrast, the higher income tax deduction would be a *function* of the higher loss arising under an unlimited liability regime. Yet with unlimited liability, the tax subsidy is on the firm's liquidation, not on its survival. Thus, if one were to look solely from a tax perspective, shareholders' incentives to monitor the management of the corporate firm so as to ensure that the firm stays in business would unfavorably be affected by unlimited liability.

Apart from disrupting the monitoring functions of the corporate form, the introduction of general unlimited liability would adversely affect the corporation's ability to raise funds through the issuance of shares, and it would probably raise the firm's cost of capital. First, unlimited liability would reduce the overall supply of equity capital in as far as it discourages investments by risk averse investors.

Second, on the assumption that investors' valuation of shares varies with their anticipated level of risk, with unlimited liability, investors would pay less for a corporation's shares than the amount they would be willing to pay if they were to enjoy limited liability. In effect, unlimited liability depresses the amount of capital a firm can obtain from the issue of shares.

Third, the price investors are likely to pay for a share carrying unlimited liability would be further reduced because of investors' anticipated costs of monitoring other shareholders' relative wealth, their prospective costs of designing and enforcing restrictions on the transfer of shares to investors of less wealth than the seller, and because of the opportunity costs of investment illiquidity which such restrictions and increased transaction costs in stock markets might entail.

Fourth, unlimited liability would reduce the ability of investors in corporate equity to diversify away firm-specific risks. When firm-specific risks cannot be diversified away, minimizing the number of holdings would be a risk-minimizing strategy for investors. This strategy is likely to result in a further discount on share prices because of the extra risk associated with non-diversified holdings which investors would incorporate in their bids.

True, under an unlimited liability regime, lenders may be prepared to charge lower interest rates on loans as they have greater security for repayment. However, because of the reasons mentioned above, with unlimited liability the firm is likely to raise less money from the sale of shares and as a consequence, it will have to borrow more in order to obtain the same amount to finance its operations. A firm's total interest *payments*, therefore, may be larger with unlimited liability, even if interest *rates* were lower.

In addition, although creditors' increased security for repayment would, in principle, have a downward effect on interest rates, in other respects unlimited liability may push up interest rates. It may have such an effect because with unlimited liability, creditors face certain costs which they would not face under a limited liability rule. Such costs may, wholly or partially, offset the reduction in interest rates creditors would be prepared to accept because of shareholders' individual liability. In particular, unlimited liability makes it necessary for creditors to expend resources in investigating the recoverable wealth of individual shareholders, in collecting corporate liabilities from individual investors, and in designing and enforcing arrangements to prevent shareholders from reducing creditors' security after the latter have agreed to provide credit to the corporation.

Finally, the more money a firm were to borrow because of the reduced funds it would be able to raise through the sale of shares carrying unlimited liability, the greater the risk of bankruptcy, given that the firm would usually be also obliged to pay interest (and to meet repayment obligations) in the event of commercial adversities. In other words, with general unlimited liability, high debt-equity ratios may raise the number of corporate bankruptcies because interest and repayment obligations represent fixed costs to a firm [Posner (1992), 395]. Bankruptcy imposes a cost on society not only where creditors' claims remain wholly or partially unpaid, but also because of the transaction costs involved in the collection of liabilities from large numbers of personally liable corporate shareholders and because of the costs of business restructuring in bankruptcy, and finally because it is indicative of the use of resources at less than their opportunity costs (meaning that the resources used by the bankrupt firm would have generated more value for society if used elsewhere, which implies a waste of socially valuable resources).

To recapitulate, abolition of the statutory limited liability principle in favor of general unlimited liability would produce a cost to society, as described in the preceding pages, in that it would adversely affect the ability of the corporate form to raise capital for investment and to bring about effective monitoring of productive activity.

Where unlimited liability were to result in more expensive and less effective monitoring of input behavior, output quality and quantity are likely to suffer, while production costs and, hence, output prices are apt to go up. And where unlimited liability would detrimentally affect the firm's ability to obtain capital to finance its operations, the overall level of productive activity would shrink. Moreover, where higher costs of capital were to raise the firm's costs of production, again, output prices would go up.

In effect, to the organizers of a firm, unlimited liability would raise the opportunity costs of the corporate form of organization and lessen, or even remove, the corporate form's comparative advantage over other forms of business organization. If subsequently the use of alternative forms of organization were to raise the costs of establishing any firm, transaction cost savings of firms over market exchange transactions would diminish, and ultimately economic activity would less likely come to be organized in a firm. In that event, the advantages associated with large-scale production and specialization of production factors would not, or to a lesser degree only, be realized (see the discussion in Chapter 1).

A shift to unlimited liability, then, would involve considerable social costs, primarily consisting in the forgone benefits of limited liability. Where the social cost of abolishing the limited liability rule would outweigh the social benefit of the greater efficiency in corporate decision-making that unlimited liability would bring about, substitution of unlimited liability for the limited liability principle would produce a net loss to society.

Taking into account the social cost of introducing general unlimited liability, the relevant question now facing us would seem to be how the external costs problem can be remedied while concurrently maintaining the beneficial effects of limited liability (described extensively in Chapter 3): how can we maintain the virtues of limited liability, while at the same time remedying its sins? We examine this question in the remainder of this chapter.

Unlimited Liability for Corporate Torts?

The Proposal for Pro Rata Liability

Hansmann and Kraakman [1991] have proposed the abolition of the limited liability rule in respect of torts committed by corporations. According to their proposal, shareholders' limited liability should be preserved in relation to debts arising from *contracts* entered into by the corporation. The distinction between contract creditors and tort creditors is based on the assumption that unlike tort creditors, contract creditors, as voluntary creditors, are able to negotiate credit terms providing adequate compensation for the risk which limited liability shifts to them [1991, 1919-1920]. However, in Chapter 7 we set out several reasons why contract creditors, like tort creditors, are unlikely to receive such adequate compensation in every case. Hence, unlimited shareholder liability for corporate *torts* would not solve the problem of uncompensated *contract* creditors and corporate decision-making that ignores the cost of corporate insolvency to contract creditors.

Unlimited, joint and several liability for corporate torts has similar disadvantages as the introduction of general unlimited, joint and several liability for shareholders would have. To avoid at least some of those disadvantages, Hansmann and Kraakman have proposed a rule of *pro rata* (or *proportionate*) liability. As we saw in Chapter 3, pursuant to a *pro rata* liability rule, a shareholder's liability is determined by the proportion he holds of the total number of shares issued by the corporation. For instance, a 10 percent shareholder is liable for 10 percent of the corporation's tortious liabilities exceeding the marketable value of corporate assets.

The proposal for *pro rata* shareholder liability for corporate torts is based on the idea that by increasing shareholders' exposure to liability, proportionate liability creates incentives for shareholders and for corporate managements driven by shareholder interests to adjust corporate behavior to take into account its full social cost. In other words, the idea is that *pro rata* liability changes incentives by increasing shareholders' risk.

Hansmann and Kraakman submit that *pro rata* liability will influence corporate decision-making by causing share prices to reflect potential costs to shareholders of tortious liability in excess of corporate assets. In their own words: "If shareholders faced full liability for potential tort losses, share prices would incorporate available information about the full extent of these possible losses" [1991, 1907]. According to this reasoning, the greater the perceived probability of tortious liability exceeding corporate assets and the larger the perceived magnitude of such liability, the lower the market price of the shares in the corporation concerned. Hence, if a corporation were to engage in activities having a substantial risk of triggering excessive tortious liability, such behavior would be reflected in a decline in share prices. Indeed, the very purpose of the proposed *pro rata* liability rule is "to make share prices reflect tort costs" [1991, 1903].

The asserted fact that with *pro rata* shareholder liability, market prices would decline to reflect the actual probability and magnitude of future tort losses, including losses exceeding corporate assets, is said to provide incentives to both shareholders and managers to consider the full expected social costs of corporate torts [Hansmann and Kraakman (1991), 1907]. As set forth in Chapter 4, wealth maximizing shareholders desire managers to maximize the value of their shares, and various market mechanisms operate which, to a certain extent, provide incentives to managers to behave accordingly. According to the analysis presented by Hansmann and Kraakman, under a *pro rata* liability rule, maximizing share value requires managers to internalize the tort risks of corporate activities in corporate decision-making so as to reduce shareholders' potential exposure to proportionate liability.

This, in turn, requires the adoption of higher standards of care towards third parties and the selection of less hazardous business activities, based on cost-benefit calculations which incorporate the full extent of the tort losses that the corporation's activities may generate. In addition, to keep stock prices up, managers will be induced to take out liability insurance covering the full costs of corporate torts. Such insurance would not merely eliminate prospective losses for shareholders resulting from proportionate liability, thereby boosting share prices, but it would also provide compensation for the victims of corporate torts. Managers would have incentives to expend corporate resources for these purposes until the marginal benefit to shareholders of measures reducing their exposure to liability claims in excess of corporate assets, equals the marginal expected *social* costs of corporate torts.

Effects of Pro Rata Liability

With *pro rata* liability, the amount a shareholder can lose is legally independent of the wealth of his fellow shareholders. Wealthy or poor, any one shareholder is liable for only a percentage of the corporation's unsettled tortious liabilities in proportion to his share ownership. He does not have to make up for the deficit arising from other shareholders' inability to pay their proportionate part of the burden. Consequently, Hansmann and Kraakman [1991, 1906] submit, individual shareholders would not have an interest in expending resources to monitor other shareholders' wealth levels. Similarly, would-be acquirers of shares would not have incentives to examine the wealth of the seller and the relative wealth of existing shareholders. In these ways, *pro rata* liability would save transaction costs in comparison with joint and several shareholder liability.

Moreover, at first glance, *pro rata* liability may be deemed to remove the demand for restrictions on share transfers to investors of less wealth than the seller as shareholders' potential exposure to liability is no longer interdependent. By taking away the need for such restrictions and by avoiding the transaction costs incurred in monitoring other shareholders' wealth levels, proportionate liability would purportedly enable the continuous operation of a flexible securities market which a joint and several liability regime would threaten.

However, despite the fact that under *pro rata* liability, any one shareholder's potential legal liability is exclusively determined by the proportionate size of his investment, individual shareholders would still have well-defined incentives to monitor their fellow shareholders' personal wealth levels. As we set out in Chapter 3 (in our discussion of the significance of limited liability to the functioning of stock markets), even under a *pro rata* rule, a relatively wealthy shareholder's risk of being pursued by the corporation's creditors for his proportionate share of the corporation's unsettled debts would be greater than that of an investor of modest means, given positive costs of collection. Collection costs might be quite substantial particularly if there are many different shareholders, especially if they are situated in different jurisdictions [Cooper Alexander (1992)]. Thus, not as a result of the liability rule *per se*, but as a result of positive collection costs under any form of unlimited liability, investors' *de facto* liability risk would be correlated to other shareholders' relative wealth even if *pro rata* liability were the rule.

Also, the joint shareholders' capacity to pay (*i.e.* the sum of every single shareholder's non-invested wealth) is likely to influence the terms on which the firm will be able to obtain credit, including the interest rates creditors will charge it, and thus, the value of the firm and the value of each shareholder's shares in it [Woodward (1985), 604]. For these reasons, the personal wealth levels of the other shareholders would continue to be relevant to individual investors if they were subject to *pro rata* liability (instead of joint and several liability), which would induce them to monitor accordingly – not necessarily to the same extent as under joint and several liability, but in any event to a larger degree than under limited liability. For the very same reasons, demands for restrictions on share alienability may continue to arise – not merely on the part of the shareholders, but also on that of creditors desirous to secure the joint shareholders' capacity to pay corporate debts in the event of the corporation's bankruptcy.

Furthermore, apart from the fact that shareholders would continue to have an interest in one another's personal wealth, *pro rata* liability would not remedy certain other disadvantages associated with joint and several liability. Given that with *pro rata* liability, as under a joint and several liability regime, an investor's entire non-invested wealth is at risk, investors have risk-minimizing incentives to become actively involved in the firm's management. As discussed previously, such involvement would both raise the firm's costs of decision-making and interfere with the specialization rationale underlying the separation of management and investment functions which is one of the core advantages associated with the corporate form. As proportionate liability, like joint and several liability, raises their risk relative to limited liability, even if they would not actively participate in the firm's management, investors would be induced to spend more resources in monitoring corporate activity and corporate liabilities, which would effectively reduce returns on investment, with a negative effect on stock prices.

In addition, no different from joint and several liability, *pro rata* liability entails that, *ceteris paribus*, investors cannot readily reduce their investment risk by simply increasing the number of corporations in which they hold shares: any increase in his number of shareholdings would increase an investor's potential exposure to liability (but see Grundfest's [1992] predictions on the use of alternative diversification techniques under *pro rata* liability, discussed in the next sections). It is true, of course, under *pro rata* liability no less than under limited liability, that an increase in the number of shareholdings will reduce average *expected* losses for each holding in an investor's portfolio and thus, reduce expected losses for the portfolio as a whole. However, under *pro rata* liability (as under joint and several liability), each additional holding would expose an investor to the *risk* of suffering a potentially catastrophic loss in absolute terms, which might exhaust his entire personal wealth (including the other investments in his portfolio). In a portfolio in which equity is present, this possibility cannot as such be diversified away and it is precisely the *possible* magnitude of losses (*i.e.* the mere possibility of a catastrophic loss occurring), rather than the *expected* value of possible losses, which concerns risk averse investors most and which they would wish to diversify away most. Limited liability enables them to do so by simply increasing their number of holdings, unlimited, whether *pro rata* or joint and several, liability does not. Proportionate liability, therefore, reduces the prospects for assembling diversified equity portfolios which dispose of firm-specific risks. As a consequence, similar to joint and several liability, *pro rata* liability is likely to reduce the supply of risk capital by discouraging investments from risk averse investors. By reducing investors' ability to relieve themselves of firm-specific risks through diversification, proportionate liability is also apt to lower the amount investors are prepared to pay in exchange for shares in a corporation, thus raising the firm's cost of capital.

Finally, a *pro rata* liability rule does not remedy the transaction costs *creditors* are to incur in order to assess the repayment capacity of individual shareholders with a view to setting risk-commensurate interest rates, and to recover liabilities in tort from the assets of dispersed shareholders. In all these ways, *pro rata* liability would adversely affect the corporate form as a vehicle for attracting capital into a firm.

Alleged Responses by Capital Markets

In the preceding section we have argued that a shift to a *pro rata* liability regime for corporate torts would produce some of the same detrimental effects as joint and several unlimited liability. Grundfest [1992] has criticized *pro rata* liability from a different perspective. His emphasis is not on the costs of introducing proportionate liability, but, rather, he submits that, regardless of such costs, a shift to *pro rata* liability would not produce the benefits asserted by Hansmann and Kraakman at all.

Grundfest's criticism is based on the argument that a change in shareholders' exposure to liability by the introduction of *pro rata* liability will be countered by financial instruments and transaction techniques available in today's capital markets. In brief, he holds that the dynamics of the capital markets will deprive a *pro rata* liability rule of its purported effects of increasing investors' risk and causing stock prices to reflect the risk that corporate liabilities will exceed corporate assets. As a result, so he contends, proportionate liability will *not* induce managers to internalize the full-expected social costs of corporate torts.

According to Grundfest, if proportionate liability were the rule, investors with few assets which can be reached to cover tortious liabilities of the corporation, would specialize in holding the shares in corporations whose activities might generate tort losses in excess of corporate assets. Investors having substantial investable wealth but few assets susceptible to third party damage claims (denoted as "attachment-proof" investors), have a comparative advantage in holding shares in corporations with high expected tort costs because they will lose little in the event of third party claims for proportionate damages. Attachment-proof investors include both investors with little non-invested wealth and investors who have shielded their personal assets from claims under a *pro rata* liability rule, for instance, by transferring assets to jurisdictions which do not recognize proportionate liability judgments or by placing their shares with nearly insolvent nominee owners. Attachment-proof investors would also include offshore investors, *i.e.* investors domiciled in jurisdictions in which *pro rata* liability is unenforceable [Grundfest (1992), 397-399].

Investors having substantial wealth at risk would, in contrast, specialize in holding shares in corporations, the activities of which are unlikely to generate proportionate liability exposure. Moreover, to enable investors to evade proportionate liability exposure, corporations may, instead of equity shares, issue debt instruments (for example, bonds) and equity substitutes, *i.e.* securities (such as warrants) which are not equity and thus not subject to unlimited liability but the characteristics of which are more or less similar to those of equity shares. In addition, specialized intermediaries holding shares in corporations with high tort risks may design schemes which separate unlimited liability from equity shares by the issue of equity derivatives and debt instruments.

The risk and return characteristics of shares in corporations that may generate proportionate liability exposure are likely to differ from those of corporations with low expected tort costs as the economic features of both types of firms are different. Firms of the latter category normally engage in less hazardous economic activities (for example, trade and the rendering of services) than firms belonging to the former category (including for example, manufacturing industry, chemicals and construction). To obtain a balanced portfolio, Grundfest submits that both attachment-proof and other investors will want to hold equity securities relating to safe firms and to firms having high expected tort costs. To satisfy their diversification demands while at the same time shielding investors with assets susceptible to third party claims for proportionate damages, attachment-proof investors and investors with assessable assets can use a variety of arbitrage techniques such as futures, options or swaps transactions.

Futures, options or swaps transactions in the capital markets could provide both classes of investors with diversified investment portfolios, the risk and return characteristics of which would not substantially differ from those attainable under the existing limited liability regime. Such transactions would in fact arbitrage away the effects of a *pro rata* liability regime. In effect, Grundfest concludes, *pro rata* liability for corporate torts will *not* produce changes into shareholders' and managers' incentives.

First, given that investment portfolios will purportedly reflect the same risk and return characteristics as under a limited liability regime, market prices of shares will be unchanged from prices under limited shareholder liability: the equilibrium prices of shares carrying *pro rata* liability will be "identical to those in a limited liability regime" [Grundfest (1992), 404]. Hence, *pro rata* liability will not occasion stock price signals inducing managers to select business activities and to adopt standards of care which reflect the full social costs of corporate activities. Second, as attachment-proof investors will hold the shares in corporations, the activities of which may generate proportionate shareholder liability, there will be no net increase in the pool of assets available to tort creditors of such corporations. For both reasons a *pro rata* liability rule arguably will not result in corporate decision-making which internalizes the costs of corporate torts in excess of corporate assets.

The proposition that in reality, share prices will not be different from those under limited liability is supported, to some extent, by Grossman's study of market trading in American Express shares during the 1950s [Grossman (1995)], to which we referred in Chapter 3. In these years, American Express shares were subject to *pro rata* unlimited liability with respect to both contractual and tortious liabilities incurred by the American Express Company. Still, Grossman found no indication that these shares traded at a discount in the market to make up for the additional risk in comparison with shares in other companies that carried limited liability: "(...) there is no clear indication that the stock was, in fact, discounted because of its liability status" [1995, 80]. However, the apparent absence of a discount because of unlimited liability may have been due to investors perceiving the *actual* risk that the American Express Company would incur liabilities in excess of its assets as zero or close to zero, so that the *pro rata* liability rule would not in fact expose them to a risk of personal liability of any significance. Indeed, Grossman [1995, 80] concludes: "American Express was considered a low-risk stock, and the market did not appear to regard unlimited liability as adding special riskiness (...)". This finding leaves open the possibility that market prices of *pro rata* liability shares in companies to which investors would attach a significant positive risk of liability in excess of corporate assets, would be depressed by a risk premium compensating investors for the risk of personal liability.

To prevent the evasion of proportionate liability discussed by Grundfest, Hansmann and Kraakman [1992] have proposed the adoption of legal measures to preserve a core of shareholders who have assets which can be assessed for the corporation's excess tortious liability, and to block routes for evasion of proportionate liability. In particular, they propose "regulatory measures to facilitate collection from small domestic shareholders and to discourage a wholesale flight of equity in risky firms" to jurisdictions which do not allow the enforcement of *pro rata* liability [1992, 435]. Grundfest [1992, 391 fn. 13] has replied that such restrictions "would prove impossible to implement and would add further costs to a proportionate liability regime". One may add that any regulatory measures which impose restrictions on capital flows are likely to impede the operation of capital markets, increase transaction costs and curb the supply of equity capital.

Prospects for Diversification

Central to Grundfest's criticism of *pro rata* liability described above is that under a *pro rata* liability rule, investors will be able to achieve the same reduction of risks by portfolio diversification as with limited liability, through arbitrage techniques and financial instruments available in the capital markets. This view is based on a rather optimistic perception of the ability of capital markets to adapt to proportionate liability. In contrast, in our view, *pro rata* liability does raise serious impediments to portfolio diversification along the lines described by Grundfest, both on the supply side and on the demand side of the capital markets.

As regards the supply side, portfolio diversification as contemplated by

Grundfest requires first, that corporations and intermediaries issue debt instruments and equity substitutes instead of equity shares carrying unlimited liability and second, that such alternatives for shares shall enable the construction of investment portfolios having risk and return characteristics identical to those of portfolios under a limited liability regime. Indeed, corporations can limit the issue of equity shares and sell bonds (or other debt instruments) instead but, as discussed in Chapter 3, the risk and return characteristics of bonds and debt in general are essentially different from those of equity shares. Corporations may also choose to sell equity substitutes such as warrants and convertible bonds but, again, the economic features of such instruments do not exactly match those of shares. Therefore, it would seem at best questionable whether debt instruments and equity derivatives enable investors to construct investment portfolios which do not contain equity shares but which do have the same risk and return characteristics as portfolios including shares carrying limited liability.

Intermediaries will only enter capital markets to sell equity substitutes (options, futures) if they expect to make a profit from carrying on such a business. Consequently, equity substitutes created by intermediaries would probably sell at a premium over the value that would be commensurate to the stock market price of the shares in the corporation concerned. Such a premium would increase the costs to investors of assembling a balanced portfolio and these added costs may discourage investors from doing so. Likewise, solely if they can earn a profit, intermediaries will offer to organize arbitrage transactions enabling diversification, with similar effect.

In any event, the creation and sale of debt instruments and equity derivatives would not enable corporations to avoid the issue of shares carrying unlimited liability: apart from legal requirements compelling corporations to issue shares, any corporation desiring to raise equity capital to finance its operations cannot avoid issuing shares. If investors with assessable assets were to exclude equity shares from their portfolio to evade liability exposure, as Grundfest suggests, this would substantially change the nature of their portfolio in comparison with a portfolio including equity shares, in such measure as equity substitutes would not bring about the same risk and return characteristics as shares.

Furthermore, as pointed out by Hansmann and Kraakman [1992, 428-429], Grundfest's assertion that with *pro rata* liability, investors will be able to assemble diversified portfolios resembling those achievable under general limited liability, is contingent upon the existence of a pool of attachment-proof investors who will hold the shares in corporations having a large exposure to tortious liability. Only if non-assessable investors hold high-risk shares can potentially assessable investors confine their investments to equity substitutes and low-risk shares. Accordingly, the supply of equity substitutes carrying limited liability in a world of unlimited shareholder liability will depend on the existence, and the size, of a pool of attachment-proof investors. To become attachment-proof, investors of non-trivial wealth will have to surmount substantial transaction costs (for instance, by transferring assets to other jurisdictions, by placing non-invested wealth with straw men or by hiring nominee owners to hold high-risk shares). Such transaction costs might well threaten the generation of the requisite pool of attachment-proof investors capable of holding high-risk shares. To the extent that transaction costs would prevent the capital markets from procreating attachment-proof investors, prospects for assembling balanced investment portfolios that diversify away *pro rata* liability are diminished.

Diversification under an unlimited liability regime will not merely be troubled with supply side problems of the kinds referred to above, but also with problems on the demand side.

Investors with assets assessable for excess corporate liabilities in tort and desiring to achieve portfolio diversification by adding firms in areas of business which run substantial tort risks, would have to incur higher costs than under general limited liability. First, they would have to incur the transaction costs of arbitrage transactions in the capital markets. Such costs may be quite significant if buying and selling commission payments to market traders (brokers) are included. Second, as indicated above, investors presumably have to pay intermediaries (or the corporations themselves if they are the issuers) for their efforts to create equity substitutes, in addition to the payment of the bare value of the investment instrument itself. Third, insofar as equity substitutes are derived from existing shares, the ultimate holders of those shares (attachment-proof investors) may well demand compensation for bearing the risk of proportionate liability. The same applies in relation to any investment instrument requiring the issuer to assume the liability risk, such as put options; we refer to our discussion of put options and unlimited shareholder liability in Chapter 3.

Each of the aforesaid costs would increase an investor's cost of assembling a diversified portfolio when compared with a limited liability world, thereby impeding diversification strategies. To the extent that these costs exceed an investor's expected benefit from evading proportionate liability, they would inhibit portfolio diversification. In such an event, investors obviously would not achieve the same degree of diversification as under limited liability and would not arbitrage away the effects of *pro rata* liability.

We recall that Grundfest's theory that *pro rata* liability will not influence share prices and corporate decision-making depends on the assumption that investors can and will assemble diversified investment portfolios with risk and return characteristics equal to those attainable under a limited liability rule. This assumption is contradicted by the supply side and demand side problems discussed above. If in fact a *pro rata* liability rule will not enable investors to evade liability exposure by diversification, as we believe, *pro rata* liability would create incentives inducing corporations to internalize the full expected costs of torts. However, such beneficial effect of proportionate liability would be at the cost of the disadvantages of such a liability regime described earlier. In particular, as *pro rata* liability would threaten investors' ability to diversify away risks, it would impede the corporation's capital-raising ability.

If, in contrast, a *pro rata* liability regime *would* permit the evasion of liability exposure, as claimed by Grundfest, it would not bring about its asserted benefit. In such event, a shift to proportionate liability would "simply impose additional transaction costs on investors and issuers alike", as Grundfest [1992, 420] has stated. The higher the transaction costs which investors face in the capital markets, the harder it will be for corporate firms to raise capital by the sale of shares because investors will discount share prices by the amount of those transaction costs.

Alternative Remedies

The Special Case of Close Corporations

For the reasons discussed above, a shift to *pro rata* liability for corporate torts would not, in our view, establish a viable solution to the problem of externalization of risk which is posed by limited shareholder liability. Either it would not accomplish the asserted benefit of bringing greater efficiency to corporate decision-making or it would do so only at the expense of raising decision-making costs, thwarting the separation of the functions of management and residual risk-bearing, and crippling the corporation as a capital-raising device.

General unlimited liability may only be preferable to limited liability in cases in which limited liability is not instrumental to the effective monitoring of input behavior, or to the inflow of capital into the corporate firm. In such cases, unlimited liability would induce managers motivated by shareholder interests to consider the full social costs of corporate activity whilst it would not at the same time impede the monitoring or financing functions of the corporate concept. A particular class of corporations can be identified in which limited liability would seem to be rather unimportant to the monitoring of input behavior and the procurement of capital. This class consists of closely held corporations, the shares of which are owned by a single shareholder or by a few shareholders, with no active stock market trading in the corporation's shares.

As stated in the introductory chapter, this book is concerned primarily with publicly held corporations, which were defined as corporations, the shares of which are scattered amongst a large number of shareholders and which can be readily traded on an organized stock exchange or in an over-the-counter or other private market. Hence, the bulk of the observations advanced so far focuses on these publicly held corporations. This should not conceal the fact that limited liability also creates incentives for shareholders of closely held corporations to engage the firm in a socially excessive level of risk-taking, both when determining what activities the firm should undertake and when selecting the level of care that should be exercised at a given activity level in order to avoid injury to third parties. In addition, the subject of the close corporation is related to that of its publicly held counterpart not merely because they share the limited liability feature, but also because publicly held corporations frequently incorporate distinct parts of their business as separate close corporations, all or virtually all of the shares of which they directly or indirectly own and of which they control the management.

Different from publicly held corporations, however, the degree of shareholder involvement in the management of close corporations would seem to be largely independent of the limited liability rule. In the present limited liability world, closely held corporations with one or few shareholders, whether private individuals or corporations themselves, are predominantly shareholder-managed or have a large degree of shareholder involvement in managerial decision-making. In effect, the ownership of the residual claim in this class of corporations is largely restricted to the firm's decision-makers [Fama and Jensen (1983a), 303, 322]. Limited liability, then, does not operate to separate the management function from that of residual risk-bearing, at least not in a similar degree as in respect of publicly held corporations [Easterbrook and Fischel (1985), 110; (1986), 271]. Given that in closely held corporations the shareholders are in control of the firm's management and own the residual claim, the incentive to externalize risk which limited liability creates for such shareholder-managers is prone to be more severe than it is for the specialized managers that run publicly held corporations (as Easterbrook and Fischel [1985, 110] have noticed). This is because in close corporations, the shareholder-managers will capture all of the benefits if a risky venture becomes a success, whereas in publicly held corporations such benefits are diluted in a multitude of shareholders, with salaried managers benefiting only to the extent that their incomes are tied to corporate performance and to the extent that other disciplining mechanisms discussed in Chapter 4 will reward them, for instance, through an increase in the rental value of their human capital.

Not only does limited liability in close corporations not operate to separate management from residual risk-bearing, other advantages associated with limited liability for shareholders of publicly held corporations are also absent. For instance, as there is only one or a small number of shareholders, limited liability does not bring about significant savings in shareholders' expenses incurred in monitoring fellow shareholders' wealth. For the same reason, limited liability cannot be construed as a response to a perceived "free rider" problem among the shareholders relating to the monitoring of productive activity. Moreover, the operation of a securities market in which shares can be freely traded is relatively unimportant as a mechanism for promoting effective corporate management, given that the shareholders of closely held corporations are subject to restrictions to the alienability of shares (the rationales of which were briefly touched upon in Chapter 5) which limit their ability to move their invested wealth to alternative investment opportunities promising greater returns. Hence, limited liability does not play any meaningful role in facilitating the operation of such a market.

Furthermore, the significance of limited liability to the raising of capital by closely held corporations is rather limited and tends to be overestimated. True, limited liability may be regarded as encouraging investments by risk averse investors but, as we discussed in Chapter 3, risk-aversion cannot in itself explain limited liability given that risk averse investors could invest in bonds issued by the corporation or purchase third-party liability insurance where available. In addition, investors in closely held corporations who choose to run the firm themselves or to be closely involved in its management and who accept being subject to exit restrictions limiting their ability to liquefy their investment, can hardly be considered risk averse. Thus, they are quite unlikely to belong to the category of investors whose making of investments limited liability may be thought to promote.

Perhaps more fundamentally, in reality, limited liability for shareholders of closely held corporations towards professional lenders, including banks and other financial institutions, is largely a myth. Such creditors more often than not require shareholders to voluntarily assume unlimited liability as a condition for the extension of a loan to the corporation, or they demand that shareholders assume liability up to an amount greatly exceeding the subscription price of their shares. Accordingly, shareholders must waive their right of limited liability towards these creditors in order for the corporation to attract loans [Posner (1992), 423]. The "shareholder guarantee" would seem to be the legal instrument most commonly used for this purpose. In this way, the statutory principle of limited liability is subverted by private transactions in the market place.

Where creditors demand and shareholders are prepared to accept unlimited liability, shareholders' statutory limited liability is irrelevant to the corporation's ability to raise equity capital. Creditors demanding unlimited liability apparently take for granted the additional costs of assessing individual shareholders' repayment capacity and bringing collection suits against individual shareholders. In these circumstances, statutory limited liability *raises* rather than lowers transaction costs by compelling lenders and shareholders to contract around the limited liability rule.

Finally, investors' prospects of diversification are not as important to the ability of closely held corporations to acquire capital as they are to corporations with multiple non-controlling shareholders. Diversification is a risk-minimizing strategy available to passive investors who are unwilling to become actively involved in the management of any of the firms in their portfolio. However, as indicated, shareholders in closely held corporations generally do not bestow the management of the firm upon a specialized management and are not averse to actively participating in managerial decision-making themselves. They are not, generally, passive investors assembling a portfolio composed of manifold unrelated investments to diminish risks. And even if they did wish to pursue diversification in order to reduce their investment risk, their ability to do so effectively would be less than that of shareholders of publicly held corporations, because there is a physical limit to the number of firms they could manage or co-manage simultaneously and because increasing their number of holdings would not reduce risk if lenders stipulated for personal liability of shareholders. With respect to close corporations, limited liability as a prerequisite for diversification is not, therefore, as important to the procurement of capital from investors as it is with respect to publicly held corporations.

What, then, does limited liability do for closely held corporations?

Firms operated in different organizational forms compete against each other in the markets for investment capital and managerial labor with a view to attracting both capital for investment and management skills to run the firm. Both investors and managers are free to choose one form of organization over another when deciding where to invest or to work. In order to survive, any one firm competing in these markets must offer to investors, a risk and return package and to managers, a reward package that, on the whole, is competitive with the packages offered by other firms. The meaning of limited liability for shareholders of close corporations is probably best understood in the context of this competition rather than from the perspective of its contribution to the operation and organization of the firm.

As is apparent from our discussion so far, close corporations may be deemed to have several comparative disadvantages over publicly held corporations in the competition among differently organized firms to attract equity capital: shareholders of close corporations largely forgo the benefits of specialization of function (as the firm is not run by a specialized management), investment liquidity through easy transferability of shares (given that transfer restrictions apply) and diminution of investment risks through diversification. Also, there being no liquid market for their shares, closely held corporations lack the benefit of the stock market both as a mechanism through which investors could easily determine the value of their residual claim (by simply looking at the market price of the corporation's shares), and as a mechanism creating incentives for value-maximizing management through the impact of managerial decisions on the market price of the shares and the threat of a takeover [Easterbrook and Fischel (1986), 275-276]. Similarly, close corporations have a comparative disadvantage in the market for managerial labor: whereas publicly held corporations seek to recruit managers who have to supply management skills only, close corporations are looking for persons who are prepared to provide to the firm management services, investment capital and risk-bearing (as residual claimants), which forces the number of qualified (and willing) managers down [Easterbrook and Fischel (1986), 274].

Statutory limited liability for shareholders of closely held corporations may be conceived as being a premium for investors which serves to secure the close corporation's ability to compete in the markets for investment capital and managerial labor notwithstanding the aforementioned competitive disadvantages and which, thus, serves not only to encourage investment in firms operated as close corporations but also to enhance the joint supply of management and risk-bearing services to such firms. It is in fact a reward for the supply of joint management and investment rather than an organizational instrument which it is in the framework of the publicly held corporation. As closely held corporations tend to organize small-scale firms and starting businesses in particular, limited liability may be viewed as a premium encouraging investment in these types of firms – not, at least not primarily, a premium to overcome risk-aversion on the part of investors, but a premium to enhance the close corporation's power to compete against firms organized differently in the markets for investment capital and managerial labor.

Unlimited Liability for Shareholders of Close Corporations

Although the upside of limited liability is different for publicly held and closely held corporations, the downside is essentially the same: it permits shareholders and those acting on their behalf to ignore losses exceeding the amount of shareholders' investment that the corporation's activities may generate, and compels both involuntary creditors and voluntary creditors unable to contract around the limited liability rule to subsidize corporate activity by bearing the risk of such excess losses, thus forcing them to suffer the costs of corporate insolvency if and when the business fails. In this way, subject to shareholders' obligation to pay the subscription price of their shares only, it places the cost of developing and promoting new businesses on the creditors of the corporation [Landers (1975), 593]. As a result, in the words of Halpern, Trebilcock and Turnbull [1980, 148], limited liability of shareholders of close corporations creates incentives for investors "(...) to exploit a moral hazard and transfer uncompensated business risks to creditors", as it enables them to pursue personal benefit irrespective of the costs of their strivings to the latter.

As explained in the preceding section, this downside of limited liability is not offset by monitoring and financial benefits similar to those that limited liability creates for publicly held corporations with numerous shareholders and a separate management. In addition, the fact that limited liability may be understood as a premium which supports firms organized as a close corporation in their competition against differently organized firms, does not mean that limited liability is indispensable for the survival of closely held firms or for the survival of the close corporation as a form of organization. Other factors independent of the limited liability principle (and independent of possible tax advantages) may exist explaining why a firm's organizers may choose the close corporation to set up a business.

For instance, where the cost of separating management and residual risk-bearing is greater than investors' expected return from such specialization of function, the close corporation, to the extent that it concentrates management and residual risk-bearing, has an advantage over organizational forms that are characterized by strict separation of these functions (such as its publicly held counterpart). Similarly, Fama and Jensen [1983a, 322; 1983b, 346] have interpreted the close corporation as a device to avoid the agency costs associated with separation of management from risk-bearing. This could explain why close corporations have become prominent in two types of firms in which the costs of separating these functions are likely to be prohibitive: firms in which the number of cooperating input owners is small and in which the shirking problem among the input owners, therefore, is unlikely to be so significant as to justify the costs of specialized monitoring by a separate management, and firms in which there are no important economies of scale in the production of output that demand large accumulation of wealth from a variety of suppliers for investment in firm-specific assets [Fama and Jensen (1983b), 346].

Inasmuch as in closely held corporations the same persons are both managers and residual claimants, the close corporation also allows greater flexibility in the size and format of managerial rewards than organizations run by a specialized management. In publicly held corporations, for instance, the management usually receives the bulk of its compensation through agreed-upon salaries, which are quite independent of the firm's earnings and present fixed costs to the firm it is also obliged to pay in the event of business adversities that diminish the firm's earnings. By contrast, in close corporations, shareholder-managers may choose to lower their fixed income as managers in order to reduce the firm's costs and, if the firm's earnings so allow, to raise their income component from the possession of the residual claim, *i.e.* the part of their income that is contingent on the firm's results. This may help to explain why the close corporation is often chosen to organize starting firms, the earnings of which tend to be subject to a greater degree of uncertainty than those of existing firms with established product markets and for which, therefore, it is necessary to keep their cost structures flexible (*i.e.* adjustable) if they wish to stay in business when actual earnings fall short of projections.

Furthermore, as discussed in Chapter 5, given that close corporations generally have a limited number of shareholders who are concurrently closely involved in the firm's management, restrictions on the alienability of shares which are typical of this class of corporations (but not of its publicly held counterpart), may operate to preserve for investors relationship-specific investment value that would be forgone if individual shareholders were free to dispose of their shares to any third party purchaser.

Not only does the close corporation possess certain features apart from limited liability which may account for its use in the organization of small-scale and starting businesses, also if, as a matter of public policy, it were considered desirable to subsidize firms operated as close corporations in order to support small businesses and to promote the development of new firms, it is not at all obvious why such a subsidy should be provided strictly by the firm's creditors, through the bearing of uncompensated business risk and the suffering of losses in the event of business failure. If subsidizing closely held firms is judged to be desirable as a public policy goal, it would seem more plausible to have such a subsidy provided by the state on behalf of society as a whole, paid from the state's tax revenues.

Therefore, taking into account that limited liability in closely held corporations is a premium for investors and not an organizational essentiality, that it does not yield monitoring and financial benefits as in publicly held corporations and that the close corporation form bears advantages for the organization of (small-scale) businesses other than limited liability, we support the view (advanced, among others, by Halpern, Trebilcock and Turnbull [1980, 148] and by Shavell [1987, 176]) that in order to induce shareholders, including shareholder-managers, to internalize the full social costs of corporate activity when making decisions on behalf of the firm, unlimited liability would be the preferred statutory regime for closely held corporations. On the assumption that they have assets at stake in addition to their shares in the firm, unlimited liability will give the shareholders a direct pecuniary interest in controlling the corporation's activities in order to avoid it taking excessive risk, whilst their involvement in the firm's management will give them both the knowledge and the ability to reduce risks and to enhance care. This applies to cases in which all the corporation's shares are held by a single shareholder as well as to cases in which there are several shareholders who are jointly involved in the management of the firm. In both cases, therefore, unlimited liability should be introduced.

However, if a close corporation has several shareholders, unlimited *joint and several* liability may well create monitoring costs among the shareholders and demands for a complete ban on share transfers to purchasers with less wealth than the seller similar to those which would be provoked by unlimited liability for shareholders of publicly held corporations. A rule providing for *pro rata* liability instead of joint and several liability would obviate such side-effects. Moreover, in order to avoid the transaction costs that creditors were to surmount if they had to collect the corporation's debts from individual shareholders, creditors should first be required to seek payment from the corporation itself [Halpern, Trebilcock and Turnbull (1980), 148 fn. 51]. In the event that the corporation would have insufficient assets to cover its payment obligations or would simply refuse to pay, they should be required to file a petition with the appropriate court for the establishment of the corporation's insolvency (meaning bankruptcy) and for the appointment of a trustee to handle the case. The trustee appointed by the court should subsequently enforce *pro rata* liability upon the individual shareholders on behalf of the corporation's joint creditors and distribute the proceeds to the latter in proportion to their respective claims. Creditors themselves should not be permitted to bring independent collection suits against individual shareholders. For the same reason (avoidance of transaction costs), an unlimited liability regime should preserve the corporation as a legal entity capable of contracting debts and incurring tortious and other liabilities in its own name so that parties wishing to deal with the firm would not have to transact with individual shareholders. The individual shareholders, then, should be vicariously liable for the obligations incumbent on the corporation, subject only to the corporation's inability to pay.

Prima facie, an unlimited liability regime would work only if shareholders were unable to relieve themselves of personal liability by disposing of their shares in the face of corporate insolvency. If solvent shareholders were able to evade liability by simply transferring their shares to, probably, less solvent acquirers who would then become liable in their place (or by causing the corporation to repurchase shares previously issued), it would seem that unlimited liability would not have its proclaimed beneficial effect on shareholders' incentives and corporate decision-making as shareholders would *de facto* enjoy limited liability. This proposition, however, is not entirely, at least not necessarily, true.

To the extent that potential purchasers of shares would anticipate future personal liability arising from corporate activities prior to their acquisition of the shares, they would most likely attach negative value to the shares in question as they would expect the same to consume all or part of their personal wealth rather than add to it. This would practically render the shares unsalable, except to purchasers who are already judgment proof at the time of purchase and to purchasers who are unaware of the imminence of liability. This, in turn, would give existing shareholders an interest in avoiding excessive risk-taking, not merely to keep down the risk of their own personal liability but to secure the shares' alienability in fact and to enhance the shares' value to potential purchasers and accordingly, the price the latter will be prepared to pay [Shavell (1987), 176]. Such incentives are likely to be inadequate in cases where existing shareholders anticipate that imminent personal liability can be hidden from would-be purchasers or that the latter will be unaware of past corporate activities that may trigger liability following their acquisition of the shares, where the transaction costs facing potential purchasers to obtain correct information on the risk of personal liability will be prohibitive (given that existing shareholders ordinarily have an information advantage over the former), and where the existing shareholders expect that they will be able to evade liability in any event through the use of evasive constructions (for instance, by transferring their shares in the face of corporate bankruptcy to an insolvent figurehead purchaser, possibly located in another jurisdiction). In each of these cases, existing shareholders would not have adequate incentives to reduce risk if they could relieve themselves of imminent liability by transferring their shares. Therefore, we propose that unlimited liability should extend to former shareholders that owned shares prior to the corporation's insolvency, at the moment or during the period in which the activity generating losses in excess of the corporation's assets was carried out.

On December 21, 1989, the Council of the European Union adopted a directive addressed to the Union's member states which specifically deals with close corporations of which the shares are owned by one shareholder only (and which does not cover close corporations with more than one shareholder). This directive, named Council Directive (EEC) 89/667, is known as the twelfth European directive on company law. The directive aimed to harmonize, to a rather limited extent, the laws of the Union's member states pertaining to statutory close corporations with a single shareholder and obliged the member states to take such implementing measures as were necessary to make their national laws comply with the directive's provisions.

Contrary to abolishing limited liability with respect to single-shareholder corporations, the twelfth directive aims to ensure that throughout the European Union, the limited liability principle will be available to single shareholders of close corporations so as to enable individual business owners to limit their liability for the obligations incurred by the business. Consequently, as a rule, any sole shareholder, owning all of the shares in a close corporation incorporated in a member state of the European Union, should be able to enjoy limited liability, irrespective of whether he has become the corporation's sole shareholder at the occasion of its formation or at a later date.

However, the twelfth directive grants the member states the discretion to deny the limited liability privilege to sole shareholders who are corporations or other legal entities themselves and also to natural persons who hold all of the shares in more than one close corporation (Section 2 (2) of the directive). Accordingly, the directive does not oblige individual member states to confer limited liability on corporations desirous to establish wholly owned subsidiary corporations, or on individuals who are the sole shareholder of two or more corporations at the same time [Boschma (1997), 20]. The reason that limited liability is not prescribed in these instances – although member states are free to allow it –, does not lie in a policy judgment by the European legislature against corporations establishing wholly owned subsidiary corporations or against natural persons owning all shares in several corporations but rather, in the fact that the laws of the various member states differed on these points and that there was no legislative desire, at least no political majority, amongst the member states to uniform their laws with a view to eliminating such differences.

The twelfth directive embracing limited liability as the general rule for single-shareholder close corporations, albeit with the above-mentioned qualifications, must not be interpreted such that the European legislature disavowed the possibility of limited liability hurting creditors or that such possibility has been ignored in the directive. However, instead of attempting to altogether remove the perverse incentives limited liability entails by prescribing unlimited liability for sole shareholders of close corporations, the directive relies on other techniques to protect creditors.

First, whenever all of the shares in a close corporation come to be held by a single shareholder, this fact and the identity of the sole shareholder must be made public, either through its registration with the appropriate official commercial registers or by its entering into a register kept by the corporation itself which must be accessible to the public (pursuant to Section 3 of the directive). Which manner of making the information public will apply, depends on the implementing legislation enacted by the individual member states and, thus, can vary between the different states. The disclosure requirement concerning the fact that all the corporation's shares are owned by a single person, together with this person's identity, serves to feed information into credit markets, thus enabling would-be creditors of single-shareholder close corporations to take appropriate measures in order to protect themselves against the risk of being exploited by the corporation's sole shareholder. Moreover, the disclosure requirement economizes on the transaction (*i.e.* search) costs which would-be creditors would have to incur if they had to collect the same information through investigations of their own. All of this, however, applies to voluntary creditors only: *in*voluntary creditors, by definition, are unable to collect and respond to corporate and shareholder information before being forced into a transaction.

Second, the twelfth directive seeks to directly protect both voluntary and involuntary creditors by prescribing certain formalities which, to some extent, restrict the sole shareholder's discretion to intermingle the affairs of the corporation with his personal affairs. The directive contains two such requirements: any decision that is made by the shareholder on the basis of the powers residing in the shareholders as a body must be properly recorded in writing (Section 4 (2)), as must be any contract between the sole shareholder and the corporation if the latter is represented by the shareholder in respect of the contract concerned, with the exception of contracts concluded in the ordinary course of business (Section 5). These requirements further that the corporation be operated as a separate business and may in addition, be conceived as opposing improper self-dealing (including fraud) by the shareholder at the expense of the corporation and its creditors. This in turn helps voluntary creditors to set risk-commensurate terms when extending credit to the corporation and, to the extent that the cited requirements oppose the arbitrary appropriation of corporate resources by the sole shareholder, they enhance both voluntary and involuntary creditors' ability to collect from the corporation.

Third, in its fifth recital, the directive states that it does not intend to prejudice the laws of individual member states of the European Union which, in exceptional circumstances, provide for imposition of personal liability on a corporation's sole shareholder in spite of limited liability being the rule. Accordingly, the twelfth directive allows member states to set aside the limited liability of a close corporation's sole shareholder in "exceptional circumstances", the definition of which is left to member state jurisdictions and which in all likelihood require seriously improper conduct on the part of the relevant shareholder [Boschma (1997), 17]. This exception to the rule would seem to endorse member states' right to impose unlimited liability as an after-the-fact remedy once the sole shareholder has used his limited liability to externalize losses to creditors, with a view to allowing creditors to recover such losses from the shareholder's non-invested assets. The disclosure and recording requirements described above are essentially *ex ante* techniques devised to oppose externalities before they arise, whilst the imposition of personal liability is an *ex post* remedy which may come into play when preventive instruments have failed. To what extent this remedy is available under the laws of one member state of the European Union, the Netherlands, and under the laws of a non-member state, the United States, is examined in Chapter 9 *infra*.

Prior to the adoption and implementation of the twelfth directive, unlimited liability for shareholders owning all of the shares in a close corporation used to be the statutory rule in several member states, Italy being one. Section 2497 of the Italian Civil Code used to provide that in the event of insolvency of the corporation, the sole shareholder was personally liable for the debts the corporation had incurred during the period in which he had been its sole shareholder. Experience in Italy under this rule revealed that exposure to unlimited liability was easily avoided by the issue of one or a small number of shares to an associate of the corporation's majority shareholder, who held all remaining shares. Similar evasive constructions were reportedly used in Greece and in the United Kingdom, where the national corporation statutes also provided for unlimited liability of single shareholders in certain cases. This experience would seem to support the view that for unlimited liability to be effective, its realm should not be limited to single-shareholder corporations.

As indicated, under Section 2 (2) of the twelfth directive, the member states of the European Union may provide for unlimited shareholder liability if all shares in a corporation are owned by a different corporation or by another legal entity. Thus, until the Council of the European Union adopts legislation to the contrary, member states' national laws are at liberty to provide that a parent company which owns all of the shares in a subsidiary corporation, shall be liable without limitation for the latter's obligations. Indeed, in our view, an unlimited liability regime for shareholders of close corporations should extend to close corporations whose shares are owned by another corporation such that parent companies shall be liable for the obligations of their subsidiaries. Such liability would create incentives for the shareholders of parent corporations and for parent company management to avoid liabilities by subsidiary corporations in excess of the latter's assets. Similarly, Shavell [1987, 176] has argued that a parent company liable for the debts of its subsidiary would have both the motive and the ability to reduce risks created by the subsidiary. Where a subsidiary has a management different from that of its parent, through the operation of markets for managerial labor inside corporate groups, managers of subsidiary corporations would have similar incentives.

In what is probably one of the first comprehensive explorations of the law and economics of corporate groups, Berle [1947] associated the imposition of liability on a parent company with the existence of one underlying firm, of which the parent and the subsidiary represent integrated, more or less indistinguishable parts. According to his "theory of enterprise entity", where the activities of affiliated corporations together form one firm, this economic reality should lead to their joint liability for the liabilities generated by the enterprise, irrespective of the legal entity in the name of which they were incurred [1947, 348]; a theory that was later embraced and refined by Landers [1975]. Thus, liabilities should follow the economic enterprise from whose operations they have ensued rather than the legal entity nominally accountable. However, it is not the integrated firm *per se* but the very use of separate affiliated corporations to avoid liability which shifts business risks to third parties. This can also be observed in the absence of a single underlying firm. Therefore, in our view, there would seem to be a good case in favor of holding parent corporations liable for the debts of their subsidiaries regardless of whether they carry on an integrated business collectively.

Unlimited liability for parent corporations would discourage the use of "special purpose" subsidiary corporations established to perform activities with a high risk of generating excessive liabilities. As described earlier, such special purpose corporations are used to isolate high-risk activities from the other activities of a corporate group. In particular, they are aimed at insulating the assets of other group companies from the liabilities generated by such high-risk activities. In this way, the risk of failure of the activity in question is shifted to creditors of the subsidiary concerned who have been unable to obtain parent company guarantees. Unlimited liability for parent companies would discourage such practices and would compel parent companies, including their shareholders and managements, to incorporate the costs of high-risk group activities into their private cost-benefit calculations up to the combined value of the joint assets of the member companies of the corporate group concerned.

Finally, with limited liability, corporations may seek to reduce risks by setting up incorporated joint ventures with other, non-affiliated corporations for the purpose of performing activities carrying a substantial risk of generating excessive liabilities. In order to avoid externalization of risks through the establishment of such joint ventures, each company participating in an incorporated joint venture should be liable, on a *pro rata* basis, for the unsettled debts of the joint venture company. Such "dual liability" would induce each participating corporation to incorporate a proportional part of the expected social costs of the joint venture's activities as part of their internal cost structures and, in consequence, to have the joint venture company exercise appropriate care in order to avoid its operations generating liabilities exceeding its assets (which would have to be paid by the respective parent companies). Likewise, in the case of torts committed by multiple injurers acting in concert, imposition of liability on each injurer has been shown to create incentives for each injurer to take optimal care, it being in their mutual interests to avoid liability [Shavell (1987), 165-166].

The Publicly Held Corporation

We have argued that the advantages of limited shareholder liability to publicly held corporations do not apply to closely held corporations which by definition have only small numbers of shareholders and the shares of which are not traded in regular stock markets. Similarly, the rationales for limited liability in respect of publicly held corporations do not apply to subsidiary corporations and to incorporated joint ventures, the shares of which are held by other corporations. In order to remedy the externality problem posed by limited liability, therefore, unlimited liability would seem to be the preferred rule for these classes of corporations.

However, as we have also seen, unlimited liability does not provide a viable alternative with regard to publicly held corporations with multiple diversified shareholders and with freely transferable shares. Still, the advantages of limited liability to this class of corporation do not alter the fact that limited liability induces shareholders and managers driven by shareholder interests to ignore the social costs of corporate activity exceeding the value of shareholders' investment, which may result in uncompensated transfers of the risk of business failure to creditors. Is there a remedy which preserves the advantages of statutory limited liability while at the same time aligning corporate decision-making, particularly corporate cost calculating, with the full social costs of corporate activity?

Independently of his proposal (with Hansmann) for *pro rata* liability of shareholders, Kraakman [1984] has promoted the idea that expansion of personal liability of *managers* for corporate liabilities, especially corporate liabilities in tort, towards third parties, would induce the internalization of external costs in management decisions: personal liability purportedly would give managers incentives to avoid excessive risk-taking by the corporate firm, and to ensure that liability insurance levels be adequate to cover injury sustained by third parties as a result of corporate activities. Much of our discussion in Chapter 5 relating to the social costs of managerial liability for injury inflicted on shareholders also applies here: imposition of personal liability on managers would create both direct costs (compensation payments to management for the bearing of undiversified liability risk and for litigation expenses) and indirect costs (shrinkage of the pool of recruitable managers, over-investment in risk avoidance, stock price discounts for compensation payments to management and anticipated costs of litigation), whilst most likely D&O liability insurance would only be able to partially alleviate such effects for essentially the same reasons that were discussed at the end of Chapter 5. However, making managers liable for corporate liabilities towards third parties would also give rise to another, more fundamental problem.

Personal liability for liabilities generated by the corporation's activities would effectively force managers to assume the risk of those activities. Accordingly, managers would not merely be in charge of running the firm but they would also perform a risk-bearing function. This would interfere with the separation of business management and risk-bearing functions underlying the corporate form and defy the specialization rationales from which that separation has emerged (as discussed in Chapter 2). As McKean [1978, 89] has pointed out, managers would no longer be specialists in managerial tasks but, rather, in some mixture of managerial and risk-bearing responsibilities, whilst the shouldering of business risk would no longer be concentrated in the shareholders. This would both limit the possibility of specialization in any one of these functions according to comparative advantage and create a demand for a different type of manager, who should combine management and risk-bearing features. We are afraid that this type of manager is quite similar to a non-specialized shareholder-manager, whom the publicly held corporation has long overthrown precisely to avail investors of the benefit of an organizational structure in which management and risk-bearing functions are each assigned to specialists. In effect, imposition of personal liability upon managers would both threaten the effectiveness of the firm's management and reduce the attractiveness of the corporate form to investors which would be reflected in fewer investments, higher operative costs, lower output levels and higher prices for consumers [McKean (1978), 89].

In a different theory, Posner [1976, 520] has suggested that every corporation engaged in high-risk activities should be obliged to post a bond equal to the "highest reasonable estimate of the probable extent of its tort liability". By restricting the corporation's discretion to pay out resources to its shareholders, the posting of such a bond would unquestionably raise the assets available to satisfy the corporation's tortious liabilities, thereby not merely increasing shareholders' potential loss but also compelling them to bear more of the *expected* losses from torts caused by the corporation's activities. This in turn would induce corporations to consider in their decision-making processes a greater part of the costs of corporate activity to tort victims so that they would be less likely to engage in activities where anticipated social costs exceed expected benefits to the shareholders. In addition, the posting of a bond may create extra incentives to exercise care as wealth maximizing shareholders would not want to forfeit the value of the bond. For these reasons, we empathize with the object of Posner's proposal. However, having at least four objections to his proposal, it cannot persuade us.

First, requiring corporations to post a bond to provide for future liabilities in tort may accommodate tort victims, but it ignores the problem of uncompensated risk transfers to other involuntary creditors such as the tax authorities and to voluntary creditors unable to obtain *ex ante* compensation for the risk of corporate asset insufficiency. Posner's suggested remedy, then, is unlikely to promote greater efficiency in corporate decision-making with respect to these categories of creditors.

Second, the "highest reasonable estimate of the probable extent" of a corporation's tortious liability may prove difficult to implement as a standard for determining the amount of the bond to be posted. What is a "reasonable estimate" and who should be responsible for making such an estimate? Who should be responsible for acquiring the relevant information to estimate the corporation's probable liability in tort, and who should administer the bond posted? Should there be a fall-back if the odds change and the estimated amount turns out later to be insufficient to cover the corporation's probable (or actual) liability in tort?

Perhaps more important, at least from the perspective of providing adequate compensation to tort victims, the "probable extent" of the corporation's tortious liability, which is at the center of Posner's bond formula, is rather unlikely to generate sufficient means to compensate tort creditors for losses exceeding corporate assets if such losses actually occur: except in extraordinary cases (in particular, where the corporate form is deliberately used to commit torts and shield shareholders from the resulting liabilities), a corporation's *probable* liability in tort will be less than its *actual* liability if a tort is committed so that the amount of the bond posted will be insufficient to cover tort victims' actual losses. For instance, if the likelihood of a severe loss exceeding corporate assets is small, the amount of the bond will be equally small and, thus, be grossly inadequate to compensate tort victims in the event of occurrence of such a loss. To summarize, although the "bond" remedy could work, at least in theory, from a deterrence perspective as it would compel corporate decision-makers to face the expected tort losses associated with the corporation's activities, it would still be inadequate from the point of view of providing compensation to tort victims for non-prevented losses exceeding corporate assets.

Fourth, if we understand Posner's proposal correctly, it requires corporations engaged in dangerous activities to earmark a part of their resources as security for future tortious liabilities and assumes that the same resources may not also be pledged as security for the repayment of loans extended by voluntary creditors. (If the bond to be posted for the benefit of tort victims were unsecured, the intended beneficiaries would only have a general, non-preferential claim against the corporation's assets alongside the claims of voluntary creditors. In that event, posting a bond would not provide any advantage over the situation that would apply if no bond were posted at all.) Accordingly, the bond requirement would proportionately reduce the collateral the corporation may put up to banks and other voluntary lenders. In effect, the corporation's ability to attract capital by raising debt would be harmed. Thus, the greater protection for tort creditors and the perceived increased efficiency in corporate decision-making the bond requirement is intended to bring about, would come at the expense of the corporation's capital-raising ability. Obviously this would have an adverse effect on the level of corporate investments, including investments in projects *un*likely to generate excessive liabilities.

The basic idea underlying Posner's bond proposal is that the benefit of limitation of liability should require the reservation of a minimum amount to cover future liabilities in tort and that this amount should be correlated to the extent of such future liabilities. The same idea has been applied, even before Posner advanced his proposal, in the International Convention on Civil Liability for Oil Pollution Damage which was agreed on November 29, 1969. Article III of this Convention provides that, as a rule, the owner of a sea-going vessel carrying oil in bulk as cargo shall be liable for any pollution damage resulting from the escape or discharging of oil from the vessel. However, Article V (1) entitles the owner of the ship to limit his liability under the Convention in respect of any one incident causing pollution damage to an amount calculated on the basis of the ship's tonnage, except if the incident occurred due to "the actual fault or privity of the owner" (Article V (2)). In order to avail himself of such a limitation of liability, the owner of the vessel must "constitute a fund for the total sum representing the limit of his liability" with a court or other authority indicated in the Convention (Article V (3)). Article V (3) provides that this fund can be constituted "either by depositing the sum or by producing a bank guarantee or other guarantee, acceptable under the legislation of the Contracting State where the fund is constituted, and considered to be adequate" by the relevant court or other authority.

Only two years after the adoption of the International Convention on Civil Liability for Oil Pollution Damage, the compensation system for victims of pollution damage set forth by this Convention was considered to be inadequate by the Convention's contracting states. On December 18, 1971, they adopted a supplementary convention entitled the International Convention on the Establishment of an International Fund for Compensation for Oil Pollution Damage. The supplementary convention states in its recitals, as one of the reasons of its being agreed, that the compensation system provided in the earlier convention "does not afford full compensation for victims of oil pollution damage in all cases while it imposes an additional financial burden on shipowners". The similarity with the objections raised above against Posner's bond proposal is notable. The supplementary convention of 1971 has established the "International Oil Pollution

Compensation Fund" which both provides compensation to persons suffering pollution damage if the compensation obtainable pursuant to the earlier convention proves inadequate (Article 4) and which relieves the financial burden of shipowners under the earlier convention (Article 5). A shipowner is, subject to certain limitations, entitled to reimbursement from the International Fund for liability payments made under the convention of 1969, including payments from the private fund he may have constituted pursuant to that convention in order to limit his liability, if the aggregate amount of liability exceeds a certain threshold (to be calculated on the basis of Article 5 (1) of the supplementary convention). In effect, a shipowner's cost of limiting his liability for oil pollution damage under the convention of 1969 is reduced by the amount he can recover from the International Fund in the event of an incident triggering liability.

Compulsory Insurance

An alternative to the bond remedy discussed above could be, in principle, to complement the limited liability rule with a legal requirement that corporations take out insurance against any liabilities, whether arising from contracts or torts, that may exceed corporate assets. Such a requirement might take the form of requiring corporations to purchase third-party insurance coverage against tortious liabilities generated by the firm and against corporate liabilities based on the non-performance of contractual obligations and would, in fact, oblige corporations to carry insurance against their own insolvency. By taking out third-party liability insurance, a corporation would obtain coverage against having to pay for other parties' losses resulting from its activities, and the latter's ability to recover such losses would be secured to the extent that losses are covered by the firm's insurance policy.

The major advantage associated with a compulsory insurance requirement as described above is that in a competitive insurance market, insurance companies would charge premiums at rates approximating the full extent of the corporation's anticipated liabilities (instead of anticipated liabilities limited by the value of corporate assets), so that insurance premiums would also cover the risk that corporate assets fall short of the liabilities generated by the business. Hence, corporations engaging in activities with a high risk of generating excessive liabilities would have to pay high insurance premiums, whereas corporations engaging in less risky areas of business would be charged proportionately lower premiums. Through the amount of insurance premium due, corporate decision-makers would be compelled to internalize the full anticipated social costs of contemplated activities in their cost-benefit calculations. This in turn would cause the firm to engage in risky activities only up to the level at which marginal expected social costs equal marginal expected benefits to the shareholders. Thus, corporate decision-makers would take socially efficient decisions on whether or not to engage the firm in an activity and accordingly, make socially efficient investment decisions.

However, there are serious disadvantages, too, to a requirement that corporations purchase third-party liability insurance. First, although to the extent that they reflect expected corporate liabilities, insurance premiums would induce corporate decision-makers to engage the firm in a socially efficient level of activities that may trigger liabilities exceeding corporate assets, their incentives to exercise care in order to avoid liability at a given level of activity (*i.e.* once the investment is made), might be diluted. Thus, although the level of risky activity would be socially efficient, the corporation's level of care (*i.e.* its efforts to prevent losses) might not be. This is because the presence of insurance coverage may itself alter the corporation's incentives to take care as it would not have to bear the losses resulting from failure to do so, which would be paid from the insurance policy [Shavell (1982), 127; (1987), 195-196; 241-242]. (The changing of incentives by the insurance policy is known as the "moral hazard" problem, the implications of which are further discussed on pages 317-318 *infra*.) The presence of insurance coverage would diminish incentives to prevent loss particularly where insurers are unable to observe the corporation's level of care and consequently fail to link the insurance premium payable, or the other terms of the insurance policy, to the corporation's taking of preventive measures (for instance, the use of safety devices) aimed at avoiding liability (see our discussion of the effects of D&O liability insurance in Chapter 5 *supra*). In the extreme, if the corporation has full liability insurance coverage and insurers are unable to control its level of care in any respect, corporate decision-makers would have no motive at all to invest in loss prevention.

Second, insurance markets, as any other markets, are tainted by positive transaction costs, which attend the supply of insurance: insurers must examine firms' risk levels in order to determine risk-commensurate insurance premiums, they have loss-minimizing incentives to monitor the firm's actions after the insurance is provided in order to oppose changes in behavior that would increase their risk, they must incur administrative expenses in order to both devise and administer insurance policies and premiums and to cope with claims made under a policy, they will often incur expenses in negotiations with other insurance companies in order to reinsure their risks, and they have to maintain an organizational infrastructure (overhead) capable of performing all of these tasks. To the extent that liability insurance premiums will cover the transaction costs facing the insurer in addition to his expected payments under the policy (*i.e.* the insurer's risk), transaction costs may cause insurance premiums to be significantly higher than a corporation's expected liabilities. If corporations are subject to a requirement to purchase liability insurance coverage, this would result in a corporation desirous to engage in an activity being forced to pay more than the expected liabilities it would generate. In consequence, when evaluating the activity in question, through the insurance premiums associated with it, corporate management would be induced to consider *more* than the anticipated losses from the activity, so that it might well decide against the activity although in reality, its anticipated social costs would be less than anticipated returns to the shareholders and although it would, therefore, be socially desirable that the activity be undertaken. Accordingly, when insurance premiums exceed expected liabilities as a result of the transaction cost component included in premiums, the firm may *under*invest in risky activities: the level of risky activity might simply be too low in relation to the anticipated losses associated with the activity (which, indeed, would be the exact opposite from the situation we seek to remedy but which from the perspective of efficiency, would be equally undesirable).

Third, limited shareholder liability combined with a requirement for corporations to take out third-party liability insurance would change the nature of the insurance that would be obtained as compared with the situation under limited liability without an insurance requirement: if corporations are not subject to an obligation to carry liability insurance, it will be for the corporation's voluntary and involuntary creditors to purchase insurance against their own losses in the event of corporate insolvency. Thus they would have to take out "first-party" insurance (*i.e.* insurance against the insured's personal loss) if they wish to reduce their risk (provided, of course, that such insurance would be available in the market). Accordingly, the introduction of an insurance requirement for corporations would involve a shift from first-party insurance to third-party insurance, which in turn would most likely have an upward effect on the level of insurance premiums, for the following reasons.

As Priest [1988, 207] stated with respect to United States insurance markets, the administrative costs associated with third-party insurance are considerably higher than those accompanying first-party insurance (he estimates the former at 2.75 to 5.75 times higher). In effect, the component of insurance premiums covering transaction costs under third-party insurance will be higher than the same component under first-party insurance, with the consequences described above. The difference in transaction costs follows, at least in part, from the fact that third-party insurance gives rise to more extensive litigation – particularly on the establishment of liability, meaning a right to claim under the insurance policy –, than first-party insurance, which generally does not require that a liable party be identified. Furthermore, as also indicated by Priest [1988, 207] on the basis of United States data, coverage for the same potential loss under third-party insurance tends to be clearly higher than coverage under first-party insurance (by a factor 2.34, on average) which again entails higher premiums. To the extent that this implies that under third-party insurance, coverage would exceed potential liabilities, with the firm carrying too much insurance relative to the losses it might cause and, consequently, that insurance premiums would be higher than the anticipated losses associated with an activity, the corporation would, through the insurance premiums, have to bear *more* than the activity's expected social costs. In this event, corporate decision-makers would, once more, have incentives to decide against some activities, the anticipated social costs of which would be less than their anticipated returns to the shareholders and which, hence, would be socially desirable to undertake.

Alternatively, where demand for the firm's products is sufficiently inelastic and the firm can increase returns from an activity at its own discretion by raising output prices in order to offset high insurance premiums, corporate decision-makers can decide to undertake the activity at a higher price, so that consumers would collectively pay for the firm's over-insurance and for additional transaction costs and would, therefore, other things equal, be worse off than under first-party insurance. On assumption that they could not claim more than the amount of their loss, third-party liability insurance coverage exceeding the losses that the firm could cause, would also not better the position of victims of corporate activity.

Fourth, perhaps most important, a compulsory insurance requirement would only work if insurance markets were to produce insurance policies providing (more or less) full coverage against the tortious and contractual liabilities entailed by the corporation's operations, including liabilities exceeding corporate assets. Yet it is questionable whether insurance companies will be prepared to offer such coverage, in particular, with respect to liabilities based on non-performance of the corporation's contractual obligations. Indeed, Arrow [1970, 139-140] has associated the very origin of statutory limited liability with a failure of insurance markets: through limited liability, he argues, "[t]he law (...) steps in and forces a risk-shifting not created in the market place" [1970, 140]. Although we agree with Woodward [1985, 605] that failure of insurance markets cannot alone account for the prevalence of statutory limited liability because insurance presupposes risk-aversion (only parties willing to eliminate the risk of suffering potentially large losses choose to buy insurance) and because risk-aversion, as mentioned earlier, cannot in itself explain limited liability, Arrow's basic point that the market's ability to produce insurance is subject to limitations, can hardly be disputed (as has been demonstrated in Chapter 5 with respect to D&O liability insurance). He observed that generally, the insurance available in the market is limited with regard to scope (the range of insurable risks) and amount (the insured amount usually being limited to a certain maximum and insurance policies often stating deductibles to be paid by the insured). Moreover, insurance policies frequently include provisions that restrict the insured party's liberty of action and subject him in one way or another to the insurer's control [Arrow (1970), 141-142].

Two factors can be identified which, apart from prohibitively high transaction costs in some situations, limit the insurability of risks through market supplied insurance: the "moral hazard" problem and the "adverse selection" problem. "Moral hazard" refers to the fact that when protected by insurance coverage, insured parties might cause losses which they would have endeavored to prevent in the absence of insurance, that is, which would not have arisen if they had had to bear the loss themselves. More generally, it refers to the incentives for the insured party created by the insurance policy to increase either the probability of a loss or its possible magnitude or both. Such behavioral changes would be detrimental to the insurer inasmuch as they would alter the assumptions upon which he relied when setting the insurance premium and defining the other terms of the policy: he would then be exposed to more risk and, thus, to potentially higher losses than he agreed to insure. Where a significant "moral hazard" problem is present that cannot be resolved by the insurer through active monitoring of the insured's conduct or through the terms of the insurance policy, he may not be prepared to supply coverage at any premium as his risk would be indefinite and as, therefore, he would not be able to set risk-commensurate premiums (and other contract provisions). Thus, insurance coverage diminishing the insured's incentives to avoid losses could not merely lead to too little exercise of care (as we discussed above), in the end it could lead to the non-availability of insurance *per se*.

The "moral hazard" factor is likely to be especially important in relation to the insurance of corporate liabilities following from inadequate performance of contractual obligations: if the corporation were insured against having to pay for losses caused by the non-performance of a contract previously entered into, its incentive to properly perform the contract in question (for instance, to repay a loan or to pay the agreed interest rate) would be greatly reduced. In other words, the presence of insurance coverage would allow corporations to default on obligations it has contracted without having to face the losses so imposed on others. For the same reason (diminishment of incentives to perform properly), one may safely assume that insurers will be reluctant to provide third-party insurance covering corporate liabilities to voluntary creditors, except where they are able to control the corporation's performance of its obligations to such creditors (which in turn would require them to actively survey corporate behavior). Similarly, in Arrow's view the "moral hazard" factor explains why "(...) insurance against failure of businesses or of research projects has not arisen; the incentive to succeed may be too greatly reduced" [1970, 143]. This view is shared by Shavell [1987, 198], who maintains that the problems with incentives entailed by the presence of insurance coverage are responsible for the fact that parties "do not generally have insurance against business losses".

Apart from the "moral hazard" problem on the part of the corporation, there is also a "moral hazard" on the part of creditors that contract with a corporation which carries insurance against inadequate performance of its contractual obligations. Such creditors have little reason to set credit terms in accordance with the corporation's actual risk of becoming insolvent or to avoid becoming a creditor of a corporation with assets which may prove insufficient to meet its obligations, given that in the event of corporate default, their losses would be covered by the firm's insurance policy anyway. In other words, they would have little to fear from the corporation's failure.

The "adverse selection" problem, which operates in addition to the "moral hazard" factor, refers to the fact that insurers may lack the information necessary to adequately define risks in advance of offering insurance and may, therefore, fail to segregate high-risk insureds from low-risk ones when creating separate risk pools according to expected risk levels and setting insurance premiums. As a result, low-risk insureds might have to pay insurance premiums higher than their expected losses (*i.e.* their risk), meaning that they will pay more than they get from the insurance, and will therefore be induced to cancel the insurance. In the extreme, risk pools will completely unravel and the insurer will be left with high risks only, in respect of which he may find himself unable to sell coverage at a profit so that insurance will become unavailable. A requirement for corporations to carry third-party insurance against any liabilities that they might generate would impede the definition of risks and the creation of separate risk pools consisting of risks of similar value in several ways.

Priest [1988, 208-209] has explained that in addressing third-party insurance, it is more difficult for insurers to define risks appropriately than when addressing first-party insurance (that is, under limited liability without an insurance requirement for corporations) because in the case of third-party insurance, insurers' risk is contingent on the interpretation and application of legal liability rules by the judiciary, which could create substantial uncertainty concerning both the probability of a claim against the insurance policy arising and the possible magnitude of such claims. For instance, the courts may expand liability beyond the level anticipated by the insurer when calculating his odds by imposing greater liability awards (*i.e.* higher amounts of damages) or by expanding the range of events covered by the liability rule to which the insurance policy relates. Indeed, as we discussed in Chapter 5 in relation to D&O liability insurance, in the mid-1980s, such developments have caused insurance companies in the United States to reduce coverage or to completely withdraw insurance from the market in areas where their risk had become largely undefinable. With respect to first-party insurance, on the other hand, insurers' risk is predominantly determined by the probability that the insured will incur a personal loss (not: will have to pay for a loss suffered by another party) and by the possible size of such losses, which relieves insurers of the uncertainty and consequent difficulty in determining risk described above.

Given that the application of liability rules (*i.e.* how far courts will extend liability) is beyond the insurer's control, not merely are absolute risks harder to predict, in third-party liability insurance it is also more difficult for insurers to distinguish high-risk insureds from low-risk insureds than in first-party insurance. This will make it more difficult for them to pool risks of similar size, with the above-mentioned consequence that low-risks will be induced to drop out and that coverage may be denied [Priest (1988), 209]. Indeed, as Viscusi [1991, 35] has observed, rational insurance companies will deny liability insurance coverage "when risks cannot be effectively pooled and spread or when risks are highly unpredictable".

Furthermore, if every corporation were required to carry third-party insurance in respect of corporate liabilities to both voluntary and involuntary creditors, the risks facing various firms would, to some extent, be correlated (that is, an increase in one firm's risk would mean an increase in other risks in the same pool) and, consequently, become even more difficult to predict and to segregate: if every corporation had to take out insurance, insurers' risk in respect of each corporation would increase should an event occur affecting all or most corporations that raises the probability or the possible amount of a claim against any one insurance policy, for instance, an economic depression that would raise the rate of corporate defaults, a natural disaster or a war, a change in product liability laws increasing all manufacturers' exposure to liability, or the manifestation of a defect in a product manufactured by an entire industry. If risks are correlated in this way, insurers' ability to diminish their aggregate risk through pooling would be reduced. Insurers would then be inclined either to deny or limit coverage or to charge premiums higher than their expected payments under the policy in order to protect themselves against unanticipated risk increases and this, again, would mean than corporations would have to bear more than the expected losses their activities could cause to others.

The above discussion should not be misinterpreted to suggest that if corporations were made subject to a requirement to carry third-party insurance against the liabilities generated by the business, insurance markets would not supply such insurance at all. Obviously, under the present limited liability rule without a complementary insurance requirement, insurance against liability in tort is available in many cases and this is unlikely to change if an insurance requirement were introduced. However, with respect to liabilities based on the non-performance of contracts, the situation is different. In addition, because of the reasons discussed above, if corporations were required to take out liability insurance covering the full size of their potential liabilities, there would most likely be limitations to the insurance coverage that would be available in the market, whilst the insurance premiums charged by insurers might well exceed the expected losses from the corporation's activities to third parties (which in turn would induce them to decide against certain activities that might be socially desirable to undertake). One may argue that to the extent that markets would fail to produce private insurance, the government should step in and arrange for the supply of social insurance against corporate liabilities. However, in a way, social insurance would do exactly the same as limited liability: it would impose the costs of corporate insolvency on society at large instead of on those who reap the fruits from the firm's activities in the event of success.

In the preceding pages, we discussed an insurance requirement complementing the existing limited liability rule. At least in theory, it is also possible to altogether abolish statutory limited liability and oblige either the shareholders or the corporation itself to purchase third-party insurance against corporate liabilities to voluntary and involuntary creditors, such that the insurance requirement would function as a substitute for limited liability. However, an insurance requirement combined with unlimited shareholder liability would not merely give rise to the very same problems as limited liability with complementary insurance, it would even exacerbate them. If insurers had to negotiate with each individual shareholder on the purchase of liability insurance, transaction costs would be huge. In addition, in order to determine their risk, insurers would not only have to evaluate the value of the corporation's assets, but also the individual shareholders' personal wealth levels, which would create additional transaction costs [Easterbrook and Fischel (1985), 101]. Furthermore, as Woodward [1985, 605] observed, conflicts might arise among shareholders on the amount of insurance coverage that should be purchased as shareholders' levels of non-invested wealth would be different and, thus, the risk to which each of them would be exposed under unlimited liability. Hence, it would seem difficult to rebut Posner's conclusion that a requirement to take out liability insurance would not be a "satisfactory alternative to limited liability" [1976, 520].

Establishment of a Compensation Fund

For the reasons discussed above, private insurance requirements would at best provide only a partial remedy to the externality problem posed by limited liability. However, the principle of obliging corporations to pay risk-reflecting premiums for the purpose of providing compensation to creditors whose claims exceed corporate assets and creating appropriate incentives to reduce risks, is a promising starting point for a more complete remedy. Based on the same principle, we submit that publicly held corporations should be required to pay a certain fee, for example on an annual basis, into a newly established fund from which creditors of the corporation should be satisfied in the event of corporate failure, to the extent that the corporation's assets prove insufficient to meet its payment obligations.

Such a fund should be administered independent of any particular corporation and the fees payable by individual corporations should be based on each corporation's risk of insolvency. Even if this risk could not be completely defined, the marketable value of the corporation's assets relative to the size of its potential liabilities would provide some indication of the risk of failure. The higher the insolvency risk, the higher the fee a corporation should be required to pay into the creditors' compensation fund. Thus, firms engaged in activities which are generally acknowledged as sources of potentially excessive liabilities, such as chemicals manufacturing, hazardous waste, oil and chemicals transport, medical drugs and equipment industries and manufacturing of potentially hazardous (for example, toxic) products, should be required to pay higher fees than firms engaged in less dangerous lines of business. Similarly, ideally fees should be responsive to the level of care that a firm exercises in order to prevent excessive liabilities from arising and also to the size of its insurance coverage protecting creditors against such liabilities.

Through the fees payable, firms would be compelled to internalize the costs of failure to their creditors: as they have to pay for the risk that is shifted to creditors, they will have incentives to match the marginal anticipated benefits of a particular project to the shareholders with the marginal anticipated costs to both shareholders and creditors in the event of failure. In effect, the level of risk selected will reflect the project's anticipated *social* costs, and not only projected costs to the *shareholders*. The same will apply to the firm's level of care and to the extent of its insurance coverage, provided that fees respond to these factors.

If corporate management were to select activities, the anticipated social costs of which in the event of failure would exceed the anticipated benefits to shareholders in the event of success, the shareholders would have to bear the deficit (*i.e.* the risk of a default occurring) through the fee which the corporation must pay into the compensation fund and which would eventually come at the expense of shareholders' return. Hence, on condition that fees increase if more risk is shifted, where managers would ignore potential losses that corporate activities may cause to creditors, thus increasing their risk of non-payment, shareholders would be harmed through the operation of the fee mechanism. Accordingly, the disciplining market forces described in Chapter 4 would provide incentives to managers to balance expected benefits to shareholders with the social costs of corporate activities in order to avoid fee increases, at least to the extent that such fee increases are not outweighed by higher returns to the shareholders. In effect, the market mechanisms operating to induce managers to act in the shareholders' best interests, will now also operate to induce managers to choose activities in the best interests of society as a whole: instead of inducing managers to externalize risk in order to maximize the value of shareholders' residual claim, they will now create incentives to internalize the full social costs of corporate activity as this would maximize the residual claim's value (by saving fees), thereby enhancing social efficiency in corporate decision-making.

The notion of a compensation fund established for the purpose of compensating creditors of corporate activity who are unable to obtain payment from the corporation itself, is not new. Especially in relation to involuntary creditors who have suffered property damage or personal injury as a result of corporate activity, compensation funds have occasionally been mentioned as an alternative to the payment of damages through the tort system, particularly in cases involving a large number of victims practically unable to obtain reparative damages from the injurer on the basis of a tort claim [Bocken (1987); (1988); Dommering (1996)]. Cases in which the tort system fails to provide adequate compensation include cases involving multiple victims whose combined damage greatly exceeds the injurer's assets, or in which no specific liable party can be identified, or in which the legal requirements for tortious liability are not satisfied despite the fact that third parties did suffer significant harm that in all likelihood is attributable to the activities of one or more identifiable corporations (for instance, as the relevant standard of causation cannot be fulfilled).

In the real world, compensation funds have been set up in a number of settings characterized by one or more of the aforementioned features in which victims of corporate activity were unable, or were deemed to be unable, to obtain damages through the tort system. One may think of, to name a few, the compensation fund for sufferers of asbestos related diseases which was set up by the United States' leading asbestos producer, the Manville Corporation in 1988 (the "Manville Personal Injury Settlement Trust"), the fund established by A.H. Robins, the manufacturer of the Dalkon shield (a contraceptive), to pay damages to women who suffered injury from the use of the Dalkon shield (the "Dalkon Shield Claimants Trust"), the Air Pollution Fund that was set up by the Dutch government pursuant to Section 15.24 of the Dutch Environmental Control Act in order to redress harm caused by unexpected exposure to air pollution and irrecoverable from the polluter, and the International Oil Pollution Compensation Fund referred to a few pages ago.

The establishment of a compensation fund to make up for external costs ensuing from corporations' activities is not a panacea but has its own demerits, which to a greater or lesser extent may threaten the fund's effective performance and which have led to a rather critical appraisal of the fund remedy in academic circles. In relation to funds operative in the United States to compensate victims in mass tort cases (and with express reference to the Manville and Robins' funds referred to above), Viscusi [1991, 167] reports that major problems facing such funds are (i) inadequacy of the financial resources available to meet claims for damages, (ii) uncertainty concerning the fund's ability to pay claims arising in the future, and (iii) high administrative costs associated with the operation of the fund itself, including high litigation costs (legal fees), which may absorb a considerable part of the resources intended as compensation. Thus, the fund's capitalization may be insufficient in relation to the total damage for which compensation is sought and the fund's long-term viability may be questionable as the number of claims on the fund may be greater than originally anticipated, especially in cases in which more claims arise as the years evolve, such as in the event of asbestos related claims and other cases involving long tail liability risks. There could also be continued expensive litigation concerning the validity of claims and the amount of damages to which claimants on the fund are entitled. For all these reasons, compensation funds are not generally viewed as the "ideal solution" to the compensation problem which exists if parties suffering injury from corporate activity are unable to obtain damages on the basis of existing liability rules [Viscusi (1991), 169].

Compensation funds have been criticized not only with respect to their ability to efficaciously provide compensation but also on the basis of their potential detrimental effect on the prevention of injury, in particular, their effect on injurers' incentives to take care [Faure and Hartlief (1996), 38]. If the existence of a compensation fund would in fact relieve injurers of the obligation to pay damages due to victims being entitled to receive compensation from the fund, potential injurers' motives to take measures aimed at preventing personal injury or property damage to third parties would be diminished. In this case, the fund's existence would *add to* the problem of external costs rather than resolve it as less prevention by injurers would lead to more injury and greater losses to other members of society (meaning more externalization of costs).

The preservation of loss-avoiding incentives on the part of injurers would in any event require that the compensation fund's managers have the right to recover from the injurer any payments made from the fund, which in turn requires that victims should assign to the fund their rights to receive damages from the injurer, as a condition for being entitled to compensation from the fund. Through a recovery action by the fund, the injurer could be compelled to reimburse the fund if a claim is made on it in respect of an injury attributable to him, so that indirectly he would have to bear the injury's costs. His incentives to take care would then be more or less similar to the incentives he would have if he were to pay damages directly to the victim (on the assumption that the latter can claim from the fund, and the fund can recover from the injurer, an amount similar to the amount that the victim could otherwise have claimed directly from the injurer on the basis of existing liability rules). Indeed, Dutch legislation concerning the Air Pollution Fund referred to above expressly provides that if compensation is paid from the Air Pollution Fund, the fund automatically acquires the victim's rights to receive compensation in the same amount from other sources (Section 15.26 (4) of the Environmental Control Act). The International Oil Pollution Compensation Fund has a similar right to recover any amount of compensation for pollution damage paid by the fund from the owner of the polluting vessel or his liability insurer (pursuant to Article 9 (1) of the 1971 Convention on the Establishment of an International Fund for Compensation for Oil Pollution Damage).

There are several reasons why none of the above concerns are likely to pose a fundamental threat to the compensation fund we propose to establish. With respect to the fund's ability to make payments to claimants, insufficiency of financial resources is mostly a problem for funds that are established *after* a particular loss-causing event has occurred, for the purpose of providing compensation to victims of that event who could not obtain compensation through the tort system (such as in the Dalkon shield and asbestos cases). In such a case, the financial resources necessary for the operation of the fund need to be assembled on an *ad hoc* basis, once it has become clear that the injurer himself has insufficient means to pay appropriate damages (or cannot be traced at all). Thus, the injurer's ability to contribute to the fund will be less than the total compensation sought. This *ad hoc* nature is at least partly responsible for the perceived difficulty in raising adequate financial resources (who will make up for the injurer's failure to pay?).

In addition, if a fund is set up to compensate losses resulting from an event which occurred in the past (for example, the marketing of a medical device or the release of a hazardous substance), typically the fund is called into being to cope with losses not anticipated at the time, the ultimate amount of which is subject to a substantial degree of uncertainty that does not disappear with the establishment of a compensation fund. For instance, new losses may reveal themselves many years after the loss-causing event took place (such as in the case of asbestos related disease), and the number of victims (claimants) may be unknown at the time the fund is established. Such factors may interfere with the original estimate of the total resources that would be required to enable the fund to compensate the relevant losses, and threaten the long-term viability of funds set up to deal with historical loss-causing events, in particular, events involving long tail liability risks.

A compensation fund set up to compensate creditors of corporations in the event of the corporation's insolvency, however, would neither be an *ad hoc* fund created for the purpose of satisfying creditors of one or more specific insolvent corporations, nor a fund set up to cope with the consequences of a particular loss-causing event that occurred in the past. The proposed fund would be of a general nature, intended to provide relief to the creditors of each corporation participating in the fund in the event of non-payment, and it would be financed *in advance of* the loss-causing event (viz. the relevant insolvency) through the fees that individual corporations would be required to pay in: corporations would pay *ex ante* to repair future losses that would fall should the corporation fail. If fees are set appropriately, this should warrant that the fund will always have sufficient resources to meet the costs of creditors' claims.

Moreover, unlike funds which are set up to provide compensation for losses in respect of which no compensation is available on the basis of existing liability rules, the fund we propose would not act as a substitute for existing liability rules. Rather, it would *complement* the existing rules and provide a guarantee to creditors of corporations effecting that if on the basis of an existing liability rule they have a claim on a particular corporation, payment of that claim is guaranteed by the fund should the corporation prove insolvent. Thus, creditors would remain bound by the requirements of existing liability rules and must have a valid claim against an insolvent corporation under these rules before they could claim from the fund. Accordingly, the fund would be a mere fall-back of, not an alternative to, existing liability rules, ensuring that creditors will in fact receive the amount to which they would be entitled under these rules [Bocken (1988), 4]. As a *guarantee fund*, the scope of the fund we propose would be more limited than that of funds established to provide compensation in lieu of payment of damages through the tort system, and this would also be likely to support the fund's financial soundness and long-term viability.

The fact that the proposed fund would not in any respect limit or prejudice existing liability rules means that the deterrent effect of such rules would remain basically unchanged as corporations would not be relieved of any liability they incur. Rather, the continued operation of existing liability rules would entail that liability of the corporation would have to be established before a claim could be made on the compensation fund. Thus, as before, the corporation's assets could be wiped out completely by the liabilities it incurs (and should be wiped out completely before a claim on the fund were possible), so that the incentives of corporate decision-makers to prevent external loss would not be diminished by the existence of the proposed compensation fund. Granted, the fact that the fund will provide compensation for losses exceeding the corporation's assets will induce corporate decision-makers to treat such losses as imposing liabilities only equal to the corporation's assets but, as we have seen in Chapter 7, this is no different from the situation which exists in the absence of a fund. In addition, such effect could be alleviated by conferring on the fund the right to recover the costs of claims on the fund from the remaining assets of the insolvent corporation. Furthermore, in order to effect that the incentives of the individuals behind the corporate veil (shareholders and managers) to avoid external loss will not be reduced by the existence of a compensation fund, the fund should be given the right to recover from such individuals any payments made from the fund in cases in which under the applicable law, individual creditors of the corporation would have a right to hold such individuals personally liable. Accordingly, claimants on the fund should be required to assign to the fund any such right and any rights they have against the corporation itself in respect of the amount paid by the fund.

The final threat to the effective performance of compensation funds consists of the operational costs of the fund itself and the costs of litigation between the fund and claimants wishing to collect from it. Neither of these factors, however, is apt to form an insurmountable hurdle to a fund set up to provide relief to unpaid creditors of insolvent corporations.

First, it is rather unlikely that the fund will provoke new litigation on a large scale as a claim on the fund would be no different from a claim on the corporation that failed to pay and as, hence, the validity of a claim on the fund would have to be established no different from a claim on the corporation itself; there would, in other words, not be a material change in the claim concerned or in the claimant's position except that the claim must be brought against a different entity. In addition, given that the proposed fund would compensate creditors of insolvent corporations only, the procedural rules applying to the submission of claims to the fund should link up with the rules that apply to the bringing of claims in any bankruptcy case. Thus, if under the applicable law a claim against an insolvent corporation would have to be acknowledged by the trustee in charge of that corporation before any payment may be made from the corporation's estate, the same principle should apply with respect to claims submitted to the fund, and claimants should have the same rights to challenge a decision by which the trustee refuses to acknowledge their claim. In other words, the rules concerning the treatment of claims in any bankruptcy case should extend to claims directed at the compensation fund so that no new prospects for litigation would emerge.

Second, the costs of operating the compensation fund, including the costs of administering claims and payments, could probably be kept down if the fund were organized as a separate branch of the tax authorities and as such could take advantage of both the information already available with the tax authorities in respect of a corporation's liabilities, assets and cash flows, and the organizational infrastructure of the tax system. For instance, a rule could be introduced requiring that claims on the fund be submitted on an annual basis together with the claimant's annual income tax form, and claims could be processed in a manner similar to the processing of income tax forms, with payments from the fund being administered similarly to income tax returns.

The compensation fund that we propose to establish should, in principle, pay compensation to both voluntary and involuntary creditors in the event of corporate failure. However, if *any* unsatisfied creditors were permitted to collect their claims from the compensation fund, regardless of whether they could have avoided their losses, the existence of such a fund may unintentionally and counterproductively add to the aggregate social costs of corporate insolvency by diluting creditors' incentives to take care themselves in order to prevent the occurrence of a loss. If creditors were to be satisfied irrespective of whether they had taken precautionary measures to protect themselves against the corporate debtor's insolvency, it would not pay them to expend resources in order to avoid losses from bankruptcy. Voluntary creditors might even deliberately enter into contracts with nearly insolvent corporations intending to collect claims pursuant to such contracts from the compensation fund should the corporation prove insolvent. In this manner, creditors could realize gains from trade which, taking into account the value of the debtor's assets, they would not normally have been able to accomplish and which in reality would not probably have existed given the debtor's inability to perform the contract as agreed. On the other hand, if creditors were assured that they would obtain payment of their claims notwithstanding the corporation's bankruptcy, they would have stronger incentives to aim at the corporation's bankruptcy and involuntary liquidation rather than to collaborate with management to achieve a restructuring of the business and to preserve the corporation's assets as a going concern.

If the establishment of a compensation fund for creditors of insolvent corporations were accompanied by the above-mentioned side-effects, the envisaged internalization of the costs of insolvency in corporate decision-making would come at the expense of an increase in the total costs of corporate bankruptcies. Such an increase would be reflected in the fees which corporations would have to pay into the compensation fund and through which corporate decision-makers would balance anticipated benefits to shareholders against anticipated costs of corporate activity to society as a whole. As a consequence, corporate decision-makers would probably abstain from projects to which they would have dedicated resources (and which would have had a positive net present value to society) if total insolvency costs (as reflected in the fees payable to the compensation fund) were less.

The costs of business insolvency invariably present a loss to society, as noted earlier, because insolvency cases by definition are liable to involve uses of scarce resources at less than their opportunity costs, not to mention the transaction costs (including costs of business restructuring) they entail. The problem currently facing us, then, is how to promote the internalization of insolvency costs in corporate decision-making through the fees corporations should pay to our proposed compensation fund, whilst at the same time avoiding the situation that the existence of such a fund would raise total insolvency costs by rewarding careless creditors or creditors opportunistically dealing with nearly insolvent corporations.

For this purpose, we propose that access to the compensation fund should be restricted to those creditors who could not reasonably have avoided the non-payment of their claims, for example, by obtaining appropriate security for payment or by not extending credit at all in cases in which the corporate debtor was already approaching bankruptcy when credit was extended. In relation to voluntary creditors, therefore, a "reasonable care" standard should be introduced which would restrict access to the compensation fund to unsatisfied creditors who had exercised reasonable care in order to prevent the non-payment of their claim. For instance, creditors dealing with a corporation that was visibly approaching bankruptcy at the time, and whose single most important aim was apparently to seek compensation from the fund, should be denied access. Similarly, creditors who failed to protect their interests against non-payment by the corporate debtor but, rather, relied upon having recourse to the compensation fund should not be entitled to receive compensation from the fund. "Reasonable care" tests are already applied elsewhere in private law, especially in tort law, in order to discourage socially costly behavior, and the test proposed here should therefore be a feasible instrument for encouraging creditors to avoid bankruptcy costs.

Whether an unsatisfied creditor meets the "reasonable care" standard should be assessed by the trustee in the corporation's bankruptcy as he has, or is best equipped to obtain, appropriate information on the merits of the insolvency case concerned. If, according to the trustee, a creditor has passed the "reasonable care" test, the trustee should refer the claim concerned to the compensation fund which should then pay the part of the claim which cannot be satisfied from the assets of the insolvent corporation. No change in the rules concerning the distribution of the proceeds from the liquidation of the business should be necessary.

In relation to tort creditors, there is no need to introduce a special "reasonable care" test as a requirement for access to the compensation fund considering that such a test is, in one form or another, already present in existing tort laws: in determining whether or not a victim of injury is entitled to receive damages from a third party based on tort, the courts usually take the victim's own behavior into account. A victim who suffered injury primarily through his own negligence is not, or is to a limited extent only, entitled to damages. In this manner, a tortfeasor's liability to pay damages is limited by the requirements of care which tort law imposes on victims. As regards the payment of compensation to victims of torts committed by corporations unable to fulfil obligations to pay damages, the compensation fund should adhere to the requirements of care inherent in existing tort laws and not introduce new standards.

In relation to involuntary creditors other than tort victims, a "reasonable care" standard similar to that proposed for voluntary creditors would not make sense either, as such other involuntary creditors are generally unable to limit their losses by exercising care. For instance, the claims of the tax authorities (and, hence, their potential losses) are fixed by statute law and are essentially unrelated to the tax authorities' own behavior. The same applies to claims for the payment of social security premiums. Requiring such involuntary creditors to exercise "reasonable care" in order to avoid becoming creditors of an insolvent corporation would not alter the corporation's liabilities to them or the amount they may be unable to recover from the corporation's assets, given that those liabilities follow directly from statute law. Therefore, their access to the compensation fund should not be restricted by the "reasonable care" test set out earlier.

9. In Search of Souls to Damn – Legal Responses to the External Costs Problem

WE HAVE SEEN that the corporate form of organization is tainted by two conflicts of interests: that between utility maximizing managers and wealth maximizing shareholders, and that between the corporate entity and its shareholders on the one hand and other members of society (in particular, the corporation's voluntary and involuntary creditors) on the other.

The first conflict arises as utility maximizing managers may pursue objectives irreconcilable with maximization of the value of shareholders' residual claim, thus furthering their personal self-interests at the expense of the shareholders. The second conflict of interests arises as shareholders shielded by limited liability have wealth-maximizing incentives to ignore the social costs of corporate activity beyond the maximum amount they may lose in the event of default, given that limited liability insulates them from losses exceeding corporate assets. By virtue of the limited liability rule, shareholders may use the corporate form to pursue personal gain potentially at the expense of other members of society. It is in the interest of society at large, however, that corporate activity be based upon cost-benefit calculations which incorporate not merely the shareholders' anticipated private costs but the full social costs of the activity concerned.

Prima facie one may object that the first conflict of interests facing the corporation is irreconcilable with the second or that, in any case, both conflicts of interests are incapable of being remedied simultaneously. For instance, Fischel [1982, 1265] has accused proponents of reforms in corporate governance of a "failure to recognize that management cannot be at the same time too little and too much dedicated to profit maximization".

Our discussion, in Part II of this book, of the conflict of interests between shareholders and managers suggests that the latter may pay *too little* attention to the former's wealth-maximizing interests. However, the argument that limited liability encourages shareholders (and managers, to the extent they do act in shareholders' interests) to partially ignore the social costs of corporate activity, suggests that the corporate form may well suffer from over-subservience to the shareholders. In other words, our discussion of the conflict between shareholders and managers implies that the efficiency of the corporate form is threatened by the neglect of shareholders' interests, whereas the discussion of the discrepancy between shareholders' and society's interests may be construed to mean that managers should not pay *too much* attention to shareholders' private interests.

The reasoning summarized above, although perhaps having some intuitive appeal, oversimplifies the issues and is therefore largely incorrect. The first conflict of interests is essentially independent of the second, both conflicts originate from different and competing incentives and involve different behavior patterns (utility maximization versus wealth maximization), and both conflicts can, and should, be tackled simultaneously. It is true, however, that that each conflict requires a solution of itself, precisely because both conflicts have different origins.

A utility maximizing manager may neglect the wealth-maximizing interests of the shareholders *and* the interests of the corporation's actual or prospective creditors. A wealth maximizing shareholder may desire that that manager ignore social costs exceeding the value of his investment and at the same time he may sustain wealth losses (including opportunity losses) as a result of the manager's pursuit of personal utility. Devices aimed at inducing managers to maximize the value of shareholders' residual claim would mitigate the divergence of interests between shareholders and managers, but they would also induce managers to pay less attention to the interests of society at large, thus adding to the conflict of interests between shareholders and society. On the other hand, devices aimed at inducing shareholders and managers to incorporate the full social costs of envisaged corporate activity into business decisions would mitigate the conflict between shareholders and society, but not that between managers and shareholders.

Utility maximizing managers may endeavor to raise the value of the residual claim by ignoring a part of the social costs of corporate activity, and concurrently usurp a part of the added value by allocating corporate income to uses aimed at maximizing managerial utility. Thus, managerial self-interest seeking at shareholders' expense and externalization of risk to other members of society may in fact occur at the same time. To utility maximizing managers, the interests of such other members of society are relevant only to the extent that they have entered into their personal utility functions. This applies regardless of whether or not shareholders desire that managerial decisions reflect the full social costs of corporate activity. Permitting managers to depart from shareholders' interests, hence, will not remedy the externality problem posed by limited liability – such permission does not mean that they will duly incorporate the social costs of corporate activity in business decision-making.

Suppose that the externality problem posed by limited liability *were* resolved, so that maximization of the value of shareholders' residual claim would now require managers to balance the anticipated benefits from corporate activity to the shareholders with the anticipated costs of the activity concerned to society at large. To the extent that managers have discretion to depart from shareholders' interests, they may still not act accordingly and fail to fully incorporate the social costs of corporate activity in business decisions. For instance, rather than scrutinizing the long-term external effects of a contemplated project, managers may limit themselves to their expected tenure of office, or they may intentionally disregard such external effects and pursue high short-term profits in order to maximize the flexible part of their personal income depending on short-term corporate earnings. For other examples of aberrant activities we refer to Chapter 4.

The larger the degree to which managers are motivated to pursue shareholders' wealth-maximizing interests, the more pressing the need for society to create incentives for shareholders to demand that management fully consider the social costs of corporate activities. On the other hand, the more effectively such incentives are created, the greater will be the benefit to society if managers adhere to shareholders' interests.

In Chapter 4, we saw that corporate managers' discretion to pursue personal self-interests at shareholders' expense is primarily due to imperfections in the market mechanisms that discipline them. Likewise, as discussed in Chapter 7, the inefficiencies in corporate conduct that arise from limited liability are largely a matter of market failure, *i.e.* the market's failure under limited shareholder liability to establish appropriate incentives for shareholders and managers to consider in their decision-making the full social costs of corporate activities and set risks accordingly. In the previous chapter we discussed, from a theoretical perspective, several remedies that might be pursued in order to correct this failure. Now we will survey how in reality one possible remedy, viz. extended liability of shareholders, is applied under U.S. law and under Dutch law.

Some two centuries ago, Edward, Baron Thurlow, who was at the time the Lord Chancellor of England, referred to the corporation's perceived indifference to the interests of other members of society in the now classic phrase: "Did you ever expect a corporation to have a conscience, when it has no soul to be damned, and no body to be kicked?" [Coffee (1981), 386]. In the present chapter, we explore where and when U.S. law and Dutch law impose personal liability on shareholders in deviation from the prevailing general limited liability rule so as to enforce a conscience on at least the corporation's shareholders, prompting them to do the same to the corporation.

As for our survey of legal remedies to the problem of managerial self-interest seeking at shareholders' expense in Chapter 6, we concentrate on major issues as our purpose, again, is not so much to give an exhaustive description of the relevant laws. Rather, we intend to see whether existing legal concepts under U.S. law and under Dutch law providing for unlimited shareholder liability can be understood from the perspective of the economics underlying the corporate form of organization and the limited liability rule as an organizational principle.

The External Costs Problem: U.S. Law

Personal Liability and Other Remedies

Personal liability is not merely applied as an instrument to induce managers to refrain from shifting the costs of furthering their own self-interests to shareholders. Deviating from the limited liability rule, both U.S. and Dutch courts have also occasionally imposed liability upon shareholders in instances in which the corporation's assets have fallen short of its obligations to creditors. In such cases, personal liability serves to confront shareholders with the costs of the operations of the business exceeding their invested wealth. Yet personal liability is not the only legal means employed to tackle the problem of externalization of costs to creditors of corporations.

The law of fraudulent conveyances, for instance, known in both the U.S. and the Netherlands, limits shareholders' ability to shift costs to creditors through the transfer of funds or property belonging to the corporation to a shareholder [Clark (1977), 505]. When such a transfer is harmful to a creditor in that it renders the corporation unable to fully meet its obligations to him (or exacerbates existing payment difficulties), the creditor may have the transaction set aside on conditions specified by the law, in particular, if the transfer is deemed to be deceitful or made without fair consideration being paid by the shareholder. In effect, the creditor will be able to collect corporate debts from the funds or assets that were conveyed from the corporation to the shareholder concerned.

Furthermore, mandatory disclosure requirements do not only feed information into market mechanisms disciplining managerial behavior, they also provide would-be creditors with information about the corporation's creditworthiness and the risk of a default. Creditors can take advantage of such information in determining whether they are willing to extend credit and in setting risk-commensurate interest rates and other terms on which they are prepared to grant credit. Accordingly, public disclosure requirements facilitate bargains for *ex ante* compensation for the risk shifted to creditors. As we saw in Chapter 7, mandatory disclosure requirements economize on creditors' information costs and thus lower the transaction cost hurdle they must surmount to obtain such compensation. However, as also argued in Chapter 7, mandatory disclosure of corporate financial information may operate to prevent externalities from arising only in relation to voluntary creditors whose bargaining power is more or less equal to that of the corporation.

Another category of legal responses to the externality problem posed by limited liability (also addressed in Chapter 7) includes minimum initial capital requirements, capital maintenance rules, dividend limitations and other statutory restrictions on the distribution of corporate funds to shareholders. Such rules exist, in one form or another, both in various U.S. jurisdictions and in the Netherlands. All such rules aim to ensure that the corporation actually has assets from which its debts can be collected once due. Whilst disclosure requirements oppose externalities from an *ex ante* perspective, by facilitating risk-reflecting credit arrangements, rules belonging to the present category aim to do so *ex post*, by opposing the occurrence of uncompensated losses after the credit terms are set.

Minimum capital requirements, capital maintenance rules and restrictions on distributions to shareholders purportedly oppose externalization of costs to creditors in three manners. First, they should directly increase the probability that creditors will duly receive payment of their claims once they have extended credit. Second, capital maintenance rules and restrictions on corporate distributions serve to stabilize the capital on which creditors relied when they agreed to extend credit. In this manner, they try to establish that the *ex ante* risk premium and other terms contained in credit arrangements will continue to accurately reflect the risk of a default after the arrangement is made so that no externality will arise. Third, minimum capital requirements, capital maintenance rules and restrictions on corporate distributions oblige shareholders to commit a certain part of their wealth to the corporation and this they may lose in the event of failure. By raising shareholders' potential loss, these rules ideally increase the level of costs shareholders wish management to consider in the making of business decisions.

Fraudulent conveyance law, mandatory disclosure requirements and the capitalization rules discussed above do not prejudice the distinguishing organizational characteristics of the corporate form (legal entity status, transferable shares, centralized management and limited liability). Imposing personal liability upon shareholders for corporate debts, by contrast, does have such an effect. It interferes both with the principle that shareholders' non-invested wealth is secured from the corporation's creditors and with the principle that the corporation is an entity legally distinct from its shareholders, with independent rights and obligations. The first aspect is emphasized in the expression "piercing the corporate veil", the second in the expression "disregard of corporate entity", both of which are interchangeably used by U.S. courts and commentators to refer to imposition of shareholder liability despite statutory limited liability.

Given that unlike the other remedies mentioned above, personal liability of shareholders is a clear departure from the basic rules of the corporate form, in the remainder of this chapter we will have a closer look at when and how, this response to the externality problem is applied. While acknowledging that deficiencies in the formalities for incorporating a business may also be a reason for personal liability of shareholders, we focus on personal liability as it may arise in the course of the operation of the firm, assuming that the firm has been incorporated properly. As with managerial liability, we concentrate only on the major issues.

Piercing the Corporate Veil

Where the corporate veil is lifted to impose personal liability upon a shareholder, creditors of the corporation may collect the latter's debts from that shareholder's personal assets, up to the full extent of his wealth. A collection suit intended to inflict personal liability upon a shareholder for a corporate obligation is brought against the individual shareholder in question, in his capacity as a shareholder, and is based on the obligation incurred by the corporation. If the court finds for the plaintiff, the obligation concerned remains that of the corporation but the shareholder is held liable for its fulfillment.

Although the concept of piercing the corporate veil is, as such, accepted universally throughout the U.S., deviations from the limited liability rule in different U.S. jurisdictions seem united in the following respects only.

First, imposition of personal liability on shareholders is a matter of case law as developed and applied by the courts, with no statutory standard of shareholder liability existing and with state and federal legislatures largely silent on the subject. The concept of piercing the corporate veil, then, has developed from the common law and leaves considerable discretion to the courts as to its interpretation and its application to individual cases. This discretion is well recognized by the courts.

Second, personal liability of shareholders is limited to cases in which the assets of the corporation are insufficient to pay its debts once they have fallen due, meaning that the corporation's creditors have no discretion to choose whether to collect from the corporate entity or from its shareholders. In *Anderson* v. *Abbott* [321 U.S. 349, 362 (1944)], the U.S. Supreme Court expressly acknowledged that "[l]imited liability is the rule, not the exception (...)", whilst the court in *Carpenters' Dist. Council* v. *W.O. Kessel Co.* [487 F. Supp. 54, 57 (W.D. Pa. 1980)] noted that "the general rule [is] that the corporate entity should be recognized and upheld except in the most unusual circumstances". Creditors are bound by that rule and there is only scope for attempts to invoke personal shareholder liability as the exception to the rule if the corporation's collectable assets have fallen short of its debts due, regardless of whether substantive law requirements for shareholder liability (to be discussed below) can be met.

If personal liability is imposed, however, the shareholder in question is liable for the full amount of the corporation's outstanding debts, irrespective of the percentage of the shares he owns. Thus, the corporation and any shareholder whose defense the court has rejected will become jointly and severally liable for the former's unsettled debts, and so will be all individual shareholders upon whom liability is imposed; if the court rules to lift the corporate veil to reach the non-invested assets of a number of shareholders (*i.e.* more than one), each shareholder involved ordinarily becomes subject to the same joint and several liability rule as prevails in partnership law [Hansmann and Kraakman (1991), 1893].

Third, cases in which courts have decided to pierce the corporate veil are reportedly limited to closely held corporations, including corporations with shares owned by one or a small number of private individuals as well as corporations whose shares are held by another corporation in a corporate group context [Barber (1981), 372-373; Easterbrook and Fischel (1985), 109; Thompson (1991), 1055]. Indeed, consistent with our analysis in Chapter 8 suggesting that personal liability should not be imposed on shareholders of publicly held corporations, in an extensive study of about 1,600 cases from all over the U.S. in which piercing-the-veil claims had been instituted, Thompson [1991, 1047] found that "[i]n the entire data set, piercing did not occur in a publicly held corporation". Earlier, on review of the case law,

Barber [1981, 372] had made a similar observation.

In addition, Thompson [1991, 1055] found that the success rate of piercing-the-veil claims against shareholders of close corporations decreased as the number of shareholders increased. In respect of close corporations whose shares were held by a single private individual, courts reportedly entered judgment for the plaintiff in 49.64 percent of the cases. However, if the number of private shareholders amounted to more than three, plaintiffs' success rate dropped to 34.98 percent. This finding is consistent with our hypothesis in Chapter 3 that the reduction in transaction costs brought about by statutory limited liability becomes more significant as the number of shareholders increases. Taking into account the upward effect of unlimited liability on transaction costs as the number of shareholders rises, then, it is no surprise that courts are more reluctant to depart from the limited liability rule as the number of shareholders becomes greater.

Fourth, courts have imposed personal liability on shareholders both for corporate obligations arising from contract and for tortious liabilities generated by the operations of the firm. Thus, courts have decided to lift the corporate veil for the benefit of voluntary as well as involuntary creditors. The substantive criteria which are applied to impose personal liability do not differentiate between claims based on a contractual obligation incumbent on the corporation and claims based on tortious liability of the corporation: courts tend to approach both categories of claims in a materially identical manner [Barber (1981), 380-381].

In his above-mentioned study, Thompson [1991, 1058] found that courts were prepared to pierce the corporate veil more often in cases involving claims based on transactions between the plaintiff and the corporation entered into in a bargaining situation than in cases involving claims based on corporate torts (41.98 percent compared to 30.97 percent success rate of piercing claims). Thus, the requirements for imposing personal liability were considered satisfied more often in contract than in tort situations. Judging from the numbers, the greater success rate of contract claims is well recognized by creditors' attorneys: of the total number of piercing claims (both successful and unsuccessful) in the cases in Thompson's study, claims were based more frequently on contractual than on tortious liabilities incurred by the corporation (contract claims outnumbering claims based on tort by a factor of 3.45, with successful contract claims outnumbering successful tort claims by a factor of 4.67).

When holding a shareholder liable for the contractual obligations of the corporation, courts are in fact finding that voluntary creditors have not willingly assumed the risk of corporate insolvency and have not already been compensated through the terms of the contract. Thompson's findings are, therefore, at odds with the theory that voluntary creditors bargain for *ex ante* compensation for the insolvency risk that limited liability shifts to them, and support our competing view set out in Chapter 7 that they are relatively unlikely to receive adequate compensation through the terms of the contract.

Finally, as regards the substantive standards for imposing personal liability on shareholders, the various U.S. jurisdictions are united primarily by the lack of a uniform, unambiguous concept of the substantive criteria by which piercing-the-veil claims are adjudicated. As the federal court in *Bucyrus-Erie Co.* v. *General Products Corp.* [643 F.2d 413, 418 (6th Cir. 1981)] admitted, "[n]o precise test for disregarding the corporate fiction has been articulated by the courts, each case being regarded as "sui generis" and decidable on its own facts".

Case law has induced one commentator to state that veil-piercing cases are characterized by "their general failure to articulate reasoned grounds of decision, thus affording little predictability in an area in which conduct is ordinarily highly planned" [Note (1958), 1123]. Likewise, Clark [1986, 73] has observed that lifting-the-veil cases are unified "more by the remedy sought (...) than by repeated and consistent application of the same criteria for granting the remedy". A similar observation had been made by Ballantine [1946, 312] several decades earlier: "The formulae invoked usually give no guidance or basis for understanding the results reached".

Still earlier, the same Ballantine [1925, 15] had referred to the case law on veil-piercing as "a legal quagmire", whilst Justice Cardozo in *Berkey* v. *Third Ave. Ry. Co.* [244 N.Y. 84, 94, 155 N.E. 58, 61 (1926)], in a corporate group context, stated that this area of law was "enveloped in the mists of metaphor". Although little seems to have changed since then, through these mists certain minimum requirements can be identified which must be satisfied before courts will impose personal liability upon a shareholder. Although variations exist between different state jurisdictions, both in the terminology used and in the application of the law, these requirements form the bedrock of the law of piercing the corporate veil throughout the U.S. We explore this bedrock a little further in the next sections.

As a preliminary observation, we note that courts adjudicate piercing-the-veil claims on the basis of the same set of standards regardless of the identity of the defending shareholder concerned. Thus, the same rules apply whether the shares in a corporation are owned by a private individual or are held by another corporation in a corporate group context.

Nonetheless, in his above-mentioned study, Thompson [1991, 1055-1057] found that courts are somewhat less inclined to pierce the veil when the shares are held by another corporation (the parent company) than they are when the shares are owned by one, two or three private individuals (a combined piercing rate of 48.05 percent for corporations belonging to the latter category compared with 36.79 percent when the shares are held by a parent corporation). In our view, this finding may be explained by the fact that parent corporations frequently incorporate subsidiary companies in the pursuit of diversification policies aimed at minimizing risk for both shareholders and creditors of the parent company, with a view to enhancing the group's aggregate capital-raising ability. Limited liability of the parent in this context has a clear function in facilitating such diversification, which courts may be willing to uphold when the parent's holding is intended for the cited purposes only and the parent does not actively use its limited liability to inflict injury on creditors of the subsidiary company.

By contrast, when a corporation has a small number of private shareholders (in Thompson's study: less than four), such shareholders are less likely to hold their shares purely for diversification purposes which the courts will respect. As the number of private shareholders rises, however, transaction cost considerations as well as diversification observations similar to those made for parent companies become relevant and this may explain why courts then become less inclined to impose personal liability.

The Instrumentality Test

The first hurdle that creditors seeking to lift the corporate veil in order to access any one shareholder's non-invested wealth must surmount is the "instrumentality" (or "alter ego") test. According to this test, the corporation must have been the "mere instrumentality" of its shareholders, meaning that there was virtually no separation in fact between the shareholders and the corporate entity. The corporation, then, although being a separate legal entity, did not in reality function as an entity distinct from its shareholders.

In *Automotriz del Golfo de California* v. *Resnick* [47 Cal. 2d 792, 796, 306 P.2d 1, 3 (1957)] the court indicated that for satisfaction of the instrumentality requirement there must be "such unity of interest and ownership that the separate personalities of the corporation and the individual [shareholders] no longer exist". Slightly more specifically, the court in *United States National Bank of Omaha* v. *Rupe* [207 Neb. 131, 135, 296 N.W.2d 474, 477 (1980)] held that the instrumentality criterion requires that "the corporation is a mere facade for the personal dealings of the shareholder and that the operations of the corporation are carried on by the shareholder in disregard of the corporate entity".

When precisely a corporation may be deemed a "mere facade" for its shareholder(s) is highly dependent on the facts and circumstances of the particular case. In *Herbert* v. *Wiegland* [207 So.2d 882, 887 (4th Cir. 1968)], the court considered that "[e]very act purportedly to have been done by or in the name of the corporation was entirely dictated and controlled by, and was in fact the act of, [the defending shareholder] personally". Similarly, in *Lowendahl* v. *Baltimore & Ohio R.R.* [247 App. Div. 144, 157, 287 N.Y.S. 62, 76 (1936)] and in *Zaist* v. *Olson* [227 A.2d 552, 558 (Conn. 1967)], the courts, using similar wording, maintained that the instrumentality criterion required "complete domination" of a corporation by a shareholder, including domination "not only of finances, but of policy and business practice in respect to the transaction attacked so that the corporate entity as to this transaction had at the time no separate mind, will or existence of its own". The domination requirement captures the essence of the instrumentality rule, and explains why the concept of piercing the corporate veil is not invoked in respect of publicly held corporations with multiple non-controlling shareholders and run by specialized managers.

Elements recognized in case law as indicating that a shareholder dominated a corporation in such a manner that he turned it into a mere instrumentality of himself, include *de facto* control of managerial decision-making by the shareholder, intermingling of funds and other assets belonging to the corporation with the shareholder's personal assets, the use of corporate assets or funds by the shareholder personally (including acts of self-dealing), failure to maintain separate corporate and financial records and to pursue separate accounting policies, the shareholder representing his personal business and that of the corporation as being identical, and other such interference of the shareholder in the affairs of the corporation. In *United States National Bank of Omaha* v. *Rupe* [207 Neb. 131, 135, 296 N.W.2d 474, 477 (1980)], for instance, the court related the instrumentality criterion to the "[d]iversion by the shareholder or shareholders of corporate funds or assets to their own or other improper uses". Courts and commentators frequently cite such instances of shareholder interference with the corporation as "disregard of corporate formalities" [Barber (1981), 377].

In the context of parent-subsidiary relationships, courts have also considered important such factors as: identity of the managements of the parent and the subsidiary corporation, operations of both companies being organized in and conducted from the same offices, commingling of the commercial activities of the parent and the subsidiary, the activities of the subsidiary being directed by the management of the parent company, virtual absence of distinct business attributable to the subsidiary except for business conducted with affiliated companies, absence of separate meetings of the shareholders and directors of the corporations concerned, similarity of the trade names which the parent and the subsidiary use when dealing with third parties, control of the subsidiary's capital flow by the parent, in particular, systematic "milking" of the subsidiary's financial resources by the parent, and payment of the salaries of the employees of the subsidiary by the parent corporation. From such facts the court may deduce that the subsidiary corporation is not in reality an entity distinct from its shareholder, the parent company, but, rather, a puppet of the parent.

In the ancient case of *Finnish Temperance Soc'y Sovittaja* v. *Finnish Socialistic Publishing Co.* [238 Mass. 345, 355, 150 N.E. 845, 848 (1921)], for instance, the court found that parent company intermeddling in the affairs of the subsidiary corporation had resulted in "complete identity of interest", which led the court to infer that the subsidiary in reality was no more than a "creature or mouthpiece" of the parent company. However, the mere existence of a parent-subsidiary relationship, without more, is not *per se* sufficient to trigger veil-piercing, as, for example, the court in *Miller* v. *Dixon Industries Corp.* [513 A.2d 597 (R.I. 1986)] noted [Kindlund (1987), 370]: the parent company must have impinged on the subsidiary in one or more of the manners described above.

In summary, if a court is requested to disregard the corporate entity, on the basis of the instrumentality rule, the plaintiff must prove that the shareholder in question disregarded the corporation's distinct entity status and treated it as if the corporation's dealings were his own. To this effect, the plaintiff has to demonstrate that the degree of shareholder domination was substantially beyond the level of influence that an ordinary majority shareholder would exercise and that it extended well beyond the incident use of voting rights. There must have been active, direct shareholder intermeddling in the affairs of the corporation, to such an extent that the corporation's dealings can hardly be distinguished from those of the shareholder, the borderline between the two having become dim if not virtually invisible; there must have been "a pattern of ignoring the separateness of the corporation", as the court in *Solomon* v. *Greenblatt* [812 S.W.2d 7, 19 (Tex. 1991)] has put it.

Some courts demand, moreover, that the domination by the shareholder must have resulted in the non-fulfillment of the specific corporate obligation for which the creditor concerned seeks to impose personal liability upon the shareholder. In other words, the acts of the shareholder must have been the proximate cause of the particular corporate liability the creditor seeks to collect. Accordingly, the courts in *Lowendahl* v. *Baltimore & Ohio R.R.* [247

App. Div. 144, 157, 287 N.Y.S. 62, 76 (1936)] and *Zaist* v. *Olson* [227 A.2d 552, 558 (Conn. 1967)] have construed the instrumentality rule to require that the shareholder's "control and breach of duty must [have] proximately cause[d] the injury or unjust loss complained of".

However, such a specific "proximate cause" requirement is not consistently applied by the courts throughout the U.S. Often it is sufficient for the plaintiff to convince the court that the involvement of the shareholder in the affairs of the corporation has been the predominant factor in causing the corporation to incur the liabilities which it incurred, including the liability in respect of which the plaintiff has requested the court to lift the corporate veil. In *Glenn* v. *Wagner* [313 N.C. 450, 457, 329 S.E.2d 326, 331 (1985)], for instance, the North Carolina Supreme Court maintained that if a corporation is a "mere shell, created to perform a function for an affiliated corporation", in order to pierce the veil, the assessment of shareholder domination need not be "narrowly limited to control over the particular transaction attacked". According to such case law, it is sufficient that a reasonable relationship can be shown between the domination by the shareholder and the injury suffered by the plaintiff (the non-fulfillment of the corporation's obligation to him), without the plaintiff having to prove that the shareholder has directly caused the particular injury of which he complains [Krendl and Krendl (1978), 27].

The instrumentality requirement protects non-controlling investors from personal liability. By doing so it encourages proportionately small, passive investments and makes diversification a rational investment strategy, thereby enhancing firms' ability to raise equity capital. In addition, it discourages shareholder intrusion on managerial decision-making, thereby encouraging investors to take full advantage of specialized management when the benefits of having specialized managers outweigh the costs and, in effect, promoting efficacy in monitoring.

In contrast, when a corporation is found to be the mere instrumentality of a dominant shareholder who "used the corporate entity for solely personal purposes and disregarded the corporate form" [*Canario* v. *Lidelco, Inc.*, 782 F.Supp. 749, 760 (N.Y. 1992)], the advantages associated with incorporation discussed in Chapter 2 are not realized.

First, there are no productivity gains and cost reductions from specialized management, the dominant shareholder himself dictating virtually all managerial decision-making.

Second, the corporation's legal entity status will not produce significant transaction cost reductions in the operations of the business and the administration of its assets. As described in Chapter 2, legal personality serves to maintain the assets in the firm as a going concern, insulates the firm's assets from the individual investors, and enables the firm to operate in the market as a concern independent of the shareholders. Transaction cost advantages are realized because there is no need for the individual shareholders to become involved in the ownership of the assets in the firm and in transactions pertaining to such assets, or in other business transactions. However, if a corporation is found to be a mere instrumentality of its shareholder, there is virtually no divide between the assets and dealings of the business firm and those of the shareholder. Thus, the very source of the cited transaction cost advantages does not exist. By contrast, as they cannot readily distinguish between the personal assets and business of the shareholder and those of the corporation, legal entity status will *increase* transaction costs to would-be creditors, it becoming more difficult for them to identify what security the corporation (or the shareholder) provides and to determine the risk they would take by extending credit to the corporation.

Third, a shareholder choosing to dominate a firm on the basis of a majority shareholding is unlikely to take advantage of limited liability to assemble a diversified portfolio so as to reduce that firm's cost of capital. Instead of becoming a passive diversified investor, he has deliberately elected to become an active investor in the firm concerned and to shoulder the investment risk of holding a majority of the shares in that firm. This decision points to risk-preference rather than to a desire to reduce risk through diversification. Moreover, if the dominant shareholder of one firm were to diversify by making substantial investments in other corporations, each of them subsequently being operated as his puppets (or as puppets of the others), that, again, would raise transaction costs to creditors. Where the latter would be precluded from ascertaining the insolvency risk of the relevant debtor accurately, the shareholder's reduction of risk would come at the expense of creditors.

Fourth, if a firm is dominated by a majority shareholder, there is unlikely to be an active market for the stock of that firm promoting efficacy in managerial decision-making by that shareholder. Thus, there is no reason to retain limited liability in order to ensure stock market discipline.

As the above observations reveal, when a shareholder uses a corporation as a mere instrumentality of himself, the economic rationales for upholding the separateness of the corporate entity are absent. Shareholders' limited liability then raises transaction costs in credit markets and may be used as a shield to externalize costs to creditors while the corporate form as such, including limited liability, does not produce its desired social benefits. When a shareholder uses the corporation as an instrumentality, therefore, there is a "perversion of the privileges to do business in a corporate form", as the court in *Walkovszky* v. *Carlton* [18 N.Y.2d 414, 420, 223 N.E.2d 6, 10 (1966)] has put it. This is what the instrumentality test reflects. The threat of personal liability posed by the instrumentality test will not only induce dominant shareholders to duly consider the costs of the firm's operations to creditors but also to let the corporate firm function as one economic entity, whose ability to pay off creditors will first and foremost depend on its own fortune.

The Inequity Test

In addition to the instrumentality requirement, when adjudicating piercing-the-veil claims, courts ordinarily apply a second test which creditors must also pass in order to obtain permission to access shareholders' non-invested wealth. This second test entails that in the case concerned, it must also be shown that retention of the limited liability rule would have an "inequitable effect" on creditors of the corporation, to the extent that the principles of equity would call for a correction of the rule in that case. The "inequity" hurdle encourages would-be creditors not to rashly extend credit to potentially insolvent shareholder-dominated corporations, thereby reducing the likelihood and social costs of corporate bankruptcy and, in effect, opposing the use by corporate firms of scarce resources below their opportunity value.

In *Automotriz del Golfo de California* v. *Resnick* [47 Cal. 2d 792, 796, 306 P.2d 1, 3 (1957)], the court defined this requirement to mean that "if the acts [of the corporation] are treated as those of the corporation alone, an inequitable result will follow". Likewise, the court in *DeWitt Truck Brokers, Inc.* v. *W. Ray Flemming Fruit Co.* [540 F.2d 681, 686-687 (4th Cir. 1976)] stated that there must be "an element of injustice or fundamental unfairness". The inequity (or "unfairness") test and the instrumentality requirement discussed above constitute a cumulative, "two-prong" test which a creditor seeking to lift the corporate veil must satisfy [Barber (1981), 376].

When will retention of the limited liability rule have an inequitable result that may prompt a court to set it aside? Courts have given various, often rather inconclusive, answers to this question. In *United States* v. *Milwaukee Refrigerator Transit Co.* [142 F. 247, 255 (Wis. 1905)], in a classic formulation the court noted that "when the notion of legal entity is used to defeat public convenience, justify wrong, protect fraud, or defend crime, the law will regard the corporation as an association of persons", that means, hold the shareholders personally liable. In *Lowendahl* v. *Baltimore & Ohio R.R.* [247 App. Div. 144, 157, 287 N.Y.S. 62, 76 (1936)] and in *Zaist* v. *Olson* [227 A.2d 552, 558 (Conn. 1967)], the courts stated a requirement that the defending shareholder had used his domination of the corporation "to commit fraud or wrong, to perpetrate the violation of a statutory or other positive legal duty, or a dishonest or unjust act in contravention of the plaintiff's legal rights". Accordingly, some courts and commentators have referred to the inequity test as the "improper purpose" requirement [Krendl and Krendl (1978), 18].

There are three factors that are generally recognized which may cause limited liability to produce inequitable effects on the corporation's creditors: fraud, undercapitalization, and misrepresentation. *Fraud* (deceit) by a shareholder ordinarily satisfies the inequity test but it is not in itself required to impose personal liability upon a shareholder: "[t]he corporate identity can be pierced to prevent not only fraud, but any injustice", as the court in *Paumier* v. *Barge B.T. 1073* [395 F. Supp. 1019, 1039 (1974)] noted. Likewise, in *Anderson* v. *Abbott* [321 U.S. 349, 362 (1944)], the U.S. Supreme Court acknowledged that cases of fraud make up part of the exception justifying that the corporate veil be lifted, but that fraud cases do not exhaust that exception.

A shareholder's desire to take advantage of limited liability so as to shield his personal wealth against claims from creditors is not in itself fraud *and* is not sufficient on its own to give rise to injustice. Indeed, courts have recognized that a business may be incorporated precisely to afford shareholders the benefit of limited liability. In *Elenkrieg* v. *Siebrecht* [238 N.Y. 254, 262, 144 N.E. 519, 521 (1924)], for instance, the court acknowledged that an investor is entitled to incorporate a business "for the very purpose of escaping personal liability". Avoidance of liability was also recognized as an acceptable reason for incorporation in, for example, *Anderson* v. *Abbott* [321 U.S. 349, 361 (1944)] and *Walkovszky* v. *Carlton* [18 N.Y.2d 414, 223 N.E.2d 6 (1966)]. Thus, a shareholder's motives for incorporation do not subject him to personal liability: it is not for the courts to judge whether a firm was "incorporated in good faith, or whether incorporation was (...) an evasive device (...) to escape an individual responsibility for the conduct of the business", as was established in *Werner* v. *Hearst* [177 N.Y. 63, 67, 69 N.E. 221, 222 (1903)].

Whether or not a court will lift the corporate veil depends on its evaluation of the *effects* of limited liability, not on the reasons that prompted incorporation. It comes down, thus, to the actual use that is made of limited liability. If it is used to defraud creditors, courts have consistently maintained that it would then be inequitable if limited liability were upheld. For instance, the court in *Chase Manhattan Bank* v. *264 Water Street Ass.* [571 N.Y.S.2d 281, 282 (1991)] denied the application of the principle of limited liability to a parent company which had employed a scheme devised "to denude the subsidiary of its assets in order to render it unable to honor its obligations" to the complaining creditor. Fraud cases by nature involve externalization of costs to creditors, and veil-piercing in the event of fraud counters such effect both directly and by correcting shareholders' perverse incentives. Moreover, the protection created by the ability to access shareholders' non-invested wealth will reduce the transaction costs would-be creditors' are to incur to ascertain a corporation's true payment capacity and to detect or prevent fraud.

A second factor which may cause limited liability to be deemed to be inequitable to the corporation's creditors is *misrepresentation*, which does not require plaintiffs to demonstrate fraud (deceitful or dishonest artifices) on behalf of the controlling shareholder(s) [Krendl and Krendl (1978), 31]. When adjudicating veil-piercing claims that invoke misrepresentation, courts examine whether creditors were misled as to the identity or solvency of the party with which they were dealing as a result of the behavior of, or acts attributable to, the dominating shareholder(s).

Misrepresentation cases in which courts have lifted the corporate veil, such as *Paumier* v. *Barge B.T. 1073* [395 F. Supp. 1019 (1974)] and *Zaist* v. *Olson* [227 A.2d 552 (1967)], involved cases in which a prospective creditor had been given an incorrect, overly favorable picture of the extent or the value of the assets of the company seeking credit (and to which he would eventually have recourse should he wish to collect the company's debt to him). For instance, a creditor may have received the impression that he was dealing with the more solvent parent company (or majority shareholder) rather than the less solvent subsidiary, that the debtor corporation owned more (or more valuable) assets than it did, or that the dominating shareholder would repay a loan extended to the corporation if the latter failed to do so. Facts such as the mixing up of the assets and operations of the corporation with those of the shareholder, the use of similar trade names, and the direction of operations from the same offices that may suggest the corporation to be an instrumentality of the shareholder, may also prompt a finding of misrepresentation. A corporation's simple inability to pay, however, does not constitute misrepresentation (or fraud).

Where a prospective creditor is misled into believing that there are more (or more valuable) assets providing security for the fulfillment of the corporate debtor's obligations, he may be lulled into extending credit which he would not have provided if he had known the actual financial situation of the debtor, or into extending credit at terms more favorable to the debtor. If the creditor could then only collect his claim from the assets of the corporation in the event of a default, limited liability would have increased his loss compared to the loss he would have suffered if he had possessed accurate information, the misrepresentation having deprived him of the ability to refuse credit or to assume the undercapitalization risk and charge *ex ante* compensation through the credit terms.

Piercing the corporate veil on the basis of misrepresentation by a dominant shareholder is not merely a means to prevent externalization of costs to creditors, it is also an application of the "cheapest cost avoidance" principle: to ascertain the true identity or the real payment capacity of the corporate debtor and to set credit terms accordingly, a would-be creditor would have to incur higher expenses than the dominating shareholder would have to incur in order to inform him correctly. Put another way, misrepresentation, like fraud, raises transaction costs in credit markets, and the threat of personal liability for shareholders serves to reduce such costs [Posner (1976), 520-521].

The Undercapitalization Factor

Undercapitalization is a third factor which courts may deem to result in injustice if limited liability is retained. In *Automotriz del Golfo de California* v. *Resnick* [47 Cal. 2d 792, 797, 306 P.2d 1, 4 (1957)], for instance, the court considered that "inadequate financing, where such appears, is a factor, and an important factor, in determining whether to remove the insulation to stockholders normally created by the corporate method of operation". "An obvious inadequacy of capital, measured by the nature and magnitude of the corporate undertaking" was also quoted by the U.S. Supreme Court in *Anderson* v. *Abbott* [321 U.S. 349, 362 (1944)] as a factor which may trigger veil-piercing, "even in the absence of a legislative policy which undercapitalization would defeat". Undercapitalization is used by the courts as a catch-all term referring to situations in which the equity capital that shareholders have invested in the assets of the corporation has proven grossly insufficient to meet its liabilities. There must be a gross disproportion, then, between the capital that shareholders have paid in as reflected in the value of the corporation's assets and the debts it has incurred.

Whether such a disproportion exists needs to be analyzed on the basis of the facts of each case and is largely a matter of hindsight. Although there are no absolute quantitative standards for determining whether a particular corporation is undercapitalized, courts often consider the following questions. Have shareholders furnished the corporation with sufficient capital to enable it to carry on its business as a distinct economic entity, operating independently of the shareholders? Does the amount shareholders have invested provide a reasonable cushion for the corporation's creditors, taking into account the business's prospective liabilities, or have they created a financial structure prone to unduly jeopardize creditors in the event of commercial adversities? Is the portion of total corporate assets represented by the capital that shareholders have contributed reasonably sufficient to withstand the ordinary stresses and strains of the business [Note (1958), 1128]? The answers to such questions vary with the nature of the business concerned, the scope of its operations, the amount of risk (hazard) it involves, the normal financial requirements of the business, and the reasonable foreseeability of the adversities encountered and the liabilities incurred, and occasionally depend on a comparison with other firms in the same industry.

Courts have sometimes applied the undercapitalization factor by reviewing whether the corporation had "substantial capital reasonably regarded as adequate to enable it to operate its business and pay its debts as they matured" [*Ohio Edison Co.* v. *Warner Coal Corp.*, 79 Oh. App. 437, 72 N.E.2d 487 (1946)]. Such a phrase, however, does not set a fixed measure for assessing the adequacy of a corporation's capital but, rather, restates the issue so as to require the court to evaluate whether shareholders have paid in enough capital to cover the business's reasonably foreseeable liabilities.

Courts have frequently pierced the corporate veil in cases where a single shareholder has incorporated a business with virtually no assets of its own, where the business is heavily dependent on the assets of the shareholder to conduct operations, and all the while its revenue is being siphoned off by the shareholder. Early examples of such case law are *Garden City Company* v. *Burden* [186 F.2d 651 (C.A. 10th, 1951)] and *Wallace* v. *Tulsa Yellow Cab Taxi and Bagage Co.* [178 Okl. 15, 61 P.2d 645 (1936)]. However, as the court in *Walkovszky* v. *Carlton* [18 N.Y.2d 414, 419, 223 N.E.2d 6, 9 (1966)] noted, "[t]he corporate form may not be disregarded merely because the assets of the corporation (...) are insufficient to assure (...) the recovery [of its debts] sought".

Absence of sufficient capital to satisfy corporate obligations, then, is, according to this case law, not in itself enough to impose personal liability upon a shareholder: the corporation must be undercapitalized by the standards cited above, this undercapitalization must have given rise to injustice, and the instrumentality test must have been satisfied. Thus, there must be something more, and clearly more, than mere inability to pay. If insufficient capital alone were decisive, the limited liability rule would become meaningless and this is what the court's above-cited consideration in *Walkovszky* v. *Carlton* expresses. Consistent with this, Thompson [1991, 1063, 1065-1067] found that in just over 26 percent of the cases in his study in which courts found a case for undercapitalization, limited liability was nonetheless retained (the corporate veil being pierced in 73.33 percent of undercapitalized corporations).

The significance of the undercapitalization factor in the adjudication of piercing-the-veil claims lends indirect support to our view in Chapter 7 that statutory minimum equity capital requirements and capital maintenance rules are unlikely to eliminate the perverse incentives created by limited liability. Despite such requirements, shareholders may deliberately shelter themselves behind the limited liability rule and have the corporation engage in activities the costs of which to creditors in the event of failure may by far exceed the amount shareholders have invested, minimum capital requirements and restraints on corporate distributions being no assurance that the corporation will have sufficient assets to pay its creditors. It is when a court finds that a corporation was both undercapitalized and operated as a mere instrumentality of its shareholder(s) that it will find that the corporate shield was in fact used to externalize a part of the costs of the business to the corporation's creditors. Veil-piercing then corrects the externality that limited liability has provoked, whilst the *threat* of personal liability serves to discourage such use. By treating undercapitalization as a factor relevant to the adjudication of piercing-the-veil claims, courts admit that minimum capital provisions, where existing, and capital maintenance rules may not prevent externalization of costs to creditors.

The failure of minimum capital requirements to protect creditors has come to be recognized by the custodians of the Model Business Corporation Act (in the Official Comment at Section 6.21). For this reason, the requirement that the articles of incorporation must state a minimum equity capital which shareholders are to pay in, was deleted from the Model Act in 1980. Similarly, modern state corporation statutes have reportedly dropped minimum equity capital requirements of any meaning as a condition for incorporation [Clark (1986), 67].

Some commentators have suggested that the presence of undercapitalization would trigger veil-piercing earlier in state jurisdictions which do not have statutory minimum capital requirements than in jurisdictions which do impose such requirements [Conard (1976), 432]. However, consistent with our view concerning the relative unimportance of minimum capital requirements to opposing externalities, Thompson [1991, 1050-1052] has not reported statistically significant differences in piercing rates for different state jurisdictions.

The External Costs Problem: Dutch Law

Statutory Concepts

In the preceding sections, we have surveyed the two-prong test of instrumentality and inequity applied by U.S. courts in piercing-the-veil cases. We do not aim to argue, however, that every U.S. court in every single piercing case consistently and systematically investigates whether the instrumentality and inequity requirements described above have been satisfied. Rather, we submit that U.S. courts are *guided* by these requirements, and that they can be observed in one form or another in the bulk of existing case law. In some cases, instrumentality and inequity standards are applied explicitly, whilst they (or one of them) are rather implicit in other cases. For instance, a typical fraud case hinges on inequity, with instrumentality being implicit when fraud is established (for fraud by a shareholder via the corporate entity ordinarily presupposes shareholder dominance). All in all, in our view, the instrumentality and inequity tests provide a key to understanding U.S. case law with respect to piercing the corporate veil.

Let us now see how the concept of shareholder liability is applied in the Netherlands to remedy externality problems arising from limited liability. Our focus on liability should not conceal, however, that Dutch law relies more on other techniques to protect creditors than on the imposition of personal liability on shareholders. These other techniques include mandatory disclosure requirements, minimum capital requirements, statutory limitations on distributions to shareholders, and restrictions on the use of corporate funds to repurchase stock.

Dutch corporate legislation traditionally attaches greater importance to minimum equity capital requirements than U.S. corporation statutes tend to do. As a condition for incorporating a business, Dutch law demands that shareholders put up at least NLG 40,000 in equity capital if they intend to establish a close corporation ("*Besloten Vennootschap*") (Section 2:178 (2) of the Civil Code). Based on European Community law (viz. the second European Community directive on company law), a minimum equity capital of NLG 100,000 is prescribed to found a publicly held corporation ("*Naamloze Vennootschap*") (Section 2:67 (2) and (3) Civil Code). After incorporation these amounts must be maintained in the assets of the business at book value, and represent shareholders' minimum permanent investment. For the reasons stated earlier, we are rather skeptical of the efficacy of such requirements. If anything, they are misleading to creditors as they suggest that the assets of the business are worth at least the relevant minimum capital, which may not be true at all. Hence, there would not seem much to be lost if the aforesaid capitalization requirements were abolished.

The same applies to another, *de facto* minimum capital requirement contained in the Dutch corporation statute. This second requirement is the result of a combination of the following three rules. First, business corporations may only issue equity shares having a par value (Sections 2:67 (1) and 2:178 (1) Civil Code) and, generally, shares may not be issued at less than their par value (which must be stated in the articles of incorporation) (Sections 2:80 (1) and (2) and 2:191 (1) Civil Code). Second, when purchasing a share from the corporation, investors must put up either the entire par value of the share or, if expressly agreed, a lower amount equal to at least one quarter of the par value and in this case the corporation (or the trustee in the event of corporate bankruptcy) is entitled to demand payment of the remaining amount later (Sections 2:80 (1) and 2:191 (1) Civil Code). Purchasers of bearer shares (which only publicly held corporations may issue), however, must always directly pay up the full par value of the shares (Section 2:82 (3) Civil Code). In any event, the initial consideration paid by the joint shareholders must equal at least the relevant minimum capital stated above. Third, no distributions may be made to shareholders from the consideration which investors have paid in as payment of the par value of their shares (Sections 2:105 (2) and 2:216 (2) Civil Code). These rules combined aim to effect the situation that the corporation will always have a minimum cushion of capital for creditors equal to at least the number of shares issued times the par value of the shares.

However, the salable value of the corporation's assets from which creditors may seek payment, may be far less than the cited amount. The par value concept and the legal restraints on distribution that are based on it, have a bearing on the *volume* of shareholders' equity capital as shown on the corporation's balance sheet, but not on the *value* of corporate assets. Par value merely represents an *illusion* of value, the sum of par values being no reflection of the actual worth of the assets in the firm. The par value/ no distribution-requirement, therefore, does not provide creditors with any security of payment or with reliable information on the creditworthiness of the corporation, but may instead mislead them. Creative legal accounting methods may create an accounting profit and a corresponding earned surplus on the equity side of the balance sheet so as to allow for a distribution of funds to be made entirely out of the earned surplus. Such a distribution would *reduce* the net worth of corporate assets and, so, reduce creditors' capital cushion, although the above-mentioned legal restraint on distributions would be properly complied with.

We agree in principle that statutory limitations on corporate distributions encourage shareholders to take into account potential losses to creditors up to the amount which, pursuant to the limitations, must remain in the business and that such limitations protect creditors up to this amount, but restrictions on distributions based on the sum of the par value of equity shares issued fail to serve such purposes. The par value concept, then, does not provide creditors with any significant protection and may therefore, from a creditor interest perspective, be abolished as well. The same observations and conclusion apply to the statutory requirement (Sections 2:67 (1) and 2:178 (1) Civil Code) that the total of the par values of the shares which the corporation *may* issue, at its inception or at a later date, must be stated in the articles as the corporation's "legal capital" (which must satisfy the minimum capital requirements described earlier): the salable value of the assets, and not the stated "legal capital" ("*maatschappelijk kapitaal*"), determines the size of the capital cushion protecting creditors.

Moreover, regardless of the corporation's legal capital and the par value of its shares, it is the capital *market* which determines how much money the corporation can raise from the sale of shares, and it is the corporation's perceived capacity to earn money for its shareholders, not par value and legal capital, which determines the capital market price of the shares. The legal capital and par value requirements suggest that the shares represent a value that in reality may not exist. Thus, for the purpose of raising equity capital, these concepts need not be maintained either. (Indeed, the custodians of the U.S. Model Business Corporation Act reached the conclusion many years ago that the notions of "par value" and "legal capital" do not serve a meaningful purpose, and they were thus eliminated from the Model Act in 1980.)

We share the view of the custodians of the Model Business Corporation Act that restraints on distributions which are based on insolvency tests related to the value of corporate assets rather than on the volume of the equity capital, provide more effective protection to creditors than do minimum capitalization, par value and legal capital concepts like those embraced by Dutch corporate law. The Model Act states such insolvency tests in Section 6.40 (c), as follows: "No distribution [to or for the benefit of shareholders] may be made if, after giving it effect: (1) the corporation would not be able to pay its debts as they become due in the usual course of business; or (2) the corporation's total assets would be less than the sum of its total liabilities plus (unless the articles of incorporation permit otherwise) the amount that would be needed, if the corporation were to be dissolved at the time of the distribution, to satisfy the preferential rights upon dissolution of shareholders whose preferential rights are superior to those receiving the distribution." In our view, a provision like this one, directly aimed at maintaining sufficient assets in the firm to pay creditors, would be preferable to the current Dutch concepts discussed above.

Personal Liability of Shareholders

The concept of piercing the corporate veil, meaning rendering shareholders personally liable in their capacity as shareholders for the fulfillment of obligations incumbent on the corporation, does not exist in the Netherlands.

Dutch law does recognize the notion of personal liability of shareholders in spite of statutory limited liability. However, unlike U.S. law, the legal basis of such liability does not lie in the obligations of the *corporation*, but in the obligations of the individual *shareholder* concerned towards the corporation's creditors. In other words, when personal liability is imposed by a court, the shareholder will not be ordered to fulfill a *corporate* obligation but to fulfill an obligation of his *own*. Accordingly, creditors of a corporation desirous to collect payment of a corporate debt from a shareholder must demonstrate that the latter is subject to a personal obligation to pay an amount equaling that debt. There are several sources from which such an obligation may arise and these we explore below.

The first source of shareholder liability is Section 2:403 of the Civil Code, which applies in corporate group contexts only. In brief, this section provides that a corporation belonging to a corporate group is exempt from the requirement to make up and to disclose a detailed annual balance sheet and income statement in the manner statutorily prescribed if, *inter alia*, the following conditions are met: the financial figures of the company concerned must be consolidated into the financial statements of another company of the same group (which is usually the group's parent company), and the latter company must have stated in writing that it has assumed joint and several liability for debts of the first company ensuing from juridical acts (including, in particular, debts arising from contract). The "statement of liability" is to be filed with the Chamber of Commerce at which the corporation claiming the exemption is registered.

From Section 2:403 it follows that creditors of a subsidiary company may hold the subsidiary's shareholder, the parent company, liable for certain debts of the subsidiary if the parent has filed a statement of liability as described in order to relieve the subsidiary of financial disclosure requirements. However, the liability which the parent company would so assume does not extend to involuntary creditors. Victims of torts committed by the subsidiary, then, will find themselves unable to recover judgments for damages from the assets of the parent company. Likewise, the tax authorities will not be entitled to collect payment of taxes owed by the subsidiary from the parent.

The basis of shareholder liability pursuant to Section 2:403 of the Civil Code is not the liability of the subsidiary corporation itself but the statement of liability given by the shareholder (the parent company) in compliance with this section. Obviously, both U.S. law and Dutch law permit shareholders to voluntarily guarantee the due fulfillment of corporate obligations as they wish, notwithstanding the limited liability rule. However, shareholder liability pursuant to Section 2:403 is different from genuine voluntary liability, as this section creates a statutory *obligation* on the shareholder to accept unlimited liability for certain corporate debts if the debtor (the subsidiary) is to be relieved of public disclosure requirements.

If a subsidiary corporation is exempt from its legal obligations to disclose financial statements, its financial figures being consolidated into the parent company's annual financial report, would-be voluntary creditors of the subsidiary would have to incur higher information costs to ascertain the creditworthiness of that corporation. They would now have to gather for themselves the information that they would otherwise have been able to deduce from the subsidiary's balance sheet and income statement. As information costs become higher, the threat of externalization of risk would increase. The obligation of the parent company to assume liability for debts of the exempted subsidiary serves to avoid such higher information costs and consequent externalities. The result of the parent assuming liability is that it becomes unnecessary for would-be voluntary creditors of the subsidiary to examine in detail that company's creditworthiness: they can rely upon the joint payment capacity of the subsidiary and the parent company and may obtain information on their joint ability to pay from the latter's consolidated financial report, which must satisfy the statutory requirements concerning financial disclosure.

The above reasoning does not, however, apply to *in*voluntary creditors. Debts to involuntary creditors by definition do not arise out of bargaining situations. As there is no bargaining before credit is extended, disclosure of less financial data by a particular corporation will not result in higher information costs for prospective involuntary creditors. To them, the extent of the data the corporation discloses is irrelevant. Thus, shareholder liability would not reduce *in*formation costs of involuntary creditors and this probably explains why Section 2:403 excludes this category from the statement of liability it prescribes.

However, the exclusion of involuntary creditors makes Section 2:403, in our view, a topsy-turvy rule: given that involuntary credit is not extended in a bargaining situation, involuntary creditors cannot protect themselves against corporate insolvency by reviewing the financial figures disclosed and as they could not in any case have protected themselves even if the relevant subsidiary corporation was under an obligation to disclose elaborate financial information, they are denied the protection which Section 2:403 affords voluntary creditors, although they might well have bargained for the same protection if they *could* have bargained. Thus, the weaker party (involuntary creditors) is denied the protection given to the stronger party (voluntary creditors), for the very reason that it *is* the weaker party, being unable to bargain. In effect, Section 2:403 rewards rather than discourages the use of subsidiary companies to externalize risk to involuntary creditors, thereby adding to the externality problem in relation to this class of creditors rather than reducing it. We propose, therefore, that the shareholder liability prescribed by Section 2:403 be extended to include involuntary creditors.

There is yet another ambiguity relating to the kinds of creditors protected by Section 2:403. The statement of liability which Section 2:403 prescribes is a substitute for the protection that voluntary creditors could derive from the subsidiary's annual financial report if it had not been exempted from statutory disclosure obligations. Therefore, the statement of liability should be filed no later than the date on which the relevant subsidiary was to disclose its annual financial report had it not been exempted [Maeijer (1994), 609]. Does it follow also that only creditors of the subsidiary who extended credit after the statement's filing, that means, who lacked the information of the subsidiary's financial report, are entitled to invoke the stated liability?

Although the wording of Section 2:403 is inconclusive, the answer to this question must be negative. If creditors who extended credit prior to the filing of the statement of liability were excluded from its scope, they would become unable to keep track of their risk once the debtor ceased to satisfy the statutory disclosure requirements. The consolidated financial statements released by the parent company that issued the statement of liability would be irrelevant to this category of creditors as they would be unable to invoke liability of the parent. As a consequence, they would be unable to take risk-reducing measures if their risk of non-payment increased after the debtor had become exempt from disclosure. For instance, they would be unable, because of lack of knowledge, to demand additional security in the event of an increase in the insolvency risk (though the credit terms may have entitled them to do so), to sell and assign their claim to a third party in exchange for cash, or to renegotiate the terms of the credit arrangement in order to incorporate the additional risk.

For this reason, would-be creditors of a corporation currently complying with statutory disclosure rules but which may be exempted later (that is, a corporation which belongs to or may become part of a corporate group), would have risk-minimizing incentives to demand contractual devices limiting the corporation's liberty of action so as to prevent unilateral increases in the insolvency risk, to install costly monitoring and detection mechanisms, and to oblige the prospective debtor to keep disclosing certain financial data to the creditor even if it were legally exempt from disclosure. Obviously, any such devices would raise the transaction costs attending corporate borrowing. Alternatively, potential creditors might limit risk by not extending credit at all, in particular, if the prospective corporate debtor refuses to accept devices like those described above. Such effects are avoided if existing creditors also be afforded the protection of the statement of liability issued pursuant to Section 2:403. Therefore, we share the view of Maeijer [1994, 610] that Section 2:403 should be construed to include creditors who extended credit prior to the statement's filing, in addition to new creditors.

Liability Based on Misrepresentation

The second source of shareholder liability in Dutch law is *misrepresentation*. However, the scope of misrepresentation as a basis of shareholder liability is more limited than the equivalent concept in U.S. case law relating to the piercing of the corporate veil.

Misrepresentation, according to Dutch law, is present when a shareholder made such statements or behaved in such a manner that a creditor of the corporation could have reasonably presumed that he was either contracting with the shareholder instead of the corporation, or that the shareholder was personally guaranteeing the obligation entered into by the corporation. In such an event, the shareholder is deemed to have dealt personally with the creditor and the latter may hold him liable for the fulfillment of his consequent personal obligation (on the basis of Section 3:35 of the Civil Code). Likewise, in *De Vos* v. *De Kort* [NJ 1977, 119 (Hof A'dam 1975)], a case pertaining to two affiliated companies (not involving a shareholder-corporation relationship), the appellate court found that one affiliate was bound by a contract which according to that affiliate had been entered into by the other company given that the first affiliate had created the impression that *it* was the contracting party.

Alternatively, the statements or conduct of a shareholder may have furnished creditors with the impression that the corporation was not acting in its own right but on behalf of the *shareholder* [Maeijer (1994), 896]. If in the circumstances the relevant creditor could have reasonably relied upon the accuracy of such an impression, the shareholder is deemed to have been duly represented by the corporation as his legal agent and, consequently, the obligation contracted by the corporation is considered that of the shareholder personally: not a corporate obligation but a *shareholder* obligation has arisen, which the creditor concerned may subsequently demand the shareholder to fulfill (by reference to Section 3:61 (2) of the Civil Code).

Misrepresentation as a source of shareholder liability is limited to the instances described above. In both cases, the legal basis of the shareholder's liability is the shareholder's *own* obligation as a contracting party: the shareholder is deemed either to have directly contracted with the creditor concerned (the first case) or to have been represented by the corporation acting as his agent (the second case), and creditors may hold the shareholder liable based on his *personal* obligation which is presumed to have so arisen.

A misrepresentation action against a shareholder is most likely to succeed if the shareholder was involved in the day-to-day business of the corporation and he mixed his personal dealings with those of the corporation, which may have misled creditors as to the identity of the party with which they were contracting. However, mere *confusion* on the part of the creditor-plaintiff is not enough, as the Supreme Court has noted in *Blok* v. *De Haan* [NJ 1985, 446 (HR 1984)]; there must have been some positive act attributable to the defending shareholder which occasioned the creditor-plaintiff to presume that the shareholder was bound. For instance, in *NBM* v. *Securicor* [NJ 1995, 170 (HR 1994)] concerning an action not formally based on misrepresentation (but on tort; see below), liability was imposed upon a shareholder (the parent company) for non-performance of a contract by a subsidiary corporation in a case in which employees of the parent company had been involved in the contract negotiations, had made it known that they were parent company employees, and had verbally represented that the parent would treat the subsidiary's creditors decently.

Misrepresentation, by its very nature, may only lead to shareholder liability in relation to voluntary creditors; this is no different from its U.S. equivalent. As we saw in our discussion of misrepresentation and shareholder liability under U.S. corporate law, misrepresentation is apt to raise voluntary creditors' information costs and promotes externalities. Personal liability of shareholders is the law's response, which aims to avoid such effects.

Liability Based on Tort

A *tort* committed by a shareholder is the third source of shareholder liability recognized in Dutch law. A creditor of a corporation may hold a shareholder liable for damages based on tort (Section 6:162 of the Civil Code) if the shareholder behaved wrongfully towards the creditor concerned and if such wrongful behavior resulted in the corporation's failure to pay, wholly or partially, its debt to that creditor. If in a tort action the court enters judgment for the creditor-plaintiff, the shareholder will be ordered to repair the loss which that creditor has sustained through the corporation's failure to pay; the shareholder must then pay damages to make up for the corporation's unsettled debt.

The shareholder, again, is not held liable to fulfill a corporate obligation but to fulfill a personal obligation, viz. an obligation to pay compensatory damages. Liability is not imposed upon him in his capacity as a shareholder but as a tortfeasor. Accordingly, the creditor-plaintiff for whom the court has found is not permitted access to the shareholder's assets in order to collect a corporate debt but, solely, to collect the amount of the shareholder's personal liability for damages. Thus, the corporate veil *per se* is not lifted. The *amount* of the shareholder's liability, however, is determined by the extent of the corporation's unpaid debt.

Most litigation by creditors of a corporation who seek to inflict personal liability upon a shareholder is based upon alleged torts by shareholders. A prerequisite for a successful tort action against a shareholder is the corporation's failure to pay the creditor-plaintiff: unless the corporation has defaulted on the payment of its debt to that creditor, the creditor has not suffered a loss for which he may seek reparation from a shareholder. Such a prerequisite does not apply to actions based on misrepresentation or on a statement of liability issued pursuant to Section 2:403 of the Civil Code.

Whereas only voluntary creditors may successfully claim liability on the basis of misrepresentation or on the basis of the cited statement of liability, in a tort action voluntary as well as involuntary creditors of the corporation may claim damages from a shareholder. Thus, tort actions against shareholders may be brought for any unpaid debts of the corporation, regardless of whether the relevant debt has arisen from a contract entered into by the corporation or from a corporate tort. In practice, however, plaintiffs in shareholder tort actions are mostly voluntary creditors.

A tort action against a shareholder may be brought irrespective of whether the shareholder is a private individual or a corporation. The same applies to misrepresentation actions but not to actions based on the liability statement pursuant to Section 2:403, which require a corporate group context. If the court in a tort action directed against several shareholders holds more than one shareholder liable for the creditor-plaintiff's damage from the corporation's default, each shareholder whose defense is rejected will be jointly and severally liable for the damages payable (Section 6:102 Civil Code).

Tort actions may be brought by individual creditors of the corporation or, in the event of corporate bankruptcy, alternatively, by the trustee appointed by the court acting on behalf of the creditors as a class. The trustee's right to bring a tort action for the benefit of the joint creditors was recognized by the Supreme Court in its decisions in *Peeters* v. *Gatzen* [NJ 1983, 597 (HR 1983)] and *Nimox* v. *Van den End* [NJ 1992, 174 (HR 1991)]. It will be appropriate for the trustee to bring a tort action against a shareholder if the latter's allegedly tortious conduct harmed the creditors as a class and not merely a single individual creditor. The right of the trustee to bring a tort action against the shareholder is then efficient as it saves the litigation costs of a variety of suits for damages by individual creditors.

The trustee is not entitled, by contrast, to bring proceedings based on the statement of liability issued pursuant to Section 2:403 as that statement does not create rights for the bankrupt corporation or for the joint creditors as a class but solely for the corporation's voluntary creditors. If the trustee, in the right of the joint creditors, were entitled to bring proceedings based on the cited statement of liability, both voluntary and involuntary creditors would benefit from subsequent payments made by the shareholder concerned to the trustee because according to Dutch bankruptcy law, such payments would have to be distributed to *all* creditors in proportion to their respective claims (with due observance of creditors' differing preferential rights). That would water down the protection which the statement of liability affords voluntary creditors, and contrast with the tenor of Section 2:403 as it currently stands.

Likewise, only a creditor may bring an action based on misrepresentation as described in the preceding section, given that such an action hinges on the presumption that the creditor-plaintiff has contracted with the individual shareholder, not with the corporation; as the action assumes that there has been no involvement by the corporation in its own right, there is no role for the trustee to play.

To date, like the concept of piercing-the-veil in U.S. jurisdictions, the concept of personal liability of shareholders based on tort has resided in the domain of (shareholders of) close corporations, covering both close corporations whose shareholders are private individuals and close corporations belonging to a corporate group. The same applies to shareholder liability on the basis of misrepresentation, whilst shareholder liability based on the statement of liability given pursuant to Section 2:403, as noted, is limited to a corporate group context.

When may creditors, based on tort, claim compensatory damages from a shareholder for unpaid debts of the corporation? In other words, when do Dutch courts find that a shareholder committed a tort subjecting him to personal liability for damages?

Generally, courts have broad discretion in adjudicating tort claims against shareholders brought by creditors of a corporation, or by the trustee in the event of bankruptcy, and in determining whether or not the defending shareholder(s) acted tortiously. Like U.S. legislatures, the Dutch legislature has left this domain to case law, and like the decisions of U.S. courts in piercing-the-veil cases, the decisions of Dutch courts are highly dependent on the facts of each case.

Categories of Tortious Liability

Judging from existing case law, instances of shareholder liability based on tort may be grouped into the following three different categories.

First, a shareholder may have caused the corporation to incur an obligation which it was unable to fulfill from the outset while at the time the obligation was incurred the shareholder was aware, or should reasonably have been aware, that the corporation was inadequately equipped or had insufficient assets to properly perform that obligation, and lacked assets to pay damages for its non-performance. Cases in which a shareholder used a deliberately undercapitalized corporation to do business belong to this category, as do certain instances of fraud. The courts have initially applied the aforesaid standard of tortious liability to members of the management board, but it equally applies to shareholders who control the management of the corporate firm. In *Stimulan* v. *Klaas* [NJ 1990, 286 (HR 1989)], for example, the Supreme Court confirmed an appeal court decision quoting that standard which imposed liability on a member of the management board who was at the same time the corporation's single shareholder.

A shareholder is likely to become liable in tort, for instance, if he caused the corporation to enter into a contract for the purchase of goods at a price that he knew it was unable to pay. Decisive is what the shareholder actually knew, or should reasonably have known, at the time the contract was entered into. The existence at that time of a mere *possibility* that the corporation might later become unable to perform the contract does not subject the shareholder to tortious liability, as is apparent from the judicial decisions in *Romme* v. *Bakker* [TVVS 1994, 188 (HR 1994)] and *BASF Nederland* v. *Van Ommen* [NJ 1989, 92 (Hof Arnhem 1988)]. A shareholder may also become subject to liability in tort along this line of case law if he caused the corporation to engage in activities prone to generate corporate tortious liability, although he was, or should have been, aware that the corporation's assets were insufficient to indemnify prospective tort victims for the damage inflicted upon them.

Secondly, liability in tort may be imposed upon a shareholder for having deprived the corporation of the ability to duly perform an existing obligation, *i.e. after* the obligation was incurred, in particular, by depriving it of the assets or funds necessary to fulfill the obligation concerned. For example, the shareholder may have rendered the corporation unable to pay an outstanding debt by occasioning it to assign corporate property or distribute corporate funds to himself. Similarly, he may have caused the corporation to mortgage or pledge assets to himself or for his private benefit; as a consequence, creditors may have become unable, or less able, to collect on corporate liabilities. Tortious liability may also arise if the shareholder willfully precluded the corporation from fulfilling an obligation resting on it which it *could* in fact have performed, as is apparent from the Supreme Court's decision in *Van Waning* v. *Van der Vliet* [NJ 1992, 411 (HR 1992)].

The second category includes cases in which creditors of the corporation were defrauded after they had extended credit, as well as cases of asset stripping after a corporate liability had arisen in which the shareholder(s) did not have a fraudulent intent. For instance, in *Commission of the European Community* v. *Theal et al.* [NJ 1985, 124 (Arr. A'dam 1981)], the district court imposed liability in tort on, *inter alia*, a shareholder who had stripped the corporation of its assets in an alleged restructuring operation after that corporation had incurred a fine payable to the Commission of the European Community based on European competition law. As a consequence of the asset transfers, the corporation had become unable to pay the aforesaid fine. The court found that the defending shareholder had acted tortiously by wrongfully neglecting the Commission's interest in the payment of the fine due to it by the corporate entity.

Another good example of a case belonging to the second category is *Nimox* v. *Van den End* [NJ 1992, 174 (HR 1991)]. In this case, the corporation's single shareholder had decided that the corporation should distribute certain reserves to himself. Such a distribution was in itself permitted by statutory dividend restrictions. No physical distribution of funds took place but the shareholder received a claim against the corporation equal to the amount of the reserves concerned. This claim was merged with another, pre-existing claim of the shareholder. Subsequently, the shareholder sold his entire claim to a creditor (in fact, another creditor) of the corporation in exchange for a consideration in cash. Earlier that creditor had received security from the same corporation in relation to other claims of his against the corporation, which enabled him to also obtain payment of the shareholder's claim assigned to him.

As a result of the distribution decision and the subsequent assignment by the shareholder of his claim, the corporation became unable to pay creditors other than the secured creditor to whom the shareholder's claim had been sold. The court held the shareholder liable in tort based on the injury sustained by the other creditors, a decision which is consistent with our view that dividend restrictions (capital maintenance rules) may *mitigate*, but not *eliminate*, the perverse incentives created by shareholders' limited liability: the court's decision confirms that a shareholder's conduct may be tortious, that is, may inflict externalities on the corporation's creditors, even though statutory limitations on corporate distributions are duly observed [Maeijer (1994), 895].

Thirdly, a shareholder may have given creditors the impression that the corporation was financially sound or at least worthy of credit whereas in reality it was not, for instance, by deliberately having failed to inform would-be creditors that the corporation, although seemingly solvent, had virtually no assets from which they could collect payment. Such acts or omissions may give rise to tortious liability if the shareholder was involved in the corporation's management and thus had sufficient insight into its affairs to know better *and* to know that creditors erroneously relying on the corporation's soundness in all likelihood would face injury whereas the creditor-plaintiff himself was unaware, and could not reasonably have been aware, of the real facts. Creditors may in this way be tempted to extend credit which they would not otherwise have done had they known the corporation's true financial situation, or at the very least they would have extended it on different terms. This category includes cases in which creditors were somehow presented with an inadequate picture of the corporation's capacity to pay its debts and could not reasonably have known better, with the relevant shareholder being aware, or having to foresee, that they would be likely to incur loss if they relied on that picture and having neglected a positive duty to correct them.

Cases belonging to the third category include *Albada Jelgersma Holding* v. *Intercoöperatieve Zuivelfabriek van Antwerpen* [NJ 1988, 487 (HR 1988)] and *Osby-Pannan* v. *Las Verkoopmaatschappij* [NJ 1982, 443 (HR 1981)].

In the first case, the defending shareholder had acquired the shares in a nearly insolvent corporation. Upon acquisition, the shareholder had publicly announced that he would revitalize the corporation in question and enhance its liquidity. Accordingly, trade creditors were given the impression that credit extended to that corporation would be properly repaid. However, the corporation was adjudicated bankrupt within a year of the acquisition, as a result of which its debt to the trade creditor-plaintiff remained unsettled. The court imposed tortious liability upon the shareholder for having suggested that extending credit to the corporation was safe although he was aware of its financial difficulties, and subsequently having failed to take measures to protect creditors when the corporation proved to be irreparably insolvent.

In the second case, *Osby-Pannan* v. *Las Verkoopmaatschappij*, the defending shareholder (the parent company) had occasioned the subsidiary corporation to assign virtually all of its assets to the parent. However, the assets were physically left with the subsidiary. As a consequence, *prima facie* the subsidiary appeared to afford new creditors a reasonable capital cushion but in reality it had virtually no assets from which they could be paid. The court held the parent company liable in tort, considering that the parent had such insight into the subsidiary that it must have been aware, or should reasonably have anticipated, that the aforesaid assignment of assets would harm new creditors of the subsidiary as it practically deprived them of the opportunity to enforce their claims, and that the parent had nonetheless ignored the interests of such creditors.

The three categories described above do not constitute completely separate realms. Claims and allegations falling within different categories may be advanced in a single tort action and courts may base their decisions on considerations from more than one category. In particular, there may be overlaps in court decisions between the third category on the one hand and the first or second category on the other. However, the basis for tortious liability set out for each category, once established, may independently and on its own merit result in the imposition of shareholder liability.

As a rule, Dutch courts do not apply an express "instrumentality" or "alter ego" test similar to that applied in U.S. piercing-the-veil cases. However, in all three categories described above, courts do require that the defending shareholder effectively dominated the corporation to such a degree that the non-payment of the corporation's debt to the relevant creditor-plaintiff is attributable to the conduct of the shareholder. Some court decisions refer explicitly to shareholder dominance or control, especially if the case falls within the third category described above, whilst the same requirement is rather implicit in decisions in other cases, especially in those belonging to the first or second categories. The economic rationales behind the dominance requirement were described in our discussion of the instrumentality test in U.S. piercing-the-veil law; we may refer back to that discussion.

Shareholder dominance may most obviously be present when the shareholder is concurrently a member, or the sole member, of the corporation's management board. However, membership of that board is neither a necessary nor a sufficient condition for deemed presence of shareholder dominance and tortious liability of a shareholder. Moreover, if the defending shareholder is found to have effectively dominated the corporation, that does not in itself expose him to liability in tort. According to consistent case law including *Keulen* v. *BLG* [NJ 1986, 792 (HR 1986)], *Deniz Naklyati* v. *Glorywave Shipping* [NJ 1992, 247 (HR 1991)] and *Bato's Erf Beheer* v. *the Netherlands* [NJ 1996, 214 (HR 1995)], shareholder dominance alone is insufficient for liability: it must be accompanied by wrongful acts falling within one or more of the tort categories identified above.

The U.S. "inequity" test does not have a direct equivalent in Dutch law relating to shareholder liability. Whereas in the "inequity" test, the emphasis is on the result if limited liability were to be upheld, the starting point in Dutch tort (and misrepresentation) cases is the conduct of the defending shareholder(s) *per se*. However, the instances of liability in tort in the three categories described above reflect essentially the same notion of inequity: if the shareholder were not liable to pay compensatory damages in the instances described, "an inequitable result" (quoting *Automotriz del Golfo de California* v. *Resnick*) would follow and creditors would sustain "an element of injustice" (quoting *DeWitt Truck Brokers, Inc.* v. *W. Ray Flemming Fruit Co.*) by the very same standards as those set out in the U.S. inequity test. Like the U.S. inequity test, the three Dutch categories of shareholder tortious liability protect creditors against fraud, misrepresentation as applied in U.S. piercing-the-veil law and against dealing with an undercapitalized corporation; we have already discussed the rationales behind these factors in relation to shareholder liability. The inequitable element present in all three Dutch categories set forth above may be defined as wrongful neglect by a shareholder of the interests of creditors.

The notion of inequity is also reflected in the Supreme Court's consideration in *Manifattura Tessile Erba* v. *Amsterdamsche Bank* [NJ 1957, 514 (HR 1957)] requiring creditors to look after their own interests and take protective measures so as to limit the risk of non-payment wherever appropriate. Although the relief sought in this case was not shareholder liability but liability of a bank towards a creditor of a borrowing corporation, the aforementioned requirement is also relevant to tort actions against shareholders. Thus, creditors' prospects of having tortious liability imposed on a shareholder are mitigated by the rule that they should endeavor to avoid losses by looking after their own interests properly themselves. This restriction serves to prevent extension of credit to *de facto* insolvent corporations and, thus, to reduce the social costs of corporate bankruptcy.

In the above-mentioned cases, *Osby-Pannan* v. *Las Verkoopmaatschappij* and *Albada Jelgersma Holding* v. *Intercoöperatieve Zuivelfabriek van Antwerpen*, the creditor-plaintiffs could not reasonably have protected themselves from the losses they sustained because of lack of accurate information, and liability in tort was imposed on the parent companies in question as they had neglected creditors' interests. By contrast, in a somewhat similar U.S. case, *Fisser* v. *International Bank* [282 F.2d 231 (2d Cir. 1960)] involving a subsidiary corporation with minimum assets which was dominated by its parent company, the parent had duly informed creditors of the subsidiary company that the latter lacked substantial assets and was being operated primarily for the purpose of furthering the interests of the parent company. In that case, the U.S. court concluded that it would not be inequitable to uphold the limited liability rule and so refused to lift the corporate veil. Judging from the decisions in the Dutch cases quoted above, the outcome would have been no different had the case been decided by a Dutch court.

Liability Based on Mismanagement

The final source of shareholder liability in Dutch law, which is in fact a species of liability in tort (especially of the second category mentioned in the previous section), is contained in Sections 2:138 and 2:248 of the Civil Code.

According to these sections, if a shareholder manages the corporation, either as a member of the management board or by *de facto* participating in the management (*i.e.* by acting as a quasi-manager), in a manner so woefully inadequate that the corporation is forced into bankruptcy, he will be liable for the corporation's deficit in the bankruptcy. However, liability is imposed not in his capacity as a shareholder but in his capacity as a member or quasi-member of the corporation's management board.

Proceedings based on Section 2:138 or 2:248 of the Civil Code may only be brought by the trustee appointed by the court in the corporation's bankruptcy, who will distribute any subsequent payments from the shareholder-manager among the corporation's various creditors. In such proceedings, the trustee must demonstrate to the satisfaction of the court that the defending shareholder actively participated in the management of the corporation, that the corporation was manifestly mismanaged, and that moreover such mismanagement was an "important cause" of the corporation's bankruptcy.

The trustee's right to hold shareholders personally liable as managers or quasi-managers in bankruptcy cases prompted by mismanagement is the final recourse under Dutch law for the protection of creditors against exploitation by the shareholders. The rigid requisites for a successful action (viz. active shareholder involvement in the firm's day-to-day management, bankruptcy, manifest mismanagement and mismanagement having been an important factor in causing the bankruptcy) preclude such actions from being more than a means of last resort for the remedy of externalities arising from limited liability.

Concluding Remarks

THE FIRM IS more than a production function, a series of inputs from which output is obtained. The inputs that make up the firm cooperate as a *team* to jointly effect output, their individual efforts being combined into team product. Within the team, the ordinary market mechanism does not operate to allocate resources among alternative uses; intra-firm coordination takes its place.

The corporate form organizes the team and substitutes centralized management for the market to direct productive activity. The corporate form so enables exploitation of the advantages associated with the organization of productive activity in a firm: specialization of production factors, specialization in the assessment of business risks, avoidance of the costs of market exchange transactions, resolution of shirking problems in team productive actions, and elimination of hold-up problems in production processes involving relationship-specific assets. However, the corporate form does not merely organize the team, it also promotes the supply of two particular inputs to it: effective monitoring and risk capital. The distinguishing features of the corporate concept of organization all advance the supply of these inputs to the firm.

The desire to avoid market exchange transactions as an organizational instrument, to ensure effective monitoring of input performance in team productive activity, and to foster the influx of capital inputs into large-scale, capital-intensive production processes, all induced the emergence of the corporate form. As such, the corporation is a creature of market forces, not an invention of state bureaucracies.

The relationships between the cooperative input owners in the firm are of a voluntary associative nature and so is the adoption of corporate features to organize the firm. Accordingly, the relationships between the cooperative input owners, including the relationship between the residual claimants and the other team members, involve private contractual and quasi-contractual arrangements, which are reflected in the corporate concept. Incorporation under a public statute serves to avoid the transaction costs of establishing corporate characteristics through private contracting. The cost reduction attained is greatest if the statutory rules mimic the voluntary arrangements upon which the private parties involved in the corporate firm would agree if they were not impaired by transaction costs.

Promotion of effective monitoring and supply of risk capital to team productive processes and avoidance of transaction costs in the organization of such processes, particularly in the effectuation of corporate features, are the upside effects of the corporate form as standardized in public corporation statutes. However, there are downside effects, too.

The first downside effect of the corporate form arises as the corporation institutionalizes the conflict of interests between utility maximizing managers and wealth maximizing residual claimants. This conflict is responsible for the existence of agency costs, which raise the operational costs of the corporate firm, threaten the allocation of resources to their highest value in use, reduce returns to shareholders, discourage investment and raise output prices. Competition in product and factor markets, incentive contracts for managers, the market for corporate control, and managerial labor markets all operate to align managers' interests with those of the shareholders and so mitigate agency costs. However, these mechanisms do not *eliminate* the divergence of interests between managers and shareholders and consequent agency costs. Product and factor market competition are incapable of disposing of economy-wide agency costs, incentive contracts absorb at least a part of the agency costs they purport to reduce and managers may pursue evasive strategies offsetting their intended effects on incentives, the law of diminishing marginal utility of wealth by definition limits the effectiveness of pecuniary incentives such as those created by stock options, the market for corporate control and managerial labor markets both involve substantial transaction costs impairing their effective operation, labor market discipline also suffers from adverse selection and moral hazard problems, and excessive retained cash balances may pervert corporate control transactions.

The law may mitigate managerial departures from shareholders' wealth-maximizing interests by strengthening market disciplinary forces, particularly by facilitating the supply of information into the above-mentioned markets in order to reduce transaction costs in these markets, and, to a limited extent, by extending the instruments available to shareholders to monitor managerial behavior. In addition, the law may enhance capital market discipline on managers and purify the operation of the market for corporate control by entitling the shareholders to challenge corporate policies concerning retention of profits and to demand pay-out of cash reserves, either through direct distributions of cash or through corporate stock repurchase programs, so as to prevent large retained cash balances insulating management from monitoring by capital markets. Personal liability of managers for injury sustained by shareholders as a result of managerial behavior is not generally a desirable means to tackle the agency costs problem, for the cost of a rule subjecting managers to potential personal liability (higher managerial salaries, over-cautiousness, avoidance of profitable business, litigation costs) may well outweigh its purported benefit of fewer aberrant activities by managers. Consistent herewith, both in United States jurisdictions and in the Netherlands, imposition of personal liability on managers is limited to exceptional cases, in particular, to cases in which the rationales for management by specialist managers (greater effectiveness in the monitoring of input behavior at lower costs) are absent.

In June 1997, a private committee (the "*Commissie Corporate Governance*"), established under the auspices of Amsterdam Exchanges N.V. (the corporation which organizes the Amsterdam stock exchange), published a series of non-binding recommendations on the governance of publicly held corporations in the Netherlands, primarily intended for corporations listed on the Amsterdam exchange. These recommendations, mostly of a practical nature, seek to improve the technical functioning of supervisory boards and management boards as well as the intra-corporate relationships between supervisory directors, managers and shareholders. They also promote greater accountability of top management and supervisory directors to the shareholders and independence of the supervisory board in the performance of its supervising tasks, and they oppose possession of shares and stock options by corporate insiders for the purpose of realizing short-term gains.

The committee proposes to enhance shareholders' ability to monitor corporate management in several ways: first, by awarding shareholders who own at least one percent of a corporation's outstanding shares or whose shares represent a stock market value of at least NLG 500,000, the right to nominate items for discussion at the company's general meeting of shareholders; second, by introducing a system of "proxy solicitation" (currently virtually non-existent in the Netherlands) in order to facilitate greater influence of individual shareholders on the decision-making in the general meeting of shareholders; and third, by inviting the management and the shareholders of a particular corporation to re-evaluate the actual powers of the shareholders and thus, the corporation's internal "balance of power". In this context, the committee emphasizes that both the corporation's top management and its supervisory directors should require the confidence of the shareholders.

The committee's recommendations do not contain or debate proposals for *structural* reforms in the concept of the corporation, or in the Dutch corporate law governing it (and therefore fall outside the scope of our study). That is somewhat surprising in view of the fact that, as we have emphasized throughout this book, conflicts of interests between those governing the corporation and the shareholders subject to their governance are *inherent* in the concept of the corporation, and greatly influence both investor-management relations and the corporation's decision-making. It is remarkable moreover, that the committee's report does not contain a single reference to the extensive economic scholarship on matters of corporate organization, including the relationships between the corporation's various constituents. However, the "*Commissie Corporate Governance*" certainly deserves credit for having placed the delicate but important subject of conflicting interests inside the corporation on the agenda for public debate.

A follow-up study published in December 1998, which examines whether and to what extent the committee's recommendations have been implemented by individual corporations listed on the Amsterdam exchange, has meanwhile revealed that although corporations appeared generally supportive of the recommendations, on the whole shareholders' powers vis-à-vis corporate management have not substantially increased in the year following their publication. The follow-up study states (on page 370) that "(...) severe limitations on the influence of shareholders [on the management continue to] exist and no fundamental changes of governance structures have been announced in this regard. (...) Few companies decided to augment the influence of shareholders." Accordingly, the study concludes (on page 371): "The evidence suggests that companies felt no need to change substantially the relations with their shareholders", *i.e.* to improve the latter's monitoring opportunities.

Following these findings, in May 1999, the Dutch government announced that it is to prepare new legislation intended to increase corporate managers' accountability to the shareholders. Such legislation is to include, *inter alia*, provisions aimed at facilitating proxy solicitation and a statutory right for individual shareholders satisfying certain quantitative thresholds to add items to the agenda of the corporation's general meeting of shareholders, like the "*Commissie Corporate Governance*" proposed earlier (save on a non-binding basis). Such legislation could serve to limit managers' discretion to depart from value maximization and to complement market disciplinary mechanisms, without creating socially undesirable side-effects, and would therefore, in our view, deserve Parliament's support.

The second downside effect of the corporate form ensues from statutory limited liability of shareholders. Limited liability does support the operation of the corporate firm in various ways: it facilitates centralization of management, enhances transferability of shares, thus promoting liquidity of investments, enables risk reduction through diversification, and economizes on transaction costs in the capital markets. However, limited liability also creates perverse incentives to externalize business risk (*i.e.* the risk of failure) to other members of society, viz. the corporation's voluntary and involuntary creditors. As a result of limited liability, corporate decision-makers are induced to ignore a part of the social costs of corporate activity, namely that part which exceeds the value of the corporation's assets. This in turn may lead them to have the corporation engage in over-risky ventures, underinvest in care to reduce risks and take out inadequate third party liability insurance, thus increasing the risk of loss to which parties external to the corporation are exposed as well as their actual losses in the event of business failure. Accordingly, limited liability permits shareholders to pursue private wealth improvements potentially at the expense of other members of society.

In the case of publicly held corporations, the social costs of abolishing statutory limited liability, that means, relinquishing its above-mentioned advantages, presumably outweigh its detrimental effects to creditors. For this class of corporations, establishment of a compensation fund to be sponsored by the publicly held corporations may serve both to compensate limited liability's costs to creditors and to correct the perverse incentives it creates. In the case of closely held corporations, however, the advantages of limited liability mentioned above are unlikely to be significant, and instead personal liability for shareholders may be introduced to enhance social efficiency in corporate decision-making. Consistent with our analysis, courts in the United States and in the Netherlands invariably uphold limited liability for shareholders of publicly held corporations, but they have imposed liability on shareholders of closely held corporations in cases in which the limited liability rule had resulted in the externalization of costs to creditors of the corporation and the defending shareholders had not exploited the above-mentioned advantages of statutory limited liability.

Given the socially undesirable effects summarized above attending the conflicts of interests between shareholders and managers and between shareholders protected by limited liability and other members of society, the question which almost inevitably faces policy makers is how to manage these private conflicts of interests accompanying the corporate form of organization in the interest of society at large. Generally, debate on the answers to this question should, in our view, explore three potential routes (or combinations thereof): (i) structural reform of the concept of the corporation, (ii) enhancement of market mechanisms operating to create incentives for socially desirable behavior, and (iii) where such market mechanisms fail, regulation devised to ban socially undesirable behavior, in particular, to mitigate agency costs and to avoid externalization of business risk and in the event of failure, costs.

As the conflicts of interests discussed in this book may be interpreted as structural deficiencies of the corporate form, any agenda concerning the resolution of these conflicts in the public interest should pay attention to the structure of the corporation itself as embedded in, and governed by, the applicable corporate law. Given the effects of market mechanisms upon corporate behavior and the incentives they create for the individuals in the firm, it is also impossible to ignore the significance of such mechanisms and the prospects they offer to induce socially desirable behavior. And given both the constraints on market forces in a world tainted by positive transaction costs and the impact of the choices of the individuals inside the corporate firm on other members of society and on the use of society's valuable resources, the option of public regulation may not be ruled out either.

However, regulatory authorities should always recognize that the corporate form is nothing but the exponent of the voluntary associative activities of private individuals. Corporate law-makers should therefore strive to mimic the arrangements upon which contracting individuals would voluntarily agree, with which regulation should only interfere if required to serve the public interest. This in turn requires that the social benefits of the interference be carefully balanced against its social costs. With regard to the nature of the corporate law, it follows that corporate law should be enabling as a rule and mandatory as the exception in respect of rules devised to preclude the externalization of costs to corporate insiders (shareholders) or outsiders (creditors).

The strengthening of shareholder control over corporations' retained cash, the enhancement of shareholders' monitoring abilities vis-à-vis top management and the abolishment of statutory limited liability for shareholders of close corporations would all follow the route of structural reform. Yet, as noted, a right for the shareholders to demand distribution of excessive cash in whatever way would also enhance the disciplining of managers by the capital markets and by the market for corporate control. Disclosure of specific information relating to individual managers' remuneration packages would feed information into managerial labor markets that discipline managerial behavior. Regulation would serve to implement structural and market-oriented reforms, and to establish the proposed compensation fund for creditors of publicly held corporations.

Pejovich [1981,257] has conceptualized law as a "public capital good", costly to create but yielding a flow of benefits to society over a lengthy period of time by enhancing the predictability of behavior. In effect, he maintains, people are encouraged to "exploit beneficial exchange opportunities that have long-run consequences" [1981, 258]. The same is true for the legal concept of the corporation: it specifies the rules of the game for the relationships between those involved in, or doing business with, a firm furnished with corporate attributes and so it encourages private individuals to exploit long-term value-creating opportunities of cooperative productive action in, or exchange transactions with, the corporate firm. Any changes in the concept of the corporation, or the law governing it, should preserve these benefits.

Finally, it is not our intention whatsoever that our book should explain every economic aspect of the corporate form of organization or resolve the manifold questions arising from it. Nor do we pretend that our proposed remedies for the downside effects attending the corporate form provide full answers to the complex problems observed; little would be less true. It is our aspiration, however, that this study may contribute to the understanding of the economic rationales and effects of the corporate form, help to appraise its upside effects, and contribute to the debate concerning the appropriate legal responses to its downside effects. Harold Demsetz [1987, 4] once wrote: "The test of the quality of an idea is in the questions it raises". If our book, or a single part of it, were to fulfill this test, we would be more than satisfied.

References

Albach, H., 1981, *The Nature of the Firm – A Production-Theoretical Viewpoint*, 137 Journal of Institutional and Theoretical Economics/ Zeitschrift für die gesamte Staatswissenschaft 717.

Alchian, A.A., 1975a, *The Basis of Some Recent Advances in the Theory of Management of the Firm*, in: Manne, H.G., (ed.), The Economics of Legal Relationships – Readings in the Theory of Property Rights, St. Paul, Minn.: West Publ., 487.

Alchian, A.A., 1975b, *Corporate Management and Property Rights*, in: Manne, H.G., (ed.), The Economics of Legal Relationships – Readings in the Theory of Property Rights, St. Paul, Minn.: West Publ., 499.

Alchian, A.A., 1977, *Some Economics of Property Rights*, in: Idem, Economic Forces at Work – Selected Works by Armen A. Alchian, Indianapolis: Liberty Press, 127.

Alchian, A.A., 1984, *Specificity, Specialization, and Coalitions*, 140 Journal of Institutional and Theoretical Economics/ Zeitschrift für die gesamte Staatswissenschaft 34.

Alchian, A.A., 1991, *Development of Economic Theory and Antitrust: A View from the Theory of the Firm*, 147 Journal of Institutional and Theoretical Economics/ Zeitschrift für die gesamte Staatswissenschaft 232.

Alchian, A.A., 1993, *Thoughts on the Theory of the Firm – A Tribute to Eirik G. Furubotn*, 149 Journal of Institutional and Theoretical Economics/ Zeitschrift für die gesamte Staatswissenschaft 365.

Alchian, A.A., and H. Demsetz, 1972, *Production, Information Costs, and Economic Organization*, 62 American Economic Review 777.

Alchian, A.A., and S. Woodward, 1987, *Reflections on the Theory of the Firm*, 143 Journal of Institutional and Theoretical Economics/ Zeitschrift für die gesamte Staatswissenschaft 110.

American Law Institute, 1958, *Restatement (Second) of Agency*, St. Paul, Minn.: American Law Institute Publ.

American Law Institute, 1977, *Restatement (Second) of Contracts*, St. Paul, Minn.: American Law Institute Publ.

American Law Institute, 1994, *Principles of Corporate Governance: Analysis and Recommendations*, as Adopted and Promulgated on May 13, 1992, Vol. 1 and 2, St. Paul, Minn.: American Law Institute Publ.

Amsler, C.E., Bartlett, R.L., and C.J. Bolton, 1981, *Thoughts of Some British Economists on Early Limited Liability and Corporate Legislation*, 13 History of

Political Economy 774.
Anderson, G.M., and R.D. Tollison, 1983, *The Myth of the Corporation as a Creation of the State*, 3 International Review of Law and Economics 107.
Arrow, K.J., 1969, *The Organization of Economic Activity*, in: Joint Economic Committee, 91st Congress, 1st Session, The Analysis and Evaluation of Public Expenditure: The PPB System, 47.
Arrow, K.J., 1970, *Insurance, Risk and Resource Allocation*, in: Idem, Essays in the Theory of Risk-bearing, Amsterdam: North-Holland Publishing Co., 134.
Arrow, K.J., 1974, *The Limits of Organization*, New York: Norton and Co.
Arrow, K.J., 1985, *The Economics of Agency*, in: Pratt, J.W., and R.J. Zeckhauser (eds.), Principals and Agents: The Structure of Business, Cambridge, Mass.: Harvard Business School, 37.

Bainbridge, S.M., 1997, *Community and Statism: A Conservative Contractarian Critique of Progressive Corporate Law Scholarship*, 82 Cornell Law Review 856.
Ballantine, H.W., 1925, *Separate Entity of Parent and Subsidiary Corporations*, 14 California Law Review 12.
Ballantine, H.W., 1946, *Law of Corporations* (revised edition), Chicago: Callaghan and Co.
Barber, D.H., 1981, *Piercing the Corporate Veil*, 17 Willamette Law Review 371.
Baumol, W.J., 1962, *On the Theory of Expansion of the Firm*, 52 American Economic Review 1078.
Baumol, W.J., 1967, *Business Behavior, Value and Growth* (revised edition), New York: Macmillan.
Baumol, W.J., 1973, *The Firm and Its Objectives*, in: Palda, K.S., (ed.), Readings in Managerial Economics, Englewood Cliffs, N.J.: Prentice-Hall, 15.
Berle, Jr., A.A., 1947, *The Theory of Enterprise Entity*, 47 Columbia Law Review 343.
Berle, Jr., A.A., 1950, *Historical Inheritance of American Corporations*, 3 Social Meaning of Legal Concepts – An Annual Conference Conducted by the New York University School of Law 189.
Berle, Jr., A.A., and G.C. Means, 1991, *The Modern Corporation and Private Property* (originally published in 1932), New Brunswick: Transaction Publ.
Blaug, M., 1958, *The Classical Economists and the Factory Acts: A Re-evaluation*, 72 Quarterly Journal of Economics 226.
Block, D.J., Barton, N.E., and S.A. Radin, 1987, *The Business Judgment Rule – Fiduciary Duties of Corporate Directors and Officers*, Clifton, N.J.: Prentice-Hall.
Blumberg, P.I., 1993, *The American Law of Corporate Groups*, in: McCahery, J., Picciotto, S., and C. Scott (eds.), Corporate Control and Accountability – Changing Structures and the Dynamics of Regulation, Oxford: Clarendon Press, 305.
Bocken, H., 1987, *Alternatives to Liability and Liability Insurance for the Compensation of Pollution Damages (Part 1)*, 1 Tijdschrift voor Milieuaansprakelijkheid/ Environmental Law Review 83.

Bocken, H., 1988, *Alternatives to Liability and Liability Insurance for the Compensation of Pollution Damages (Part 2)*, 2 Tijdschrift voor Milieuaansprakelijkheid/ Environmental Law Review 3.
Boschma, H.E., 1997, *De Eenpersoons-bv*, Deventer: Kluwer.
Boulding, K.E., 1960, *The Present Position of the Theory of the Firm*, in: Boulding, K.E. and W.A. Spivey (eds.), Linear Programming and the Theory of the Firm, New York: Harper, 1.
Brealey, R.A., and S.C. Myers, 1988, *Principles of Corporate Finance* (third edition), New York: McGraw-Hill.
Buchanan, J.M., and G. Tullock, 1965, *The Calculus of Consent – Logical Foundations of Constitutional Democracy*, Ann Arbor: University of Michigan Press.
Butler, H.N., 1986, *General Incorporation in Nineteenth Century England: Interaction of Common Law and Legislative Processes*, 6 International Review of Law and Economics 169.
Butler, H.N., and L.E. Ribstein, 1988, *State Anti-Takeover Statutes and the Contract Clause*, 57 University of Cincinnati Law Review 611.

Carr, J.L., and G.F. Mathewson, 1988, *Unlimited Liability as a Barrier to Entry*, 96 Journal of Political Economy 766.
Chandler, Jr., A.D., 1977, *The Visible Hand – The Managerial Revolution in American Business*, Cambridge Mass.: Belknap Press.
Chapman, B., 1996, *Corporate Tort Liability and the Problem of Overcompliance*, 69 Southern California Law Review 1679.
Chayes, A., 1959, *The Modern Corporation and the Rule of Law*, in: Mason, E.S., (ed.), The Corporation in Modern Society, Cambridge, Mass.: Harvard University Press, 25.
Cheung, S.N.S., 1983, *The Contractual Nature of the Firm*, 26 Journal of Law and Economics 1.
Clark, R.C., 1977, *The Duties of the Corporate Debtor to Its Creditors*, 90 Harvard Law Review 505.
Clark, R.C., 1985, *Agency Costs versus Fiduciary Duties*, in: Pratt, J.W., and R.J. Zeckhauser (eds.), Principals and Agents: The Structure of Business, Cambridge, Mass.: Harvard Business School, 55.
Clark, R.C., 1986, *Corporate Law*, Boston: Little, Brown and Co.
Coase, R.H., 1937, *The Nature of the Firm*, 4 Economica (n.s.) 386.
Coase, R.H., 1960, *The Problem of Social Cost*, 3 Journal of Law and Economics 1.
Coase, R.H., 1984, *The New Institutional Economics*, 140 Journal of Institutional and Theoretical Economics/ Zeitschrift für die gesamte Staatswissenschaft 229.
Coase, R.H., 1988a, *The Nature of the Firm: Origin*, 4 Journal of Law, Economics, and Organization 3.
Coase, R.H., 1988b, *The Nature of the Firm: Meaning*, 4 Journal of Law, Economics, and Organization 19.

Coase, R.H., 1988c, *The Nature of the Firm: Influence*, 4 Journal of Law, Economics, and Organization 33.
Coase, R.H., 1988d, *The Firm, the Market, and the Law*, Chicago: University of Chicago Press.
Coase, R.H., 1992, *The Institutional Structure of Production*, 82 American Economic Review 713.
Coase, R.H., 1993, *Concluding Comment*, 149 Journal of Institutional and Theoretical Economics/ Zeitschrift für die gesamte Staatswissenschaft 360.
Coffee, Jr., J.C., 1981, *"No Soul to Damn: No Body to Kick": An Unscandalized Inquiry into the Problem of Corporate Punishment*, 79 Michigan Law Review 386.
Cohen, L.R., 1979, *The Firm: A Revised Definition*, 46 Southern Economic Journal 580.
Cohen, L.R., 1990, *Why Tender Offers? The Efficient Market Hypothesis, the Supply of Stock, and Signaling*, 19 Journal of Legal Studies 113.
Commissie "Corporate Governance", 1997, *Aanbevelingen inzake Corporate Governance in Nederland*, Amsterdam.
Conard, A.F., 1976, *Corporations in Perspective*, Mineola, N.Y.: Foundation Press.
Cook, W.W., 1921, *"Watered Stock" – Commissions – "Blue Sky Laws" – Stock Without Par Value*, 19 Michigan Law Review 583.
Cooper Alexander, J., 1992, *Unlimited Shareholder Liability through a Procedural Lens*, 106 Harvard Law Review 387.
Cutler, L.N., 1979, *Economic Efficiency as the Focus of Structural Reform*, in: Schwartz, D.E., (ed.), Commentaries on Corporate Structure and Governance: The American Law Institute-American Bar Association Symposiums 1977-1978, Philadelphia: American Law Institute-American Bar Association, 346.

Dahlman, C.J., 1979, *The Problem of Externality*, 22 Journal of Law and Economics 141.
De Alessi, L., 1973, *Private Property and Dispersion of Ownership in Large Corporations*, 28 Journal of Finance 839.
Demsetz, H., 1966, *Some Aspects of Property Rights*, 9 Journal of Law and Economics 61.
Demsetz, H., 1969, *Information and Efficiency: Another Viewpoint*, 12 Journal of Law and Economics 1.
Demsetz, H., 1975, *Toward a Theory of Property Rights*, in: Manne, H.G., (ed.), The Economics of Legal Relationships – Readings in the Theory of Property Rights, St. Paul, Minn.: West Publ., 23.
Demsetz, H., 1983, *The Structure of Ownership and the Theory of the Firm*, 26 Journal of Law and Economics 375.
Demsetz, H., 1986, *A Commentary on Liability Rules and the Derivative Suit in Corporate Law*, 71 Cornell Law Review 352.
Demsetz, H., 1987, *An Appreciation of Armen A. Alchian's Contribution to the*

Theory of the Firm, 143 Journal of Institutional and Theoretical Economics/ Zeitschrift für die Gesamte Staatswissenschaft 3.
Demsetz, H., 1988, *The Theory of the Firm Revisited*, 4 Journal of Law, Economics, and Organization 141.
Demsetz, H., 1997, *The Firm in Economic Theory: A Quiet Revolution*, 87 American Economic Review 426.
Dewing, A.S., 1953, *Financial Policy of Corporations* (fifth edition), New York: Ronald Press.
Dobb, M., 1928, *Russian Economic Development*, New York: F.P. Dutton and Co.
Dommering-Van Rongen, L., 1996, *Schade Vergoeden door Fondsvorming*, Deventer: Kluwer.
Dooley, M.P., 1978, *Should Management's Control of the Corporation Be Weakened and That of the Shareholder Strengthened?*, in: Johnson, M.B., (ed.), The Attack on Corporate America, New York: McGraw-Hill, 82.

Easterbrook, F.H., and D.R. Fischel, 1981, *The Proper Role of a Target's Management in Responding to a Tender Offer*, 94 Harvard Law Review 1161.
Easterbrook, F.H., and D.R. Fischel, 1985, *Limited Liability and the Corporation*, 52 University of Chicago Law Review 89.
Easterbrook, F.H., and D.R. Fischel, 1986, *Close Corporations and Agency Costs*, 38 Stanford Law Review 271.
Easterbrook, F.H., and D.R. Fischel, 1991, *The Economic Structure of Corporate Law*, Cambridge, Mass.: Harvard University Press.
Eisenberg, M.A., 1979, *A Larger Role for Shareholders*, in: Schwartz, D.E., (ed.), Commentaries on Corporate Structure and Governance: The American Law Institute-American Bar Association Symposiums 1977-1978, Philadelphia: American Law Institute-American Bar Association, 133.
Eisenberg, M.A., 1988, *The Nature of the Common Law*, Cambridge, Mass.: Harvard University Press.
Ekelund, Jr., R.B., and R.D. Tollison, 1980, *Mercantilist Origins of the Corporation*, 11 Bell Journal of Economics 715.
Ekelund, Jr., R.B., and R.D. Tollison, 1991, *Economics* (third edition), New York: Harper Collins Publishers Inc.

Fama, E.F., 1980, *Agency Problems and the Theory of the Firm*, 88 Journal of Political Economy 288.
Fama, E.F., and M.C. Jensen, 1983a, *Separation of Ownership and Control*, 26 Journal of Law and Economics 301.
Fama, E.F., and M.C. Jensen, 1983b, *Agency Problems and Residual Claims*, 26 Journal of Law and Economics 327.
Faure, M.G., and T. Hartlief, 1996, *Een Asbestfonds als Alternatief voor de Aansprakelijkheid van de Werkgever?*, 11 Nederlands Tijdschrift voor Sociaal Recht 37.

Fischel, D.R., 1982, *The Corporate Governance Movement*, 35 Vanderbilt Law Review 1259.
Fischel, D.R., and M. Bradley, 1986, *The Role of Liability Rules and the Derivative Suit in Corporate Law: A Theoretical and Empirical Analysis*, 71 Cornell Law Review 261.
Franke, G., 1987, *Reflections on the Theory of the Firm – Comment*, 143 Journal of Institutional and Theoretical Economics/ Zeitschrift für die gesamte Staatswissenschaft 143.
Friedman, M., 1953, *The Methodology of Positive Economics*, in: Idem, Essays in Positive Economics, Chicago: University of Chicago Press, 3.
Friedman, M., 1970, *The Social Responsibility of Business Is to Increase Its Profits*, New York Times Magazine, September 13, 32.
Fuller, W., 1938, *The Incorporated Individual: A Study of the One-Man Company*, 51 Harvard Law Review 1373.
Furubotn, E.G., and S. Pejovich, 1974, *Two Essential Concepts: Transaction Costs and Attenuation*, in: Idem (eds.), The Economics of Property Rights, Cambridge, Mass.: Ballinger Publ., 45.

Gaastra, F.S., 1991, *De Geschiedenis van de VOC*, Zutphen: Walburg Pers.
Galbraith, J.K., 1967, *The New Industrial State*, Boston: Houghton Mifflin Co.
Garrett, R., 1967, *Corporate Donations*, 22 Business Lawyer 297.
Gilson, S.C., 1990, *Bankruptcy, Boards, Banks, and Blockholders: Evidence on Changes in Corporate Ownership and Control when Firms Default*, 27 Journal of Financial Economics 355.
Goetz, C.J., 1986, *A Verdict on Corporate Liability Rules and the Derivative Suit: Not Proven*, 71 Cornell Law Review 344.
Golbe, D.L., 1988, *Risk-taking by Firms Near Bankruptcy*, 28 Economics Letters 75.
Gordon, J.N., 1989, *The Mandatory Structure of Corporate Law*, 89 Columbia Law Review 1549.
Grossack, I.M., and Martin, D.D., 1973, *Managerial Economics – Microtheory and the Firm's Decisions*, Boston: Little, Brown and Co.
Grossman, P.Z., 1995, *The Market for Shares of Companies with Unlimited Liability: The Case of American Express*, 24 Journal of Legal Studies 63.
Grundfest, J.A., 1992, *The Limited Future of Unlimited Liability: A Capital Markets Perspective*, 102 Yale Law Journal 387.

Halpern, P., Trebilcock, M., and S. Turnbull, 1980, *An Economic Analysis of Limited Liability in Corporation Law*, 30 University of Toronto Law Journal 117.
Hansmann, H., and R.H. Kraakman, 1991, *Toward Unlimited Shareholder Liability for Corporate Torts*, 100 Yale Law Journal 1879.
Hansmann, H., and R.H. Kraakman, 1992, *Do the Capital Markets Compel Limited Liability? A Response to Professor Grundfest*, 102 Yale Law Journal 427.

Hart, O., 1989, *An Economist's Perspective on the Theory of the Firm*, 89 Columbia Law Review 1757.
Henn, H.G., 1970, *Handbook of the Law of Corporations and Other Business Enterprises* (second edition), St. Paul, Minn.: West Publ.
Henn, H.G., and J.R. Alexander, 1983, *Laws of Corporations* (third edition), St. Paul, Minn.: West Publ.
Herman, E.S., 1984, *The Limits of the Market as a Discipline in Corporate Governance*, 9 Delaware Journal of Corporate Law 530.
Hessen, R., 1979, *In Defense of the Corporation*, Stanford: Hoover Institution Press.
Hicks, J., 1982, *Limited Liability: The Pros and Cons*, in: Orhnial, T., (ed.), Limited Liability and the Corporation, London: Croom Helm, 11.
Hol, A.M., 1990, *Efficiëntie als Instrument en als Norm – Enkele Rechtstheoretische Kanttekeningen bij de Economische Analyse van het Recht*, 39 Ars Aequi 632.
Holderness, C.G., 1990, *Liability Insurers as Corporate Monitors*, 10 International Review of Law and Economics 115.
Hunt, B.C., 1936, *The Development of the Business Corporation in England, 1800-1867*, Cambridge, Mass.: Harvard University Press.

Jarrell, G.A., Brickley, J.A., and J.M. Netter, 1988, *The Market for Corporate Control: The Empirical Evidence since 1980*, 2 Journal of Economic Perspectives (nr. 1), 49.
Jensen, M.C., 1983, *Organization Theory and Methodology*, 58 Accounting Review 319.
Jensen, M.C., 1986, *Agency Costs of Free Cash Flow, Corporate Finance, and Takeovers*, 76 American Economic Review 323.
Jensen, M.C., 1989, *Eclipse of the Public Corporation*, Harvard Business Review, September-October (nr. 5), 61.
Jensen, M.C., and W.H. Meckling, 1976, *Theory of the Firm: Managerial Behavior, Agency Costs and Ownership Structure*, 3 Journal of Financial Economics 305.
Jensen, M.C., and W.H. Meckling, 1979, *Rights and Production Functions: An Application to Labor-managed Firms and Codetermination*, 52 Journal of Business 469.
Jensen, M.C., and K.J. Murphy, 1990, *Performance Pay and Top-Management Incentives*, 98 Journal of Political Economy 225.
Jensen, M.C., and Ruback, R.S., 1983, *The Market for Corporate Control: The Scientific Evidence*, 11 Journal of Financial Economics 5.
Jensen, M.C., and J.B. Warner, 1988, *The Distribution of Power among Corporate Managers, Shareholders, and Directors*, 20 Journal of Financial Economics 3.

Kahn-Freund, O., 1944, *Some Reflections on Company Law Reform*, 7 Modern Law Review 54.

Kaplan, S.N., and D. Reishus, 1990, *Outside Directorships and Corporate Performance*, 27 Journal of Financial Economics 389.
Kindleberger, C.P., 1997, *Economic Laws and Economic History*, Cambridge, U.K.: Cambridge University Press.
Kindlund, J.M., 1987, *Case Comment at Miller v. Dixon Industries Corp., 513 A.2d 597 (R.I. 1986)*, 21 Suffolk University Law Review 370.
Klein, B., 1988, *Vertical Integration as Organizational Ownership: The Fisher Body-General Motors Relationship Revisited*, 4 Journal of Law, Economics, and Organization 99.
Klein, B., Crawford, R.G., and A.A. Alchian, 1978, *Vertical Integration, Appropriable Rents, and the Competitive Contracting Process*, 21 Journal of Law and Economics 297.
Knight, F.H., 1921, *Risk, Uncertainty and Profit*, Boston: Houghton Mifflin Co.
Knight, F.H., 1942, *Profit and Entrepreneurial Functions*, 2 Journal of Economic History 126.
Kraakman, R.H., 1984, *Corporate Liability Strategies and the Costs of Legal Controls*, 93 Yale Law Journal 857.
Krendl, C.S., and J.R. Krendl, 1978, *Piercing the Corporate Veil: Focusing the Inquiry*, 55 Denver Law Journal 1.
Kripke, H., 1976, *Can the SEC Make Disclosure Policy Meaningful?*, 2 Journal of Portfolio Management 32.
Kwang, C-W., and Y-L. Wu, 1971, *Mathematical Programming and Economic Analysis of the Firm: An Introduction*, Scranton: Intext Educational Publishers.

Landers, J.M., 1975, *A Unified Approach to Parent, Subsidiary, and Affiliate Questions in Bankruptcy*, 42 University of Chicago Law Review 589.
Landers, J.M., 1976, *Another Word on Parents, Subsidiaries and Affiliates in Bankruptcy*, 43 University of Chicago Law Review 527.
Landes, W.M., and R.A. Posner, 1987, *The Economic Structure of Tort Law*, Cambridge, Mass.: Harvard University Press.
Lease, R.C., McConnell, J.J., and W.H. Mikkelson, 1983, *The Market Value of Control in Publicly Traded Corporations*, 11 Journal of Financial Economics 439.

Machlup, F., 1967, *Theories of the Firm: Marginalist, Behavioral, Managerial*, 57 American Economic Review 1.
MacNeil, I.R., 1981, *Economic Analysis of Contractual Relations*, in: Burrows, P., and C.G. Veljanovski (eds.), The Economic Approach to Law, London: Butterworths, 61.
MacNeil, I.R., 1985, *Reflections on Relational Contract*, 141 Journal of Institutional and Theoretical Economics/ Zeitschrift für die gesamte Staatswissenschaft 541.
Maeijer, J.M.M., 1964, *Het Belangenconflict in de Naamloze Vennootschap*, Deventer: Kluwer.

Maeijer, J.M.M., 1994, *Vertegenwoordiging en Rechtspersoon*, Vol. 3: De Naamloze en de Besloten Vennootschap, Zwolle: Tjeenk Willink.
Maeijer, J.M.M., 1995, *Note at Poot v. ABP (HR December 2, 1994)*, Nederlandse Jurisprudentie 1995 (nr. 288), 1346.
Manne, H.G., 1962, *The "Higher Criticism" of the Modern Corporation*, 62 Columbia Law Review 399.
Manne, H.G., 1964, *Some Theoretical Aspects of Share Voting – An Essay in Honor of Adolph A. Berle*, 64 Columbia Law Review 1427.
Manne, H.G., 1965, *Mergers and the Market for Corporate Control*, 73 Journal of Political Economy 110.
Manne, H.G., 1975, *Our Two Corporation Systems: Law and Economics*, in: Idem (ed.), The Economics of Legal Relationships – Readings in the Theory of Property Rights, St. Paul, Minn.: West Publ., 511.
Manne, H.G., 1981, *The Publicly Held Corporation as a Market Creation*, 137 Journal of Institutional and Theoretical Economics/ Zeitschrift für die gesamte Staatswissenschaft 689.
Marris, R., 1964, *The Economic Theory of Managerial Capitalism*, New York: Free Press.
McCulloch, J.R., 1965, *The Principles of Political Economy* (fifth edition), originally published in 1864 (fifth edition), New York: Augustus M. Kelley.
McKean, R.N., 1978, *Should Corporate Managers' Liability for Third-Party Injuries Be Expanded?*, in: Johnson, M.B., (ed.), The Attack on Corporate America, New York: McGraw-Hill, 86.
McNulty, P.J., 1984, *On the Nature and Theory of Economic Organization: The Role of the Firm Reconsidered*, 16 History of Political Economy 233.
Meiners, R., 1978, *Does Limited Liability Subsidize Corporations at the Expense of Society?*, in: Johnson, M.B., (ed.), The Attack on Corporate America, New York: McGraw-Hill, 223.
Meiners, R., Mofsky, J., and R.D. Tollison, 1979, *Piercing the Veil of Limited Liability*, 4 Delaware Journal of Corporate Law 351.
Mill, J.S., 1965, *Principles of Political Economy* (originally published in 1848), edited by W. Ashley, New York: Augustus M. Kelley.
Monitoring Commissie "Corporate Governance" and Economisch Instituut Tilburg, 1998, *Monitoring Corporate Governance in Nederland*, Amsterdam.
Monsen, R.J., and A. Downs, 1965, *A Theory of Large Managerial Firms*, 73 Journal of Political Economy 221.
Morck, R., Shleifer, A., and R.W. Vishny, 1988, *Management Ownership and Market Valuation: An Empirical Analysis*, 20 Journal of Finance 293.
Morgan, T.D., 1978, *Are Shareholders' Remedies for Improper Acts of Corporate Officials Sufficient?*, in: Johnson, M.B., (ed.), The Attack on Corporate America, New York: McGraw-Hill, 92.
Murphy, K.J., 1985, *Corporate Performance and Managerial Remuneration: An Empirical Analysis*, 7 Journal of Accounting and Economics 11.

Note, 1958, *Liability of a Corporation for Acts of a Subsidiary or Affiliate*, 71 Harvard Law Review 1122.
Nutzinger, H.G., 1978, *The Firm as a Social Institution*, in: Backhaus, J.G., Eger, T., and H.G. Nutzinger (eds.), Partizipation in Betrieb und Gesellschaft, Frankfurt am Main: Campus Verlag, 45.

Pejovich, S., 1981, *Law as a Capital Good*, in: Sirkin, G., (ed.), Lexeconics: The Interaction of Law and Economics, Boston: Martinus Nijhoff Publ., 257.
Polinsky, A.M., 1983, *An Introduction to Law and Economics*, Boston: Little, Brown and Co.
Pollock's *Principles of Contract* (twelfth edition), 1946, by P.H. Winfield, London: Stevens and Sons.
Posner, R.A., 1976, *The Rights of Creditors of Affiliated Corporations*, 43 University of Chicago Law Review 499.
Posner, R.A., 1992, *Economic Analysis of Law* (fourth edition), Boston: Little, Brown and Co.
Pratt, J.W., and R.J. Zeckhauser, 1985, *Principals and Agents: An Overview*, in: Idem (eds.), Principals and Agents: The Structure of Business, Cambridge, Mass.: Harvard Business School, 1.
Priest, G.L., 1988, *Understanding the Liability Crisis*, in: Olson, W., (ed.), New Directions in Liability Law, New York: The Academy of Political Science, 196.

Robertson, D.H., 1923, *The Control of Industry*, London: Nisbet.
Romano, R., 1989, *What Went Wrong With Directors' and Officers' Liability Insurance?*, 14 Delaware Journal of Corporate Law 1.
Romano, R., 1991, *The Shareholder Suit: Litigation without Foundation?*, 7 Journal of Law, Economics, and Organization 55.
Romano, R., 1993, *The Genius of American Corporate Law*, Washington, D.C.: American Enterprise Institute Press.
Ross, S.A., and Westerfield, R.W., 1988, *Corporate Finance*, St. Louis: Times Mirror/ Mosby College Publ.

Sanders, P., and Westbroek, W., 1994, *BV en NV – Het Nieuwe Ondernemingsrecht* (seventh edition), by Buijn, F.K., and P.M. Storm, Deventer: Kluwer.
Scherer, F.M., 1988a, *Corporate Ownership and Control*, in: Meyer, J.R., and J.M. Gustafson (eds.), The U.S. Business Corporation: An Institution in Transition, Cambridge, Mass.: Ballinger Publ., 43.
Scherer, F.M., 1988b, *Corporate Takeovers: The Efficiency Arguments*, 2 Journal of Economic Perspectives (nr. 1), 69.
Scott, W.R., 1951, *The Constitution and Finance of English, Scottish, and Irish Joint-Stock Companies to 1720*, Vol. 1, New York: Peter Smith.
Shavell, S., 1982, *On Liability and Insurance*, 13 Bell Journal of Economics 120.

Shavell, S., 1984, *Liability for Harm versus Regulation of Safety*, 13 Journal of Legal Studies 357.
Shavell, S., 1986, *The Judgment Proof Problem*, 6 International Review of Law and Economics 45.
Shavell, S., 1987, *Economic Analysis of Accident Law*, Cambridge, Mass.: Harvard University Press.
Simon, H.A., 1962, *New Developments in the Theory of the Firm*, 52 American Economic Review 1.
Smiley, R., 1976, *Tender Offers, Transaction Costs and the Theory of the Firm*, 58 Review of Economics and Statistics 22.
Smith, A., 1981, *An Inquiry into the Nature and Causes of the Wealth of the Nations* (originally published in 1776), Vol. 1 and 2, edited by Campbell, R.H., Skinner, A.S., and W.B. Todd, Indianapolis: Liberty Fund.
Sowards, H., 1974, *Corporation Law*, Buffalo, N.Y.: Dennis.
Stano, M., 1975, *Executive Ownership Interests and Corporate Performance*, 42 Southern Economic Journal 272.
Stein, E., 1950, *Comment*, 3 Social Meaning of Legal Concepts – An Annual Conference Conducted by the New York University School of Law 218.
Stephen, F.H., 1988, *The Economics of the Law*, Ames: Iowa State Press.
Stigler, G.J., 1951, *The Division of Labor is Limited by the Extent of the Market*, 59 Journal of Political Economy 185.

Thompson, R.B., 1991, *Piercing the Corporate Veil: An Empirical Study*, 76 Cornell Law Review 1036.

Vanberg, V., 1982, *Das Unternehmen als Sozialverband – Zur Sozialtheorie der Unternehmung und zur juristischen Diskussion um ein neues Unternehmensrecht*, 1 Jahrbuch für neue Politische Ökonomie 276.
Van der Goot, L.R.T., and R.H. van het Kaar, 1997, *Beschermingsconstructies, Structuurregime en Ondernemingswaarde*, 71 Maandblad voor Accountancy en Bedrijfseconomie 497.
Van der Grinten, W.C.L., 1992, *Handboek voor de Naamloze en de Besloten Vennootschap* (twelfth edition), originally by E.J.J. van der Heijden, Zwolle: Tjeenk Willink.
Van Horne, J.C., 1973, *The Objective of the Firm*, in: Palda, K.S., (ed.), Readings in Managerial Economics, Englewood Cliffs, N.J.: Prentice-Hall, 3.
Van Schilfgaarde, P., 1995, *Van de BV en de NV* (tenth edition), Arnhem: Gouda Quint.
Viscusi, W.K., 1990, *The Performance of Liability Insurance in States with Different Products-Liability Statutes*, 19 Journal of Legal Studies 809.
Viscusi, W.K., 1991, *Reforming Products Liability*, Cambridge, Mass.: Harvard University Press.

Williamson, O.E., 1964, *The Economics of Discretionary Behavior: Managerial Objectives in a Theory of the Firm*, Englewood Cliffs, N.J.: Prentice-Hall.

Williamson, O.E., 1973, *Markets and Hierarchies: Some Elementary Considerations*, 63 American Economic Review 316.

Williamson, O.E., 1975, *Markets and Hierarchies: Analysis and Antitrust Implications – A Study in the Economics of Internal Organization*, New York: Free Press.

Williamson, O.E., 1981, *Contract Analysis: The Transaction Cost Approach*, in: Burrows, P., and C.G. Veljanovski (eds.), The Economic Approach to Law, London: Butterworths, 39.

Williamson, O.E., 1985, *The Economic Institutions of Capitalism – Firms, Markets, Relational Contracting*, New York: Free Press.

Williamson, O.E., 1986, *Economic Organization – Firms, Markets and Policy Control*, Brighton: Wheatsheaf Books Ltd.

Williamson, O.E., 1993, *The Evolving Science of Organization*, 149 Journal of Institutional and Theoretical Economics/ Zeitschrift für die gesamte Staatswissenschaft 336.

Williston, S., 1927, *The Law of Contracts*, Vol. 1, New York: Baker, Voorhis and Co.

Wolfson, N., 1984, *The Modern Corporation – Free Markets versus Regulation*, New York: Free Press.

Woodward, S., 1985, *The Economics of Limited Liability*, 141 Journal of Institutional and Theoretical Economics/ Zeitschrift für die gesamte Staatswissenschaft 601.

Case Index

U.S. Cases

Dutch Cases

Subject Index

GPSR Compliance

The European Union's (EU) General Product Safety Regulation (GPSR) is a set of rules that requires consumer products to be safe and our obligations to ensure this.

If you have any concerns about our products, you can contact us on ProductSafety@springernature.com

In case Publisher is established outside the EU, the EU authorized representative is:

Springer Nature Customer Service Center GmbH
Europaplatz 3
69115 Heidelberg, Germany

Batch number: 10755284

Printed by Printforce, the Netherlands